SSSP

Springer
Series in
Social
Psychology

SSSP

Ronald J. Fisher

The Social Psychology of Intergroup and International Conflict Resolution

Springer-Verlag New York Berlin Heidelberg
London Paris Tokyo Hong Kong

Ronald J. Fisher
Department of Psychology
University of Saskatchewan
Saskatoon, Saskatchewan, S7N 0W0
Canada

and

Canadian Institute for International Peace and Security
Ottawa, Ontario, K1R 7X7
Canada

With 14 Illustrations

Library of Congress Cataloging-in-Publication Data
Fisher, Ronald J.
　　The social psychology of intergroup and international conflict
　resolution/Ronald J. Fisher.
　　　p.　cm. – (Springer series in social psychology)
　　Includes bibliographical references.
　　ISBN 0-387-97073-8 (alk. paper)
　　1. Intergroup relations.　2. Conflict management.
3. International relations.　I. Title.　II. Series.
HM131.F525　1989
303.6'9 – dc20　　　　　　　　　　　　　　　　　　89-35512

Printed on acid-free paper.

© 1990 by Springer-Verlag New York Inc.
All rights reserved. This work may not be translated or copied in whole or in part without the written permission of the publisher (Springer-Verlag, 175 Fifth Avenue, New York, NY 10010, USA), except for brief excerpts in connection with reviews or scholarly analysis. Use in connection with any form of information storage and retrieval, electronic adaptation, computer software, or by similar or dissimilar methodology now known or hereafter developed is forbidden.
The use of general descriptive names, trade names, trademarks, etc. in this publication, even if the former are not especially identified, is not to be taken as a sign that such names, as understood by the Trade Marks and Merchandise Marks Act, may accordingly be used freely by anyone.

Typeset by Caliber Design Planning, Inc.
Printed and bound by R.R. Donnelley & Sons, Harrisonburg, Virginia.
Printed in the United States of America.

9 8 7 6 5 4 3 2 1

ISBN 0-387-97073-8 Springer-Verlag New York Berlin Heidelberg
ISBN 3-540-97073-8 Springer-Verlag Berlin Heidelberg New York

Contents

1. **Introduction: The Pervasive Enigma of Intergroup Conflict** 1

   Protracted Social Conflict: The Ultimate Enigma 3
   The Social-Psychological Study of Intergroup Conflict............. 5
   Challenges for the Study of Intergroup and International Conflict 8
   The Scope and Plan of This Book 16

2. **Classic Contributions to the Study of Intergroup Conflict** 21

   Ethnocentrism and Realistic Group Conflict Theory 22
   The Field Studies: Sherif, Blake, and Mouton, and Zimbardo 25
   Social Identity Theory 28
   The Groundwork for Eclectic Theory 30
   Conclusion: Implications for Theory, Research, and Practice 37

3. **Cognitive Theories Applied to Intergroup Conflict**
   (Peter R. Grant) 39

   The Effects of Categorizing Individuals into Groups:
   The Experimental Evidence 39
   Cognitive Theories of Intergroup Relations....................... 45
   Implications for Conflict Resolution 54
   Conclusion 57

4. **Group Factors in the Escalation of Intergroup Conflict** 59

   A Primer on Group Dynamics 59
   Self-Esteem, Identity, and Ethnocentrism 62
   Intergroup Conflict and Group Cohesiveness 64
   Conformity, Polarization, and Groupthink 68
   Crisis Decision Making Versus Effective Problem Solving 74

	Leadership and Constituent Pressure	82
	Implications for Conflict Escalation and De-Escalation	84
5.	**An Eclectic Model of Intergroup Conflict**	87
	The Approach to Theory Building	88
	Variables of the Model	91
	Principles or Laws of Interaction	97
	Boundaries of the Model	105
	System States of the Model	108
	Propositions of the Model	112
	Conclusion	115
6.	**The Intergroup Conflict Simulation** (Peter R. Grant, Ronald J. Fisher, Donald G. Hall, and Loraleigh Keashly)	117
	Development of the Initial ICS Design	119
	The Testing and Refining of the Initial ICS Design	133
	Testing the Final ICS Design	136
	Conclusion	141
7.	**International Conflict: The Question of Survival**	143
	The Sources of International Conflict	146
	Perception, Cognition, and Images	150
	Communication and Interaction	156
	The Social Psychology of International Negotiation	163
	The De-Escalation of International Conflict	170
8.	**Social-Psychological Approaches for Resolving Intergroup and International Conflict**	177
	The Facilitative Conditions of Intergroup Contact	180
	Approaches to Managing and Resolving Conflict	186
	The GRIT Strategy for De-Escalating Conflict	196
	Problem-Solving Workshops for Improving Intergroup Relations	202
	Conclusion	208
9.	**Third Party Consultation as a Method of Intergroup and International Conflict Resolution** (Ronald J. Fisher and Loraleigh Keashly)	211
	Third Party Consultation	213
	The Social-Psychological Rationale of Third-Party Consultation	218
	Toward a Taxonomy of Third Party Intervention	223

	Comparing Consultation and Mediation Using the ICS	229
	A Contingency Approach to Third Party Intervention	233
10.	**Conclusion: Paths Toward a Peaceful World**	239
	Major Themes	239
	Implications for Conflict De-Escalation and Resolution	242
	The Agenda for the Future	245
References		251
Author Index		269
Subject Index		275

Chapter 1

Introduction: The Pervasive Enigma of Intergroup Conflict

Destructive intergroup conflict is the most complex and costly enigma facing humankind. It is the preeminent social issue of our time in that it ruthlessly saps the resources required for human development and productivity, and in the extreme threatens our very survival. Poorly handled intergroup cleavages occur in a variety of settings—organizational, communal, international—and the costs of destructive escalation are readily apparent to all. In organizational settings, badly managed conflict between workers and management, and among various departments and units, results in lost work time, lowered morale, and wasted energy. In communal settings, racial prejudice, discrimination, and tension among ethnic groups breeds inequality and debilitates the quality of life for many. At the international level, many parts of the world are aflame with violence while others smoulder, all against the backdrop of an impending nuclear holocaust.

Yet, immediately, we must also acknowledge the functional aspect of intergroup conflict as a source of often necessary social change and movement toward justice and equality. Developed and sustainable societies, while still harboring noticeable inequities, are those that have found apparently adequate means of addressing conflicting group interests, at least for the time being. Many other societies are racked by cleavages between various interest and class groups, each seeking a place in the sun. Thus, on the moral question of the desirability of intergroup conflict, there are initially two answers. The first is that conflict simply exists and as such it is neither good nor bad. It is a central fact of human existence and the first task of social scientists is to describe and explain it. The second answer is conditional—intergroup conflict can be good or bad depending on whether it is handled constructively or destructively. The ideal is that differences are confronted and resolved nonviolently and in ways that are mutually acceptable to the groups involved. On this question, the challenge to the concerned social scientist/practitioner is to search for means by which the destructiveness of intergroup conflict is reduced while the benefits of social change are simultaneously realized—an order so tall as to be immediately labeled as unrealistic by many. Nonetheless, to accept the realists' prescription—do nothing—is tantamount to accepting the ongoing tragedy of intergroup conflict as well as the inevitability of eventual annihilation, and must therefore be rejected. The study of intergroup conflict and its resolution is an imperative if we are concerned about understanding human social behavior and improving the human condition.

There are a number of types of destructive intergroup conflict but nowhere are the costs more obvious and severe than in that most abhorrent form at the international level which we label "war." Yet surprisingly, this virulent form of violent confrontation continues unabated. Since World War II, depending on the criteria used, somewhere in the order of 100 wars have occurred, threatening the well-being of millions of people in dozens of countries. According to Kende (1978), in the 32 years following World War II, a total of 120 wars were fought on the territories of 71 countries. Put in different terms, the total duration of wars in the 32-year period was more than 369 years, and on any single day in the period, an average of 11 wars were being fought. Kende's criteria include an armed conflict involving activities of regular armed forces on at least one side, organized fighting on both sides, and a degree of continuity between armed clashes, however sporadic. The types of wars identified include "antiregime wars" fought within the territory of a country against the government in power; "tribal wars" fought between tribal, ethnic, or religious groups over territory or autonomy; and "border wars" wherein two or more countries fight across their boundaries for territory or other objectives. Kende's analysis indicates that the most frequent type of war in the modern era is the antiregime war (73 of 120), often with foreign participation. Tribal wars and border wars are less frequent (29 and 18 of 120, respectively) and foreign participation in these wars is not as pronounced. Kende's interpretation is that this pattern is a consequence of the current political situation in which the disintegration of the colonial system coincides with conflict among antagonistic social and political groups, classes, and tendencies within the same country. Congruent with this interpretation, the vast majority of wars are occurring in the Third World, specifically in Asia, Africa, the Middle East, and Latin America. These wars are primarily internal ones, and as countries have gained independence, the conflict is more and more between groups or factions within the same country. The trends identified by Kende (1978) continue into the present. In its 1987 yearbook, the Stockholm International Peace Research Institute lists 36 wars currently being fought, all but one in the Third World, and almost all internal conflicts. These wars involve over 5 million soldiers from 41 countries, with various forms of support from many other countries.

Behind this painful picture of Third World conflagration stands the even more ominous conflict between the superpowers and their allies holding the horrendous possibility of worldwide nuclear "omnicide." Although recent moves toward détente between the Soviet Union and the United States are to be applauded and encouraged, it must be realized that the arms race continues almost unabated. The agreement on Intermediate Nuclear Forces in Europe will only reduce the number of nuclear warheads by approximately 5%. This still leaves each side with approximately 10,000 strategic weapons. The total nuclear arsenal of tactical and strategic weapons is close to 50,000 and represents over 5,000 times all the explosive force used in World War II. The first atomic bomb dropped on Hiroshima, a tactical weapon by today's standards, killed or maimed 160,000 people and devastated an area of 4½ square miles. If a modern, 20-megaton nuclear warhead fell on a typical North American metropolitan area, for example San Francisco, 2 million people would die within the first 10 minutes. Another million would be seriously injured, suffering third-degree burns, deafness, and blindness. As the Physicians for Social Responsibility point out, medical facilities, many of them destroyed, would be totally inadequate to deal with such a calamity. On a global scale, the use of even a fraction of existing nuclear warheads, perhaps as low as 1000, could trigger nuclear winter, an environmental catastrophe of unheralded proportion (P.R. Ehrlich, 1983; Sagan, 1983; Turco, Toon, Ackerman, Pollack, & Sagan, 1983). Dust from groundbursts and ash and soot from firestorms in burning cities and forests would blot out the sun, temperatures would drop to below freezing, photosynthesis would stop, crops would die, and all life would be threatened. Oxides of nitrogen injected into the atmosphere by nuclear detonations would break down the ozone layer, allowing increased ultraviolet radiation to strike the earth when the skies eventually cleared, blinding animals and birds, and killing aquatic life that starts the food chain. While estimates of the severity of nuclear winter vary, the fact is that a nuclear war between the superpowers would set civilization back centuries at a minimum and at a maximum could annihilate all life on this planet.

The costs, both direct and indirect, of war and the preparedness for war are staggering. In 1986, ironically the United Nations International Year of Peace, total world military expenditures approached 900 billion U.S. dollars (Sivard, 1986). The United States accounts for about 30% of these expenditures and is ranked 1st in a number of categories of military activity, yet it stands 10th in public health expenditures per capita and 17th in infant mortality rate. Worldwide, three in five governments spend more on the military than on fighting all the enemies of good health. One and one-half *billion* people have no effective medical care and 570 million are malnourished (Epp-Tiessen, 1987). Of the $950 billion owed by developing countries to the developed ones, arms imports account for 25% thus accentuating the discrepancies between the North and the South. At the same time, the continuing militarization of the planet consumes significant human resources. An estimated 45 million people make up the work force of the world's armed forces, and in developing countries the recruitment of highly skilled workers for military purposes means that civilian needs go begging. About 20% of the world's scientists and technicians are engaged in research and development for military purposes, and they spend about 25% of the resources devoted to such activities. In 4 days, military expenditures equal the total yearly budget of the United Nations for international development. In a world where 40,000 children die in agony every day from starvation and related illness, this situation can only be regarded as inexplicable and unconscionable. And yet it exists.

Protracted Social Conflict: The Ultimate Enigma

Intergroup conflict arises in many forms and there are a number of typologies for categorizing it. Galtung (1965) distinguishes conflict at the individual level from that at the collective level which may be either intrasystem or intersystem. Thus, collective conflict may be intranational or international, and Galtung notes that the introduction of a group level to the scheme would account for conflict within and between class, ethnic, racial, or other interest groups. Beres and Schmidt (1982) use Galtung's scheme to help distinguish four predominant areas of conflict research: social conflict involving structures of dominance and inequity between class or interest groups within a society, industrial conflict between organized labor and management groups within an established adversarial system, organizational conflict involving small groups (units, departments, etc.) within a cooperative system, and international conflict between nations within the loosely defined global system. Dahrendorf (cited in Angell, 1965) delineates conflict between various levels of social units including "groups" (e.g., males and females), "sectors" (e.g., the army and the navy), and "societies" (e.g., Protestants and Catholics). Suprasocietal relations, then, involve conflict between countries or blocs. Dahrendorf's scheme also distinguishes among conflicts between equals, and unequals and between the whole versus a part (e.g., the state versus the criminal gang).

Building on these schemes, the current analysis distinguishes various forms of intergroup conflict primarily on the basis of the level of the overarching system. Thus, intergroup conflicts can be located at the organizational, communal, societal, and international levels. Intergroup conflict in organizations occurs between various structural groupings such as departments, between levels such as executive and middle management, and between labor and owners/managers as in classic industrial conflict. In communal settings, intergroup conflict is often expressed between ethnic, racial, religious, and gender groups and is usually noticeable through the existence of prejudice and discriminations as well as the occasional outburst of violence. These intergroup cleavages may also be expressed at the societal level in the form of social issues (e.g, racism, poverty) and are joined by conflict between classes, political groups, or other broad sectors of society, such as the military–industrial complex, the environmental lobby, and various other social movements. Finally, at the international level there is conflict between nations and blocs that is often intertwined with intergroup cleavages at the societal and communal levels. It is this intermixing of levels and issues that produces the most enigmatic and irresolvable form of intergroup cleavage – protracted social conflict.

There exist in the world today a number of intense intergroup conflicts, some between and some within nations, that appear intractable. A continuing state of tension is heightened by episodes of escalation often involving violence, which is typically terminated by mutual exhaustion and/or some form of peacekeeping. Traditional approaches to conflict management prove ineffective and the underlying issues move no closer to resolution. Examples of such conflicts at various points of longevity and expression include those in the Middle East, Northern Ireland, Cyprus, Lebanon, United States–Soviet Union, India–Pakistan, South Africa, Kampuchea, Sri Lanka, Iran–Iraq, the Horn of Africa, El Salvador, and Nicaragua. Numerous other conflicts of a similar but less intense nature exist throughout the world, awaiting the process of escalation to increase their intensity and visibility.

This type of seemingly intractable intergroup conflict has recently been labeled "protracted social conflict" by Azar (1983) to denote its ongoing and seemingly irresolvable nature. The sources of protracted social conflict are not to be found in the traditional loci of economics or power but in the frustration of compelling needs including those for security, identity, and participation, which are essential to human development. Protracted social conflict is therefore typically rooted in a combination of economic underdevelopment, structural inequality, and unintegrated political systems. Thus, historical intergroup cleavages are often combined with continuing inequity to produce the irrepressible nature of protracted social conflict. In a similar vein, Burton (1987a) speaks of "deep-rooted conflicts," which are not based on interests that are negotiable, but on underlying needs that cannot be compromised. The most conspicuous of these are violent conflicts between communities and nations over the preservation of cultures, values, and needs, but such conflict can occur in any relationship where inequality exists and needs for identity and participation are frustrated. Traditional methods of conflict management, which deal only with surface issues, simply suppress underlying needs and help lay the seeds for more intense conflict in the future.

An appealing aspect of the analyses by Azar and Burton, both of whom are political scientists, is the inherent social-psychological perspective, which links universal needs of individuals through their identity group to intergroup and international conflict. Thus, the conceptualizations of protracted or deep-rooted conflict are highly compatible with the approach taken to understanding intergroup conflict by the field of applied social psychology, that is, social-psychological research and practice in real world settings directed toward the understanding of human social behavior and the amelioration of social problems (Fisher, 1982). In particular, the humanistic value base of applied social psychology asserts that individuals and social groups have undeniable needs and rights for security, dignity, respect, and a "place in the sun" in both physical and psychological terms, that is, involving identity, recognition, participation, and control over their own destiny. Denial or suppression of these needs and rights creates a dynamic for social change that must be considered along with traditional sources of intergroup and international conflict in the areas of economics and power. Realizing that the most intense and protracted conflicts in the world today are inherently social-psychological opens the door for the wider analysis of intergroup conflict employing a wide range of concepts and methods drawn from social psychology and related disciplines. This analysis asks questions not only about the sources of intergroup conflict, but also about the processes of escalation that render such conflicts intractable. In this endeavor, consideration needs to be given to the integration of concepts from multiple levels of analysis within the context of a social-psychological approach. Therefore, it is important to spell out the general nature and parameters of this perspective.

The Social-Psychological Study of Intergroup Conflict

The study of intergroup conflict and, more broadly, that of intergroup relations have attracted the attention of social psychologists since the inception of the discipline (Fisher, 1985). The approach that has been taken in this endeavor, while varying considerably from study to study, can be characterized as phenomenological, interactive, and multilevel within a systems orientation. These same qualities can be seen to describe the overall discipline in its most powerful and useful form (Fisher, 1982).

The social-psychological approach is based on the philosophy of phenomenology, which maintains that we develop our picture of the world through our senses and that our subjective experience thereby provides the reality out of which we operate. Thus, the perceptions, cognitions, attitudes, and values held by individual actors in intergroup conflict are seen as important influences on their behavior in relation to the other party and the conflict. The theorizing about conflict by Deutsch (1987) provides one of the strongest illustrations of the phenomenological approach. Deutsch maintains that parties in conflict respond to each other in terms of their perceptions and cognitions of each other and that their behavior is influenced by their expectations of each other. On a broader scale, the social-psychological study of intergroup relations generally takes the perspective that perceptions, motivations, and actions of individuals influence, and in turn are affected by, the interaction between groups (D.M. Taylor & Moghaddam, 1987). It should immediately be pointed out, as noted by Condor and Brown (1988) in their overview of psychological factors in intergroup conflict, that the perceptual and cognitive processes of interest are both normal and collective. That is, the emphasis is on the perceptual and cognitive functioning that all normal human beings engage in, rather than on the pathological aberrations of a minority of abnormal, disturbed individuals. Second, since intergroup conflict is a collective phenomenon, the focus should be on collective social perception, cognition, and motivation, that is, elements that are shared at the group level and have relevance to the relationship between groups.

It follows from the phenomenological stance that the social-psychological approach sees conflict as involving considerable subjectivity, both in the experiencing of the situation and in the valuing of alternative outcomes. Although conflict is not regarded typically as unrealistic—that is, as simply a matter of misperception or misunderstanding—it is seen as having an unrealistic component, the extent of which will vary in any given situation. Conflict is defined in this book as *a social situation involving perceived incompatibilities in goals or values between two or more parties, attempts by the parties to control each other, and antagonistic feelings by the parties toward each other.* The subjective side of conflict thus enters in through the processes of perception, cognition, communication, motivation, valuing, and emotion. Subjectivity also enters into the process of decision making that the parties engage in with respect to the conflict. Again, this is seen as a predominantly, but not exclusively, rational activity; that is, decision making is seen as involving a limited rationality, with the mix of objectivity and subjectivity varying over different situations. A final implication of the phenomenological stance of the social-psychological approach is that conflicts can often be resolved in the sense of a mutually satisfactory and self-sustaining outcome, as opposed to simply being settled through a compromise that leaves neither party satisfied. This is because the perception and valuing of interests and positions is again a subjective process that, over time, can result in changes, thus allowing parties to reperceive priorities and to create integrative combinations that may in fact resolve the conflict. It is somewhat ironic that the same subjective processes that in part create and escalate the enigma of intergroup conflict may also make it possible in part to fashion creative and mutually acceptable resolutions.

The second key element of a social-psychological approach to understanding intergroup conflict is an emphasis on the behavioral interaction between the parties. Deutsch (1973) puts forward basic principles stating that interaction is initiated by motives and in turn generates new motives. The interplay between interaction and the subjective side of conflict is therefore paramount to understanding the phenomenon. How parties perceive and interpret each other's actions will be a prime determinant of how they will respond and thereby of how the conflict interaction will unfold. Interaction between the parties takes a number of forms, each of which is worthy of study in its own right. Parties enter into communication in various forums and formats, and the nature of this process can have important implications for the escalation and resolution of the conflict. In particular, the openness, accuracy, and complexity of communication are dimensions of importance. Wider interaction between the parties can vary in terms of the competitiveness or cooperativeness of their orientations, and this element will have profound implications for how the conflict is played out. In particular, mutually competitive orientations are seen as fueling the escalatory spiral that is the hallmark of destructive intergroup conflict. In this regard, the norm of reciprocity is worthy of much attention as to how it influences the interactive behavior of the parties in escalating, but also in potentially de-escalating, conflict. Specific forms of interaction are also worthy of study, and social psychologists have shown considerable interest in the process of negotiation as a means of settling differences between groups. On a wider scale, the emphasis on interaction leads to questions about the conditions and circumstances under which members of conflicting groups may come into intergroup contact that leads to beneficial outcomes, that is, greater understanding and more positive attitudes. The importance of interaction also leads social psychologists to look for face-to-face, interactive methods of de-escalating and resolving intergroup conflict. In particular, the development of small-group, problem-solving methods is based on the assumption that interaction between the parties is essential for any moves toward resolution to occur.

A third element of the social-psychological approach is the attention to multiple levels of analysis within a systems perspective. In its most powerful form, social psychology asks questions about the functioning of human social behavior at the individual, interpersonal (including role), group, intergroup, organizational, communal, societal, and international levels of analysis (Fisher, 1982). Particular concern is directed to how variables from different levels interrelate in the multiple causation of behavior within the context of a social system. Thus, in approaching the study of intergroup conflict, attention must be directed toward a wide range of factors at various levels of analysis that seem to be essential, if not critical, in the development, escalation, and resolution of the phenomenon. Thus, Deutsch (1973), for example, posits that parties to a conflict are composed of subsystems and yet are capable of unified action, and that their interaction takes place within a social environment that must be considered. This point has been echoed more recently by

Condor and Brown (1988), who emphasize the fact that motivational and cognitive processes (in which social psychologists have shown great interest) necessarily operate in a social context. The systems perspective carries an additional imperative, which is that the analysis of conflict should start at the level of the system in question and blend in variables from other, usually lower, levels as they appear to be useful in understanding the conflict. Thus, emergent properties at each level, especially the one in focus, must be given their due. Thereby, higher level events are less likely to be spuriously explained through the use of lower level concepts — the error of reductionism.

Thus, in approaching intergroup conflict, one maintains an intergroup perspective while blending in consideration of individual-level variables, such as personality characteristics or conflict management style, and group-level variables, such as cohesion or problem-solving competence. Certain concepts that inherently link levels of analysis are especially useful. For example, the concept of social identity links the individual to the group and the concept of boundary role links the group representative to the intergroup relationship. Similarly, at the international level, the concept of nationalism connects the individual to the national structures and processes that are central to relations among states. The greatest challenge is, of course, identifying those variables at different levels of analysis that seem to have particular significance for the escalation and resolution of intergroup conflict. The potential contribution of a social-psychological approach is to help ascertain and to study critical variables at multiple levels that influence complex social interaction within the system in question. In this way, the enigma of destructive intergroup conflict might be eventually illuminated and implications for peaceful forms of management and resolution developed.

Challenges for the Study of Intergroup and International Conflict

The enigma of destructive intergroup conflict lays down a gauntlet to the social science disciplines that is both complex and urgent. Can we offer insights for understanding this perplexing, ultimate conundrum? Can we contribute policy recommendations and practice strategies that may help the world break out of the spiral of increasing destructiveness and potential annihilation? All pursuits, disciplines, and professions have, of course, contributions to make to the understanding and management of intergroup conflict, but the social sciences are intrinsically relevant by their very subject matter, which is the understanding of human social behavior in the context of social systems. Unfortunately, the social sciences, and social psychology in particular, suffer from a variety of deficiencies which limit both relevance and utility in addressing pressing social issues such as intergroup conflict (Fisher, 1982). Thus, social psychology must meet a number of challenges in general, and in relation specifically to the study of intergroup conflict, if it is to make a useful contribution to understanding and practice.

First, there is a challenge to integrate theory, research, and practice in the study and resolution of intergroup conflict. The existing and potential relations among these three elements within the field of social psychology is shown in Figure 1.1

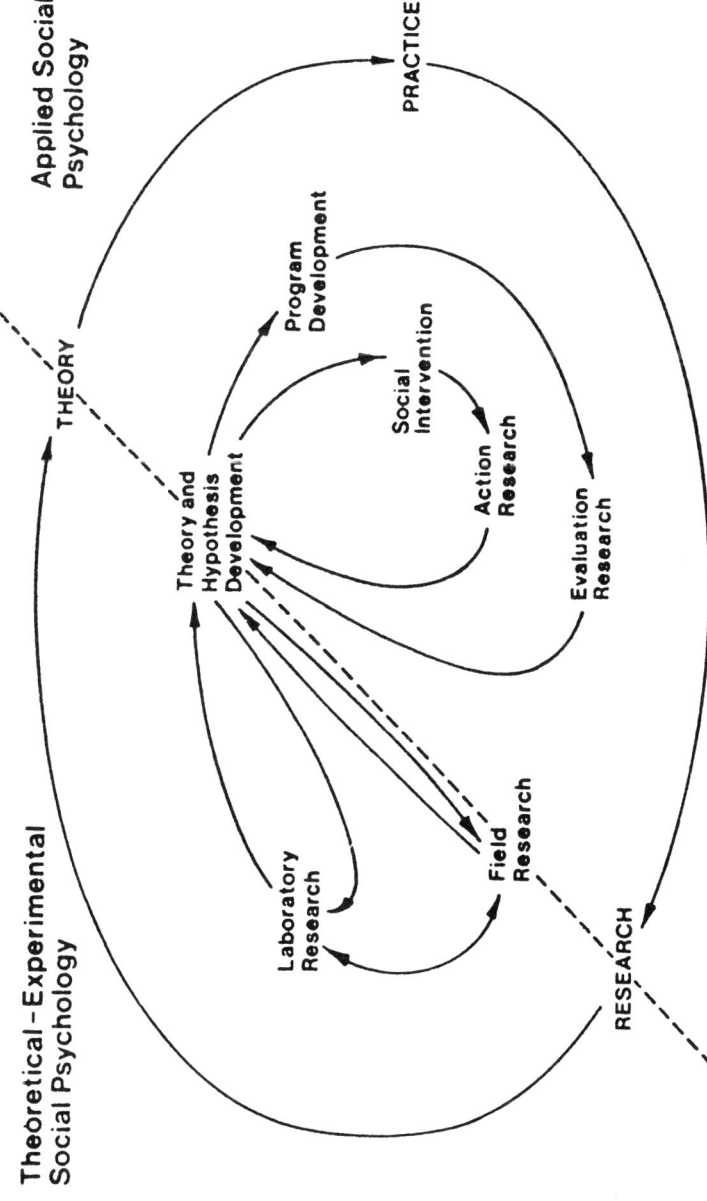

Figure 1.1. Theory, research and practice in social psychology (copyright 1981 Canadian Psychological Association, reprinted by permission).

(Fisher, 1981). The broad cycle connecting the elements can be entered at any point, but the emphasis is placed on research informing theory, primarily through the process of induction. Theory is used to guide practice, that is, direct applications of knowledge to address social issues. The effects of practice can be evaluated using research and this reflects back on, and further informs, theory. Within the discipline, there are of course more limited and specific cycles between theory and research and among theory, research, and practice. Theoretical development may stimulate research through the process of deduction, and the results from research may be related back to theory with no connections to practice. Parenthetically, this is seen as one of the deficiencies of mainstream social psychology that underlies its general lack of relevance to social problems. However, the development of applied social psychology throughout the 1970s and 1980s is starting to rectify this situation (e.g., Fisher, 1982; Oskamp, 1984; Weyant, 1986). Within the theoretical-experimental side of the discipline, the interplay between laboratory and field research is seen as a very important aspect of informing theory in a more comprehensive and valid manner. Within the applied side of the discipline, assistance in the development and implementation of social programs, policies, and interventions based on theoretical understanding is seen as one of the unique contributions that social psychology can make to society. In addition, the use of research—specifically evaluation and action research—to assess and help further plan such practice activities is highly prescribed. The continuous interplay of theory, research, and practice is thus seen as a necessary element of a vibrant, relevant, and useful social psychology and, more generally, social science.

In approaching the enigma of intergroup conflict, the integration of theory, research, and practice is essential to adequate understanding and the development of effective methods of resolution. In the area of conflict, the social-psychological enterprise has been largely restricted to the interplay of theory and research. Practice interventions have been almost nonexistent, although more recently, policy recommendations have been provided based on research results and conceptual models. Deutsch (1983), for example, provides a set of policy suggestions for deescalating the superpower conflict between the United States and the Soviet Union based on his understanding of the escalatory spiral that has led them to the point of intense and dangerous stalemate. More to the point, the developing practice of third party consultation is a rare example of the direct involvement of social scientist/practitioners in the study and resolution of intergroup conflict (Fisher, 1983). When practice interventions like third party consultation are carried out, research evaluations of these interventions are usually nonexistent or based on the simplest of methods such as case study description. Thus, not only is there a paucity of practice, but there are also severe limitations in the assessment of practice. It is therefore not surprising that practice interventions have had very little input in terms of developing or testing theory, and that theory in turn is rarely used to develop practice interventions—common sense and experience being much more available and usable repositories of knowledge. A rare example is the problem-solving work of Kelman (1982) on the Middle East conflict in which ideas from a social-psychological understanding of intergroup conflict are woven into the practice interventions, and theory is in turn informed by the experience of practice. In the domain of research, lines of investigation in the laboratory have too often been separated from studies in the field. Thus, each methodology attempts to inform theory in ignorance of the other. A prime example is the area of games research, where more than 1,000 studies have been largely unconnected to the results of other methodologies, and in fact have failed to cumulate toward any form of comprehensive theory (Pruitt & Kimmel, 1977). Deutsch (1973) is one of the few who have attempted to integrate the findings from games research with those from field studies and other investigations in order to develop a broader and more valid understanding of conflict. By and large, however, the need for greater integration of theory, research, and practice in the study and resolution of intergroup conflict is very apparent and constitutes one of the greatest challenges facing the field. This, in turn, is linked to other issues that must be addressed.

There is a significant challenge in the social-psychological study of intergroup and international conflict to clearly distinguish levels of analysis and to then creatively integrate these toward comprehensive understanding. In studying intergroup conflict and intergroup relations in general, there has been an overreliance on concepts and theories from the individual level of analysis such as attitudes, cognitive dissonance, attribution theory, etc. (Fisher, 1985). While these ideas have utility, they are not adequate by themselves to account for intergroup-level phenomena such as prejudice, discrimination, or destructive conflict. Much more attention needs to be paid to group-level variable such as identity, cohesion, and conformity and to intergroup concepts, such as competitive versus cooperative orientations and mutual ethnocentrism, in order to understand the development, escalation, and resolution of intergroup conflict.

A related distinction that needs to be made is to clearly demarcate the interpersonal level from the intergroup level, and to proceed with caution when attempting to explain behavior at the latter level using concepts from the former. Intergroup relations go beyond interpersonal relations in a number of important respects. As Sherif (1966) has indicated, the study of intergroup relations must consider the properties of the groups themselves and the consequences of membership in the groups on the individual members. Intergroup behavior occurs only when members of two groups interact across group boundaries in terms of their group identifications, and not if they are simply interacting interpersonally as individuals who happen to be members of different groups. Blake, Shepard, and Mouton (1964) indicate that when an individual is interacting as a representative (or member) of a group, additional forces beyond the interpersonal level come into play, not the least of which are the perceptions and evaluations of other members of the representative's behavior. The role of the leader or member interacting with another group becomes one of representing and not violating the goals, values, and convictions of the group. Building on this analysis, Blake and Mouton (1984) emphasize how rules and standards of behavior—that is, group norms—regulate the behavior of members through sometimes subtle but powerful pressures. In a negotiation context, these influences have come to be referred to as constituent pressure (e.g., Thomas, 1976). Additional influences at the intergroup level identified by Blake and Mouton (1984) include group pride, which fuels suspicion and resentment toward outsiders who are critical of the group; high cohesion, which leads members to put loyalty before logic in judging their group's position; invidious comparisons between groups; and a shared win-lose, competitive orientation, which feeds mistrust and hostility.

Another useful way of distinguishing interpersonal from intergroup behavior is in terms of the concept of identity. According to Turner (1982), interpersonal relations involve personal identity, whereas intergroup relations involve social identity that is defined in terms of group memberships. Social identity includes the common attributes of the group, and leads members to view both their own group and other groups as more homogeneous than they really are. Thus, intergroup behavior will tend to be more uniform than interpersonal behavior. Furthermore, forces that affect the group as a whole will have important implications for members' behavior. Hence, intergroup behavior will be influenced by characteristics of intergroup relations such as power, status, and equity rather than by qualities of the interpersonal relations between members from different groups (Hewstone & Brown, 1986b).

The conclusion is that concepts and theories from the interpersonal level are inadequate and should not be used as the sole or even primary explanations of intergroup behavior. Thus, we will see that the use of interpersonal attraction theory to explain the rationale of the intergroup contact hypothesis is incomplete if not misdirected (Hewstone & Brown, 1986b). Similarly, explanations of the potential efficacy of Osgood's (1962) de-escalation strategy of Graduated Reciprocation in Tension-reduction, (GRIT), which are based on individual processes of perception and interpersonal conceptualizations regarding attraction and trust, are bound to be inadequate by themselves. What are eventually required in both these instances and others are explanations using concepts derived primarily from the intergroup level with some assistance from theorizing at the individual, interpersonal, and group levels.

In a similar vein, explanations of international conflict cannot be restricted to conceptualizations from the intergroup and/or lower levels of analysis. As Withey and Katz (1965) have pointed out, a social-psychological analysis of international conflict must deal with psychological factors that are relevant to understanding national social structures and the cooperative or hostile relations between structures. Thus, understanding modes of national integration and the assumption of national roles must be blended with awareness of the essential characteristics of national structures and the dynamics that move nations toward war. One appealing aspect of the concept of protracted social conflict (and similar ideas) is that it holds the potential of combining theories from the intergroup and international levels of analysis. In many instances, the concept of the identity group and all that goes with it will be as indispensable in understanding such conflicts as the concept of the nation state and all that goes with it.

A further challenge for the social-psychological study of intergroup conflict is for the use of multiple methods of study and for the integration of results derived from them. Contemporary social psychology is noted for its reliance on experimental, laboratory methods for generating data. The appeal of such methods is their manageability—some would say their simplicity—and their capacity to allow for the study of causal relationships through the manipulation and control of variables. The primary concern with experimental methods is that of external validity—do the conditions and operationalizations of the laboratory adequately represent the real world? A second concern, more directly relevant to the study of conflict and related to the challenge of studying intergroup conflict at the intergroup rather than the interpersonal level, is that a large amount of the laboratory research in this area uses paradigms that involve interpersonal and not intergroup interaction. The prime example is that of games research, which has predominantly used two-person games, such as the Prisoner's Dilemma, as the central vehicle for studying conflict and cooperation. Irrespective of the pros and cons of games research in general (see Pruitt & Kimmel, 1977, and Schlenker & Bonoma, 1978, for example arguments), the fact remains that the Prisoner's Dilemma and most other laboratory games used in the study of conflict involve interpersonal interaction. All of the significant elements of group and intergroup reality are not represented. This is also true of most laboratory studies of negotiation and of de-escalation strategies, such as GRIT, which often use the Prisoner's Dilemma. In some studies of negotiation, bargainers are instructed that they are representing certain groups, but given that the groups do not exist in the form of real persons and that there is no group or intergroup interaction, the external validity of this technique is highly questionable. Thus, while laboratory studies may test causal hypotheses about relationships among selected variables, these statements must be taken as only tentative and restricted possibilities about the complex reality of intergroup conflict.

Field studies have been used sparingly in the social-psychological study of intergroup conflict, but with notable success. In particular, the field experiments of Sherif (1966) and his colleagues using boys camp groups have probably generated more research and theorizing than any other single piece of research in the area. Using this methodology, the researchers were able to generate and study a considerable amount of the complexity of the development, escalation, and resolution of intergroup conflict. A similar but less well-known line of investigation using adult Americans in management training workshops was undertaken by Blake and Mouton (1961) and generally produced results that paralleled those of Sherif. In addition, field studies including survey work on intergroup relations have helped to provide the research base on which principles relating to positive intergroup contact have been developed. Finally, case study descriptions of intergroup conflicts in organizational and community settings have helped round out the use of field methods for understanding this complex enigma.

The use of simulations for the study of intergroup conflict has unfortunately been practically nonexistent. One recent exception is the work of Love and her colleagues (1983) on the process of bargaining between interreligious social service agencies engaged in prison work. At the international level a well-known and notable example is the work of Guetzkow and his colleagues (1963) on the Inter-Nation Simulation, which has been used among other things for an evaluation of the effectiveness of the GRIT strategy (Crow, 1963). Simulations require a great deal more effort than laboratory games and this makes it difficult to carry out the numerous runs required for the statistical testing of hypotheses. Nonetheless, it is proposed that simulation methodology has a great deal to offer the social-psychological study of intergroup conflict, because it has the potential of blending the experimental control necessary for internal validity with a degree of complexity required for adequate external validity.

At the level of international conflict, the use of content analysis for the study of communication and interaction among national actors continues to produce significant payoffs. This endeavor tends to be an interdisciplinary enterprise with political scientists taking the lead, but with useful contributions by social psychologists. These analyses are particularly valuable when they focus on an intergroup or interstate relationship over time, or when they produce comparative analyses that allow for the study of important variables in the process of conflict escalation or alternative strategies in conflict management and termination. While this work lacks the power of experimental control to assess causal relationships, it represents a very useful window on reality in the field of intergroup and international conflict.

Given this brief overview of different research methods with some selective comment on their strengths and weaknesses, what conclusions can be drawn with respect to the methodological challenge for the study of intergroup conflict? First, it is clear that all methods have their place, and that within a sense of moderation and balance, all should be encouraged. However, the much more important agenda is to begin comparing and integrating the results of the different methods within the overall study of intergroup conflict. Too often, lines of investigation are pursued with great vigor but in utter isolation of potentially related endeavors. Clearly, research results that are supported by data from different methods are to be accepted and valued over those that are not. Theoretical principles of conflict escalation, de-escalation, and resolution that stand up under the scrutiny of a range of different methods are bound to entail greater validity and should be given a wider hearing.

Thus, in the present treatment, analyses that draw on the results of different methodologies will be highlighted whenever possible. A laudable trend in this regard is the blending of results from laboratory methods – primarily games research – with the findings of content analyses or case studies completed either on a comparative or longitudinal basis. For example, the work of Patchen (1988) on resolving disputes between nations integrates results on conflict management strategies used in laboratory games with those derived from historical case analyses of actual international conflicts. The complementarity of principles derived from these separate lines of investigation provides a very strong base for the drawing of conclusions and the making of recommendations for real-world strategists. Another examples is the work of Lindskold (1986) on the GRIT strategy, which blends essential findings from the use of games with descriptions of partial real-world implementations of the strategy to provide a compelling case for its potential utility. Similarly, the social-psychological study of negotiation is moving more and more away from its reliance on experiments in interpersonal bargaining and toward the consideration of the social, cultural, and political context in which negotiations take place (Druckman, 1983). These types of initiatives and developments are to be encouraged and rewarded however possible because they move the field in the direction of greater validity and utility in the study of intergroup conflict and its resolution.

A final challenge facing social psychology in its attempt to contribute to the understanding and resolution of intergroup and international conflict is the need to develop models and methods of practice, which, as noted above, are almost nonexistent in the field. Specifically, the challenge is to develop conflict management and resolution practices based on social science knowledge and expertise regarding social intervention and social change. This is to be distinguished from most existing practice in conflict management, which flows from either a legal base or a base in power politics. Thus, parties typically attempt to negotiate their differences and, failing that, seek mediation or arbitration; or, they use persuasion, positive or negative incentives, or deterrence, threat, and ultimately violence to get what they want. In contrast, social science prescribes the approach of problem analysis and problem solving, based on a general understanding of the dynamics of planned social change, that is, the conscious, systematic, and experimental application of knowledge to help solve human social problems (Bennis, Benne, & Chin, 1985; R. Lippitt, Watson, & Westley, 1958).

Planned change calls for limited or moderate interventions into human affairs involving the deliberate and collaborative use of social science knowledge to improve the functioning of social systems (Fisher, 1982). It therefore occupies the middle road between nonintervention in social affairs, advocated by the doctrine of laissez-faire, and radical intervention, proposed by Marxism. Specifically, the doctrine of planned change proposes a "normative–reeducative" strategy in which individuals and groups are actively involved in discussing and planning the changes designed to reduce the social problems that they are experiencing (Chin & Benne, 1985). This strategy assumes that people are rational and will make changes that are in their best interests, but that group norms and commitments to them are also powerful determinants of behavior. Thus, individuals must engage in a process of active reeducation in which they discuss new knowledge and the possibilities for change, and examine their own values and attitudes in relation to these. In this way, a climate is created in which new group norms can emerge and new commitments can be created. This strategy is highly compatible with a humanistic value base including a democratic approach to decision making in which informed individuals and groups are involved in a process of free and active choice. This is a far cry from the all too common "power–coercive" strategy in which people are forced to change through the application of a variety of forms of social influence. The normative–reeducative strategy is represented in the activities of human relations training and organizational and community consultation that constitute a large segment of the practice domain in the field of applied social psychology and related disciplines (Fisher, 1982).

With regard to intergroup conflict resolution, the doctrine of planned change and the humanistic value base prescribe methods by which the parties themselves are actively involved in a problem-solving process, either by themselves or with the assistance of a third-party facilitator. In organizational settings, the social technology of intergroup problem solving has been pioneered by the work of Blake and Mouton (1984; Blake, Shepard, & Mouton, 1964), and is now regarded as an accepted part of the wider practice of organization development. Developments and applications in community and international settings are less advanced and less frequent, and it is at these levels that the challenge for the growth of practice is particularly acute. Methods need to be further developed by which the parties can examine their differences and the behaviors that have escalated the conflict to unmanageable levels of intensity. Mechanisms must be sought by which the parties can shift from a competitive, destructive orientation to a cooperative, constructive one in which the needs of both can be realized to a satisfactory degree. The use of action research and evaluation research to assess and further develop such practice initiatives is absolutely essential for effective development.

Based on social scientific understanding of conflict processes, policy prescriptions need to be offered that will help parties de-escalate dangerous conflicts to more manageable levels. Thus, the examination of different approaches to handling conflict and their typical effects is an important part of the knowledge that needs to underlie policy recommendations. Based on a general understanding of consultation methods, including ethical considerations, third-party approaches for conflict analysis and resolution need to be further developed and eventually institutionalized. Thus, parties involved in an intense intergroup or international conflict will have access to a forum and a format in which they can examine the conflict as a mutual problem to be solved rather than as a war to be won or lost.

At this point in the history of human social conflict, the elements of the practice challenge will appear unrealistic to many, because the power approach to conflict management continues to predominate. However, as the costs of destructive strategies escalate, as the frequency of meaningless stalemates increases, and as knowledge of alternative methods is disseminated, receptivity to nonviolent and noncoercive methods of management and resolution will grow. The ultimate challenge for social scientist/practitioners is to be ready with valid knowledge about intergroup conflict and effective methods for helping to deal with it when the possibilities for increased application and involvement present themselves.

The Scope and Plan of This Book

The intention of this book is to provide a contemporary description, analysis, and evaluation of the social psychology of intergroup and international conflict and its resolution. Thus, attention is directed toward some of the intricate and myriad ways that individual-level processes combine with group and intergroup variables in the causation, escalation, de-escalation, and resolution of intergroup and international conflict. In line with the general characteristics of the social-psychological study of intergroup conflict, an attempt is made to emphasize the phenomenological, interactive, multilevel, and systemic nature of the enterprise. A further attempt is made to draw on and integrate both classic and contemporary contributions to the field.

The scope of this book is constrained by a number of limitations and boundaries. The topic of intergroup conflict and its resolution is only a part of the wider study of intergroup relations in social psychology and social science, although many would see it as a central part. The wider interest in ongoing interaction among interdependent groups is not of interest here; the focus is on instances of intergroup relations in which the definition of intergroup conflict provided above is met. In addition, the broad issue and questions of majority–minority relations, which comprise much of the study of intergroup relations, is not directly addressed here. This is not because these issues and the theories that deal with them are not important – on the contrary, they are at the heart of the process of social change. It is simply because the necessary focus here is at the point of conflict at which minority groups have reached a level of power and assertiveness to challenge the majority over concerns of identity, security, equity, and justice. It is at this point that the relationship has the potential for either destructive escalation or constructive confrontation. This book therefore seeks concepts to help understand the past and current nature of the conflict and methods to help the parties deal more effectively and nonviolently with it.

The primary focus of the analysis is therefore on relatively equal power identity groups, however defined, that are engaged in intense conflict with each other. The intergroup relationship is seen as interdependent, that is, mixed-motive, in which both cooperative and competitive behaviors are required for the groups to meet their respective goals. More specifically, there is a central interest in protracted social conflicts in communal and international settings. However, in addressing this interest, this book will not present case study descriptions and analyses of particular intergroup conflicts as a historical or political science approach might do. Rather, the emphasis is on a generic analysis of intergroup conflict using concepts and principles drawn from the field of social psychology. Based largely on general theorizing and research about conflict, the analysis will attempt to inform our thinking about intergroup conflict in terms of core processes and outcomes. Thus, the analysis may be at a level of generality and abstractness that some will find frustrating in its lack of connection to concrete instances of conflict. However, it is proposed that the potential power of a social-psychological analysis is precisely in its generic capacity to be applied to a large number of similar conflicts. This is not to deny that full knowledge of the details of any given conflict is also essential in its understanding and its resolution. However, it is suggested that an awareness of generic and essential processes is necessary to sort the wheat from the chaff in moving toward true understanding and, it is hoped, effective mechanisms for resolution.

As a social-psychological enterprise, this book is empirically based; that is, the vast majority of theorizing that is brought forward will be linked to some form of data collection and analysis. In line with the comments above, the results that are used come from a wide range of research methods: laboratory studies including games and simulations; field studies including experiments, surveys, and participant observation; and archival studies that apply various forms of content analysis to documents representing the interaction between parties in conflict. A concerted effort will be made to move away from the overreliance on laboratory experimentation at the interpersonal level that has dominated the discipline for the past 30 years. These results will not be ignored, but an attempt will be made to blend them in with findings from broader methodologies when forming theoretical principles or constructing policy or practice implications.

This book will focus almost exclusively on the work of social psychologists, because they are most likely to take a social-psychological approach to the study of conflict by nature of their scholarly identity. This is not intended to downplay the contributions of many other disciplines in the study of intergroup and international conflict, nor of other social scientists who take a social-psychological approach. Particularly at the international level, the limited scope of the present analysis must be acknowledged. While making important contributions with regard to core processes, social psychologists rarely appreciate the numerous aspects of the national and international systems that impact upon conflict at this level. Thus, our analysis must be seen as a slice of reality that, we hope, has an important contribution to make, but which must be blended in with many other considerations in order to be useful.

The plan of this book intends to be both comprehensive and cumulative. Thus, it will attempt a degree of integration that has been largely lacking in the field. Chapter 2 will provide a review and evaluation of classic contributions to theory and research in the area. Within this, attention is directed toward the definition, sources, and escalation of intergroup conflict as discussed by social psychologists. Chapter 3 by Peter Grant, underscores the phenomenological orientation by discussing contemporary work in social perception and cognition that is relevant to intergroup conflict. The implications of these lines of investigation for the escalation and resolution of intergroup conflict will also be discussed. Chapter 4 focuses on group-level factors that feed conflict escalation. In addition to linking a number of basic elements of group dynamics to intergroup conflict, Chapter 4 will emphasize how crisis decision making too often replaces effective problem solving. Chapter 5 draws on Chapters 2, 3, and 4, plus other sources, to develop an eclectic, social-psychological model of intergroup conflict that captures the essential variables and processes at the individual, group, and intergroup levels of analysis. A systematic approach to theory building is used, which covers basic variables, core principles, important boundaries, system states of low and high intensity, and propositions that can be put to empirical test. The resulting model is recommended as a useful summarization of work to date and as a stimulating juncture for further theorizing and research. Chapter 6, co-authored with Peter Grant, Donald Hall, and Loraleigh Keashly, describes the development of a unique, innovative research paradigm for continuing study—The Intergroup Conflict Simulation (ICS). The ICS is a complex, strategic simulation designed for the systematic and controlled study of the development, escalation, and resolution of intergroup conflict in a realistic and yet manageable fashion. The validity of the simulation in terms of group development and conflict intensity is demonstrated through data collected on two successive sets of runs. Chapter 7 approaches the enigma of destructive international conflict with continuing illustrations drawn from the rivalry between the superpowers. In addition to a discussion of sources, the role of cognitive factors, and the processes of communication and interaction, Chapter 7 covers social-psychological research on negotiation and the potential for de-escalation in international conflict. Chapter 8 begins the shift to practice considerations by describing social-psychological approaches for the management and resolution of intergroup conflict. An overview of the facilitative conditions of intergroup contact is followed by an integrative discussion of alternate strategies at the interpersonal, intergroup, and international levels based on a two-dimensional model of conflict management. Two specific methods for de-escalating and resolving intergroup conflict are also discussed: Graduated Reciprocation in Tension-reduction (GRIT) and problem-solving workshops. Chapter 9, co-authored with Loraleigh Keashly, focuses on the unique and promising roles that third parties may play in intergroup and international conflict resolution as supported by social-psychological theory and research. In particular, Chapter 9 highlights the problem-solving method of third party consultation for the study and resolution of intergroup conflict. The rationale of this method is explicated and its effectiveness is compared to that of traditional mediation using the ICS. A context for consultation is provided by developing an initial taxonomy and a contingency model of third party intervention. The conclusion of the book in Chapter 10 attempts to pull together main themes that thread through the entire work. The implications of social-psychological theory, research, and practice for approaching the enigma of destructive intergroup conflict will be articulated. Finally, the necessity of further developing and institutionalizing problem-solving approaches for building a peaceful world will be highlighted.

Chapter 2

Classic Contributions to the Study of Intergroup Conflict

The discipline of social psychology can be largely characterized as the study of intergroup relations. Indeed, the history of the field is permeated with a continuing interest in topics directly or indirectly related to understanding and improving relations among groups. The early concentration on attitude measurement (e.g., Likert, 1932; Thurstone & Chave, 1929) centered largely on attitudes toward various ethnic, racial, and religious groups as shown by later compendiums of attitude scales (Shaw & Wright, 1967). Similarly, theories of attitude formation and change often reflected an interest in intergroup relations (e.g., D. Katz, 1960), while the study of ethnic and racial stereotypes directly contributed to the broader investigation of prejudice and discrimination (e.g., D. Katz & Braly, 1933; P.A. Katz, 1976; P.A. Katz & Taylor, 1988). The area of social perception and cognition also has its connections to the enigma of intergroup relations (e.g., Allport & Postman, 1945), while the study of persuasive communication is rooted in a concern with the phenomenon of wartime propaganda, a clear concomitant of destructive intergroup relations (e.g., Hovland, Janis & Kelley, 1953). Finally, the applied side of the discipline has historically shown a keen interest in intergroup relations as exemplified by the seminal work of Lewin (1948) on the use of action research as a means of improving relations among groups in community settings.

The contemporary interest in intergroup relations continues to run high in social psychology. In the United States, interest has been expressed primarily through laboratory studies evidencing great precision in the attempt to elucidate the role of specific variables in the etiology of various intergroup phenomena (e.g., Austin & Worchel, 1979; Worchel & Austin, 1986). In Europe, different but complementary lines of investigation have developed, in particular, the theory of social identity as an explanation of intergroup relations (Tajfel, 1978). In Canada, social psychologists have been especially concerned with the study of interethnic attitudes and intergroup relations within the multicultural context (e.g., Berry, Kalin, & Taylor, 1977). Indeed, it can be maintained that the 1970s evidenced a revival of interest in intergroup behavior in the field of social psychology (Tajfel, 1982), and it appears that this resurgence will continue through the 1980s and 1990s.

Unfortunately, much of the study of "intergroup relations" in social psychology, as noted in Chapter 1, has relied upon concepts and methods developed for studying individuals rather than groups or intergroup behavior. Thus, theorizing at the individual level of analysis (e.g., attitude formation, attribution) has been used to explain intergroup phenomena such as prejudice and discrimination. This type of theoretical analysis is, by its very nature, inadequate to elucidate the role of group-level variables and intergroup-level variables in intergroup behavior. Perhaps more seriously, within the general study of intergroup relations, there has been a paucity of theory and research directly devoted to the study of *intergroup conflict*. While the general study of intergroup relations contributes to our understanding of intergroup conflict as a constituent phenomenon, it is no substitute for the direct and focused analysis of conflict processes between groups. Thus, the purpose of this chapter is to set the stage for such direct study by reviewing a number of classic contributions that have significantly increased our understanding of intergroup conflict. The strengths and limitations of these contributions will be pointed out and their implications for developing an eclectic, social-psychological theory of intergroup conflict will be identified.

Ethnocentrism and Realistic Group Conflict Theory

The term *ethnocentrism* was coined in 1906 by Sumner to describe a cultural narrowness in which the "ethnically centered" individual rigidly accepted those who were culturally alike while just as rigidly rejecting those who were culturally different. According to Sumner:

> Ethnocentrism is the technical name for this view of things in which one's own group is the center of everything, and all others are scaled and rated with reference to it.... Each group nourishes its own pride and vanity, boasts itself superior, exalts its own divinities, and looks with contempt on outsiders. Each group thinks its own folkways the only right ones, and if it observes that other groups have other folkways, these excite its scorn.... Ethnocentrism leads a people to exaggerate and intensity everything in their own folkways which is peculiar and which differentiates them from others. (p. 13)

The study of ethnocentrism in social psychology was extended significantly by the work of Adorno and his colleagues in the classic study, *The Authoritarian Personality* (Adorno, Frenkel-Brunswik, Levinson, & Sanford, 1950). Given their psychoanalytic leanings, these authors saw ethnocentrism as a generalized prejudice rooted in the personality dynamics of the individual. As their starting point, these authors provide one of the most explicit definitions of the concept:

> Ethnocentrism is based on a pervasive and rigid ingroup–outgroup distinction; it involves stereotyped negative imagery and hostile attitudes regarding outgroups, stereotyped positive imagery and submissive attitudes regarding ingroups, and a hierarchical, authoritarian view of group interaction in which ingroups are rightly dominant, outgroups subordinate. (p. 150)

The Authoritarian Personality began as a study of anti-Semitism in which an attitude scale was constructed to measure prejudice towards Jews on a number of dimensions including the threatening character of Jews, their seclusiveness, and their offensive nature. As predicted, these various components of anti-Semitism showed strong relationships with each other, culminating in the development of a unitary Anti-Semitism Scale. The broader study of out-group attitudes followed with the construction of the Ethnocentrism Scale, which included items on a number of racial and ethnic minority groups as well as items measuring in-group loyalty and glorification of the "American way." Item–total correlations, correlations among subscales, and correlations with the Anti-Semitism Scale all supported the concept of ethnocentrism; that is, respondents showed a general acceptance or rejection of a variety of out-groups, and those who rejected out-groups tended to glorify and be loyal to the white Protestant American in-group. For the authors, the explanation of this phenomenon lay in the personality dynamics of the ethnocentric individual. Through the development of the F (Facism) Scale to measure antidemocratic trends and the use of clinical interviews with high and low ethnocentrics, a picture of the development and dynamics of the authoritarian personality was created. Early in their children's lives, parents who are overconcerned about social status and proper behavior use harsh autocratic discipline to rear socially acceptable children. However, this treatment results in the repression of both aggression toward the parents and child's shortcomings. Through displacement, the aggression is redirected toward out-groups in the form of antagonism and hostility. Through projection, the unacceptable faults are projected onto powerless minority groups, thus fueling prejudice. In terms of the Freudian components of personality and their interrelationships, the *id* gains expression of its aggressive impulses, while a strong but poorly internalized *super-ego* maintains power over a weak *ego* that readily submits to authority figures and defends the status quo.

The Authoritarian Personality has legitimately been criticized on several grounds for its failings in attitude measurement. Many of the items were "double-barreled," containing more than one idea, and thus making the interpretation of responses ambiguous. All the items were worded in one direction (the negative) and were thus open to a response set interpretation leading to a controversy which fueled the attitude and personality measurement literature for some time thereafter. In addition, all the scales and items followed the same format, thus increasing the common variance due to methodological homogeneity and exaggerating the potency of ethnocentrism (H.J. Ehrlich, 1964). However, the generalized prejudice identified by Adorno et al. (1950) has been documented by other studies both before and after *The Authoritarian Personality* and involving a range of additional out-groups (e.g., Campbell & McCandless, 1951; Chesler, 1965; Hartley, 1946). Unfortunately, the in-group loyalty and glorification side of ethnocentrism has received less attention. In one of the few studies addressing the in-group side, the author found that Canadian university students who tended to reject a variety of racial and religious out-groups also demonstrated greater in-group loyalty and glorification toward their family, friends, and fellow student (Fisher, 1968).

The psychoanalytic interpretations of Adorno et al. (1950) linking ethnocentrism to underlying personality dynamics have also received mixed support. Prothro (1952), for example, found a lower relationship between attitudes toward Jews and blacks in a sample of white Southerners and thereby emphasized the importance of situational factors as opposed to personality factors in the etiology of ethnocentrism. Rokeach (1960) considers the operative process in generalized prejudice to be "closed-mindedness," or *dogmatism*, thus stressing cognitive rather than dynamic processes. Nonetheless, one contribution of *The Authoritarian Personality* has been to raise the possibility that mildly pathological or unrealistic factors play a role in the etiology of ethnocentrism, and consequently in the development and escalation of intergroup conflict. Beyond that, the work stands as an early indication that the concept of ethnocentrism has potential utility in the study of intergroup relations.

An alternative explanation for ethnocentrism is to be found in the articulation of Realistic Group Conflict Theory (RCT). Based on anthropological, sociological, and social-psychological studies, Campbell (1965) postulated the basic premise of this approach that *real conflict of interest causes intergroup conflict*. Thus, Campbell saw RCT as a rejection of and an alternative to the predominant individual-level, psychological (especially psychodynamic) explanations of prejudice and intergroup conflict, which abound in the psychological literature. According to Campbell, RCT "assumes that group conflicts are rational in the sense that groups do have incompatible goals and are in competition for scarce resources" (p. 287).

Building on the work of social psychologist Muzafer Sherif (to be discussed below), sociologist Lewis Coser (1956), economist Kenneth Boulding (1962), and many other social scientists, Levine and Campbell (1972) gathered anthropological data from traditional societies to support a variety of further propositions of RCT. In summary, these are:

1. that real conflict of interest and real threat cause perception of threat,
2. that real threat causes hostility to the source of threat,
3. that real threat causes in-group solidarity and awareness of in-group identity, and
4. that real threat increases ethnocentrism.

A number of intermediate propositions articulate the entire syndrome of ethnocentrism, which is seen as being generated from the reaction to conflict and threat from out-groups. Other elements of the syndrome include increased tightness of group boundaries, reduced defections from the group, and increased punishment and rejection of defectors and deviants. A number of additional propositions explore further determinants of the level of ethnocentrism in relation to characteristics of the in-group and the out-group and the relationship between the groups. With regard to the resolution of intergroup conflict, Levine and Campbell clearly accept the major point of Sherif's work in stating their proposition: that "intergroup conflict and mutual ethnocentric hostility can only be removed by superordinate common goals or shared threats" (p. 40).

Although RCT gives less attention to individual-level variables, both normal and abnormal, it does provide a powerful integration of the group and intergroup processes involved in intergroup conflict. In doing so, it also incorporates a number of propositions from the functional approach to social conflict. Finally, RCT clearly emphasizes the seminal role that realistic sources play in the causation of intergroup conflict.

The Field Studies: Sherif, Blake, and Mouton, and Zimbardo

One of the few lines of investigation in social psychology that directly addresses the phenomenon of intergroup conflict involves the classic field studies by Sherif and his colleagues (Sherif, Harvey, White, Hood, & Sherif, 1961; Sherif, 1966) and the training laboratory studies by Blake and Mouton (1961). Both of these research programs involved the controlled and relatively complex development, escalation, and resolution of intergroup conflict with an emphasis on causative factors, common processes, and typical outcomes. The Zimbardo "Prison Experiment," (Haney, Banks, & Zimbardo, 1973), while not primarily designed to simulate intergroup conflict and while involving role playing rather than real groups, similarly provides a dramatic analogue of real and intense conflict between social groups.

The Sherif work is comprised of a series of three field experiments in which preadolescent American boys were brought into summer camp groups in order to control and study the relations that developed among them. The boys were recruited without knowledge of the study and informed consent was obtained from their parents. Three similar studies were completed, in 1949, 1953, and 1954. The last and most extensive of these is known as the "Robbers Cave Experiment" since it took place near the Oklahoma caves which the infamous Jesse James gang of outlaws once used as a hiding place.

With some variation, the field experiments included three phases:

1. An in-group development phase in which the boys were formed into two separate camp groups (in the third study with no knowledge of each other) and engaged in the usual summer camp activities. As predicted, the boys developed a sense of in-group identity and loyalty. In addition, leadership emerged, status hierarchies developed and norms and sanctions became evident, thus providing the common elements of group structure. The high degree of morale and cohesiveness that the groups typically evidenced is shown by the names that were chosen, in one case, for example, the "Eagles" and the "Rattlers."

2. An intergroup competition phase in which the groups were brought together in a series of competitive, win–lose interactions such as archery, tug-of-war, and baseball. Again as predicted, these competitions resulted in the development of in-group biases, out-group derogation and hostility, and destructive intergroup behavior. In the competitions, each group overestimated its abilities and accomplishments while underestimating those of the other group. Negative out-group stereotypes became evident and name-calling and belittling of the other group were observed, in addition to scuffles and attacks on each other's territory. Attempts to bring the groups together in peaceful social contact deteriorated into open conflict as when, for example, a dinner together escalated into a garbage-throwing war.

3. An intergroup cooperation phase in which the researchers unobtrusively imposed a series of *superordinate goals*, that is, common, compelling objectives that could only be obtained by the two groups working together, for example, having to join forces to pull and start the camp truck in order to get the food for a picnic. However, one such interaction was not enough to de-escalate the conflict; a series of superordinate goal accomplishments were required to replace hostility with positive attitudes

and behavior. One implication is that conflict escalation appears much easier to induce than is conflict resolution.

The power of the Sherif studies lies in demonstrating that a range of individual-level, but more importantly, group-level factors intertwine with intergroup variables in the development and resolution of intergroup conflict. In addition, the studies clearly show how a combination of realistic and unrealistic sources are typically involved in intergroup conflict. However, the central propositions are that real conflict of interest and the resulting intergroup competition are the fundamental cause of conflict (as articulated by RCT), and that superordinate goals are the path to conflict resolution.

The work of Blake and Mouton (1961) builds nicely on the Sherif studies by extending the line of investigation to different groups in a different setting working on different problems. Their 30 separate, repeated studies involved more than 1,000 American adults, drawn from a variety of business and industrial organizations and in management training programs on intergroup relations. Each training program and unobtrusive study ran for a 2-week period and followed five phases modeled on the Sherif work:

1. An in-group development phase in which participants engaged in 10 to 18 hours of group interaction following the sensitivity training model. This interaction typically led to the development of group cohesion, norms, goals, and power structure.

2. An intergroup competition phase, which was induced by presenting the different groups in the same training workshop with a common problem of organizational functioning, such as how to best motivate subordinates, and asking them to each develop a solution. It was indicated that only one group's solution would be chosen as the best. In this phase, the researchers observed the further development of cohesion with members putting aside differences and pulling together for victory. Pressures for conformity increased, with intolerance of disagreement and even expulsion of deviants from the group. As also observed in the Sherif studies, power relations within the groups shifted, with the more aggressive and articulate members gaining greater influence. Once solutions were developed, in-group biases led to distortions in perception and evaluation in which participants typically saw their group's solution as superior and ignored important differences between the solutions. Objective tests on the content of the competing solutions documented that similarities were often overlooked, whereas distinctions were clearly recognized, especially if they were part of one's own group's solution.

3. A win–lose outcome phase, which was imposed by having the best solution chosen by the groups or selected by an arbitrator if necessary. In this phase, the groups studied the solutions, met together to clarify the solutions, and then sent forward representatives to negotiate the final choice. The intended clarification process usually deteriorated into criticism and belittlement of the other group's solution. Observations also documented the development of hostile attitudes and negative stereotypes with antagonistic behavior, such as provocative statements being traded between the groups. When the elected representatives came forward to negotiate an outcome, the almost universal result was deadlock. When an impartial judge was called in to arbitrate, he was initially perceived as "fair" by both groups;

but once the decision was rendered, the losing group saw him as "biased" and "incompetent." The losing group often deteriorated into warring factions and the fallen leaders were ostracized. The winning group was elated, but also arrogant and complacent in a manner that did not augur well for its future.

4. A conflict reduction phase, which was then instituted by having the researchers shift to the role of human relations trainers who facilitated the process of analyzing what had transpired in the preceding three phases. Participants came to see the destructive behaviors of intergroup conflict and compared these with the alternative conditions of intergroup cooperation.

5. An intergroup collaboration phase in which the participants were trained in a sequence of problem-solving procedures designed to prevent or reduce the negative elements of intergroup competition and to create the conditions for intergroup cooperation. Participants learned to develop a range of alternatives instead of a fixed position and to look for points of similarity as well as difference in solutions. The full implementation of the problem-solving sequence was put forward as the key to the resolution of destructive intergroup conflict.

As with the Sherif studies, Blake and Mouton's (1961) workshops demonstrated that it was much easier to develop and escalate intergroup conflict than it was to de-escalate it through mutual problem solving. In addition, the workshop highlighted the power of role expectations with regard to the negotiator. The influence of constituent pressure was clearly evident both during and after negotiations between the group representatives. Rather than regarding the imposition of superordinate goals as the key to intergroup conflict resolution, the workshop studies laid the basis for developing a sophisticated social technology of intergroup problem solving as the path to peace (see Chapter 8).

The research of Blake and Mouton corroborates that of Sherif in supporting what can be termed a functional theory of intergroup behavior (Turner, 1981). That is, functional interdependence (in this case, negative) between groups for the achievement of their goals leads to competitive interaction, which produces cohesion in the groups and antagonism between them. This interpretation is similar to that of Deutsch (1973), to be discussed later in this chapter. However, Turner also points out that the studies tend to confound functional interdependence with competitive social interaction so that it is not clear whether the group and intergroup effects are due to one or the other or to both. Similarly, Dion (1979) and others have noted that the camp and workshop studies allow so many variables to operate simultaneously in the situation and in the manipulation of win–lose competition that it is difficult to know what factors were responsible for the outcomes. Drawing on the work of Rabbie (e.g., Rabbie & Wilkens, 1971), Dion points out that with regard to increased in-group cohesion, for example, it is unclear whether the effect is due to the initial high solidarity before interaction, a competitive orientation, an expectation to compete, mutual frustration during intergroup interaction, or the influence of having won or lost. For the mind of the experimentalist, these studies raise many more questions than they answer, and a number or profitable lines of investigation have attempted to sort out the effects of various independent variables on various dependent ones (see, for example, Austin & Worchel, 1979; Worchel & Austin, 1986; Turner, 1981).

A third omnibus illustration of how easily intergroup conflict can be induced is provided by the "Stanford Prison Experiment" designed by Phillip Zimbardo and his graduate student colleagues (Haney, Banks, & Zimbardo, 1973). A simulated prison was created in the basement of Stanford University's psychology building in order to study the dynamics of prison life, a central part of which was the intergroup relationship between prisoners and guards. Participants were carefully selected from among volunteers and randomly assigned to the two groups. Without warning, the prisoners were arrested, searched, handcuffed, and taken to the police station for booking. Subsequently, they were blindfolded and transported to "Stanford County Prison" where they were stripped, skin-searched, deloused, given their prisoner's garb, and informed of a list of harsh and seemingly arbitrary rules covering every basic and mundane aspect of prison life. Their keepers, the guards, were supplied with uniforms, reflector sunglasses, whistles, handcuffs, keys, and billy clubs.

At first, the prisoners attempted to revolt, directly challenging the guards' authority to impose strict rules and harsh discipline. The guards squashed the rebellion viciously and punished the ring leaders with solitary confinement. They then began to harass and intimidate the prisoners, demonstrating creativity in the use of arbitrary power. Prisoners were forced to do tedious and useless work, such as moving cartons back and forth between closets and picking thorns out of blankets dragged through bushes by the guards. Prisoners were ordered to sound off their numbers endlessly, repeatedly made to do push-ups, and forced to curse and vilify each other. In short, the relationship between prisoners and guards became a perverted, symbiotic one in which the prisoners became increasingly passive, dependent, and self-deprecating while the guards became more and more aggressive and self-aggrandizing. Stereotyping, suspicion, and hostility came to characterize the intergroup relationship. The personal stress on the prisoners began to show, and after the release of five prisoners, the experiment was terminated before reaching the intended 2-week duration. Debriefing sessions and follow-up interviews indicated that the mental anguish was situational and temporary, but that the learnings for both prisoners and guards were permanent.

The implication of this work is congruent with, but even more shocking than, that of the camp and workshop studies: well-adjusted individuals can slip very easily into roles and intergroup behavior that is myopic, destructive, and inhuman. In the prison experiment, the power of institutional structures to create and support intergroup conflict is additionally apparent. In particular, the pervasive influences of roles (perhaps overplayed in the prison simulation) on the attitudes and behavior of individuals involved in intergroup conflict was clearly demonstrated. At the same time, all three demonstrations are compatible with RCT in that real conflict of interest, competitive interaction, and ethnocentrism lie at the heart of destructive conflict between groups.

Social Identity Theory

A line of investigation pioneered by European social psychologists and complementary to RCT is the work on Social Identity Theory (SIT) by Henri Tajfel and his associates (Tajfel, 1970; Tajfel & Turner, 1979). The initial research supporting SIT involved experiments indicating that the mere perception of belonging to a group—that is, social categorization—is sufficient by itself to produce intergroup discrimination favoring the in-group. In a series of studies in which subjects have been arbitrarily or randomly classified as members of two groups and then have made decisions awarding small amounts of money to in-group and out-group members, subjects have consistently discriminated in favor of their own group (Billig & Tajfel, 1973; Tajfel, 1970; Tajfel, Flament, Billig, & Bundy, 1971).

It is important to note that, in apparent contradiction to RCT, this intergroup discrimination occurs without real conflict of interest, a history of antagonism, or any intergroup interaction. Since minimal intergroup discrimination is not based on incompatible group interests and occurs with simple social categorization, Tajfel and his colleagues suspected that they were dealing with a process that was inherent in the basic intergroup situation by itself. This led them to consider the link between the individual and the group in ways that had implications for intergroup behavior. Thus, social categorizations are seen as creating and defining an individual's place in society and thereby providing for self-reference. Social groups provide their members with identifications that define their social identity, that is, those aspects of an individual's self-image that derive from the social categories to which he or she belongs and the emotional and value significance of such membership. It is then assumed that individuals strive to maintain or enhance self-esteem and a positive self-concept, that social categories are evaluated in ways that contribute to social identity and thereby self-esteem, and that social comparison with other groups helps determine the evaluation of one's own group.

From these considerations, the basic tenets of SIT follow:

1. individuals strive to achieve or to maintain positive social identity,
2. membership in groups contributes to an individual's social identity,
3. evaluation of an individual's own group is based on social comparison with other groups, and
4. a positive social identity is based on favorable comparisons.

The basic hypothesis, then, of SIT is that pressures to gain distinctiveness for and to evaluate one's own group positively through social comparisons lead to intergroup discrimination in the in-group's favor. In cases where the intergroup comparison is unfavorable, a negative social identity and dissatisfaction with one's group result. Under certain conditions, such as the situation being seen as unjust or unstable, the individual and/or the group may attempt to improve their social identity. In cases of either positive or negative comparisons, the explanation of behavior comes through a combination of individual- and group-level concepts, primarily self-concept, social identity, and social comparison. This integrative power of SIT through an emphasis on social-psychological processes is one of its appealing elements. By highlighting the importance of individual-level variables on intergroup discrimination, the theory serves as a useful complement to RCT. It also serves as a qualification to RCT in that it demonstrates that real conflict of interest is not always necessary to create minimal intergroup discrimination. However, it is important to note that the discrimination found in supporting studies consists only of in-group favoritism—the other side of the ethnocentric reaction, outgroup rejection and hostility, is not a common finding in this line of investigation (Brewer, 1979). The potential power and scope of SIT is therefore circumscribed. In addition, some of the basic tenets of social identity have been challenged by more recent research results (D.M. Taylor & Moghaddam, 1987). For example, a field study by Brown, Wade, Mathews, Condor, and Williams (1983) found some negative relationships between group identification and intergroup discrimination and over all of the groups studied, the relationship was weakly positive. Although SIT has been a stimulating development both conceptually and in terms of research generated, its ultimate contribution to the field of intergroup relations awaits further assessment.

The Groundwork for Eclectic Theory

Each of the classic contributions above proposes or assumes a definition of social conflict, points toward certain sources of conflict, and highlights particular processes of escalation, de-escalation, and resolution. Each of these areas of conceptualization has a rich history, in its own right, in the social-psychological study of conflict. No comprehensive attempt will be made here to trace these histories, but an illustrative selection of contributions will be presented in the areas of definition, sources, and processes.

The Definition of Social Conflict

In their classic review of the study of conflict in the social sciences, Mack and Snyder (1957) maintain that:

> Obviously, "conflict" is for the most part a rubber concept, being stretched and molded for the purposes at hand. In its broadest sense it seems to cover everything from war to choices between ice-cream sodas or sundaes. (p. 212)

Nonetheless, Mack and Snyder are able to present eight basic propositions, rather than attempting a formal definition, which capture the essence of social conflict. Through a selective combination of these propositions, one can construct a working definition, which would look something like this:
  Conflict:

1. requires at least two parties,
2. arises from position scarcity and resource scarcity,
3. requires interaction among parties in which actions and counteractions are mutually opposed,
4. involves attempts to gain control of scarce resources or positions or to influence behavior in certain directions,
5. involves behaviors that are designed to destroy, injure, thwart, or otherwise control the other party, and
6. does not represent a breakdown in regulated conduct, but rather a shift in the governing norms and expectations. (pp. 218–219)

A more recent comprehensive review by Fink (1968) adopts a similar yet different approach to that of Mack and Snyder. Fink makes the case for adopting a very broad definition of social conflict so as not to prematurely restrict conceptual analysis in the area. Thus, for example, to restrict conflict to interaction wherein one party attempts to inflict physical harm on the other would rule out numerous other important instances of conflict. This may be particularly true in situations where underlying psychological patterns that motivate a struggle, for example, between economic classes, have not yet given rise to overt attempts to control, thwart, or injure. Fink thus sees conflict as a social situation or process in which the parties are linked by at least one form of antagonistic relation (e.g., incompatible goals, emotional hostility) and by one form of antagonistic interaction, (e.g., violent struggle, indirect interference). Fink therefore emphasizes the wider relationship and interaction among the parties and also acknowledges the possibility of affective elements of conflict in the antagonistic relations.

The contributions of Morton Deutsch span 40 years of conflict research and his seminal ideas on the process of social conflict will be identified below. With regard to definition, Deutsch (1973) lands solidly in the social psychology camp by asserting that conflict exists whenever *incompatible activities* occur between persons, groups, or nations. An incompatible activity is any action that prevents, obstructs, interferes with another activity, or in some way makes another activity less likely or less effective. The emphasis in Deutsch's work is thus on conflict behavior, particularly the ongoing interaction between the parties and the mutual, reciprocal influence between them.

In constructing definitions like these, social psychologists and others have confronted and attempted to deal with a number of issues or questions with regard to how conflict can best be conceptualized. Although an exhaustive list cannot be analyzed here, some illustrative points regarding the major issues can be made. First, is conflict predominantly real or imagined, that is, based in realistic or unrealistic sources? Realistic conflict is seen as arising from some objective difference in the real world, such as Mack and Snyder's (1957) resource or position scarcity. Unrealistic conflict, on the other hand, arises and exists primarily or solely in the minds (i.e., perceptions and cognitions) of those involved. The conflict is therefore a result of misperception, misattribution, miscommunication, and other phenomenological processes that create conflict where no basic incompatibilities exist. As the above definitions demonstrate, social psychologists have clearly come down on the side of realistic conflict, in which objective differences lead to conflicting behaviors intended to control the other party. This is in contrast to some analyses of individual-level psychologists, particularly those of a psychodynamic bent, who see unrealistic conflict as common and as rooted in intrapsychic processes. However, social psychologists do typically see realistic conflict growing to incorporate aspects of unrealistic conflict. Objective differences and conflicting behaviors threaten the parties leading to misperception and miscommunication which transform the interaction into a mixture of realistic and unrealistic conflict.

Another issue that runs throughout the literature on conflict is whether conflict is a destructive or constructive phenomenon. Stated in this way, the question is immediately seen as too simplistic, partly because it does not distinguish between the means of conflict and the ends of conflict. The point is often made that positive social change (i.e., toward justice and equality) often must be gained through violent means. Beyond this distinction and acknowledgment, however, lie more sophisticated questions. First, it must be maintained that conflict by itself is neither bad nor good. The former judgment is often attributed with criticism to the structural-functionalist school of social theory, as represented, for example, in the work of the sociologist Parsons, which is seen as a pretext for maintaining the superficial harmony of the status quo. The latter position, that conflict is inherently good, appears to underlie the change-oriented theories of Marx, Dahrendorf, and other more radical theorists who see conflict as the vehicle of liberation. A large number of social scientists now appear to walk the middle road, which sees conflict as a neutral process, the costs and benefits of which need to be judged in the context of any given situation. More specifically, a distinction can be made between constructive and destructive conflict based on a consideration of the processes as well as the outcomes. For example, according to Deutsch (1973), a conflict is destructive when the participants are dissatisfied with the outcomes and have a sense of loss, while a constructive conflict involves productive consequences wherein the participants are satisfied with their outcomes and feel that they have gained as a result. To see conflict as productive, destructive, or a mixture of both is compatible with the practice intent of wanting to reduce the destructiveness of conflict while realizing the potential benefits. To interpret this intent as assuming that all conflict is bad, as is sometimes done by the critics of would-be peacemakers, is both inaccurate as well as unwarranted.

Another major issue in the study of conflict has to do with the complex distinction between conflict and competition, complex because of the manner in which these two phenomena are intertwined in many social situations. Competition is often at the heart of conflict, for example, in instances of resource scarcity. The goal of each party is to achieve the valued commodity and to prevent the other from achieving it. Thus, incompatible activities derive from incompatible goals and the narrow definition of conflict is met. However, it is possible for competition to involve no direct action of one party to interfere with the activities of the other and for the activities of both to occur in parallel behaviors constrained by the adherence to rules and the imposition of sanctions for rule violations. This approach thus sees competition as indirect and regulated struggle. Conflict, on the other hand, is much more likely to be a "no holds barred" interaction with mutually destructive behaviors as its hallmark, the objective being the injury of the opponent as much as or more than the attainment of a scarce resource. Unfortunately, as the review by Fink (1968) makes clear, the distinction is not so simple, because the shifting conceptual boundaries between conflict and competition illustrate numerous choices that have been made differently by various theorists. Some adopt a broad definition of competition in which conflict becomes a special case, whereas others see competition and conflict as synonymous. How one defines conflict will, in essence, determine how the conflict versus competition issue is resolved or, at least, managed.

A final issue, related to the conflict versus competition distinction, is whether conflict requires overt antagonistic behavior for its existence or whether underlying or latent conflicts of interest constitute conflict. The definitions cited above tend toward seeing conflict as manifest rather than latent in the sense, for example, of ongoing competition and tension among societal groupings for scarce resources. The manifest approach thus emphasizes that conflict is a social interaction in which antagonistic behaviors are clearly observable. Underlying tensions are seen as necessary but not sufficient conditions for the occurrence of conflict. However, theorists who favor a social change emphasis often see latent conflict as the most significant factor in social reality, with the distinction between underlying tension versus overt struggle as being simply a matter of awareness and motivation. Again, the definition of conflict adopted will rule certain types of incompatibility in and others out with regard to further analysis (Fink, 1968).

The Sources of Conflict

Whether one adopts a broad or narrow approach to the definition of conflict, attention must still be directed to the sources of either underlying tension or overt struggle. In contrast, the narrow definition, which requires behavioral interaction, would put more emphasis on the process, particularly the escalative process, in which psychological and behavioral elements combine to fuel the conflict. This process will be considered later. In this section, the focus is on the nature and types of incompatibilities that give rise to conflict behavior.

There is of course no agreed upon typology of the sources of social conflict, as the reviews by Mack and Snyder (1957) and Fink (1968) make clear. Some theorists, for example, Coser (1956), distinguish between basic cleavages over the very nature of a society's consensual framework within which people have been operating, and conflict over the means and ends within a consensual framework. Similarly, one can distinguish between conflicts of right (over the application of agreed upon standards to specific situations) and conflicts of interest (over the changing of standards). Beyond these broader distinctions, which relate to the interplay between conflict and social change, many conflicts are seen as based in value differences (e.g., ideological conflict) and in what Mack and Snyder call resource and position scarcity. In a summary response to the question of whether there are basic facts of social life that might account for a variety of conflicts, Mack and Snyder suggest that:

> it seems generally agreed that scarcity of desired objects, states of affairs, and resources in nature and culture, the division of labor in organized society, and social differentiation lead inevitably to potentially conflictful cleavages and antagonistic interests. (p. 223)

Of the numerous typologies of conflict that have been or could be developed, that offered by Daniel Katz (1965) is one of the most concise and useful. It distinguishes three major sources, and thereby types, of conflict: economic, value, and power. *Economic conflict* involves competing motives to obtain scarce resources, including territory, and is therefore one of the clearest forms of realistic conflict. Each party wishes to acquire the most of the resource that it can without perceptible limits, and therefore directs its behavior toward maximizing its gain at the expense of the other party. In terms of management, economic conflict is most amenable to compromise or possibly to rarer integrative solutions reached through negotiation, sometimes augmented by the third-party methods of mediation or arbitration. This is assuming that the size of the resource pie is indeed fixed, as is typically assumed. If not, then it is possible to conceive of creative solutions in which the size of the pie is actually increased.

Value conflict revolves around incompatible preferences, principles, or practices that people believe in and are invested in with reference to their group identity. Differences may arise in such areas as culture, religion, politics, or ideology. At base, it is difficult to compromise or accommodate value conflicts because they lie at the center of peoples' identities. Negotiation is thereby contraindicated. Therefore, some form of peaceful coexistence may be the most likely solution, possibly involving adherence to some superordinate values that allow for differences among subordinate values. In successful multicultural societies, for example, respect for differences and a valuing of basic human rights must take precedent over the value preferences of any particular group.

Power conflict exists when each party wants to maximize its influence over the other — a possibility that is rendered impossible by the very definition. In other words, it is not possible for one party to be stronger in terms of reciprocal influence without the other being weaker. This definition, of course, assumes a fixed-pie approach to social influence, as opposed to an understanding that increasing the influence of both parties may be possible. Power conflict is particularly prone to escalation and typically ends with victory by one party and capitulation by the other. Up to that point, a continuing stalemate and state of tension may exist for a considerable period of time. The central issue in power conflict is not scarcity or incompatibility, but a question of control and related items such as pride, recognition, and the future economic rewards that power may bring.

Typologies of conflict, like all categorization systems, have the appeal of simplifying social reality through analysis, thus initially increasing our understanding. However, none can do total justice to the complexity of social life. As Mack and Snyder (1957) point out:

> Most social scientists now accept the principle of multiple causality; hence there is no one basic source of conflict. In view of the preoccupation with the evil consequences of conflict, it is not surprising that the literature on causation overbalances the rest. Indeed, so far as particular areas of conflict are concerned, underlying sources have been rather thoroughly catalogued. It is fairly easy merely to list the most significant sources of, say, war. The central problem is, of course, to determine the particular combination of underlying source factors in a given situation. (pp. 221–222)

The consensus is that most conflicts do not represent a pure type, but involve a mixture of economic, value, or power differences combined with an unrealistic ingredient of misperception and miscommunication. It is not uncommon for a conflict to originate from one source and then proliferate to include other sources and issues and to escalate through a combination of realistic and unrealistic factors. Therein lies both the challenge in understanding conflict and in approaching it with a view to developing ameliorative interventions.

The Groundwork for Eclectic Theory

The Process of Conflict

The hallmark of the social-psychological approach to understanding conflict is the emphasis on the process rather than the content of conflict, that is, on the *how* rather than the *what*. In other words, social psychologists have a particular interest in the perceptions, cognitions, attitudes, and behaviors that characterize destructive conflict and pay less attention to the substantive, specific issues that are at stake. Thus, special attention has been paid to perceptual, attitudinal, and behavioral processes that fuel the escalating spiral of destructive conflict—the unrealistic side of complex conflict.

In the study of the escalatory processes of social conflict, the name of Morton Deutsch stands out as capturing the essence of the social-psychological approach. Most of Deutsch's work, unfortunately, draws on the interpersonal level of interaction, specifically from studies of cooperative versus competitive interaction in groups and dyads, primarily within the context of laboratory games such as the Prisoner's Dilemma and the Trucking Game. Results from the interpersonal level of analysis have already been criticized as having limited validity for the study of intergroup conflict. However, Deutsch has been one of the few "games researchers" who has made an attempt to incorporate results and concepts from the intergroup level into his theorizing. In particular, Deutsch (1973) draws on the work of Sherif and Blake and Mouton in developing what is likely the most representative and acknowledged statement of the social-psychological approach to analyzing destructive social conflict.

As a social psychologist, Deutsch takes a strongly phenomenological stance in spelling out the major characteristics of his theory, but he is also sensitive to system-level determinants. The basic propositions Deutsch puts forward include:

1. The parties respond in terms of their perceptions and cognitions of each other.
2. The parties are influenced by their expectations of each other.
3. Interaction is initiated by motives and generates new motives.
4. Interaction between the parties takes place in a social environment.
5. The parties are composed of subsystems but are capable of unified action.

A major contribution of Deutsch is the specification of a cooperative versus a competitive social interaction in terms of perceptions, attitudes, communication, and the task orientation that the parties take to their relationship. In a cooperative social interaction, the parties are sensitive to similarities and hold trusting, friendly, and helpful attitudes, whereas in a competitive interaction, the parties are sensitive to differences and hold suspicious, hostile, and exploitative attitudes. In a cooperative relationship, communication is open, accurate, and relevant; in a competitive relationship, it is nonexistent or limited, misleading, and used for purposes of espionage. Task orientation in a cooperative interaction approaches the conflict as a mutual problem to be solved, whereas in a competitive interaction, each party attempts to impose its solution on the other by coercion and escalation. In terms of underlying sources, Deutsch identifies promotive interdependence (the parties' goals are positively related) and contrient interdependence (the parties' goals are negatively linked), the latter typically giving rise to incompatible activities that are the essence of the definition of conflict.

Building on the contrast between cooperation and competition, Deutsch also helps explain the enigma of social conflict by illuminating perhaps the major reason for its pervasiveness, persistence, and intransigence. The key to understanding lies in Deutsch's *crude law of social relations*: The characteristic processes and effects elicited by a given type of social relationship (cooperative or competitive) tend also to elicit that type of social relationship. In other words, in a mixed-motive conflict wherein parties are motivated to both cooperate and compete, cooperation tends to breed cooperation while competition tends to breed competition. Thus, cooperative relationships tend to become more so, while competitive relationships tend to escalate into destructive social conflict.

With regard to the escalation of conflict, Deutsch (1983) has more recently drawn on his basic propositions to describe what he terms a *malignant social process*: one that is increasingly dangerous and costly and from which the parties see no way of extricating themselves without unacceptable losses. This process of destructive escalation draws upon and bears similarity to the competitive type of interaction that is characteristic of apparently irresolvable social conflict. It occurs within an anarchic social situation in which the parties have little or no regard for the welfare of others; incorporates a competitive, win–lose orientation that assumes irreconcilability of interests; and may involve inner conflicts of the parties being expressed through the external conflict. It demonstrates cognitive rigidity (particularly stereotypes that are not confronted by reality), misperceptions and misjudgments (for example, actor/perceiver differences in attributions), unwitting commitments (in which postdecision dissonance reduction strengthens prior beliefs), and self-fulfilling prophecies (in which behavior based on prior, false expectations in fact elicits the expected response). All of these cognitive and behavioral "traps" feed into vicious, escalating spirals in which increasing risks are required to justify past investments and lead to a gamesmanship orientation in which policy analysts and decision makers play with images of power in an abstract world of scenarios that becomes removed from the awesome reality that violent confrontation would surely bring.

Overall, Deutsch's approach integrates a comprehensive coverage of the phenomenology of the individual into the level of intergroup interaction. It does this partly by generalizing interpersonal processes, such as communication, to the intergroup level and thus may involve some neglect of the group level of functioning. However, as Deutsch (1980) points out in discussing his own work, the emphasis in his early training on group processes influenced him to formulate his ideas about cooperation and competition in ways that were relevant to psychological and interpersonal processes occurring within and between groups. Although the clear majority of studies supporting his ideas are based on intermember relations within groups and dyadic interactions, limited research at the intergroup level has obtained the same basic findings (cf. Workie, 1967). The parallels between the lines of investigation stimulated by Deutsch and the classic field studies of Sherif (1966) and Blake and Mouton (1961) are therefore once again underscored.

It can also be argued that Deutsch's theory places too much emphasis on the unrealistic side of conflict analysis. However, the psychology part of the social psychology combination requires that individual concepts and processes be given their due in explanation, particularly with regard to the escalative elements of destructive conflict. The challenge is to integrate these psychological processes into the social fabric of intergroup conflict in a way that does justice to all relevant levels of analysis. As a step in this direction, Deutsch's work stands as a classic and complex social-psychological treatment of conflict, and thus serves as a major part of the base for a process-oriented, eclectic model of intergroup conflict.

Conclusion: Implications for Theory, Research, and Practice

This overview of the classic contributions to the social psychology of intergroup conflict holds within it a number of implications for theory, research, and practice. First, it is useful to identify some of the common deficiencies in contemporary theory and research. Theoretical work in the area is fragmentary and largely unconnected—the various lines of investigation are only minimally informed by each other. In relation to this problem, most theorizing fails to comprehensively integrate multiple levels of analysis, but tends to concentrate on one or perhaps two levels with limited input from others. A related problem is that results gained at the interpersonal level are too readily generalized to the intergroup and international levels. This violation of social reality is becoming the target of increasing criticism (e.g., Brown & Turner, 1981; Tajfel, 1978). With regard to research, laboratory studies often lack external validity (they are indeed games!), while the classic field studies are limited in internal validity, thus making it difficult to identify causal relationships among variables. In addition, action research that involves a practice component is almost nonexistent in the field of intergroup relations or in the study of intergroup conflict. In order to overcome these deficiencies, it is appropriate to speculate on the characteristics of valid research, the components of eclectic theory, and the directions for useful practice.

Valid and relevant research would need to embody a judicious balance between control (i.e., internal validity) and complexity (i.e., external validity). In order to do this, such research should address itself to a variety of variables at a number of levels of analysis. Thus, it would by its very nature be integrative and longitudinal, and would allow for the operation of both realistic and unrealistic sources of intergroup conflict in its execution. The use of social simulations to study the process and outcomes of intergroup conflict in these ways becomes especially appealing. Within the laboratory setting, this paradigm would allow for the study of the development and resolution of intergroup conflict in a holistic, systematic, and controlled manner. "Strategic simulations" in which conflict is created by imposing a situation of resource scarcity over which parties must then interact would appear to offer the most appropriate alternative. The development and assessment of a simulation meeting these requirements is described in Chapter 6.

An eclectic, social-psychological theory of intergroup conflict would need to include a number of essential components. It would need to begin with a comprehensive yet restrictive definition of social conflict that does not see conflict as equivalent to all forms of social opposition or difference. Antecedent conditions, including negative historical events, would need to be considered. A range of potential sources of conflict covering both the realistic and unrealistic would have to be included. Thus, the theory could build on a combination of realistic group conflict theory, social identity theory and various other social-psychological contributions. Also of importance would be the intensity of the conflict, the characteristics of the issues, the characteristics of the parties, and the functional nature of the conflict. Much attention would be given to the process of escalation and to the requirements for de-escalation. On a wider scale, an eclectic theory would be built on contributions from, and be sensitive to, relationships among variables at multiple levels of analysis, and would address itself to the similarities and the differences across different varieties of intergroup and international conflict. It is suggested that social-psychological theorizing, which is at its best multilevel and integrative, has a crucial role to play in this endeavor. An initial description of an eclectic model of intergroup conflict is developed in Chapter 5.

The implications for practice to de-escalate and resolve social conflict are numerous and complex. Methods are required that will help the parties understand the sources of their differences and the ways in which their behaviors have escalated the conflict through competitive interactions. Understandings from other areas of research, such as research on the facilitative conditions of intergroup contact, need to be built upon along with conflict theory in order to develop effective practice strategies. By and large, the challenge for practice is to replace competitive interactions with cooperative ones, possible through increasing the salience of superordinate goals, and to lay bare the insidious processes of misperception, miscommunication, cognitive rigidity, self-fulfilling prophecies, etc. that have fueled the escalation of the conflict. In doing this, attention must be directed to a variety of causative factors from a number of levels of analysis and the manner in which they have interacted to escalate the conflict. Finally, the parties need to be encouraged and invited to enter into a problem-solving process that sees the conflict as a shared difficulty to be resolved through cooperative effort. Given the intransigence of intense social conflict, it is likely that this de-escalatory process can most often and most effectively be instituted through the involvement of an impartial third party. The possibilities for the cooperative management of intergroup conflict and the constructive involvement of third parties are discussed in Chapters 8 and 9.

Chapter 3

Cognitive Theories Applied to Intergroup Conflict

Peter R. Grant

In 1963, Tajfel and Wilkes described two experiments in which subjects judged the lengths of eight lines repeatedly presented in random order over a series of six trials. In the experimental condition, the four longer lines were labeled as A and the shorter lines as B. That is, there was a relationship between each line's length and its category membership. In the control conditions, either the lines were classified at random, or the lines were not classified at all. The results showed that, in the experimental condition, intercategory differences were accentuated by the superimposition of this classification scheme but that intraclass similarities were not. Although these experiments were clearly concerned with documenting a bias in the subjective judgments of physical stimuli, the ultimate goal of the authors was to show that "shifts and biases in stereotyped judgments can be subsumed under similar shifts existing in absolute judgments of a series of physical quantities" (p. 101). That is, like Bruner (1957; Bruner & Perlmutter, 1957), they wished to explore the cognitive bases for social judgments under the working assumption that we use the same cognitive processes as those we employ to make physical judgments. Today, this assumption guides a great deal of theory and research in the area that has come to be known as social cognition. This chapter will examine the work relevant to intergroup conflict that is derived from this tradition. The first part will briefly describe the effects of categorizing individuals into an in-group and an out-group by summarizing the findings of a great deal of experimental research. The second part of the chapter will review in some detail the theories that are used to explain these findings. Finally, the third part of the chapter will discuss some practical implications of these cognitive perspectives for resolving intergroup conflict.

The Effects of Categorizing Individuals into Groups: The Experimental Evidence

Exaggeration of Within-Group Similarities and Between-Group Differences

When people categorize objects, they tend to exaggerate intraclass similarities and interclass differences (Rosch, 1978; Tversky, 1977). Similarly, when individuals are categorized as members of a particular social group they are assumed to be similar to each other and different from members of another out-group. Specifically, it has been shown that group members are assumed to be more similar to each other than members of an aggregate, that the presence of an out-group increases this assumed in-group similarity, that members of the out-group are assumed to be different from members of the in-group, and that members of the out-group are assumed to be similar to one another (see Quattrone, 1986, W.G. Stephan, 1985, and Wilder, 1986, for detailed reviews of this evidence).

Two types of experiments have been used to demonstrate these effects. In the first, subjects are asked to make judgments about members of existing social groups. For example, Doise, Deschamps, and Meyer (1978, experiment 2) asked 174 Swiss children to describe three social groups on sixteen 8-point semantic differential scales. In the control condition, the three groups were the German, French, and Italian ethnic groups that make up the majority of the population of Switzerland. In the three experimental conditions, people from Germany, France, or Italy replaced one of these ethnic groups. As predicted, the children in the experimental conditions described the two Swiss ethnic groups as more similar to each other than the children in the control condition. That is, intranational similarities were exaggerated by these children when they were asked to make international comparisons.

More precise evidence for these effects has come from the second type of research in which subjects are assigned to arbitrary social groups. For example, Wilder (1984, experiment 1) asked groups of subjects to privately express their preferences for pairs of paintings by Klee and Kandinsky. Then, supposedly on the basis of their judgments, they were told that preferences were equally divided between Klee and Kandinsky, and that they were a member of the Klee group. Subjects were then asked to predict the range of beliefs of members of their own group (I condition) or members of the other group (O condition). In the control conditions, subjects were told that everyone preferred Klee and were asked to predict the range of beliefs of the in-group (Intragroup condition), or they were not assigned to a group and were asked to predict the range of beliefs of the other subjects in the experiment (Ungroup condition). The predictions were for beliefs about artistic impressions (the basis for group assignment), political beliefs (related to artistic preferences), and opinions on a court case (unrelated to artistic preferences). In addition, the subjects in all conditions rated their similarity to the stimulus persons. The results showed that subjects rated the in-group as less homogeneous than the out-group, and in-group members as more similar to themselves than out-group members in terms of artistic preferences and political beliefs (I versus O). Furthermore, the in-group was rated as more homogeneous and similar in terms of artistic preferences in the intergroup situation (I versus Intragroup). No significant effects were found for beliefs unrelated to artistic preferences (opinions on a court case).

When a group of stimulus persons are perceived to be members of several social categories, subjects are less able to distinguish among members of the same group than among members of different groups. For example, S.E. Taylor, Fiske, Etcoff, and Ruderman (1978, experiment 1) asked white subjects to listen to a tape recorded conversation in which six men made suggestions for a play's publicity campaign.

Slides showed a picture of each of the speakers, three of whom were black and three white. The results showed that subjects were better able to match suggestions to members of different racial groups than suggestions to members of the same racial group. One reason for this may be because people chunk information about the behavior of group members into larger units as they attend to the group as a whole rather than an individual group member (Wilder, 1984, cited in Wilder, 1986). Another reason is that people seem to prefer information that confirms that they are similar to other members of their own group and different from members of an out-group resulting in selective attention to within-group similarities and between-group differences (Wilder & Allen, 1978).

One issue that is still a source of some controversy is whether the out-group is perceived to be more homogeneous than the in-group. Intuitively, one would suppose that greater familiarity and knowledge of the in-group would make this hypothesis an obvious one. Indeed, in reviewing the evidence, Wilder (1986) states that there is "strong support for the outgroup homogeneity hypothesis" (p. 311), a position also held by Rothbart and his colleagues (Rothbart, Dawes, & Park, 1984) and by Quattrone (1986). However, Stephan (1985) reviews several studies that demonstrate that evaluations of the out-group are more differentiated than evaluations of the in-group. In trying to reconcile these two positions, he uses existing evidence to argue that perhaps out-group members are perceived to be more homogeneous than in-group members on any one trait dimension, but that they are described by a more varied set of trait dimensions. Further work on this issue is needed to test this interesting notion.

Stereotyping

The study of stereotyping has had a long history in social psychology. For example, starting with the pioneering work of Katz and Braly (1933, 1935), a large number of studies have demonstrated that there is a consensus across time and subject populations on the traits that are generally ascribed to various ethnic groups (Brigham, 1971). Until the 1970s, this research was descriptive in nature: subjects were asked to indicate on a list the traits they would use to describe members of a particular social group, and the traits commonly chosen were said to form the stereotype of the group. Needless to say, this method precludes an examination of how stereotypes are represented in memory and the biases in impression formation that may result.

Subsequently, the emphasis on social cognition has led researchers to investigate stereotypes as cognitive structures. From this perspective, they are usually defined as expectations that a set of traits is associated with membership in a particular social group (Hamilton, 1979, 1981). The evidence strongly supports this view and demonstrates biases in attention and the encoding and retrieval of information such that these stereotypic expectancies are confirmed (see Stephan, 1985, for a detailed review). Specifically, attention is influenced by these expectancies so that knowing someone is a member of a particular group results in a perceiver searching for information that will confirm that the person can be characterized by stereotype attributes and selectively attending to this information when it is found. For example, Duncan (1976) asked white subjects to rate an interaction between two individuals in another room. The interaction was observed on a television monitor and, although subjects believed it was "live," they actually saw a recording of an interaction between two black and/or white actors having an increasingly heated argument over whether an engineer should keep his safe, low-paying job, or take a higher-paying job with no promise of long-term financial security. Toward the end of the videotape, subjects evaluated a scene in which one of the actors gave the other a shove. The results showed that this ambiguous action was interpreted much more negatively when a black actor was the perpetrator. For instance, 75% of the subjects in the black perpetrator–white victim condition chose the "violent behavior" category to describe this act; whereas, only 13% in the white perpetrator–black victim condition made this choice. These results suggest that the information attended to in the black perpetrator conditions confirmed the white subjects' stereotype that black people tend to be violent.

The evidence that stereotypic expectancies tend to be confirmed because they influence encoding and retrieval of information is also quite compelling, although, like the results in cognitive psychology (W.F. Brewer & Nakamura, 1984), encoding effects seem to be the stronger of the two (S.E. Taylor & Crocker, 1981; Stephan, 1985). An experiment by Rothbart, Evans, and Fulero (1979) illustrates the type of experiment used to demonstrate these effects. Subjects were shown slides that described the behavior of 50 men from a group. Prior to or following this slide presentation the group was described as either "more friendly and sociable than average" or "more intelligent than average" (p. 346), thereby manipulating the subjects' expectations. In all experimental conditions, the subjects were shown the same slides which described 17 friendly behaviors, 17 intelligent behaviors, 10 unrelated behaviors, 3 unfriendly behaviors, and 3 unintelligent behaviors. When the expectations were established before the slide presentation, subjects in the "friendly group" condition overestimated the number of friendly behaviors they had been shown and recalled more friendly behaviors in a cued recall task. Similar effects were found for subjects in the "intelligent group" condition and intelligent behaviors. These results can be interpreted as support for biased encoding, because all subjects attended to the same information. No bias was obtained when the expectancy manipulation occurred after the slide presentation. That is, the expectancies did not seem to bias information retrieval. However, biased retrieval effects have been found in other studies (e.g., Snyder & Uranowitz, 1978).

The findings summarized above suggest that people usually remember stereotype-consistent information better than stereotype-irrelevant or stereotype-inconsistent information. However, novel or unexpected information may need to be attended to closely since it represents the unknown component of a social situation, and there is evidence that salient stimuli do influence social judgments (S.E. Taylor & Fiske, 1978). Wyer and Gordon (1982, 1984) suggest that irrelevant or inconsistent information may influence judgments about a target person initially, but may decline in importance over time if this information does not fit with the perceiver's other expectancies about this person. More research is necessary to clarify this "perplexing issue" (Stephan, 1985, p. 606).

The fact that a stereotype influences the initial impression of a member of a social group would not be important if interaction with this person quickly corrected any misperception that results. However, this corrective process does not occur easily. Rather, the initial stereotypic expectancies held by a perceiver tend to be confirmed by the target person's subsequent behavior in a self-fulfilling prophecy. For example, Jussim (1986) reviews evidence that teachers form expectations about each of their pupils and that these expectations can be based upon stereotypes. Then, using these expectancies, they treat the pupils differently, giving more attention and emotional support to their "best" students, as well as more opportunities to practice difficult-to-learn skills. Disadvantaged students have trouble overcoming the negative impact of this treatment because the situation makes it difficult for them to shine in comparison to students who receive preferential treatment. This invidious process has also been documented in a variety of other social situations involving interactions between members of many different social groups (see Darley & Fazio, 1980 and Snyder, 1981, 1984 for detailed reviews).

Causal Attributions

Recently, some attention has been directed toward the causal attributions used to explain the behavior of group members. Wilder (1986) summarizes a few studies that show that when people are perceived to be members of a group, their behavior tends to be explained in terms of group rather than individual characteristics. That is, observers are less likely to make the fundamental attribution error and, therefore, are more likely to impute cause to situational factors including the presence of other group members and task characteristics. Wilder argues that this effect is obtained because the subjects in these studies have difficulty deciding whether the group member was responding to group norms or because of his or her unique disposition.

A second set of studies has focused on what has been called the *ultimate attribution error*, or *the ethnocentric bias* (Hewstone, 1988a, 1988b; Pettigrew, 1979; D.M. Taylor & Jaggi, 1974). This bias occurs when internal attributions are used to explain socially desirable actions by in-group members and socially undesirable actions by out-group members, whereas external attributions are used to explain the socially undesirable actions of in-group members and the socially desirable actions of out-group members. For example, D.M. Taylor and Jaggi (1974) showed that Hindu subjects ascribed socially desirable actions to the good character of Hindu stimulus persons, but employed situational explanations for the same behavior engaged in by Muslim stimulus persons. In contrast, socially undesirable actions were explained in terms of situational constraints faced by Hindus and the bad character of Muslims. Stephan (1985) has argued that this bias can be explained if one assumes that, in general, people expect good behavior from members of their own group and bad behavior from out-group members. That is, it is a cognitive bias based upon differing expectancies. However, because studies of the ultimate attribution error are based upon groups with a history of negative intergroup relations, other more motivational and sociostructural explanations are equally likely (see Hewstone, 1988a for a more extensive discussion).

Recently, Hewstone (1988b) has used Weiner's (1985) attributional theory of achievement motivation to discuss attributions made at the intergroup level of analysis.

He argues for a more complete examination of the attribution that people use to explain the actions of in-group and out-group members in terms of stability and controllability as well as locus of causality. Biased attributions favoring members of the in-group can occur in several ways. For example, socially desirable behavior may be explained as reflecting the ability of an in-group member (an internal, uncontrollable, stable cause), but the effort of an out-group member (an internal, controllable, unstable cause). Although in this example internal attributions are used to explain the behavior of members of both groups, there is still a bias in the suggestion that in-group members have superior abilities (see also Deaux, 1976). Hewstone (1988b) cogently argues that several types of attributions can be used to explain the behavior of an out-group member, and it is the patterning of these attributions that is important. As an example of this new approach, he cites an unpublished study in which public schoolboys attributed in-group successes to ability with or without effort; whereas, they attributed out-group successes to ability in combination with effort. Because this study used a free response format it would seem to have high ecological validity. Clearly, more work needs to be done to explore this promising new direction.

In-Group Bias

A great deal of evidence shows that categorization leads to in-group bias as was noted in Chapter 2 in the discussion of social identity theory. Most of this work uses the minimal group paradigm in which subjects are assigned to fictitious groups of no importance and then, in an unrelated task, divide points (usually worth a small amount of money) between an in-group and an out-group member. Subjects never assign points to themselves and do not gain financially if they favor a member of their own group. As an example of this paradigm, consider an early experiment by Tajfel, Flament, Billig, and Bundy (1971, experiment 2). Fourteen- and 15-year-old boys were asked to express their preference for 12 abstract paintings by choosing between pairs of reproductions shown on slides. The boys were told the paintings were by Klee or Kandinsky, but were not told the artist associated with any given painting. The boys were then assigned to a "Klee" or a "Kandinsky" group supposedly on the basis of their preferences but, actually, at random. In the second part of the experiment, the boys were taken to individual cubicles and filled out a booklet that required them to assign points worth one tenth of a penny using matrices. These matrices displayed a wide variety of payment options that the subject could select to reward two stimulus persons who were identified only as preferring the same or different painter as the subjects (in-group and out-group members, respectively). For some matrices, both stimulus persons preferred the same painter; for others, they did not. Without going into detail (see Tajfel, 1970, 1978), the matrices were constructed so that, together, they can yield a score for various payment strategies the subjects might adopt. For example, subjects may have decided to give both stimulus persons an equal amount (fairness), or to maximize the payment to both (maximum joint profit), and so on. The results showed that, when assigning points between an in-group and an out-group member, subjects consistently favored the in-group and tried to maximize the difference in scores between the in-group and the out-group. The evidence also indicated that the subjects also wished to be fair and, therefore, this discrimination was not as extreme as it might have been (Branthwaite, Doyle, & Lightbown, 1979; Branthwaite & Jones, 1975). These results are very robust and have been replicated many times (M. B. Brewer, 1979; Tajfel, 1970, 1978; Tajfel & Turner, 1979).

Cognitive Theories of Intergroup Relations

In this section, categorization theories, self-categorization theory, balance theory, and schema theory will be reviewed as they apply to intergroup relations. These cognitive theories were chosen because they have all been used to explain some of the experimental findings just summarized. However, only self-categorization theory was developed to explain intergroup relations. The others apply to object perception (categorization theories) or person perception (balance theory and schema theory) and have been extended to include intergroup relations by various authors (see Levine & Campbell, 1972; Stephan, 1985).

Categorization Theories

Exaggeration of within-group similarities and between-group differences can be explained using theories of the categorization process recently developed in cognitive psychology. Unlike classical theories of classification, in which all members of a category must possess certain defining attributes, these theories suggest that objects are grouped because they share many common attributes, although any one category member need not have all of these attributes (Lingle, Altom, & Medin, 1984). Perhaps the most influential of these categorization theories in social psychology is the Feature Matching Model proposed by Tversky (1977). In this model, similarity between two objects, A and B, is a function of the contrast between the features that A and B have in common and the distinctive features of both A and B (the matching assumption). Furthermore, A is more similar to B than C, when A and B share more common features and have less distinct features than A and C (the monotonicity assumption). On their own, these assumptions are not new. Many authors concerned with object perception and the perception of social categories have defined similarity in this way (e.g., Bruner, 1957; Campbell, 1958; Rosch, 1978; Tajfel, 1969). However, Tversky's theory is more complete in that it explicates the implications of these assumptions in detail.

Briefly, the model predicts that there will be an asymmetry in similarity judgments "determined by the relative salience of the stimuli so that the less salient stimuli is more similar to the salient stimuli than vice versa" (p. 333). This is called the *focusing hypothesis*. Tversky notes that some objects are very prototypical of a particular category because they share many features with other members of the category and have few distinctive features. These prototypes characterize the typical member of a category and, therefore, are salient. Thus, the focusing hypothesis implies that members of a category are judged to be more similar to the prototype than vice versa. The evidence supports this hypothesis and shows that people prefer to use the prototype as a referent by which they judge other members of the category.

Family resemblance is a linear combination of the common and distinctive features of all pairs of objects in a category. Rosch (1975, 1978; Mervis & Rosch, 1981) has argued that a *natural* or *basic* category is the one in which the family resemblance is highest. The evidence shows that such categories are responded to faster, are the first to be acquired by young children, are used most often in conversation, and are more likely to be associated with a mental image that reflects the whole category. However, as Tversky points out, the context determines which category is judged to be basic. Features of an object vary in diagnostic value, that is, in terms of their importance in determining the object's classification. Within a particular and restricted context, some features may have little or no importance, whereas, within a wider context, these same features may be of great value. Thus, widening the context may lead to different categories being used to classify objects as judgments of similarities are based upon a new set of features. In addition, if objects remain in the same category, they tend to be judged as more similar because they have more common features (the extension effect).

Applying this theory to intergroup relations, it can be seen that it can explain some of the findings reviewed earlier. For example, stereotypes are the prototypes that characterize the typical member of a social group. Thus, in-group members are perceived to be more similar to this prototype than they really are (perception of in-group homogeneity). The presence of an out-group changes and widens the context as the study by Doise et al. (1978) illustrates. Thus, within-group similarities should be further enhanced (the extension effect), the out-group should be seen as homogeneous, and the distinct features of the two groups relative to one another should be emphasized (perception of intergroup heterogeneity). Changing the context from intragroup to intergroup may also change the level at which information is processed from the individual to the group. That is, people switch to categorizing individuals in terms of their group membership rather than their individual characteristics.

Self-Categorization Theory

A fundamental problem with categorization theories as they apply to intergroup relations is that they are unable to explain the occurrence of in-group bias. Indeed, because they are theories of object perception, there is no basis for supposing that a systematic bias will occur. Rather, these theories predict that the salient attributes of objects in a particular context will be used to place them into categories that maximize the within-category similarities and between-category differences without regard for the value placed on these categories. Clearly this is incorrect—people value the social groups to which they belong and usually favor them over others (M. B. Brewer, 1979; Tajfel, 1978; Tajfel & Turner, 1979).

Recently, a new and very ambitious social categorization theory has been proposed by Turner and his colleagues that addresses this problem (Turner, 1985; Turner, Hogg, Oakes, Reicher, & Wetherell, 1987). Called *self-categorization theory*, it assumes that a person's self-concept is made up of many components, or *self categories*, which are activated in specific situations. While some self categories are idiosyncratic to the person (person categories), others place the self in valued social groups (social categories). The self-categorization system is hierarchical, with at least three levels: interpersonal, intergroup, and interspecies. A fundamental assumption of the theory is that the types defined by this hierarchy are not more important than one another: "the personal self reflects only one level of abstraction of self-categorization, of which the more inclusive levels are just as valid and in some conditions more important" (Turner et al., 1987, p. 46). Thus, when a person responds as an in-group member, he or she is not deindividuated (as Wilder, 1986, argues), but rather is individuated in terms of a particular self category. As in other categorization theories, a family resemblance index (called a *metacontrast*) can be calculated for any given category; this index is the ratio of intercategory to intracategory differences. The metacontrast principle, then, states that people are classified into a social group to the extent that this metacontrast is maximized in any given social situation.

On the basis of the metacontrast principle alone, systematic in-group bias would not occur. However, the fact that self categories define a person's self-concept allows the theory to overcome this problem. Salience of a particular self category is determined by accessibility and fit as well as by the size of its metacontrast ratio. Bruner's (1957) definition of an accessible category as one that is invoked by very little input is used. Because the person's past experience and current motives influence accessibility, certain self-relevant social categories become more salient. In addition, Oakes makes an important contribution to this theory by developing the notion of fit as "the degree of correlation between social behavior and group membership in *a normative consistent direction*" (Turner et al., 1987, p. 56). That is, the behavior used to classify the self with others in a particular social category must be consistent with the standards of behavior expected for members of that category. The multidetermined nature of salience in this theory allows in-group bias to occur. Essentially, individuals enhance and protect their self-esteem by identifying with social categories that reflect positively on themselves. That is, social self categories become salient for partially self-serving reasons. This argument is reminiscent of earlier ones put forward by Tajfel and Turner in their social identity theory; namely, that group members strive to maintain the positive distinctiveness of their group over an out-group motivated by a desire to enhance or maintain their self-esteem through their association with a positively valued group (Tajfel, 1978; Tajfel & Turner, 1979). Indeed, Turner asserts that social identity theory is a special case of self-categorization theory, although the latter appears to take a much more cognitive tact.

Turner's new theory is also exciting because it explicitly discusses the interaction between the interpersonal and the intergroup level of analysis. In his theory, he hypothesizes that these levels are antagonistic. Thus, to the extent that a personal self category is salient to an individual, any relevant social self category is not. Individuals evaluate themselves by comparing themselves to their ideal self, which, in this theory, is defined as the prototype for the self category that is currently activated. Thus, when a personal self category is activated, differences between in-group members are more salient and self-evaluation involves comparison of self as an individual with an ideal self. In contrast, when a social self category is salient, self-evaluation involves comparison of self as an in-group member with a prototypical or stereotypical group member. Thus, the theory provides an theoretical link between self-concept and group identity and provides a way of explaining how a group is more than the sum of its parts, without having to make the untenable assumption that groups of people think and act as one organism.

Balance Theory

Another cognitive perspective on intergroup relations is that of cognitive consistency. Wilder (1986) sums up the status of this theoretical perspective when he writes, "when differentiating between groups, persons should favor the ingroup over the outgroup in order to maintain cognitive consistency. This rationale has not been tested. Support derives chiefly from its conceptual similarity to the large literature on cognitive consistency" (p. 313). That is, although some authors have acknowledged that cognitive consistency may play a role in intergroup relations (e.g., Levine & Campbell, 1972; Dion, 1973, 1979), this perspective has not been developed or tested at the group level of analysis.

In my view, the most applicable of the cognitive consistency theories to intergroup relations is balance theory (Heider, 1958; Newcomb, 1968). This theory, or more correctly, this family of theories is based upon two key concepts: unit formation and balance. The former refers to the perception that two or more objects belong together. Factors such as similarity, common fate, and proximity suggest to the perceiver that particular patterns of stimuli form a unit within the stimulus field. In the case of intergroup relations, the labeling of persons as members of a particular group, the perception of their common fate, etc. suggest that these people are in a unit relationship. Therefore, in line with the evidence, balance theory predicts that in-group members will tend to minimize within-group differences (leveling), and exaggerate between-group differences (sharpening) in order to clarify the main features of the stimulus field.

Balance has two distinct meanings as it applies to interpersonal relations. As originally conceived, it refers to a congruence between whether a person (P) perceives himself or herself to be in a unit or a non-unit relationship with another (O), and the attitude of P toward O. Specifically, if P and O are perceived to be in a unit relationship, P is motivated to like O in order to achieve balance (Heider, 1958). Conversely, if P perceives a non-unit relationship between himself or herself and O, no such motivation exists. This type of balance predicts that similarity leads to attraction because similarities between P and O imply to P that he or she and O are in a unit relationship. More generally, any factor that indicates to P that a unit relationship exists should have the same effect. In intergroup relations, this is known as the *cognitive differentiation hypothesis* (Dion, 1973, 1979). Thus, balance theory predicts that group cohesion and in-group favoritism should be enhanced to the extent that group membership is salient and group boundaries are clear. A great deal of evidence supports these hypotheses (M. B. Brewer, 1979; Dion, 1979; Turner et al., 1987).

A second type of balance discussed in the interpersonal relations literature refers to P's attitude toward O and X, and O's perceived attitude toward X. Balance among these attitudes is said to occur if all three are positive, or two are negative and the third positive. (More generally, if the valences of the attitudes are multiplied and the outcome is positive, a state of balance exists.) For example, if P perceives O as liking and disliking the same things as himself or herself, then a balance is achieved when P likes O. Furthermore, such a balanced state among attitudes leads P to perceive a unit relationship between himself or herself and O. That is, attraction leads to the perception of similarity. When P dislikes O, Newcomb (1968) argues that a state of nonbalance is most likely. That is, in all likelihood, P will not wish to be involved with O (a non-unit relationship). If there is a relationship, then the theory implies that P must perceive that he or she and O like different things in order for balance to be achieved.

A serious flaw in balance theory is its failure to take into account context effects. As Wyer and Gordon (1984) point out, in a competitive relationship, the fact that P perceives O as wanting the same things as himself or herself may well lead P to dislike rather than like O as balance theory would predict. Similarly, in intergroup relations, a fundamental postulate of realistic group conflict theory (see Chapter 2) is that when two groups desire scarce and valued resources, intergroup conflict is likely to result (Campbell, 1965; Levine & Campbell, 1972; Sherif, 1966); yet, balance theory appears to make the opposite prediction. More generally, while balance theory does predict that intergroup hostility will lead to an exaggeration of in-group–out-group differences, it does not predict that in-group–out-group differences will cause an in-group to behave hostilely toward an out-group. This is sensible because, after all, such differences only imply that two groups are in a non-unit relationship and not necessarily that they are in a negative one. However, the theory is unable to go beyond this point. That is, because of its context-free nature, balance theory is unable to explain the conditions that favor the outbreak of intergroup hostility. This constitutes a serious theoretical limitation because, clearly, such intergroup behavior does occur (Holmes & Grant, 1979).

A second and related limitation of balance theory is its failure to distinguish between similarly valenced verbs (e.g., "like," "want," and "need"), which, therefore, renders very different psychological states equivalent (Wyer & Gordon; 1984). Extending the above example, it is because two groups want the same things that intergroup conflict is likely to result. If the same two groups like the same things, they may well develop common bonds within a harmonious relationship. Balance theory does not distinguish between these very different, positively valenced motives.

Categories as Social Schemata

In cognitive psychology, schema theories have been developed to explain how people perceive, understand, and remember objects and events in their world in the context of their past experiences (W. F. Brewer & Nakamura, 1984; Rumelhart, 1984).

Schemata are conceived to be units of generic information that organize some segment of past experience. Schemata are characterized as unconscious, active mental processes that are embedded within each other and that represent knowledge at all levels of abstraction. For example, a simple event schema, or script, for eating at a restaurant contains the generic elements of this event such as reserving a table, checking a coat, ordering a meal, etc. (Abelson, 1981; Read, 1987). In addition, schemata are active thought processes used to reconstruct specific episodic memories from generic information and memory traces of a particular occasion. Also, they are generative in that they are used as a framework within which new information is processed and given meaning. These reconstructive and generative functions are thought to operate iteratively in a "top-down," "lateral," and "bottom-up" fashion. That is, a segment of new information activates a particular schema associatively (bottom-up), which in turn activates other schemata (lateral) and attributes (top-down), and so on. The goal of such processing is to obtain an adequate understanding of new information in light of past experience. Specifically, the person seeks to instantiate new information into an existing schema by establishing its "goodness-of-fit," or prototypicality, a process characterized by Bartlett (1932) as "effort after meaning" (p. 44). Thus, continuing the example, when a person recalls a meal at a particular restaurant in the past, the restaurant event schema is evoked and guides the retrieval of specific memory traces that are used to reconstruct the occasion. Similarly, when a person goes to a new restaurant, evoking the restaurant schema gives the person a basis for understanding this new social situation in terms of his or her past. Research using this theoretical perspective has obtained results that suggest that schemata act as guides or frameworks when encoding information, interact with new information to produce new memory representations, and guide the retrieval process when locating episodic memories. In addition, there is some evidence that schemata may influence focus of attention (W. F. Brewer & Nakamura, 1984; Wyer & Gordon, 1984).

Within social psychology, it has been suggested that people use category-based cognitive schemata to represent social groups (Jones & McGillis, 1976; Markus & Zajonc, 1985; Stephan, 1985; S. E. Taylor & Crocker, 1981; Wyer & Gordon, 1984). Such schemata are described as consisting of a set of attitudes typically associated with group members along with organizational properties that specify relationships among these attributes. Examples of these organizational properties include similarity, proximity, coherence, and parsimony as well as more dynamic properties such as cognitive balance and group goals (Campbell, 1958; Markus & Zajonc, 1985; Read, 1987; Turner et al., 1987; Tversky, 1977). Schemata are conceptualized as being nested within one another in a hierarchical fashion according to level of abstraction. Thus, lower order schemata may be attributes of a higher order, more abstract schema. For example, the stereotype of a group can be conceptualized as a schema (Hamilton, 1979, 1981), but it is also one component of a more abstract schema representing this group, which might include event schemata for typical intergroup interactions, causal schemata that suggest how to interpret the behavior of the group's members, and so on. At the lowest level of abstraction are attributes, such as individual stereotype traits, probabilistic rules, and cognitive heuristics, that generate specific expectancies for interpreting the behavior of members of a group (e.g., the ultimate attribution error).

Categorization theories do not specify the cognitive strategies that people use to attend to, encode, and retrieve information. Indeed, they have been criticized as incomplete for this reason (Lingle et al., 1984; Rosch, 1978). Thus, schema theories are important because they hold the promise of being able to specify these cognitive processes and give a more complete account of intergroup relations from an individual perceiver's point of view. Unfortunately, this promise has not been fulfilled and a schema theory of intergroup relations has not been developed. Wilder (1986), for example, has developed his research program to explore the general hypothesis that the results obtained by cognitive psychologists studying the categorization of inanimate objects should also apply to the categorization of people into groups, but has not, as yet, developed a schema theory that would apply to social categories. Stephan (1985), in his very scholarly review, mentions schema theory as one perspective on attention and describes cognitive biases that result from the use of self schema, causal schema, and group schema. He does not discuss schema theory as a framework for integrating the many findings that he reviews. Finally, Turner et al. (1987) developed self-categorization theory without reference to schema theory. It appears, therefore, that categorization processes and hypotheses derived from theoretical perspectives on these processes represent the cutting edge of theoretical work in this area, rather than a systematic development of schema theory.

Perhaps one of the reasons for this lack of theory development is the magnitude of the task. At the moment, even schema theories of person perception are very rudimentary and "there is still relatively little direct empirical work on the structure and representational nature of schemas" (Markus & Zajonc, 1985, p. 145). Furthermore, theorists are still grappling with the problems of translating schema theories dealing with classification of natural objects into the social realm. For example, natural objects are usually grouped within a strictly hierarchical classification system, whereas people often are members of many social categories that overlap and are only partially hierarchical. Natural objects are usually classified according to the presence or absence of features, whereas some personality theorists classify people along trait dimensions. And, for natural objects, the association between the category name and characteristic attributes is strong, so that an attribute will evoke the category name as easily as the category name evokes the attribute. However, because attributes belong to several overlapping categories, it is more difficult for the perceiver to infer a specific social category if he or she only knows a few of these attributes (Lingle et al., 1984; S. E. Taylor & Crocker, 1981; Wyer & Gordon, 1984).

Nevertheless, some strides in the development of schema theory have been made. If schemata structure thought, then they must influence attention, encoding, and retrieval strategies in particular ways, and the empirical findings discussed earlier, as well as the much larger literature on person perception, person memory, and impression formation, is generally consistent with schema theory predictions and is often interpreted from this perspective (Markus & Zajonc, 1985). For example, schema-relevant material should be recalled better than schema-irrelevant or inconsistent material because it is organized in memory. The work on stereotype expectancies supports this hypothesis, although when inconsistent material is highly salient, then it too is recalled well (Markus & Zajonc, 1985; Stephan, 1985; S. E. Taylor & Fiske, 1979; Wyer & Gordon, 1984).

If people use cognitive schemata to represent social groups, then information that is an important part of a schema should be recalled even when evidence that the group member should be characterized this way is absent. This is because schemata serve a generative function and, therefore, fill in missing information with the typical or stereotypic characteristic. These so-called "intrusion errors" have been obtained by Cantor and Mischel (1977). In their experiment, subjects were shown 10 descriptive sentences on slides, 6 of which described a stimulus person with traits characteristic of an extrovert or an introvert. Following a brief distractor task, the subjects were asked to indicate how confident they were that they had seen each of a series of sentences describing the stimulus person. As hypothesized, subjects were more confident that they had seen sentences containing extrovert traits when the stimulus person was described as an extrovert, and sentences containing introvert traits when the stimulus person was described as an introvert, even though these sentences (and the traits they contained) had not formed part of the original stimulus set. However, Wyer and Gordon (1984) challenge the notion that people are represented in memory as exemplars of person categories. Instead, they propose that persons are represented in a series of independent, addressable storage bins containing characteristics that are associated semantically, and they reinterpret Cantor and Mischel's (1977) work in this way.

Other, more indirect, evidence also suggests that people make intrusion errors of this kind. Essentially, these studies show that people tend to overestimate the frequency with which they have seen stereotypic attributes in a stimulus set describing members of a social group (Hamilton, 1979, 1981; Stephan, 1985). For example, Hamilton and Rose (1980, experiment 1) asked subjects to read 24 sentences describing different stimulus persons by name, occupation, and characteristic trait. This stimulus set was constructed such that there were three sets of eight individuals from each of three occupational groups, and there was no relationship between membership in an occupational group and the possession of traits stereotypic of that occupation. The results showed that subjects "recalled" an illusory relationship and overestimated the frequency with which members of an occupation were characterized by stereotypic traits.

Recent theory and research suggest two important components that must be included in a schema theory of intergroup relations if it is to be developed. First, self-categorization theory clearly suggests that the study of self as a member of a social group is important (Turner, 1985; Turner et al., 1987). In particular, this theory conceptualizes the self as a series of interlinking categories that have at least three hierarchical levels: self as an individual, self as a member of social groups, and self as a member of the human race. Furthermore, an ongoing evaluative process is said to occur motivated by the person's desire for a positive self-concept. Thus, this theory suggests a particular structure and an important organizing principle for self-schemata at the group level of abstraction. In addition, when a person's self-as-member-of-a-social-group is activated, other members of this social group are equivalent to the self to some degree. This appears to extend on Heider's (1958) idea of unit relationships and suggests that such a relationship will occur in contexts that make the social self salient. The study of the relationship between self-schemata and schemata of other group members in these contexts has obvious potential for deepening our understanding of group identity and cohesion.

Second, the research that was reviewed earlier in this chapter indicates that people make quite unflattering assumptions about members of out-groups. It seems likely, therefore, that they use a schema to explain an out-group member's actions that differs from that used to explain an in-group member's actions. If this is true, a schema theory of intergroup relations will also need to specify the structure and organization of out-group schemata and how they differ from and are related to ingroup schemata. Furthermore, this perspective suggests that the way in-group members process information about an out-group is likely to differ depending on the intergroup relationship — for example, whether two groups have had a history filled with conflict or cooperation. This argument is reminiscent of the one made by a number of schema theorists (e.g., Markus & Zajonc, 1985; Taylor & Crocker, 1981) who suggest that schema theories in social cognition should be content specific and deal explicitly with context effects. In addition, it is consistent with the spirit of self-categorization theory, which takes a strong functionalist approach to the categorization process (Turner et al., 1987).

An Integration

After reading the theories just summarized, the reader may be struck, as I was, by their similarities. Clearly, self-categorization theory builds upon the work of Bruner (1957), Campbell (1958), Tajfel (1969), Tversky (1977), and Rosch (1978). However, it is noticeable that balance theory is directed at the same concerns. Indeed, the two categorization theories complement balance theory because they provide a detailed theoretical explanation for why a particular set of stimuli is perceived as a unit and how changing the context can lead to the perception of different units. Self-categorization theory and balance theory also discuss the relationship between similarity judgments, and affective and evaluative reactions. While balance theory can explain in-group cohesion, favoritism, and bias in terms of a "strain toward symmetry" (Newcomb, 1953, p. 395), it seems clear that self-categorization theory has more potential for capturing the full range of ethnocentric reactions between groups. When group members define themselves in terms of a social self-categorization, a threat to the group is a threat to the person's self-concept. Clearly, this is a powerful motivational drive that could lead to intergroup conflict. The challenge, then, is to study the manifestations of this drive within and between groups differing in terms of sociostructural variables such as status and power. Both social identity theory (Tajfel, 1978; Tajfel & Turner 1979) and self-categorization theory (Turner, 1985; Turner et al., 1987) have made a start in this direction. It is my view (Grant, 1987) that further work needs to be done to relate these theoretical perspectives to realistic group conflict theory (Campbell, 1965; Sherif, 1966) so that ethnocentrism, particularly within the context of an intergroup conflict, is understood more fully.

A schema theory of intergroup relations has not, as yet, been developed. Nevertheless, many authors refer to cognitive schemata when discussing the biases that are obtained when a person is categorized as a member of an in-group or an out-group. Indeed, because categorization theories do not specify the way information about an in-group and an out-group is structured and processed, further work on such a theory might prove to be very important. Again, it is my perspective that the examination of the structuring and processing of information about members of an in-group and an out-group should take place within a variety of situations — particularly when groups are in conflict or are otherwise under stress (Holmes & Grant, 1979). This is because the goals of a group in a certain intergroup context are likely to influence the processing of information about the in-group and the outgroup. Therefore, this needs to be an explicit part of any theory and research on the nature of in-group and out-group schemata.

Implications for Conflict Resolution

In this section, the implications of these cognitive theories for conflict resolution interventions are discussed with a particular emphasis on the intergroup contact hypothesis (see Chapter 8). It scarcely seems necessary to remind the reader that these implications should be considered in the context of other theories that explain intergroup conflict in terms of real conflicts of interest, feelings of fraternal relative deprivation in response to past injustices, and in the context of particular power and status relationships (e.g., Dion, 1986; Campbell, 1965; Levine & Campbell, 1972; Tajfel & Turner, 1979; D.M. Taylor & McKirnan, 1984). However, to do so here would be to go beyond the scope of this chapter. Furthermore, because schema theory has not been developed sufficiently, its implications for conflict resolution are largely unknown. It seems clear, however, that a schema theory of intergroup relations could be used to strengthen any intervention designed to de-escalate intergroup conflict. This is because such a theory constitutes an explanation of how group members structure and process information about in-groups and out-groups. It seems likely that, in light of this knowledge, more effective countermeasures can be designed to overcome the biases and hidden assumptions of group representatives toward their own group and the other group in the conflict.

When an intervention to reduce conflict between two groups is being developed, a cognitive perspective suggests that the perception of homogeneity within a group and heterogeneity between groups, as well as in-group favoritism, need to be countered. This includes challenging out-group stereotypes and biased causal attributions which in-group members use to "explain" out-group members' behavior. Both of the categorization theories and balance theory suggest that, to the extent that intergroup boundaries are de-emphasized and the common interests of both groups are promoted, the exaggeration of within-group similarities and between-group differences will be minimized. Furthermore, balance theory and self-categorization theory suggest that, if this occurs, in-group bias will also be reduced. These hypotheses are supported by a great deal of evidence. For example, Wilder (1986) concludes, in a detailed review of experimental work, that factors that emphasize the uniqueness of individual out-group members and/or reduce of the clarity of intergroup boundaries decreases in-group bias and discrimination. Examples of such factors include superordinate goals, cross-cutting group memberships, and a history of successful, cooperative intergroup relations.

From a balance theory perspective, these effects can be explained in terms of factors in the situation that suggest to members of the in-group that they are in a unit relationship with members of the out-group. That is, the situation is recast as one that involves members of a superordinate group. A self-categorization theory perspective can explain these findings in one of two ways. First, the situation might activate in-group members' personal rather than social self-categorizations. That is, they will switch from the intergroup to the interpersonal level of abstraction. Second, a new social self-categorization associated with the superordinate group may be activated. These theoretical alternatives warrant further investigation because the activation of a personal self-categorization versus a new social self-categorization is likely to have very different effects.

Whatever the theoretical explanation, the practical implication of these cognitive theories is that a certain type of intergroup contact is desirable in order to facilitate positive intergroup relations. That is, a cognitive perspective on intergroup relations provides one theoretical rationale for the contact hypothesis. This complex hypothesis states that attitudes and behavior between two groups in society will be improved by promoting extended interaction between members of these groups working cooperatively toward common goals, under informal and equal status conditions in which there is a strong norm of equality and institutional support for increased intergroup interaction (Amir, 1969; Hewstone & Brown, 1986b; Stephan, 1985). The factors described in this hypothesis provide the link to cognitive theories of intergroup relations as they are factors that are aimed at reducing the salience of intergroup boundaries or at emphasizing interpersonal differences among out-group members (M.B. Brewer & Miller, 1984).

The contact hypothesis has great practicality and is often used by practitioners to design interventions to help reduce conflict between groups (e.g., Hewstone & Brown, 1986a; Miller & M.B. Brewer, 1984). For example, consider the extensive work that has been done on developing and evaluating cooperative learning techniques. These techniques were designed to achieve the kind of classroom contact between children from different ethnic groups that is specified by the contact hypothesis. There is a great deal of literature that documents the positive personal and interpersonal effects of using these cooperative learning techniques while maintaining academic standards. Specifically, in comparison to students in traditionally taught classes, students taught by cooperative methods feel more liked and supported, are more aware of the feelings and thoughts of their peers, like their teacher more, and experience a gain in self-esteem (Aronson & Osherow, 1980; Johnson & Johnson, 1983; Sharan, 1980; Sharan et al. 1984; Slavin, 1980; Webb, 1982).

However, the example of cooperative learning also illustrates a recent criticism of interventions based upon the contact hypothesis that focuses on the lack of generalizability of the gains that are obtained. Although one would like children to show a general improvement in their attitudes toward members of other ethnic groups, this is not generally obtained. One reason for this lack of generalizability might be that cooperative teaching techniques emphasize the unique strengths of each child to his or her peers. For example, the jigsaw technique (Aronson, Blaney, Stephan, Sikes, & Snapp, 1978) involves breaking a topic into units and assigning a different unit to each child in a problem-solving group. Members of several such groups assigned the same unit prepare by helping each other learn. Then, in the problem-solving group, children have to teach each other the unit they were assigned in preparation for a test. This places disadvantaged minority children on an equal status with other children in the classroom. Their opinions carry weight in the group and it is counterproductive to derogate them or their contribution. However, while this technique ensures that the students recognize and respect children of different ethnicity in their group, it does not ensure that these children are perceived to be representative members of their ethnic group, and it appears they are not.

Wilder (1986) has discussed this issue in terms of a dilemma faced by any minority group member when interacting with a member of the dominant majority group. On the one hand, in order to achieve individual recognition and rewards, it is advantageous for this minority group member to emphasize his or her personal abilities that are not part of the minority group's stereotype. However, this strategy is unlikely to result in a change in attitude toward the minority group as a whole, because the minority group member will be perceived as atypical. On the other hand, public identification with the ethnic minority and behavior consistent with the majority group's stereotype of a typical minority group member are likely to confirm this stereotype in an undesirable self-fulfilling prophecy.

An additional problem with acting as a representative member of a minority group is that discrimination is likely to increase because group boundaries are made salient—precisely what cognitive theories suggest should be avoided! To counteract such a reaction, Hewstone and Brown (1986b) suggest that the slogan "separate but equal" be taken seriously. Experimental work by Lemaine (1974; Lemaine, Kastersztein, & Personnaz, 1978) has demonstrated that a competition between two groups, one of which is disadvantaged relative to the other, results in the disadvantaged groups' creating novel dimensions of comparison in order to achieve some degree of superiority (positive distinctiveness) over the advantaged group. This suggests that emphasizing the strengths of two groups along different dimensions might prevent clear group boundaries contributing to intergroup conflict. The hope is that the two groups will develop a mutual respect for each other's skills and that this will lead to harmonious intergroup relations. Initial experimental evidence reported by Brown and his colleagues (Deschamps & Brown, 1983; Brown & Wade, 1987) provides some support for this position. Brown and Wade (1987), for example. found that groups of students working toward a superordinate goal felt more friendly toward the out-group if their group had been assigned a distinctly different role from the one assigned to the out-group. This was in contrast to groups of students assigned similar roles and groups not assigned a role at all.

In sum, a current debate on how contact situations should be designed in order to lower the level of intergroup conflict focuses on whether group boundaries should be made salient. Some authors (e.g., M.B. Brewer & Miller, 1984; Ben-Ari & Amir, 1986) argue that intergroup relations will eventually be improved if interpersonal relations between members of both groups are improved under the conditions specified by the contact hypothesis. Because similarity leads to attraction, these authors suggest that interventions should highlight interpersonal similarities and de-emphasize differences, including those that are the basis of the group conflict. Others (e.g., Hewstone & Brown, 1986b) argue that is crucial to keep group membership salient so that, over time, in-group members will change their perceptions of the out-group rather than classify a particular out-group member as atypical. These authors argue that, although improved interpersonal relations will result when group representatives interact as individuals, generalization to other members of the out-group and particularly to its leadership will not take place. Self-categorization theory clearly supports the latter position (Turner et al., 1987). This is because the intergroup contact should facilitate activation of social self-categorizations in order to maximize attitude change toward a group as opposed to individual members of that group. However, if this approach to intergroup contact is followed, the in-group favoritism that results must be countered. That is, the challenge is to achieve recognition of intergroup similarities and common interests by maintaining the representatives' self-categorization at the intergroup level of abstraction. Therefore, strategies designed to help members of both groups acknowledge the strengths of the other group as well as their own are a necessary component of such a contact situation if improved intergroup relations is to result. More research is necessary to explore this important issue further.

Conclusion

This chapter summarizes empirical work on the effects of categorizing individuals into a group. Two categorization theories, balance theory, and schema theory are reviewed, and their relationship to each other is examined. Finally, the implications of these theories for conflict resolution through intergroup contact (the contact hypothesis) are discussed. To date, these theories have contributed a great deal toward understanding intergroup conflict and, more generally, intergroup relations from the point of view of the individual perceiver. Nevertheless, they need to be developed further in the context of more macro theories, such as social identity theory and realistic group conflict theory, if a more complete understanding of this complex topic is to be achieved. It is my view that further development of self-categorization theory is the most promising direction to take in this regard. In addition the structure and processing of information about in-groups and out-groups in memory needs to be addressed. The development of a schema theory of intergroup relations that takes into account the exigencies of different intergroup contexts is one theoretical approach to this problem that merits serious consideration.

Chapter 4

Group Factors in the Escalation of Intergroup Conflict

Social-psychological contributions from the individual level of analysis to the understanding of intergroup conflict emphasize the perceptual and cognitive processes, particularly biases, that distort intergroup interaction, as discussed in Chapter 3. The next level of analysis, the interpersonal, is also important, but its expression and influence typically occur within the context of yet the next level – that of the group. Intergroup relations and the management of intergroup conflict are most often and most directly approached through the functioning of each group, and especially through the process of group decision making. Whether each group is an entity unto itself in relation to the intergroup conflict, or whether it is a representative of a larger collectivity, the nature and effectiveness of its internal functioning will profoundly affect the manner in which the intergroup conflict is handled.

Thus, it is essential to examine group structure and functioning in relation to the development, escalation, and management of intergroup conflict. This will be done by first considering the basic elements of group dynamics. Subsequently, particular constructs and processes that have been identified as relevant to intergroup conflict will be discussed. These include group identity as it pertains to ethnocentrism, cohesiveness as it is affected by and affects intergroup conflict, and the processes of group conformity and polarization, which feed escalation. In addition, the effects of militant leadership and constituent pressure on representatives will be examined. The central role of decision making will be highlighted by examining the phenomenon of groupthink in contrast to effective group problem solving. Finally, the implications of group-level factors for the management and de-escalation of intergroup conflict will be considered.

A Primer on Group Dynamics

The study of group dynamics in social psychology has an uneven history. Classic work in a number of important areas came relatively early to the field, including studies of the problem-solving process (e.g., Bales, 1950), conflict in decision-making groups (e.g., Guetzkow & Gyr, 1954), the role of leadership behaviors in group functioning (e.g., Benne & Sheats, 1948), and the power of group discussion to affect individual behavior (e.g., Lewin, 1947). However, the rise of theories of social cognition and the methodology of the laboratory experiment almost pushed the study of real social groups to the point of extinction (Steiner, 1974). Much of the work that was done in the area during the late 50s and early 60s lacked a shared frame of reference or mutual purpose (McGrath & Altman, 1966). These unfortunate trends continue to hold sway in mainstream social psychology to the present day (Steiner, 1986). Nonetheless, certain topics have seen the slow accumulation of knowledge, which informs our understanding about small groups — how they form and develop, how they function, how they affect their members, how they constrain their representatives, and so on. The purpose of this section is to present a brief overview of the basic concepts of group dynamics so that they may be used in later sections to illuminate the problem at hand — the escalation of destructive intergroup conflict. More detail on group processes can be found in a number of sources including Fisher (1982), Napier & Gershenfeld (1985), and Shaw (1981).

The initial question about groups is: Why are people attracted to them? Basically, individuals join groups to meet their physical, psychological, and social needs. Furthermore, they are attracted to particular groups in large part because of the major determinants of interpersonal attraction, which are proximity, similarity, and reciprocity. In particular, similarity of opinions and attitudes is seen to be a major contributor to the choice of group memberships. Once one is a member of various groups, it can be said that one's self-concept, or individual identity, becomes in part defined by the group memberships. Thus, self-concept is intertwined with group identity. Attraction to groups flows through to one of the fundamental, emergent properties of groups, that of cohesiveness. Although cohesiveness has been defined in a number of different ways, it usually refers to the extent to which members are motivated to remain in the group (Shaw, 1981). Cohesiveness refers not simply to the individual's interpersonal attractions to other members of the group, but to the overall pattern and the strengths of attractions within and toward the group. Cohesiveness is a central variable in group functioning because it relates to a number of other important properties, in particular, social influence and productivity. It appears that members of more cohesive groups tend to be more receptive to social influence within the groups; that is, they adhere more closely to group norms. Cohesiveness also aids productivity and satisfaction with the group apparently because it increases motivation. More recently, cohesion has also been conceptualized as a functional or instrumental variable (Zander, 1979), defined, for example, as the shared commitment to the group's task (Hackman, 1976). Along with socio-emotional cohesion, this functional form would also have important implications for group performance. Thus, in many ways, a cohesive group is a more effective social unit. With regard to intergroup conflict the questions is, of course, in what directions and toward what goals are the efforts of the group directed?

Members of groups are usually quite sensitive to group norms, which may be defined as standards of behavior that are prescribed and enforced by the group through use of rewards and sanctions. In extreme cases, the costs of deviance involve condemnation, rejection, and expulsion. A considerable body of knowledge in social psychology indicates that group norms affect individual functioning in terms of perceptions, attitudes, and behavior. Thus, how one group relates to another in a situation of intergroup conflict will be largely captured by an understanding of the group norms relevant to the intergroup relationship. Conformity in groups is also expressed through obedience to authority in which the group leader is seen as the primary definer and enforcer of norms. In highly cohesive groups with autocratic leadership, the effect on individual members' behavior can be nothing short of phenomenal. Individual conformity can also be heightened in groups through a phenomenon known as *diffusion of responsibility*. In this process, the individuals experience a decrease in the sense of responsibility for decisions or actions that are taken in a group setting. Thus, more extreme behaviors may occur in the group context than if the individuals were acting separately. Finally, our understanding of conformity processes is expanded through the concept of reference group, that is, a group of similar others to which an individual refers attitudes or behavior for purposes of social comparison. Thus, the reference group not only serves as a point of comparison for the individual, but also as the holder of standards and the arbitor of behavior. The power of reference groups to affect individual attitudes and behavior has been demonstrated in a variety of field studies.

As social entities, groups evidence a number of characteristics of structure that lend stability to group interaction over time. Group norms are one element of structure in that they result in uniformity and predictability of behavior. *Communication networks*, which define the channels available to various group members, are another element of structure. A more visible aspect of group structure are the *roles* in which responsibilities are assigned to members occupying particular positions in the group. A particularly important concept in relation to intergroup relations is that of *boundary role* (D. Katz & Kahn, 1978; Holmes, Ellard, & Lamm, 1986). Boundary roles are those that operate at the boundary or interface between groups, and the study of behavior of such representatives is crucial in the study of intergroup conflict. This is because conflict is typically addressed through interaction of representatives, such as in negotiation. Two additional elements of structure are *status hierarchies*, which develop or are assigned within groups, and the related *distribution of power*, that is, the ability to influence, which can become stabilized into a relatively constant pattern.

The final and perhaps most notable element of group structure is that of *leadership*, which is central to the development of the continuing effectiveness of a group. The study of leadership has a long and varied history in social psychology and other social sciences. Attention has been directed to the concept of leadership style (e.g., autocratic, democratic, laissez-faire), leadership functions (the essential task and social behaviors required for effective group functioning), and contingency or situational approaches to leadership (wherein the success of a particular style is contingent upon characteristics of the group situation). Because leaders of groups are often boundary role persons as well, the question of leadership in intergroup conflict becomes doubly important.

The final element of group dynamics of fundamental importance is that of *problem solving*. The procedures of problem solving have received considerable theoretical and empirical attention, and it is generally agreed that a conscious and systematic process addressing both task and social requirements is most effective. One example model that effectively addresses both these essentials is discussed by Morris and Sashkin (1976). The study and practice of problem solving in social psychology was pioneered by Maier (1963, 1970), who has also commented on both the assets and liabilities of groups as problem-solving units (1967). The challenge of improving problem solving in groups is a difficult one and requires a set of ideal conditions (Napier & Gershenfeld, 1973, 1985). For example, goals are clearly understood, roles are differentiated according to skills, problems are stated as conditions, communication is open, and the group is held accountable for its decisions. It should come as no surprise that the fully functioning problem-solving group is a rare species. The negative implications for group problem solving in situations of intergroup conflict are particularly ominous.

Self-Esteem, Identity, and Ethnocentrism

One of the primary links among individual, group, and intergroup levels is found in the relationships among self-esteem, group identity, and ethnocentrism. It will be recalled that Sherif's basic approach posited that when individuals interact in terms of their group identification there is intergroup behavior. According to Tajfel (1982), group identification requires a cognitive awareness of membership, an evaluative sense of the value connotation of membership, and an emotional investment in the awareness and the evaluation. For Tajfel and his associates, the linkages between self-esteem, group identity, and invidious out-group comparisons are to be found in the basic tenets of social identity theory (See Chapter 2). Briefly, individuals strive to maintain or enhance their self-esteem, positive self-concept, and thereby positive social identity. Social groups and membership in them are associated with positive or negative value connotations, gained primarily through social comparison with other groups. Positive social identity is thus based on favorable comparisons with other groups. This approach to intergroup relations is broadened by Tajfel (1982) through using the label *CIC* for *social categorization – social identity – social comparison* theory. Social identity is defined as "that part of the individual's self-concept which derives from their knowledge of their membership of a social group (or groups) together with the value and emotional significance of that membership" (Tajfel, 1981, p. 255). Positive social identity is seen as directly related to level of self-esteem. Thus, the individual level and the group level are linked through the concept of social identity. The further connection to ethnocentrism is provided through the need to preserve or achieve a positive group distinctiveness, which in turn enhances or preserves a positive social identity. Intergroup comparisons are thus made in the direction of enhancing the qualities of the in-group and denigrating the qualities or performance of the out-group. Thus, in the CIC approach there is both a motivational and cognitive explanation of ethnocentrism (Tajfel, 1981).

Theoretical links between self-esteem, in-group glorification, and out-group denigration did not start with Sherif or Tajfel, but with Freudian psychoanalysis and with theories of personality based on self-esteem or self-concept. These earlier sources are summarized and condensed into a set of manageable propositions relating to intergroup behavior by Levine and Campbell (1972) in their statement of realistic group conflict theory. According to these authors, Freud (1948) regarded ethnocentrism as a form of narcissism at the group level. Self-love of the individual is expressed as antipathies and aversions toward strangers. However, when a group is formed, this intolerance toward others vanishes as the individual equates himself or herself with the other members of the group. Freud (1930) contended that this group narcissism then serves the purpose of facilitating the displacement of aggression from the in-group onto out-groups. Thus, in-group love as an expression of self-love becomes associated with out-group hatred. Levine and Campbell suggest in this context that the term ethnocentrism suggests a relationship of group-centeredness with self-centeredness. Ethnocentrism may be a redirected expression of individual narcissism, thus providing individual group members with narcissistic gratification. Neo-Freudians have pointed out how important this narcissistic energy can be for the survival of the group, to the point that individual members will sacrifice their lives for its survival. These considerations lead Levine and Campbell to postulate that groups that provide for more narcissistic gratification will be more ethnocentric. Thus, the link between self-esteem and ethnocentrism can be clearly made through group membership and group identification.

With regard to the concept of self-esteem itself, Levine and Campbell (1972) draw upon a number of neo-Freudian and other personality theorists who place self-esteem or self-concept near the center of their conceptualizations. Variations of "self-esteem theory" are seen in the works of Horney, Sullivan, Rogers, Fromm, and Miller, as well as numerous other theorists. The basic tenets are that self-esteem is a prerequisite for mental health, that a low level of self-esteem leads to negative attitudes toward others, and that since self-esteem is based on comparisons with others, distortions may occur to preserve or enhance one's self-esteem. It follows that low self-esteem thus requires a greater contrast between self and others, thus laying a basis for ethnocentrism. In addition, it is expected that individuals low on self-esteem would be general in their rejection of out-groups and would show a high degree of distortion in their images of out-groups. Conversely, it is expected that groups generally high in self-esteem should differentiate among out-groups to a greater degree and their images should correspond more to social reality. In some sense, group self-esteem is related to group solidarity or cohesion. However, Levine and Campbell also speculate that a group with low self-esteem will attempt to achieve solidarity through ethnocentric activity. Groups low in self-esteem therefore might react to an out-group threat by producing an in-group image of superiority, which is kept in place by wiping out any internal hostility or dissension. In these ways, self-esteem is protected both through the enhancement of in-group virtues and the derogation of out-groups. Levine and Campbell put forward a number of propositions that link low self-esteem, signaled by high internal in-group aggression, to perceptual distortions, hostility, and denigration of out-groups.

Another theoretical basis for the link between self-esteem and ethnocentrism is to be found in the functional theory of attitudes as developed by D. Katz (1960). In particular, the ego-defensive function is seen as underlying attitudes that protect the self from unpleasant realities in the world. This idea, drawn primarily from psychodynamic personality theories, holds that attitudes are formed and maintained more through the psychological functioning of the individual than they are through perceptions of reality. Ego-defensive attitudes are aroused by the posing of threats to the self, through authoritarian suggestions or through rising frustrations. All of these sources can be found in intergroup relations. If the individual, in terms of his or her group membership, feels threatened by an out-group and is experiencing frustration through competition with an out-group, this would be sufficient for the formation and expression of negative attitudes toward the out-group. Thus, the maintenance of self-esteem is linked to the development and expression of the out-group hostility side of ethnocentrism. The process of authoritarian submission would be enhanced by the in-group glorification and loyalty side of ethnocentrism. Thus, the individual level is linked through the group level to intergroup orientations and behavior.

The linkages between self-esteem, group identity, and ethnocentrism are seen as comprising a reciprocal or a cyclical process. The need for self-esteem feeds a positive group identity and the ethnocentric derogation of out-groups, all of which are seen as contributors to intergroup conflict. The results of comparisons with out-groups and the outcomes of intergroup conflict can in turn be seen as fostering a positive in-group identity and enhancing the individual self-esteem of in-group members. Social identity theorists have been able to provide some demonstration that engaging in intergroup discrimination leads to increased self-esteem (Tajfel, 1982). In particular, Oakes and Turner (1980) used the minimal group paradigm to assess directly whether the usual discriminatory responses increase self-esteem as compared to a control condition. Experimental subjects went through the minimal group paradigm and then completed an omnibious self-esteem questionnaire with instructions to focus on the immediate situation. Control subjects engaged in the first part of paradigm, but did not engage in the intergroup discrimination task. Experimental subjects reported significantly higher self-esteem than control subjects. The results are consistent with the contention of social identity theory that intergroup discrimination is motivated by a desire for positive social identity in order to increase individual self-esteem. Also, the results indicate that motivational processes are at work in intergroup discrimination and not simply the effects of cognitive categorization. In general, the findings support the propositions of social identity theory as part of the explanation for the relationship among self-esteem, group identity, and ethnocentrism.

Intergroup Conflict and Group Cohesiveness

The proposition that external conflict between groups increases internal cohesion within groups has a long history and a wide acceptance within social science. The idea is often attributed to Coser (1956), who, drawing on the work of Simmel (1955), gave the idea centrality in his functional approach to social conflict. Based on Simmel's argument that conflict is an essential ingredient of group functioning and survival, Coser stated that conflict between groups increases the internal cohesion within the groups. He cited the frequent observation that during wartime, countries forget domestic squabbles and pull together toward victory. A basis for the proposition is also found in the work of Sumner (1906), who stated that comradeship in the in-group correlates with hostility toward the out-group: In brief, "the exigencies of war with outsiders are what makes peace inside" (p. 12).

Stein (1976) provides a comprehensive review of support for the cohesion proposition, drawing on work in sociology, anthropology, psychology, and political science. In discussing the work of Sumner, Simmel, and Coser, Stein points out that, unlike Simmel, Coser recognizes that external conflict does not necessarily increase cohesion; in fact, under some conditions it can lead to anomie. In contrast to Simmel's argument that conflict results in cohesion because of the necessity for political centralization and conformity, Coser sees conflict as leading to mobilization of the group, which results in increased cohesion and which sometimes may involve centralization. Furthermore, Coser argues that there must be some degree of group consensus prior to the conflict so that the group does not disintegrate in the face of outside threat. Stein points out that the sociological work is characterized by a paucity of empirical evidence and a lack of clear definitions of either conflict or consensus.

According to Stein (1976), anthropologists have studied warfare more than sociologists have, and have generally found support for the cohesion proposition. Furthermore, the argument is advanced that the need to gain cohesion within a conflict-ridden society may also lead to external aggression, a point shared by many of the sociologists interested in the relationship. A primary contribution of the anthropological work is an attempt to delineate the conditions under which the proposition holds. The general limiter that emerges is that internal cohesion will increase as a result of external conflict only when the group or society has a centralized system and adequate political integration so that the authorities are able to intervene to create cohesion.

In the social-psychological study of intergroup conflict, the cohesion hypothesis is given a central place by Sherif (1966), who hypothesized that conflict between two groups tends to increase solidarity within the groups. The field study data indicated that cooperativeness and solidarity within groups were at their peak when the intergroup conflict was most severe. Sherif also documented that groups tended to overestimate their own performance while underestimating that of their rival. In developing realistic group conflict theory, Levine and Campbell (1972) suggest that the cohesion hypothesis is one of Sherif's most emphasized points and, parenthetically, Coser's strongest theme. Drawing on the work of these authors as well as many others, Levine and Campbell state a basic proposition of Realistic Group Conflict Theory: real threat causes in-group solidarity. The importance of the external conflict being perceived as threatening is thereby underscored.

More recent social-psychological studies on the cohesion hypothesis are reviewed by Stein (1976) and Dion (1979) in a largely independent and thereby complementary manner. Stein focuses more on experiments in which groups are placed under various forms of stress or threat, while Dion emphasizes studies involving the effects of intergroup competition on in-group cohesion. Stein points out that although none of the studies deal specifically with external conflict, the work remains relevant because some of the threat situations, such as war, are equivalent to conflict situations in the sociological and anthropological studies. Stein also notes that Coser (1956) saw threat as a necessary condition for external conflict to increase in-group cohesiveness. Among situational studies reviewed by Stein are a number showing that extreme threats, such as war, do increase cohesion and cooperative behavior in the group. Situations involving disaster and panic situations are also reviewed. The general conclusion is that, most of the time, increased cohesion is an outcome of threat. However, disintegrative behavior does occur when the group is powerless to deal with the situation or when the problem can be handled on an individual basis. Experimental studies reviewed by Stein have not dealt directly with external conflict but have examined a number of situations in which various threats or stresses have increased cohesion—for example, Schachter (1959) on affiliation under stress and Myers (1962) on competitive teams. Stein sees the importance of such work as indicating what intervening variables are important, that is, the conditions under which the cohesion hypothesis will hold. In summary, the external conflict must involve a perceived threat, the rewards for staying with the group are higher than the rewards for acting individually, and the individual must see the group as a source of support and the threat as soluble by group effort. Stein also points out the limitations of much social-psychological research in that it focuses overwhelmingly on the individual and deals with a very short time period in which a sustained group response to conflict is not available. In addition, it is difficult to extrapolate to larger collectivities in which other elements, such as subgroups and coalitions, enter in and affect the relationship. Nonetheless, Stein suggests that the cohesion hypothesis has a much broader applicability to political analysis than its current usage would lead one to believe. A study by Wang (1977) supports this contention. Using events data from 71 countries over a 6-year period (1955–61), Wang related occurrence of external hostility to internal cohesion, that is, level of conflict within the country. The findings indicated that moderate external hostility or threat was associated with increased cohesion while extreme threat was related to greater internal conflict. Wang also found that politically integrated and economically developed and equal countries tended to respond more cohesively to external threat.

In reviewing research on the relationship between intergroup conflict and group cohesion, Tajfel (1982) points out that Stein's conditions are in essence reservations regarding the cohesion hypothesis. In response to the question of what happens if these conditions are not met, Tajfel suggests that recent social-psychological research continues to have no more than piecemeal answers. For example, some studies indicate that in cases of group failure, there is a loss of cohesion (e.g., Diab, 1970; Kahn & Ryen, 1972). In general, however, much more work on the cohesion hypothesis remains to be done.

Dion (1979) provides a valuable synthesis of experimental studies on intergroup conflict and group cohesiveness. As noted, the research reviewed is largely independent of that covered by Stein (1976), partly because Dion focuses on more recent studies directly involving intergroup conflict, whereas Stein draws much of his analysis from research on groups by themselves. Dion sees the classic studies of Sherif as the first to provide evidence that intergroup conflict promotes greater group cohesiveness. Unfortunately, as later critics (e.g., Rabbie & Wilkens, 1971) point out, it is unclear what aspect of the in-group development and/or intergroup competition actually led to greater cohesion. Dion ascertains four elements that could have led to increased group cohesion and that have been separately investigated by subsequent experimental work: (a) being assigned to group membership, (b) anticipating intergroup competition, (c) engaging in competition between groups, and (d) the success or failure experienced in the intergroup competition.

Regarding the assignment of individuals into groups, the initial studies underlying social identity theory by Tajfel and his colleagues have made clear that the simple classification process elicits greater altruism toward one's co-members. It has also been found that these effects are not due to perceived attitude similarity of group members, but in fact to the categorization of individuals into different groups (e.g., Billig & Tajfel, 1973). A different line of investigation by Rabbie and his co-workers also indicates that simply assigning individuals to different groups induces a weak but reliable preference for one's own group (e.g., Rabbie & Huygen, 1974). However, in both of these lines of investigation it should be pointed out that we are not dealing directly with cohesiveness, but with behavior that may be an effect of cohesiveness. This is also true of some the measures adopted in Sherif's camp studies, such as the overestimation of the performance of one's own group members.

The effect of anticipated intergroup competition was not considered by Sherif, who saw the incompatible goals involved in intergroup competition as the prime source of group cohesion. Rabbie and his colleagues have isolated out the factor of anticipated intergroup competition by manipulating expectations of competition as well as cooperation between groups and then assessing group cohesiveness prior to actual interaction. Anticipated interaction has been found to induce greater in-group favoritism than a control condition (e.g., Rabbie & Wilkens, 1971). These investigators, however, find no differences in in-group cohesiveness under conditions of anticipated cooperation versus anticipated competition. Nonetheless, Dion points out that other studies have indicated that perceived incompatibility of goals induces greater cohesiveness than expected cooperation between groups (e.g., Kahn & Ryen, 1972).

The available evidence indicates that intergroup competition itself appears to be the strongest factor in inducing group cohesion, although direct comparison of the different factors has not been carried out in any one study. Nonetheless, Dion musters evidence from a variety of sources that indicate the power of intergroup competition. In studies of intergroup competition involving past or repeated measures, competition increases in-group cohesion. For example, J.E. Singer, Radloff, and Work (1963) found that members in pairs of discussion groups in competition reported increased liking for their own group members following competition. Druckman (1968), using the Inter-Nation Simulation (Guetzkow et al., 1963), found that following several periods of competitive decision making, members invariably rated their own group more positively. In addition, comparisons of the effects of individual versus group competition have indicated that the group condition leads to superior ratings of own product. This indicates that the findings of Sherif (1966) and Blake and Mouton (1961) on the overevaluation of in-group products appears to be due to the group context of competition. Finally, Dion cites evidence from organizational studies that clearly indicates the enhancing effect of intergroup competition on group cohesiveness. In particular, the work of Fiedler (1967) and his colleagues on college and military groups demonstrates that intergroup competition results in salutary effects such as better psychological adjustment of members and increased task performance. It is important to note, of course, that these studies, like most social-psychological research on the cohesion hypothesis, have taken place in American culture, which generally places a premium on competitiveness.

In the original camp studies, Sherif noted the beneficial effects of winning on the solidarity of the successful groups. Dion maintains that evidence from laboratory experiments likewise indicates that success in competition results in greater cohesiveness than does failure. For example, Ryen and Kahn (1975) found that cohesion decreased through three conditions from success, to ambiguous feedback, to failure in intergroup competition.

In considering the explanatory basis for the cohesion proposition, Dion considers a number of possibilities, including cognitive consistency, reinforcement theory, attribution theory, and the role of threats. The effect of threats in intergroup conflict is particularly interesting because it serves as one possible explanation for the reverse of the cohesion hypothesis, that is, the question of whether heightened in-group cohesion is itself a sufficient condition for out-group hostility. In general, Dion does not find much evidence to support the reverse hypothesis. However, a theoretical model proposed by Holmes (1975) and extended by Holmes and Grant (1979) may be useful here. When threat is low, group solidarity may be based largely on internal events such as goal attainment. However, when threat is high, intergroup differentiation will increase and in-group cohesion and out-group derogation may become directly linked. Thus, under conditions of high stress the reverse hypothesis will hold, thus pointing to the important role that threats may play in intergroup conflict.

Finally, the distinction between socioemotional and functional cohesion may be relevant to the reverse hypothesis (Forster, 1989). Tzinier (1982) proposes that these two types constitute separate and independent dimensions that groups may possess in any combination. Most studies that look at the intensifying effects of cohesion on intergroup competition use measures of socioemotional cohesion. In contrast, the heightening effects of intergroup competition on cohesion and the sometimes deleterious impact of intense conflict on group functioning may be linked to functional cohesion. Further explication of the roles that these two forms play in the cohesion hypothesis and its reverse is clearly desirable.

Conformity, Polarization, and Groupthink

Conformity to group norms is an emergent characteristic that is a primary distinguishing characteristic of intergroup behavior as opposed to interpersonal behavior. According to Tajfel (1982), interpersonal behavior is largely determined by the individual characteristics and the nature of the personal relations between two people, whereas intergroup behavior, in line with Sherif's definition, involves interactions largely determined by the group memberships of the participants. Two characteristics of intergroup behavior appear to be particularly important to Tajfel, and both are related to group conformity. The first involves the uniformities shown by members of an in-group in their behavior and attitudes toward an out-group, while the second involves uniformity in the characteristics and behaviors of out-group members as they are perceived by in-group members, that is, depersonalization, deindividuation, and stereotyping. These uniformities are accentuated in situations of intergroup conflict. Thus, conformity to group norms has particular relevance to intergroup relations and especially to situations of conflict.

The study of conformity has a long and varied history in the discipline of social psychology. In a classic study, Sherif (1936) demonstrated the effects of group influence on individual judgment in a situation of perceptual ambiguity involving the autokinetic effect. The power of conformity was shown even more strongly by Asch (1956) through using a nonambiguous situation in which subjects judged the lengths of lines. Through the use of confederates who gave bogus judgments to induce conformity pressure, Asch was able to demonstrate a surprising degree of conforming behavior. As would be expected, the influence of conformity also carries over to the more subjective and complex social variables such as opinions, attitudes, and values (Crutchfield 1955). In field situations, studies on the effects of reference groups on members' attitudes and behavior also demonstrate a conformity effect, which can be especially pronounced over time. In Newcomb's famous Bennington College study (1943), students became increasingly liberal in their social and political attitudes over 4 years, apparently due to the influence of liberal faculty members and upper year students.

Given the powerful effects of conformity on individual behavior, it is not surprising that group pressures can lead to the polarization of opinions in either conservative or risky directions. Early research in this area demonstrated the *risky shift* phenomenon, in which groups were observed to make riskier decisions than individuals acting alone. Although there were methodological difficulties with this line of investigation, it did indicate that under certain conditions, groups make more costly decisions than individuals. In addition, the risky shift research led to the general understanding that groups often engage in extremity shifts in either direction (Cartwright, 1971). For example, Moscovici and Zavalloni (1969) found that individuals' attitudes became more extreme either in positive or negative directions following group discussion toward consensus. Myers and his associates have demonstrated the effects of group polarization in the attitudinal area as well as in perceptions of others and in simulated jury decisions (e.g., Myers, 1976).

Moving to intergroup behavior, the effects of group conformity were identified in the field studies by Sherif. More dramatically, in the workshop studies involving adults, Blake and Mouton (1961) observed how greater in-group cohesion not only meant that personal differences were set aside but also that disagreement was not to be tolerated (see Chapter 2). Ideas from individuals that were out of line with the predominate thinking in the group typically triggered insidious pressures toward conformity. In extreme cases, the deviant member was ejected from the group.

The processes of conformity and polarization as they affect decision making have been highlighted by the work of Janis (1972, 1982) on *groupthink*, the term he coined to identify the process by which a cohesive and insulated group fosters concurrence seeking to the point where it overrides the realistic appraisal of alternative courses of action. In his 1982 update, Janis again analyzes a number of major American policy fiascoes and adds more recent failures in decision making, particularly the Watergate coverup, that demonstrate the processes of groupthink. Thus, his analysis indicates that the Bay of Pigs invasion, the intensification of conflict between the United States and China in the Korean war, the escalation of the Vietnam war, and the failure of the United States to anticipate Pearl Harbor are all decisions that were partly based on group decision making contaminated by groupthink. More recently, President Ford's decision to attack Cambodia and the Carter administration's attempt to rescue the Iranian hostages can be effectively analyzed from the groupthink perspective.

One of Janis's major purposes is to increase awareness of the role of social-psychological processes, particularly group dynamics, in decisions of historic importance made by elite groups. The term groupthink was chosen for its simplicity, as well as its negative connotation, in serving as a concise label for a mode of thinking that occurs when people are deeply involved in a cohesive group in which strivings for unanimity override the realistic, efficient, and moral appraisal of alternatives. Janis is struck by a paradox in intergroup relations, wherein "soft-headed groups" are predisposed to be very "hard-hearted" toward their enemies. Although many other sources of error can hamper decision making, none entail the paradoxical increases in hard-heartedness and soft-headedness that groupthink does. Thus, the central theme of Janis's analysis is summarized in the following generalization:

> The more amiability and esprit-de-corps among the members of a policy-making ingroup, the greater is the danger that independent critical thinking will be replaced by groupthink, which is likely to result in irrational and dehumanizing actions directed against out-groups. (1982, p. 13)

Based on his analysis of major policy blunders, Janis posits the groupthink syndrome as characterized by eight primary symptoms. Each symptom is identified through a variety of indicators, which in the analysis are derived from a range of sources, including participants' memoirs, historical records, and observer accounts of conversations. The symptoms can be categorized into three main types:

Type I: Overestimations of the Group and Its Power and Morality
1. An illusion of invulnerability, shared by most or all of the members, which creates excessive optimism and encourages taking extreme risks.
2. An unquestioned belief in the group's inherent morality, inclining the members to ignore the ethical or moral consequences of their decisions.

Type II: Closed-Mindedness
3. Collective efforts to rationalize in order to discount warnings or other information that might lead the members to reconsider their assumptions before they recommit themselves to their past policy decisions.
4. Stereotyped views of enemy leaders as too evil to warrant genuine attempts to negotiate, or as too weak and stupid to counter whatever risky attempts are made to defeat their purposes.

Type III: Pressures Toward Uniformity
5. Self-censorship of deviations from the apparent group consensus, reflecting each member's inclination to minimize to himself the importance of his doubts and counterarguments.
6. A shared illusion of unanimity concerning judgments conforming to the majority view (partly resulting from self-censorship of deviations, augmented by the false assumption that silence means consent).
7. Direct pressure on any member who expresses strong arguments against any of the group's stereotypes, illusions, or commitments, making clear that this type of dissent is contrary to what is expected of all loyal members.
8. The emergence of self-appointed mindguards and members who protect the group from adverse information that might shatter their shared complacency about the effectiveness and morality of their decisions (1982, pp. 174–175).

Janis's overall theoretical analysis, presented in Figure 4-1, also specifies the observable causes of groupthink in the form of "antecedent conditions" that facilitate the occurrence of the phenomenon. The primary antecedent condition is the degree of cohesiveness of the group, which is seen as a necessary yet not sufficient condition of groupthink. That is, the symptoms are not likely to occur strongly enough to interfere with decision making unless specified additional conditions are also met. These include the insulation of the policy-making group, the lack of a tradition of impartial leadership, and a lack of norms requiring methodical procedures for decision making. In the first instance, the insulation of the group provides little or no opportunity for obtaining expert information and critical evaluation from knowledgeable others. With regard to the second factor, the leader often finds it appealing to use his or her influence to gain approval of policy alternatives that he or she already favors. The third antecedent condition is highlighted by instances of nongroupthink decisions, such as the Cuban Missile Crisis and the development of the Marshall Plan, in which a variety of systematic procedures were adopted to enhance the quality of decision making. The individual and cumulative impact of these conditions is to enhance a lack of critical thinking in the decision-making group. One appeal of the antecedent conditions is that they could be assessed prior to decision-making deliberations, and predictions could be made about the level of groupthink that would be expected in any particular group.

The role of stress as a situational factor is also considered in the groupthink model, and rightly so because high stress is typically a component of crisis decision making. However, the relationship between stress and faulty decision making is not seen as a one-to-one relationship by Janis. He proposes that a "two factor" explanation is required. That is, the symptoms of groupthink are increased when there is high stress from external threats and when there is also low hope of finding a better solution than the one favored by the leader. Thus, high stress alone is not a necessary or sufficient condition for groupthink, but must be considered in relation to the behavior of the leader. If the leader conducts the deliberations in an impartial manner, setting the norm for open discussion on a wide range of alternatives, the probability of groupthink occurring is markedly reduced. When leadership behavior is not impartial, the conditions of high stress lead members to become very dependent for social support on the group in order to maintain their morale. This increases the

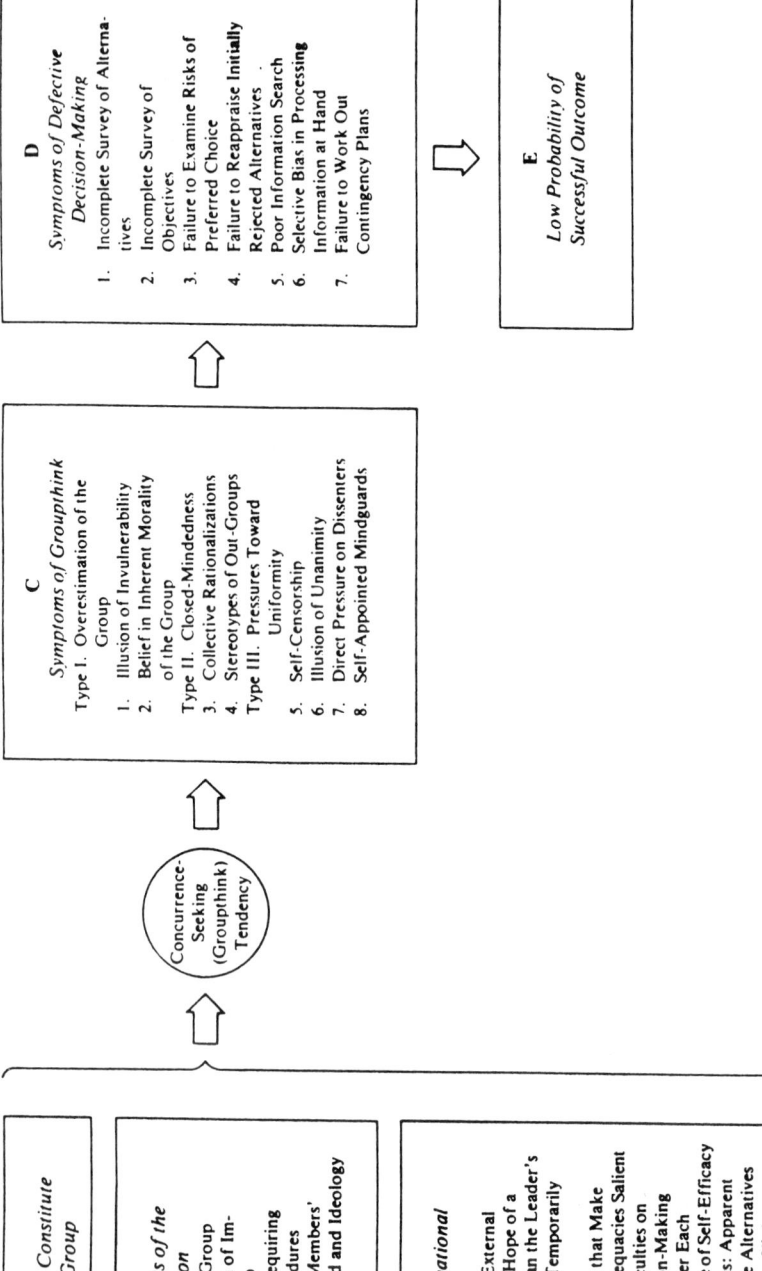

Figure 4-1. Theoretical analysis of groupthink. (From Janis, 1982 and Janis & Mann, 1977.) Reprinted with permission by The Free Press.

degree of concurrence seeking, and the groupthink syndrome unfolds. The members maintain their faith in the competence of the leader and see little chance of finding any other alternative.

The striving for mutual support through concurrence seeking leads Janis to an explanation of groupthink that draws upon the individual-level concept of self-esteem. Assuming group members are motivated to cope with the stresses of decision making, both external and internal sources of stress induce a temporary state of low self-esteem, thus increasing the need for social support. Sources include recent failures that make the members very aware of their personal inadequacies, excessive difficulties in a complex decision-making task that lower their sense of self-efficacy, and a moral dilemma in which there is an apparent lack of feasible alternatives except ones that violate ethical standards. Each time the members sacrifice moral values, their self-esteem will be further lowered by anticipatory feelings of shame, guilt, and self-depreciation. In the face of these sources of internal stress, self-esteem will be bolstered by taking part in an unanimous consensus along with respected fellow members of a congenial group. Thus, there is a joint effort to maintain emotional equanimity, and this explains the concurrence-seeking behavior. The symptoms of the groupthink syndrome form a coherent pattern when viewed in the context of this explanation.

Janis's theory of groupthink has received considerable attention, particularly in its application to decision making in international relations. However, the theory has been criticized on theoretical grounds and the small amount of empirical research it has stimulated has provided mixed results. Longley and Pruitt (1980) contend that the definition of groupthink is inadequate, that more attention needs to be given to the type of issue under consideration, and that a number of unclarities exist in the relationships among variables. The initial definition by Janis (1972) was confusing because it involved variables at three points in the causal chain from group cohesiveness to unanimity to the failure to look realistically at alternatives. Longley and Pruitt indicate that the definitional problem has been considerably alleviated in the more recent statements of the theory, which clarify the causal sequences. Also, Janis redefines groupthink as concurrence seeking, which occurs at one point in the causal chain, thus making it easier to clarify relationships. On the second point, Longley and Pruitt point out that when decisions are simple or routine, early consensus seeking may be appropriate and, furthermore, that groupthink would primarily seem to consist of premature concurrence seeking or, in other words, premature integration with inadequate differentiation in the problem-solving process. Janis (1982) agrees that premature consensus is not necessarily detrimental in dealing with routine or trivial decisions and that groupthink has negative effects when concerned with consequential issues. A number of Longley and Pruitt's concerns regarding the need for clarification in the process of groupthink appear to be answered in Janis's more complex (1982) formulation and in the explanatory hypotheses that underlie groupthink. On the research side, some studies (e.g., Courtwright, 1976; Flowers, 1977) indicate that group cohesiveness by itself may not be capable of producing groupthink, based on measures such as the number of proposed solutions and the number of facts introduced. However, it is difficult to see how the processes of groupthink in policy-making groups dealing with consequential issues can be replicated in laboratory discussion groups consisting of university undergraduates. Longley and Pruitt (1980) do perform a useful service by noting that groupthink can be linked to a number of other research lines in social psychology such as group development, integrative bargaining, and deviance in groups.

In another vein of criticism, Lebow (1981) raises the question as to whether the non-groupthink situations analyzed by Janis are indeed such good examples of effective decision making. The Cuban Missile Crisis is put forward by Janis and others as an example of how effective decision-making procedures can be used to counteract the typical symptoms of groupthink. Lebow agrees that although some of the procedures used in this case were innovative and involved a more thorough evaluation of options, the mandate of the decision-making group was constrained by President Kennedy both before and during the deliberations. In raising an alternative interpretation, Lebow is questioning the validity of Janis's analysis of both groupthink and non-groupthink situations. Lebow's treatment of the Cuban Missile Crisis highlights different behaviors and reaches different conclusions from that of Janis. At base, these discrepancies indicate the difficulties of drawing conclusions based on the historical analysis of complex events. Janis (1982) is not unaware of this difficulty when he points out that explanations inferred from historical materials need to be checked and rechecked as new evidence comes to light. Basically, he contends that groupthink is at the stage of hypothesis construction rather than hypothesis testing. In addition to proposing a systematic procedure for structuring historical inquiry, Janis suggests a number of avenues for further research of both an experimental and a field nature to test the many hypotheses involved in the model of groupthink.

Crisis Decision Making Versus Effective Problem Solving

The process of intergroup conflict can be largely seen as proceeding through parallel and reciprocal decision making by each side. Especially in times of escalation, the quality of the decision making on the part of both groups is crucial to the process and outcomes of the conflict. It is therefore not surprising that the decision-making processes of groups in conflict has received considerable attention. While some of this attention has directly focused on decision-making groups in conflict situations, much has been extrapolated from the general study of decision making in group and organizational settings. The terms *decision making* and *problem solving* are generally used in an interchangeable fashion. A distinction can be made, however, in the level of generality, in that decision making can refer to the making of choice among specified alternatives. As such it can be seen as a component of the broader problem-solving process, which is a systematic sequence of steps through which solutions to difficulties are developed, implemented, and evaluated (Fisher, 1982). However, few analysts of intergroup and international conflict make a distinction between the two processes, and that course will be followed here with one exception; that is, the decision-making process during crises induced by intergroup conflict is typically a more restricted and thereby ineffective process than that which would be prescribed by an ideal problem-solving model. The challenge is therefore how to move group decision-making processes more in line with effective problem solving.

The traditional view that decision making is predominantly a rational process has now been largely rejected within social science. This view generally held that the alternative solutions to a problem involve identifiable costs and benefits, which are weighed rationally. Thus, the decisions that are made are due largely to the reality of the problem being dealt with and the objective analysis of its characteristics and the alternatives for addressing it. Social and organizational psychologists have been among the first to challenge the rational model of decision making. In his early studies of decision making, Lewin (1947) noted that objective standards for evaluating alternative solutions are often lacking. This of course renders the individual's decision more open to both errors in thinking and social pressures of the group. Janis and Mann (1977), whose work is often seen as a major critique of the rational model, see their analysis as based on Lewin's image of the individual's vulnerability to errors in decision making through biased information processing and superficial search procedures. Janis and Mann state:

> We see man not as a cold fish but as a warm-blooded mammal, not as a rational calculator always ready to work out the best solution but as a reluctant decision maker—beset by conflict, doubts, and worry, struggling with incongruous longings, antipathies, and loyalties, and seeking relief by procrastinating, rationalizing, or denying responsibilities for his own choices. (p. 15)

In a similar vein, the work of organizational theorists, as summarized and integrated by Katz and Kahn (1978), indicates that the rational problem-solving model is inadequate. Seminal thinking in this area came from the work of March and Simon (1958), who emphasized the cognitive limits of rationality (i.e., a bounded rationality that reduces the effectiveness of decision making). They point out that knowledge of alternatives, their utility, and their consequences is always limited to the decision maker's simplified definition of the situation. Consequences of such simplification are that optimizing decision making is replaced by "satisficing," that is, the requirement that only satisfactory levels of criteria need be attained, and by a process in which decision makers deal with problems in a piecemeal fashion. The rational process of problem solving is not one of objective logic, but rather a caricature of constrained psycho-logic in which search processes are constrained by a number of limitations.

The analysis of decision making in intergroup conflict and the search for improved procedures can proceed at different levels of analysis. First, attention can be directed toward the motivational and cognitive processes of individuals that distort rationality. Second, as indicated in the previous section, forces within groups can have deleterious effects on the quality of decision making. Next, the organizational level brings into focus a broader context of decision-making processes. As indicated by March and Simon (1958) and Katz and Kahn (1978), the organizational environment helps determine what alternatives will be considered and what consequences will be anticipated. We will look at each of these levels in turn with some attention to the genesis of nonrational elements of decision making, particularly as these relate to intergroup conflict.

A great deal of the evidence on practical departures from rational decision making comes from the study of individual or psychological processes, particularly those of a perceptual or cognitive nature. Much interest in this area has occurred at the level of international relations, but the conclusions are generally applicable to intergroup conflict. For example, Lebow (1981) contends that the psychological perspective may be most relevant to understanding decision making because it offers insights into the causes and effects of misperception. Accordingly, Lebow provides a summarization and a synthesis of two of the most often quoted treatments of nonrational decision making that draw primarily on individual-level processes—Jervis (1976) and Janis and Mann (1977). An important distinction made by Lebow is that Jervis' approach is predominantly cognitive, whereas that of Janis and Mann is primarily motivational. Jervis makes good use of a popular principle coming out of social psychology (i.e., the apparent need that individuals have for cognitive consistency). The difficulty with the need for consistency is the negative implication that decision makers will be strongly biased toward information that is compatible with existing information. As with many cognitive processes, the push for consistency is a double-edged sword. According to Jervis, it can assist us in better understanding new information in relation to accumulated experience, thus providing continuity to our behavior. However, the need for consistency also may close our minds to new information or different points of view that seem incongruent with our existing beliefs, which are organized as powerful images shaping our behavior in intergroup relations. Too often, it appears that cognitive consistency leads decision makers to support and to hang on to established images that may be in need of drastic revision. Thus, rather than finding a balance between continuity and flexibility, decision makers tend toward rigidity. The existence of irrational consistency can understandably affect the decision-making process at a number of stages. As long indicated by social-psychological research on perceptual processes, consistency increases the likelihood that new information will be assimilated to the existing image through misunderstanding, adaptation, rationalization, or denial. The power of existing images and expectations also leads decision makers to reach conclusions prior to having gathered adequate new information. Images are highly resistant to revision and will change only incrementally, if at all, with decision makers being especially unlikely to develop alternative images on the basis of new information. Irrational consistency also leads decision makers to believe that their favorite alternative advances most or all of their objectives and values, whereas they tend to see other alternatives as inferior in every dimension. Finally, irrational consistency is also evident in postdecision dissonance reduction, by which decision makers come to see the chosen alternative as more desirable while the rejected alternatives become less desirable. This of course reduces any inconsistencies left by the decision, but also leads decision makers to be particularly rigid and to invest great energy in continuing to support an alterative that may have been less than adequate to begin with.

The contribution of Janis and Mann (1977) is clearly cognizant of the many perceptual and cognitive errors and biases that render decision making a nonrational process. In addition, Janis and Mann are sensitive to cognitive complexity as a prime source of inadequate decision making. Basically, when the complexity of a situation exceeds the limits of cognitive abilities, information processing becomes inadequate due to overload and fatigue. Given these various limitations, however, the major focus of their work then moves on to the causes and consequences of decision-making patterns that disrupt what they term *vigilant information processing*. Added to the cognitive elements, Janis and Mann see major sources of stress in decision making in the form of very serious threats to the decision maker's self-esteem and social status. It is this element of their approach that leads Lebow (1981) to see their model as primarily a motivational one. Thus, their theoretical framework focuses primarily on how individuals cope with the stresses of decisional conflict. Their point of departure is Lewin's (1935) concept of avoidance–avoidance conflict, which states that individuals have a tendency to withdraw from stressful conflicts in which undesirable consequences will accrue from whichever choice is made.

Janis and Mann's (1977) model specifies in detail the factors that determine whether the individual will cope with decisional conflict by withdrawing, by becoming increasingly vigilant, or by coping in other ways. They therefore develop general propositions about the conditions under which decision makers will fail to engage in vigilant information processing. The overall theoretical organization is presented as a *conflict-theory model* of decision making, which they see as applicable to all consequential decisions (see Figure 4-2). The central elements of the model are expressed in a sequence of four questions that the decision maker must ask when confronted with decisional conflict. Depending on the answer, different states or patterns of decision making occur that have important implications for the quality of the process and the products. The questions are the mediating processes anchored in observable antecedent conditions. Because much analysis in decision making looks at the influence of communication variables, these are given prominence in the formulation of antecedent conditions. The decision-making sequence begins with signs of threat that indicate that the current course of action or inaction will result in serious losses or in the failure to realize valued gains. Ignoring the risks is, of course, a dysfunctional means of avoiding stress if indeed the risks are serious. If the answer to the first question is "maybe" or "yes," the decision maker will begin to think about some new course of action. A "no" answer to question 2 will lead to an immediate adoption of that solution and a state of unconflicted change. If however, the answer to question 2 is "maybe" or "yes," the decision maker will begin considering other alternatives, and if none of these evokes a confident negative response to question 2, the decision maker will now be in a state of high decisional conflict. That is, the decision maker will want to change in order to avoid serious risk, but will at the same time not want to change in order to avoid the costs of any new course of action. A dominant pattern of unconflicted change can be indicative of the satisficing strategy, which can lead to an incrementalism consisting of a series of small changes without ever having canvased or evaluated the full range of available alternatives. Once decisional conflict has been generated by "maybe" or "yes" answers to the first two basic questions, the issue becomes the degree of optimism or pessimism about finding a better solution. If the person has no hope about finding a better solution than the objectional ones seen as available, the move is now to a pattern of defensive avoidance. Three forms of defensive avoidance are highlighted, including

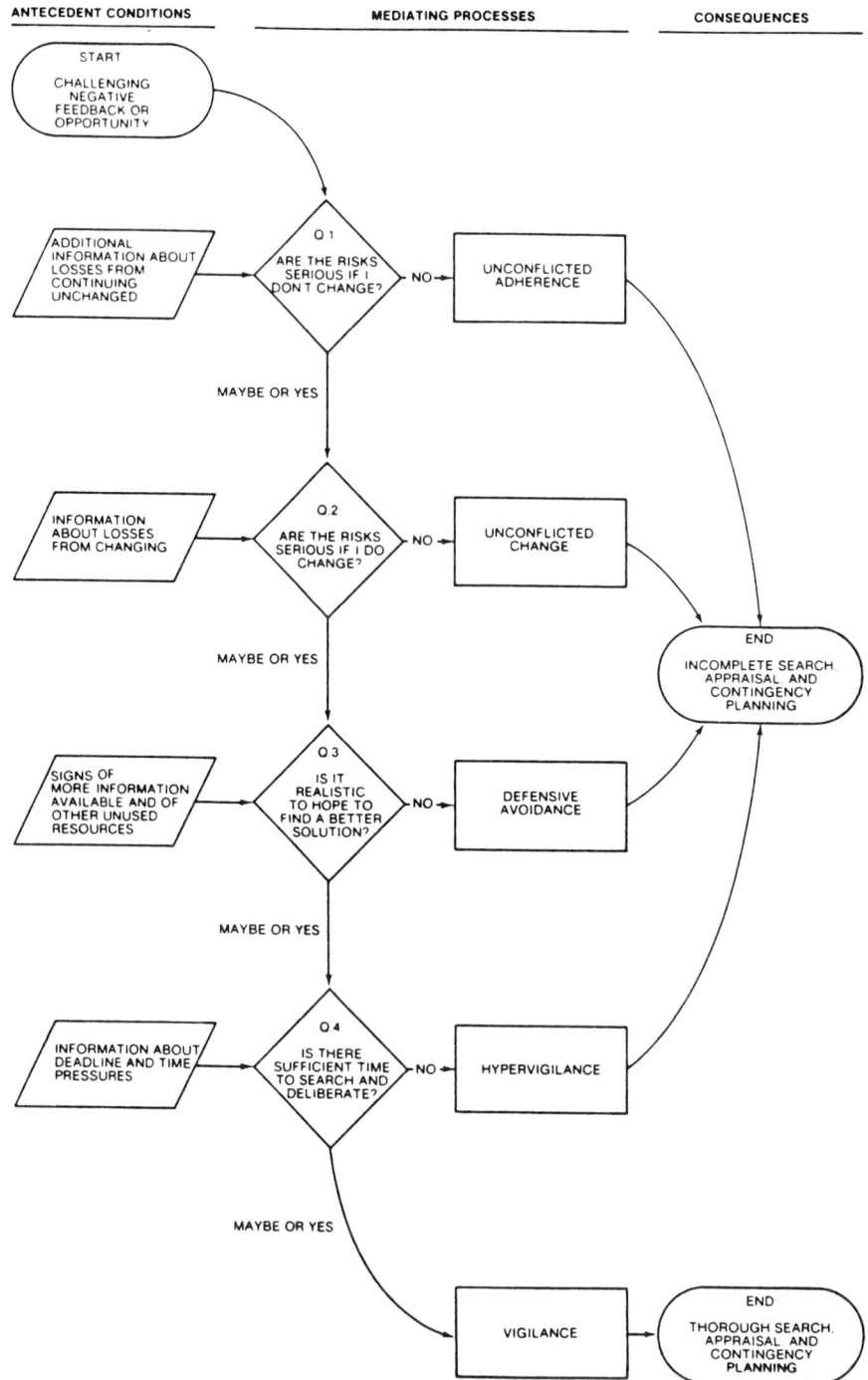

Figure 4-2. A conflict-theory model of decision making. (From Janis & Mann, 1977.) Reprinted with permission.

procrastination, shifting responsibility for the decision, and bolstering. These forms involve a high degree of perceptual and cognitive distortion. Moving to question 4, the conflict between perceiving there could be a better solution and yet not having sufficient time to find it is extremely stressful. This creates a state of hypervigilance. In this state, the decision maker is open to all sorts of information, but is unable to use it effectively. This leads to catastrophic thinking, a superficial scanning of obvious alternatives, and the use of satisficing that approaches simpleminded panic in extreme cases. In short, negative answers to any of the four questions lead to different forms of inadequate coping with the stress of decision making. In contrast, a positive answer to the fourth question lowers stress to a moderate level, in which case the person engages in a vigilant pattern that involves a thorough search for information and a careful weighing of the pros and cons of each alternative.

It is only in the case where the decision maker achieves a state of vigilance that the criteria for effective decision making are met. Janis and Mann (1977) list the following seven major criteria based on an extensive review of the decision-making literature.

> The decision maker, to the best of his ability and within his information-processing capabilities:
> 1. Thoroughly canvases a wide range of alternative courses of action;
> 2. Surveys the whole range of objectives to be fulfilled and the values implicated by the choice;
> 3. Carefully weighs whatever he knows about the costs and risks of negative consequences, as well as the positive consequences, that could flow from each alternative;
> 4. Intensively searches for new information relevant to further evaluation of the alternatives;
> 5. Correctly assimilates and takes account of any new information or expert judgment to which he is exposed, even when the information or judgment does not support the course of action he initially prefers;
> 6. Re-examines the positive and negative consequences of all known alternatives, including those originally regarded as unacceptable, before making a final choice;
> 7. Makes detailed provisions for implementing or executing the chosen course of action, with special attention to contingency plans that might be required if known risks were to materialize (p. 11).

Thus, the model presented by Janis and Mann provides a means of analyzing the moment-to-moment process of decision making. In doing so, it seems to indicate that the pitfalls and limitations of decision making are typically much greater than the likelihood of effectively implementing the criteria of good decision making. A recent study by Janis and his colleagues (1986) of the Untied States' decision making during international crises bears out this sobering proposition. Independent experts chose the gravest crises experienced since World War II and selected the sources of information, while a panel of ideologically diverse political scientists rated the harmfulness of each crisis to U.S. interest and to the threat to world peace. Using Janis and Mann's criteria, defective decision making was found to correlate with both failure to satisfy U.S. objectives and an increase in international conflict. The analysis also indicated that 37% of the crises involved poor quality decision making while 42% of the cases were rated as high quality. Further investigation found that rather than seeking vigilance, decision makers relied on simplistic rules of thumb to grapple with the dangerous complexity of international crises.

Lebow (1981) maintains that it is not possible to integrate the analyses of Jervis (1976) and Janis and Mann (1977) into a single model, because their starting points are radically different. Whereas Jervis emphasizes the need to develop simple rules for information processing in a complex and uncertain environment, Janis and Mann assume a strong need to maintain self-esteem and stature. Hence, while Jervis sees cognitive consistency as the primary organizing principle, Janis and Mann see the aversion to psychological stress as the motivator that distorts cognition. It should be pointed out, however, that in the social-psychological literature, the need for cognitive consistency is also seen as a strong motivator of behavior. In this way, both approaches are motivationally based. With regard to cognitive distortions, Lebow is able to provide some integration by seeing both approaches as resulting in certain deviations from rational decision making. These can be summarized as an overevaluation of past performance as compared to present reality, overconfidence in decisions to which commitment has been made, and an insensitivity to additional information that is critical of decisions already made. These deviations summarize how the process often departs from the criteria of effective decision making.

The controversy surrounding rational versus irrational decision making is also addressed by Kinder and Weiss (1978) in their review of the work of Jervis (1976) and Janis and Mann (1977). They also include the work of Axelrod (1976), which deals with a cognitive mapping technique to represent the manner in which decision makers reduce complex issues to simplified images. Kinder and Weiss identify four common themes in these works, including the impact of cognitive consistency on perception and information processing, systematic biases in causal analysis, the distorting effects of stress on decision making, and the cognitive construction of greater order and predictability than actually exists in the uncertain, disorderly environment of the decision maker. The inevitable conclusion is once again drawn that even at the basic level of individual functioning, the process of decision making involves much more than rational mechanisms and considerations.

Moving beyond the individual level, it is important to acknowledge that decision makers operate primarily at the level of the group. Major decisions affecting intergroup relations are seldom made by individuals acting alone. Thus, it becomes especially important to consider the assets and liabilities involved in group problem solving in combination with individual deficiencies. According to Maier (1967), based on numerous studies of the social-psychological processes involved in problem solving, group assets include greater knowledge about the problem, a greater number of approaches to the problem, better comprehension of the decision, and increased acceptance of solutions through participation. However, group liabilities are also compelling. These include social pressure, which is a major force in bringing about conformity through a need for acceptance, thereby presaging Janis's (1982) concept of groupthink. Similarly, in paralleling March and Simon's (1958) concept of satisficing, Maier's research indicates that the first moderately acceptable solution tends to be accepted by the group, thus ruling out the possibility of higher quality solutions being generated. Individual domination is an additional liability of group problem solving. Results indicate that the mere fact of appointing a leader causes this individual to dominate the discussion through greater participation, persuasive behavior, and at times stubborn persistence. In a related vein, conflict and arguments over the desired solution tend to subvert effective problem solving. The goal becomes that of winning the decision and this is typically unrelated to the quality of the solution.

Maier's liabilities relate primarily to social processes in group problem solving. In contrast, the analysis by Janis and Mann (1977), which supports the concept of groupthink, places the emphasis on task deficiencies in the problem-solving sequence. As Figure 4-1 on groupthink indicates, such symptoms of defective decision making include an incomplete survey of alternatives and objectives; failures to examine, reappraise, and plan; and inadequate searching and selective biasing in handling information. Thus, it is clear that group problem solving can evidence deficiencies in both the task or content arena and the social-emotional or process area of functioning. Hence, there must be concern with both the task and the social requirements of effective problem solving, as emphasized by Morris and Sashkin (1976), cited earlier. These authors build much of their prescription on the work of Maier as well as other social psychologists. In addition, their presentation of problem solving is paralleled by a number of others including those of Janis and Mann (1977), Holsti (1979), and Napier and Gershenfeld (1985). Thus, considerable understanding underlies a developing social technology of effective problem solving that is available to counter the typical pitfalls and liabilities that groups experience when they confront difficult decisions.

Unfortunately, difficulties at the group level of functioning are not the only barriers to effective decision making. As noted in Figure 4-1, the model of groupthink involves a number of structural faults of the organization which underlie concurrence seeking. In addition, theorists of organizational functioning point out that higher level determinants and processes bear upon the ultimate decisions that are made. Katz and Kahn (1978), in their social-psychological analysis of organizations, draw upon the work of Cyert and March (1963), who provide a behavioral analysis of organizational decision making. These authors point out that organizational decisions often reflect competing interests and goals held by various coalitions within the organization. In decision making, a considerable amount of bargaining is involved that includes politics as well as economic considerations. Often, inconsistency among competing positions is dealt with through sequential attention over a longer time period. At the level of political decision making, the analysis of Allison (1971) shows some similarity to that of the organizational theorists. In supplementing the rational actor model of decision making, Allison brings forward the organizational process model and the governmental political model. The former emphasizes the manner in which the organizational context, pressures, and standard operating procedures influence decisions, whereas the latter emphasizes bargaining among the key players who have an investment in the decision. These higher level considerations are especially important in international relations, the arena to which Allison's analysis is primarily directed.

Notwithstanding the importance of organizational and political factors in decision making, it is clear that the first requirement is effective group functioning. In relation to the task and social requirements of effective problem solving, the question of leadership becomes essential. Reality dictates that groups composed of equals seldom operate without some coordination, direction, and influence from one person who is "more than equal." According to Maier's (1967) analysis, the role of the leader is crucial. First, the leader can see that assets are capitalized upon while liabilities are prevented or minimized. Furthermore, there are elements in group decision making that can serve as either assets or liabilities, depending largely upon the social skills of the leader. The leader must move disagreement away from creating hard feelings toward a creative resolution of the conflict and thereby to an innovative and superior solution. By separating and guiding the sequence of stages in problem solving, the leader can clearly differentiate between interests, goals, obstacles, and solutions, thus removing disagreements based on misunderstanding. Finally, the leader can moderate risk-taking tendencies and can work toward the effective use of discussion time. Certainly other functions of effective leadership in group problem solving could be added to this list. Nonetheless, Maier's illustrations make the point adequately: the behavior of the leader is often the key to effective group problem solving. It therefore follows that some further consideration should be given to the role of the leader and his or her relationship with constituents.

Leadership and Constituent Pressure

The role of leadership in intergroup relations and intergroup conflict is significant, because, as Sherif (1966) and others point out, the locus of power in groups resides in the leader and other high status members. It is therefore not surprising that in critical situations, such as intergroup conflict, leaders tend to take over the reins of group decision making. A reciprocal dynamic that can occur in intergroup conflict is that the group becomes more predisposed to support aggressive leadership. For example, in the boys camp studies by Sherif (1966), the phase of intergroup competition and conflict produced changes in the status and role relationships within the group in this direction. In one group, a bully who had been castigated during the initial phase emerged as a hero during encounters with the out-group in the competition phase. In another group, the leader during the group development phase was deposed because he was not willing to take strong action against the out-group. In a similar vein, the management training studies by Blake and Mouton (1961) indicated that as intergroup conflict escalated, the more articulate and aggressive members in the group took on leadership roles. These research findings lend general support to the popular notion that intergroup conflict breeds militant leadership.

At the same time, as Sherif (1966) points out, leaders and other group representatives must remain a part of the power structure if their actions are to be effective. Although the leader cannot afford to be seen as being "soft" in dealings with the out-group, the leader is not immune from sanctions if too great a deviation in any direction from group norms occurs. The leader must pursue group goals within prevailing bounds, and any transgression in the direction of perceived weakness will expose the leader as a traitor. In a less severe fashion, Blake, Shepard, and Mouton (1964) point out that representatives of groups are influenced by pressures within the group, by which the representative is not free to negotiate according to his or her own preferences but is subject to the group's evaluation. According to Thomas (1976), group norms typically support behavior that is seen as contributing to group goals, whereas other behaviors are punished. Furthermore, this "constituent pressure" is usually in the direction of competitive and hostile behavior. This in turn may have some effect on strengthening the leadership hierarchy and the level of cohesion within the group. More recent experimental research on negotiation, as discussed by Pruitt and Rubin (1986), indicates that representatives of groups are more reluctant to yield than individuals bargaining on their own, presumably due to the effect of constituent pressure. Similarly, representatives who are more accountable to their groups in negotiations appear to be more concerned about group outcomes and are more likely to adopt a contentious approach in negotiations. It thus appears that in situations of intergroup conflict, groups are more likely to turn toward aggressive leadership and to provide leaders with the support necessary to engage in contentious behavior with the out-group.

In real world decision-making groups, the importance of leadership in fostering constructive or destructive processes and outcomes is also evident. In his continuing development of the concept of groupthink, Janis (1982) follows his analysis of the Watergate cover-up by pointing out that group cohesiveness is only a necessary but not sufficient condition of groupthink. In the light of earlier studies, as well as research on group dynamics, the Watergate case pointed out the importance of additional conditions that must be added to cohesiveness in order for the quality of the group's decision making to be significantly reduced. In addition to the insulation of the group from outside information sources and an absence of norms requiring methodical procedures for search and appraisal, Janis postulates that a lack of a tradition of impartial leadership is necessary for groupthink to occur. In this situation, the leader is unconstrained in pushing his or her pet solution and does not discourage members from mindless concurrence with this preferred course of action. This directive form of leadership is not as extreme as one-person rule, but is strong enough to discourage the open discussion of alternatives, thus promoting concurrence seeking. The occurrence of directive leadership may seem to be partly in contradiction to the phenomenon of constituent pressure. In the one case the group supports the leader's alternatives in a mindless way, whereas in interactions with the out-group, the members punish weak behavior and reinforce aggressive tendencies. In one case the group exerts influence over the leader, whereas in the other it does not. However, assuming that the alternatives put forward by the leader are in the aggressive direction, the two behaviors are compatible in that both support more contentious tactics toward the adversary. In any event, Janis concludes that the degree to which groupthink tendencies will interfere with effective information search and appraisal depends to a large extent on the leader's behavior. Janis's emphasis on the importance of open leadership in decision making is supported by a considerable amount of theorizing and research in the field of organizational psychology (e.g., Likert & Likert, 1976).

Implications for Conflict Escalation and De-Escalation

The power of group processes to affect intergroup interactions in negative and destructive directions is undeniable. At the same time, it is not clear which elements of group process would be most open to influence in positive directions. Negative dynamics related to established characteristics such as group, identity, cohesiveness, and ethnocentrism are perhaps more difficult to impact in productive ways than are the dynamics of ineffective decision making. The latter are more under the control of the parties involved and there is potential for increasing both the awareness and the competence of decision makers.

With regard to the task side of decision making, Janis and Mann (1977) draw upon the extensive research literature to bring forward ideal procedural criteria that increase the likelihood of effective decision making. With these criteria in mind, Janis and Mann then suggest a number of mechanisms for improving the quality of group decision making. In addition to decision counseling and using a balance sheet scheme, proposals are made for training and education. In particular, a design for a training workshop is presented that would sensitize decision makers to the pitfalls and provide them with alternative behaviors for effective decision making.

Janis and Mann's suggestions for improving the quality of decision making are also part and parcel of Janis's prescriptions for preventing groupthink. These prescriptions were initially presented by Janis (1972), further discussed by Janis and Mann (1977), and presented in revised form with some attention to undesirable side effects by Janis (1982). Bereft of supportive discussion, the prescriptions include the following:

1. The leader should assign the role of critical evaluator to each member, encouraging the group to give high priority to airing objections and doubts;
2. The leaders in an organization's hierarchy, when assigning a policy-planning mission to a group should be impartial instead of stating preferences and expectations at the outset;
3. The organization should routinely follow the administrative practice of setting up several independent policy-planning and evaluation groups to work on the same policy question, each carrying out its deliberations under a different leader;
4. Throughout the period when the feasibility and effectiveness of policy alternatives are being surveyed, the policy-making group should from time to time divide into two or more subgroups to meet separately, under different chairpersons, and then come together to hammer out their differences;
5. Each member of the policy-making group should discuss periodically the group's deliberations with trusted associates in his or her own unit of the organization and report back their reactions;
6. One or more outside experts or qualified colleagues within the organization who are not core members of the policy-making group should be invited to each meeting on a staggered basis and should be encouraged to challenge the views of the core members;
7. At every meeting devoted to evaluating policy alternatives, at least one member should be assigned the role of devil's advocate;
8. Whenever the policy issue involves relations with a rival nation or organization, a sizeable block of time (perhaps an entire session) should be spent surveying all

warning signals from the rival and constructing alternative scenarios of the rival's intentions;
9. After reaching a preliminary consensus about what seems to be the best policy alternative, the policy-making group should hold a "second chance" meeting at which the members are expected to express as vividly as they can all their residual doubts and to rethink the entire issue before making a definitive choice. (pp. 262–271)

Janis's prescriptions for preventing groupthink flow logically from the initial description and analysis. However, they may not be without their limitations. For example Lebow (1981) points out that all of the prescriptions are based on the assumption that leaders will make clear efforts to structure an environment that encourages critical thinking and dissent. This appears to be extremely unrealistic because, for a number of reasons, leaders are more likely to discourage the conditions associated with open decision making. For instance, criticism and dissent can threaten the leader's authority by making it more difficult to control the decision-making process, and furthermore, such expressions may be interpreted as a sign of weakness on the part of the leader. In addition, Lebow points out a more fundamental problem in that when leaders are committed to a policy, new information and constructive criticism are the last thing they will look for. In fact, case analyses indicate that leaders act to suppress or ignore dissent. However, it should be pointed out that this often occurs after the decision is made, whereas the insidious dynamics of groupthink occur during the decision-making phase itself. Of course, if the leader's mind is already made up on given course of action, the two situations are one and the same. Hence, Lebow concludes that when leaders are committed to a policy, the prescriptions have little chance of adoption and if they are adopted, it may very well be in a superficial and ritualistic manner designed mainly to reassure the decision makers that they are following the best possible path.

Even with the potential limitations and realities, it is evident that work on group processes, particularly decision making, has brought to light a variety of group dynamics that can fuel destructive intergroup conflict. In addition to creating knowledge that increases the awareness of such pitfalls, the potential exists for educating and training influential individuals and groups in more effective ways to handle decision making in approaching situations of intergroup and international conflict.

Chapter 5

An Eclectic Model of Intergroup Conflict

The purpose of this chapter is to work toward the development of an eclectic model of intergroup conflict by drawing on the classic contributions and contemporary work discussed in the preceding three chapters. In particular, an attempt will be made to develop a dynamic model of intergroup conflict with a focus on the processes of escalation, which transform a low intensity conflict into a high intensity one.

A model of intergroup conflict is only a part of a broader theory of intergroup relations and no attempt will be made here to develop that broader theory nor to place the model of intergroup conflict in that context. However, it is apparent that an eclectic theory of intergroup relations would draw on many of the same sources and would consider many of the same processes. In fact, it is noteworthy that the development, escalation, and resolution of conflict can be placed at the center of intergroup relations. For example, in a recent and comprehensive treatment of theories of intergroup relations, Taylor and Moghaddam (1987) begin with a broad definition of intergroup relations as "any aspect of human interaction which involves individuals perceiving themselves to be members of a social category, or being perceived by others as belonging to a social category" (p. 9). The authors then proceed to review the major theories in the area, that is, those that "claim to deal with the fundamental issues associated with intergroup relations: *how intergroup conflicts arise, what course they take, and how they become resolved*" (p. 14, italics added). Not surprisingly, then, a number of the major theories reviewed by Taylor and Moghaddam, as in previous coverages of intergroup relations such as that of Worchel and Austin (1986), are in fact major contributors to the study of intergroup conflict. Thus, the classic contributions reviewed in Chapter 2 are not only compatible with but may stand at the very center of the broader field of intergroup relations. At the same time, no claim is made that the model developed here is a generic treatment of intergroup relations. Consequently, a number of boundaries will be specified in order to locate the model of intergroup conflict within the broader space of intergroup relations.

The development of the eclectic model of intergroup conflict will follow a systematic and comprehensive strategy of theory construction as provided by the work of Dubin (1969, 1976). After detailing this strategy, the major conceptual units and laws, or principles, of the model will be described with limited reference to past research and theorizing. The boundaries and system states of the model will be described and illustrative propositions will be provided. Finally, the limitations and implications of the model with regard to theory development and future research will be discussed.

The Approach to Theory Building

The approach to theory building presented by Dubin (1969, 1976) is particularly appealing to scholar/practitioners of intergroup conflict resolution because it deals with guidelines for developing models that have considerable likelihood of being utilized in real life situations. In order words, the approach is tailored to developing "applied theories," which have immediate and direct application to the real world. At the same time, the general structure of theory and its development is similar whether the goal is application by the practitioner or intellectual understanding by the scholar. Dubin's primary concern is in the field of organizational psychology and with the contributions that practitioners, mainly managers, might make to theory building, particularly in defining the content of models to be developed. The scientist who builds the theory thus needs to be especially sensitive to the needs and ideas of the practitioners. In the field of intergroup conflict resolution at present, the leading edge of developments is being carried forward by scientist/practitioners who are attempting to both develop and apply theories. Examples of such work will be covered in Chapters 8 and 9. Thus, the initial developers of theory in this area will also often be the practitioners who will apply the theory. While this may initially streamline the process toward greater efficiency, the need to involve the larger population of practitioners, especially intermediaries in communal conflicts and diplomats in international relations, will become more and more pressing. Thus, initial attempts at theory building need to be widely shared at an early stage and the reactions and contributions of practitioners incorporated as soon as possible.

Dubin's approach to theory building is also appealing to scholar/practitioners in intergroup conflict resolution because of the connection between theory and the real world, where the costs of destructive attempts at conflict management are sorely felt. According to Dubin (1976),

> It is exceedingly difficult to say something meaningful about the real world without starting in the real world. Observation and description of the real world are the essential points of origin for theories in applied areas like industrial psychology, if not in all areas. (p. 18)

Thus, considerable emphasis is placed upon the rational process of induction in the early stages of theory building by which generalizations are formed based on observations and descriptions, that is, the empirical base of the social scientist. In the later stages, the emphasis shifts to the process of deduction, in which the scientist reasons from the general to the particular in the form of propositions, hypotheses, and their operationalizations. Dubin's strategy is thus compatible with the short but rich history of theory construction in social psychology wherein *empirical theories* (those based on observation and describing relationships that can be tested using the scientific method) have held sway since at least the time of Lewin (1951). Furthermore, the combination of induction and deduction holds the potential of providing powerful theories that not only organize considerable information but also yield predictions to guide future research (Marx, 1963; Shaw & Costanzo, 1970).

Dubin provides seven features or building blocks of a theoretical model. These basic conceptual components also imply the steps or series of stages that the scientist goes through in constructing a theory. Note that the terms *theory* and *model* will be used interchangeably here, as they are in Dubin's approach. Later, it will be convenient to distinguish a model as being a more limited part of a theory with broader ramifications, connections, and implications. The process of theory building moves from specifying the basic variables to specifying the laws of interaction, the boundaries and system states, the propositions and empirical indicators, and finally the hypotheses.

The first features of a model are the phenomena or variables of interest. These are the *units* whose interactions are the focus of attention for theorizing. Here, the knowledge, biases, and imagination of the scientist come into play in the selection process, which is admittedly arbitrary. In the field of conflict resolution, an awareness of variables identified as important by past research is central in the selection of units to be included in a model of intergroup conflict.

The second step in theory building is to specify the laws of interaction, or principles that specify the manner in which the variables interact with each other. Again, the judgment or lack thereof shown by the theoretician is central. The domain of the theory will be partly determined at this point because every unit included needs to be connected to at least one other unit by a law of interaction. Laws are typically statements of relationship, either positive or negative, among the units. Dubin regards the laws of interaction as the fundamental building blocks out of which a theory is constructed. In the field of conflict resolution, each of the classic contributions has brought forward statements of relationship among variables, thus providing a rich initial source of potential laws. Many of these principles have adequate logical and empirical bases so that they may be legitimately used as building blocks for an eclectic model of intergroup conflict.

The third feature of a theoretical model are the *boundaries* within which the model is expected to hold, thus specifying the limited portion of the real world to which the model is applicable. Some boundaries are benign according to Dubin—beyond them the model is not alleged to hold, but they themselves are not relevant to the way in which the model operates. Other boundaries are relevant in that they are limiting values of units or laws beyond which the model ceases to function. The boundaries define the domain of the theory within which the units interact lawfully and beyond which the units may change and/or the laws may lose their validity. Dubin points out that particularly in the social sciences there has been a "strange incapacity to recognize that a theoretical model must have a boundary" (p. 28). There is a tendency to operate with simplistic laws of interaction that are seen as universal for all situations. In the field of intergroup relations and intergroup conflict, this point requires serious consideration. There would appear to be some deficiencies in specifying the boundaries within which existing models hold and beyond which their propositions are suspect. It is likely that only attempts at constructing an eclectic theory may sensitize scholars in the area to this problem.

System states are the fourth feature in Dubin's approach to theory building. A system state is a condition of the system being modeled in which the units take on characteristic values that persist for some period of time. The system state is thus defined by the values taken by the units and by the fact that the units may interact differently in different system states. The integrity of the total system is maintained, but its condition may be markedly different in the various states. The theoretical model is defined in total by the system states over which it is operative. Dubin comments that much of social science theory is concerned with system changes over time, that is, with changes within persons and groups. The same is true of theorizing in the area of intergroup conflict, particularly with regard to the processes of escalation and de-escalation. Numerous propositions have been brought forward to illuminate these processes, but usually without an explicit attempt to specify the system states that are involved at either end or the manner in which the processes relate to these system states. The concepts of system states and system change are therefore seen as crucial to an eclectic model of intergroup conflict.

With the first four features in place through the process of induction, the sequence of theory construction now shifts to making deductions about the model in operation. *Propositions* are conclusions or truth statements that represent logical and true deductions about the system embodied in the model. Propositions are inherently true because they are statements about a theoretical system and not necessarily the real world; their only test is that they be logically consistent with the model. Two types of propositions can be distinguished—strategic and trivial. The former hold true where something of considerable significance is occurring in the relationships among units, whereas the latter differ only slightly from other propositions. Propositions also relate to two different classes of predictions that may be made based on a theoretical model. One class relates to the relationships among units; the other relates to the change among the states of the system, which should be signaled by changes in all of the units. The distinction between laws and propositions appears to be primarily one of generality, certainty, and manner of construction: laws are constructed through induction to cover fundamental relationships among variables for which considerable evidence exist; propositions are deduced from laws to cover more specific predictions on which further data needs to be gathered. Propositions are the bridge to testing the reality of the model in relation to the empirical world.

The sixth feature in theory building are the *empirical indicators* into which each term in a proposition needs to be converted. Empirical indicators connect the units of the model to observations or measurements in the real world. This feature is central to the principle of operationism in social science, which states that only propositions based on operations that are public and repeatable are admissible as scientific evidence (Stevens, 1963). Empirical indicators are often referred to as "operational definitions" of the terms or units in question.

A theoretical model only becomes a scientific or empirical model when it is put to the test. In order to do this, the final feature of the model is developed in the form of *hypotheses*, which are propositional statements with empirical indicators substituted for each term. An hypothesis is tested by measuring the values on the empirical indicators to see if the theoretically predicted relationships are achieved. Verification of hypotheses supports and confirms the related elements of the model; rejection may require modification or rejection of the model or parts of it. The seriousness and flexibility of this testing process depends on whether the scientist has the goal of proving the adequacy of the model or of improving an initial model. According to Dubin, the former approach invokes certain limitations in that data are likely to be collected only on units incorporated into the model and then only on values within the predicted ranges. The alternate approach of improving theoretical models does not suffer these limitations and should result in a constant process of theory reevaluation, modification, and, thereby, improvement (Popper, 1961). Given the relatively underdeveloped state of theory in the area of intergroup conflict resolution, the latter strategy would seem to be much more appropriate for the foreseeable future.

Variables of the Model

The short but rich history of theorizing and research on intergroup conflict has identified a large range of variables associated with the causation, escalation, and resolution of disputes. However, as Sherif (1966) points out, too many theories of intergroup relations posit one sovereign factor, such as individual frustration or leadership style, in an attempt to explain intergroup attitudes and behavior. Of course, none of these variables alone determines the course of intergroup behavior, although all may contribute. According to Sherif (1966): "Intergroup behavior can be explained only in terms of the entire frame of reference in which all these various factors operate in an interdependent way" (p. 63). Furthermore, the relative weights of the various factors will vary depending on the particular set of conditions prevailing in any given intergroup conflict.

It follows that the specification of units or variables to be included in an eclectic model of intergroup conflict must combine range with selectivity. A wide range of potentially important variables has been identified by past work, and yet to include all possibilities would render the initial model unworkable and untestable. It is therefore necessary to set priorities by selecting variables that have been identified in more than one previous model or that have stood the test of time in being consistently related to important elements of intergroup relations. Even within these restrictions, parsimony must also be achieved by choosing only one variable from an overlapping set of similar factors.

There are two dimensions and related strategies that are useful if not logically necessary in order to organize the diversity of variables that deserve inclusion in an eclectic model of intergroup conflict. These are level of analysis and time or point of influence. One weakness of many previous theoretical and empirical endeavors is the restriction of variables to only one or two levels of analysis. For example, only individual factors such as frustration might be related to intergroup conflict, or only group variables such as cohesion might be considered. At a minimum, it is posited that three levels of analysis are initially required in an eclectic theory of intergroup conflict—individual, group, and intergroup. The specification of variables at these three levels and the interplay among them are seen as the essential building blocks of such a theory.

The second dimension of importance, the temporal one, is useful not only for describing variables, but even more so for organizing the variables into the model itself. Thus, the complete execution of this strategy will become more apparent when the eclectic model is presented. Prior to this, it is important to note that the point at which a variable or a given value of a variable is formed or takes prominence is a central consideration in the development and functioning of the model. Given this, four categories of variables can be determined based on temporal identity: antecedents, orientations, processes, and outcomes. Antecedent variables exist prior to the manifest expression of intergroup conflict and can be seen as characteristics of the individuals involved, the groups involved, or the intergroup relationship itself. Orientations are predispositions, perceptions, attitudes, and approaches that are expressed in the early stages of conflict development and escalation, and that have a critical bearing on the form and intensity of the conflict. Processes refers to individual styles, group behaviors, and intergroup interactions, which both feed into and express the manifest conflict. Processes are the only variables that are dynamic in nature, as opposed to the static character of the other categories of variables, which can more or less be captured at any one point in time. Finally, outcomes are the products and effects of the conflict at the intergroup, group, and individual level. Figure 5-1 identifies the variables of the model organized by level of analysis and temporal category.

Individual-Level Variables

The potential number of individual-level variables to consider for inclusion is immense, but the task is made easier by the general finding that few personality characteristics have consistently been related to group and intergroup behavior. In the field of intergroup relations, two variables stand out as worthy of consideration: authoritarianism and self-esteem. Authoritarianism, or variants or concomitants of it, has long been implicated in the development of ethnocentrism and destructive intergroup conflict. The classic study, *The Authoritarian Personality* (Adorno et al., 1950), while deficient on numerous theoretical and methodological grounds, gave prominence to the role of authoritarianism in the etiology and expression of prejudice and discrimination (see Chapter 2). This role has generally been supported in subsequent research and the concept of authoritarianism has also been related to a range of socially significant behaviors. For example, Bixenstine and O'Reilly (1966) found that individuals higher on authoritarianism tended to use a competitive and aggressive style in playing a laboratory game involving interpersonal conflict. Self-esteem, along with its close relative, self-concept, is a personal-

Variables of the Model

	CATEGORY			
LEVEL	Antecedents	Orientations	Processes	Outcomes
INDIVIDUAL	Self-esteem	Achievement	Personal style	Self-esteem
	Authoritarianism	Affiliation	Perceptual biases	
		Dominance (power)		
GROUP	Cohesion	Trust	Problem-solving	Cohesion
	Identity	Ethnocentrism		Satisfaction
			Constituent pressure	Group Leader
		Threat		
INTERGROUP	Cultural differences		Communication	Outcome satisfaction
	History of antagonism		Interaction	Joint payoff
		Competitive/ cooperative orientation		
	Source of conflict		Dispute resolution	Resolution effects

Figure 5-1. Variables of the eclectic model.

ity characteristic of central importance in social interaction, including situations of perceived discrimination and relative deprivation (Dion, 1986). Self-esteem has been directly connected to intergroup behavior through the principles of social identity theory. Subsequent research has, for example, demonstrated that self-esteem is increased by opportunities to discriminate against an out-group (Lemyre & Smith, 1985). Its inclusion in an eclectic model, in relation to both members and representatives of conflicting groups, is essential. Both authoritarianism and self-esteem are categorized as antecedent variables.

Individual characteristics categorized as orientations include the major personal needs of achievement, affiliation, and power. This triumvirate of personal motivation has long been identified as being among the wellsprings of human behavior (e.g., McClelland, 1961, 1975; Murray, 1938). In the area of conflict resolution, there are some indications that these predispositions influence the approach that people manifest as individuals or group representatives when they interact with opposing interests. For example, Kilmann and Thomas (1975) found that individuals with a high need for achievement tend to choose a collaborating mode in dealing with interpersonal differences. They also found that on the basic personality dimension of Introversion–Extroversion, introverts tend toward avoidance of conflict, while on the dimension of Thinking–Feeling, expressive individuals have a tendency for accommodation. The latter results have been replicated by Chanin and Schneer (1984) who also found that thinking individuals tend toward a competitive or collaborative style. These examples indicate that the personality dimensions of Introversion–Extroversion and Thinking–Feeling may be worthy of inclusion in the eclectic model at some future point. Finally, with regard to the basic motives of personality, Jones and Melcher (1982) reported that the need for affiliation was positively related to smoothing conflict over and negatively related to forcing or a competitive style.

Moving into the category of processes brings us to the style and the related behavior of the individual in intergroup interaction. The construct of personal behavioral style is placed here, even though it can be seen as existing on the border between orientations and processes. In particular, attention is directed toward the individual's personal mode of managing conflict in interpersonal interaction (e.g., Thomas & Kilmann, 1974), his or her preferred style of leadership in small group interaction (e.g., Fiedler, 1967), and his or her personal style as a boundary person in negotiation (Druckman & Mahoney, 1977). How these styles are manifested in actual conflict then becomes a matter of behavior at the intergroup level. Also in the process category are the perceptual and cognitive biases of individuals that feed into the conflict, particularly its escalation. As discussed in Chapter 3, a number of biases, such as the self-confirming effects of social stereotypes and the ultimate attribution error, tend to influence information processing about the other group in simplistic and derogatory directions. Further perceptual and cognitive factors that tend to escalate and reify intergroup conflict are covered in Chapter 7 on international conflict.

Finally, the category of outcomes includes few variables because the effects of intergroup conflict are not generally seen to include individual characteristics or styles. Consequently, the only variable identified is self-esteem, which has been linked, at least indirectly, to the success or failure that groups experience as a result of conflict settlement (e.g., Blake & Mouton, 1961).

Group-Level Variables

As with the individual level, a wide range of group-level factors has been identified as potential contributors to intergroup conflict, and yet the number of these that have shown consistent relationships or have been included in major theories is manageable (see Chapter 4). As antecedents, attention will be given to group identity and cohesion. Identity is essential to the processes of self-categorization and group formation, and has partly been captured in the principles of social identity theory. Cohesion has been given prominence by many of the theorists seen as contributors to realistic conflict theory, and has received a great deal of attention in experimental research stimulated by the classic field studies of Sherif.

In the category of group orientations, the concept of ethnocentrism plays a pivotal role. Ethnocentrism is predicated upon a sense of in-group–out-group differentiation and is composed of positive in-group attitudes coupled with negative out-group attitudes. In particular, ethnocentrism involves in-group loyalty and glorification and out-group derogation and hostility. The central position of ethnocentrism in an eclectic model of intergroup conflict is supported by its inclusion, directly or indirectly, in most theories, including those that are different yet complementary, such as realistic conflict theory and the authoritarian personality. Alongside ethnocentrism is a variable that also plays an important role in realistic conflict theory—perceived threat. In Realistic Group Conflict Theory (RCT), threat may be real—based on a combination of real conflict of interest, past or present conflict between the groups, and the existence of competitive out-groups—or false—a matter of misperception. In either case, the effect is postulated to be the same (i.e., increased ethnocentrism), and the variable of significance is therefore perceived threat (Grant, 1980; Holmes & Grant, 1979).

Process variables at the group level include problem-solving competence and constituent pressure on representatives. The ability of the group to make decisions and solve problems effectively has long been considered an important contributor to the manner in which intergroup conflicts are handled. In particular, the concept of groupthink, wherein concurrence seeking overrides the realistic appraisal of alternatives, has been implicated in the creation of major foreign policy fiascoes at the international level. Social psychologists have consistently shown an interest in understanding and measuring the problem-solving processes that take place in small groups, and the current challenge is to relate this variable to intergroup conflict. The variable of constituent pressure on representatives creates the avenue by which the norms of the group vis-à-vis the conflict are brought to bear. In order to understand the intergroup behavior of representatives, the influence of the group, especially the use of positive and negative sanctions, must be considered.

Outcomes at the group level include the possible effects on cohesion following the settlement of a dispute. In addition, it is expected that satisfaction with the group, the leader, and the representatives will be affected. For example, leadership may be replaced or consolidated and representatives may be subjected to more or less constituent pressure as a result of the outcomes of a conflict.

Variables at the Intergroup Level

The intergroup level is of course the most complex in the model, and variables from other levels blend into it in ways that complicate the picture. For example, neither perceived threat nor ethnocentrism could exist without an out-group referent. If perceived threat is mutual, does it then become an intergroup variable? Are reciprocal ethnocentric attitudes a group or intergroup phenomenon? Such questions are unanswerable in any absolute sense and simply point to a basic issue in theoretical analysis: that reality cannot be completely separated into discrete categories and that somewhat arbitrary decisions need to be made. Given this qualification that certain variables cut across boundaries between levels, it is possible to describe the categories of interest at the intergroup level.

Antecedent characteristics of the intergroup relationship that require consideration include a history of antagonism, cultural differences, and, most centrally, a real conflict of interests, values, needs, and/or power. It is assumed that any valid model of intergroup conflict must accept the basic tenet of RCT that differences in disputes are real and objective and not simply misperceptions. At the same time, it is also important to acknowledge that conflict involves subjectivity, both in the perception and evaluation of real differences and in the concomitant unrealistic dynamics that affect its development and escalation. Intergroup conflict is seen as rooted in incompatible interests, primarily economic and territorial; incompatible values or ideologies; unmet needs for security, identity, or recognition; or incompatible aspirations for power. These sources of conflict are exacerbated by a history of manifest conflict between the groups and by the extent of cultural differences, in the broadest sense, between the groups.

In the area of predispositions, two variables identified in the seminal work of Deutsch (1973) require inclusion: competitive/cooperative orientation and trust. The general orientation in terms of a competitive/cooperative dimension that each group takes to a conflict is central to the path that the dispute follows. It is important to know both the willingness of each group to compete or cooperate as well as its perception of the other group's competitiveness or cooperativeness. Closely linked to this concept is the variable of trust, defined by Deutsch (1973) as confidence, or the expectation that one will get what is desired rather than feared. Orientations of mutual trust can be seen as significantly affecting intergroup behavior. Both competitive orientation and mistrust tend to be linked to ethnocentrism and thereby play a role in escalating the conflict.

The processes of intergroup conflict will vary depending on the manner in which it is confronted (see Chapter 8). In any case, broad types of variables include intergroup communication and intergroup interaction. In a situation of conflict, it is usually expected that there will be some degree of ineffective communication, some use of contentious tactics, and some amount of unproductive interaction. The specific nature of how these will be expressed will depend on the avenues of interaction that the parties have open to them and choose to engage in. The ultimate outcome of interaction will be further escalation feeding back into the competitive orientation or de-escalation moving toward some form of dispute resolution. With regard to dispute resolution, negotiation by representatives is one of the most common nonviolent means. In this case the negotiation process itself can be examined in various ways (see Chapter 7). Intervention by third parties is also a common form of dispute resolution in intense conflict (see Chapter 9). In the case of statements by group leaders, the accuracy and complexity of communication can be assessed (see Chapter 7). With regard to member interactions, behaviors such as out-group derogation and discrimination can be documented.

Finally, we come to the category of intergroup outcomes. The two major variables are joint payoff and outcome satisfaction. Given the assumption of realistic conflict, there will usually be some means of objectively assessing the benefits or costs that accrue to the groups, both singly and jointly. These tangible rewards will tend to be related to the groups' sense of satisfaction with the settlement or resolution. These variables are expected to be related as well to the nature of future relations between the groups in terms of continuance, nature, and quality. Many of these outcomes are captured by the term *resolution effects*.

Principles or Laws of Interaction

According to Dubin (1969, 1976), the laws of interaction of a theoretical model describe the general relationships among the units or variables of the system under consideration. The somewhat less imposing term *principle* will be used in this model-building exercise to denote the basic relationships on which the model is constructed. Principles are statements of general relationship that are deemed to hold for the entire range of values of the units involved. Principles are distinguished from propositions in a number of respects (Dubin, 1969), the most important being that propositions are deduced from the model, including its principles, and set forth the value of one unit that is associated with a corresponding value of another unit. Thus, the principle states what the relationship is, while the proposition indicates what the predicted values will be. Both may refer to the same units or variables. This distinction will be further elaborated in the presentation of propositions below.

The principles deserving of inclusion in an eclectic model already exist in previously developed theories of intergroup conflict, particularly in the classic contributions discussed in Chapter 2. The challenge is to integrate these sources into a cohesive and concise whole. This will require restating and combining principles from different sources and developing new principles to fill gaps in the theoretical logic of the system. Given the complexity of the empirical world being modeled and the detail of some existing theories, particularly realistic group conflict theory, this process will need to be selective as opposed to comprehensive. Thus, the principles that are included are regarded as primary, or basic, as opposed to secondary, or supplementary, and the resulting eclectic model is seen as core, or essential, rather than comprehensive, or all-inclusive. The first task in theory building is to capture the essence of intergroup conflict; a future task will involve the elaboration and extension of the basic system.

The principles will be organized roughly in order of level of analysis. However, rather than going from the individual to the intergroup level, the reverse order will be followed in order to give emphasis to the more central principles, that is, those concerned with the causation and escalation of intergroup conflict. It should be noted that the principles cannot be categorized in a completely congruent manner because some of them involve variables from two different levels of analysis. In most cases, a principle will be categorized on the basis of the variable that is a cause of

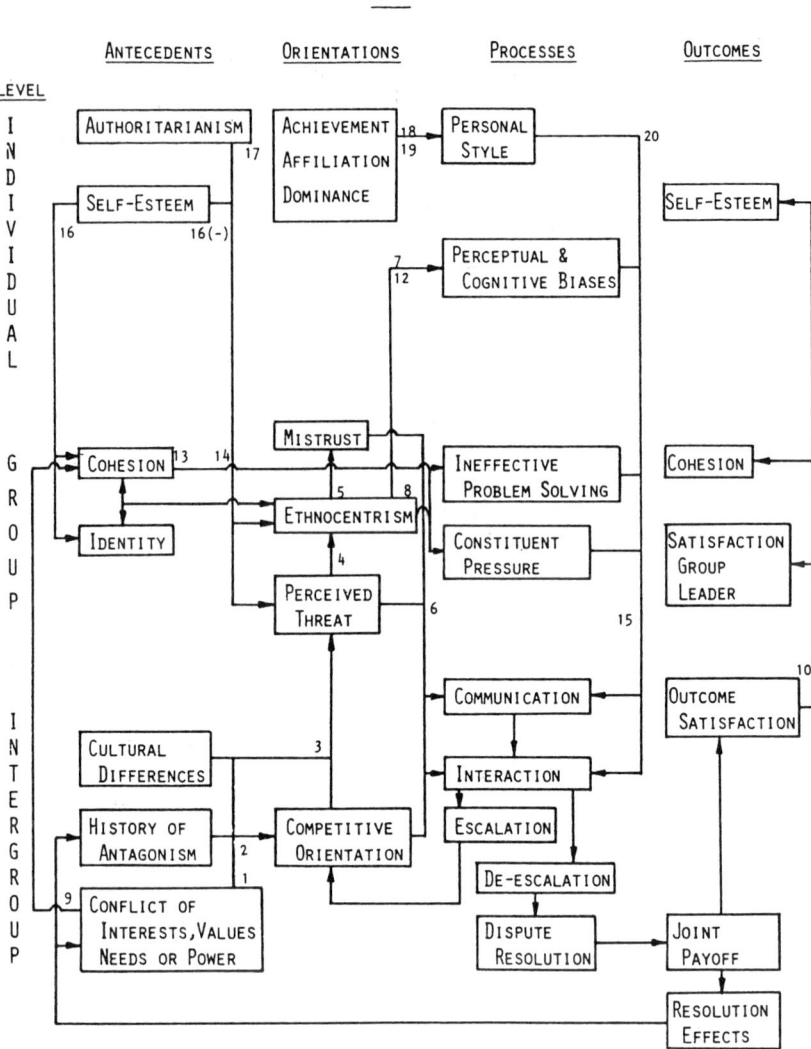

Figure 5-2. The eclectic model of intergroup conflict.

or an antecedent to the other variable involved. Although this overlap among levels complicates the conceptual task of theory building, the construction of principles that link variables from different levels of analysis is seen as one of the greatest strengths of the eclectic model. Figure 5-2 presents an overview of the eclectic model organized by level of analysis and temporal category. Note that the variables of perceived threat, ethnocentrism, and mistrust are shown at the group level, but

Principles or Laws of Interaction

through mutuality they come to be included in principles at the intergroup level. The connecting lines and arrows between variables represent the principles of the model, that is, the relationships among variables. The approximate location of the principles is shown by the numbers on the figure.

Principles at the Intergroup Level

The main emphasis at the intergroup level is on the causation and escalation of conflict. The primary sources of principles are: (a) RCT, which draws on the work of Campbell, Levine, Sherif, Coser, Boulding, and others, and (b) the contributions of Deutsch, which draw on Sherif, Blake and Mouton, and games research.

1. *Real conflict of interests, values, needs, or power causes intergroup conflict.* This principle is firmly rooted in RCT and the objective approach to understanding intergroup conflict. However, the objective stance is immediately complemented by the more subjective sources of incompatible values and unmet needs. Value conflict, in addition to economic (resource or territorial) conflict, is regarded as a basic source of intergroup antagonism following the line of argument presented by Katz (1965). The second subjective element of unmet needs comes from the more contemporary work of Burton and Azar (Azar & Burton, 1986; Burton, 1979, 1985a). These scholar/practitioners maintain that all social groups have fundamental needs for recognition, identity, security, and valued relationships, which, when denied or frustrated by other groups, result in an inexorable push for redress and satisfaction. This dynamic is seen as explaining the large number of communal and international conflicts in the world today that are protracted and apparently irresolvable (see Chapter 7). Finally, the need for power, based on the maximization dynamic of social systems (D. Katz, 1965; D. Katz & Kahn, 1978), adds a further source to the etiology of intergroup conflict. Thus, conflict is seen as having multiple sources, which may act solely or in combination. All of these sources involve basic incompatibilities, which can be summed up under Deutsch's (1973) concept of *contrient interdependence* – a condition of goal interdependence wherein the goals of two parties are negatively linked in such a way that the amount or probability of goal attainment by one party is negatively correlated with the amount or probability of the other party's goal attainment. Thus, incompatibility of goals, broadly defined, is seen as the fundamental source of conflict in the eclectic model.

2. *Real conflict causes a mutually competitive orientation and reciprocal competitive interaction.* This principle links the source of conflict to the approach that the parties then take within the intergroup relationship. Based largely on the work of Deutsch, this principle stresses the central role of competitiveness as opposed to cooperativeness in the escalation of intergroup conflict. Note that the more complex orientation of collaborativeness (a combination of assertiveness and cooperativeness) as proposed by Blake and Mouton (1964) and Thomas (1976) is also precluded by the competitive orientation. This principle also assumes Deutsch's crude law of social relations in saying that competition breeds competition in a reciprocal and mutually increasing fashion.

3. *Real conflict, cultural differences, a history of antagonism, and competitive orientation cause perceived threat.* The role of threat in the development and escalation of intergroup conflict is stressed in a number of the primary principles of RCT. The emphasis is on real threat, but because false threat is also seen as a possibility, the proper derivative is perceived threat, which then covers all situations. The use of perceived threat is also congruent with the phenomenological, social-psychological base of the eclectic model. This principle also acknowledges the importance of existing intergroup characteristics in the form of cultural differences and a history of antagonism. Although real conflict is the primary cause of disputes, the existence of historical and cultural antecedents is seen as playing an important role in escalating the conflict through the inducement of perceived threat. By identifying threat as a critical variable, this principle opens the way for threat to be acknowledged as the key in inducing the ethnocentric reaction above and beyond simple intergroup differentiation (Holmes & Grant, 1979).

4. *Perceived threat causes ethnocentrism, including in-group solidarity and out-group hostility.* Based on real conflict and perceived threat, ethnocentrism assumes a pivotal role in the eclectic model of intergroup conflict. It is seen as the primary orientation, assessed jointly at the group level, which largely determines the course and intensity of the conflict. It assumes cognitive differentiation of the in-group and out-group, and is typified by in-group loyalty and glorification and out-group derogation and discrimination. This principle is an extension of RCT, but by including competitive interaction as a source of perceived threat and thereby out-group hostility, the work of Sherif and Deutsch is also acknowledged.

5. *Ethnocentrism reduces trust and thus contributes to conflict escalation.* This principle highlights the important role of mistrust or suspicion in the etiology of intergroup conflict. A number of theorists, primarily Deutsch, have identified trust and mistrust as crucial elements in intergroup relations and intergroup conflict. The prominence of mistrust is also supported by the comments of practitioners, especially in international relations and related communal antagonisms. Again, ethnocentrism is seen as the pivotal construct in causing the mutual and reciprocal intergroup orientation of mistrust.

6. *Competitive orientation, perceived threat, ethnocentrism, and mistrust escalate conflict through ineffective communication, inadequate coordination, contentious tactics, and reduced productivity.* This principle links the major orientations of the parties to the actual behavior of intergroup conflict, and in that way is the most dynamic primary statement of the model. It is also the most complex in that four major orientations are seen as directly and indirectly causative in the escalation of conflict. Competitive orientation is seen as acting directly in influencing behavior, but also indirectly through perceived threat and thereby ethnocentrism. Similarly, perceived threat directly affects escalatory behavior, but also works indirectly through increased ethnocentrism. Ethnocentrism fuels escalation directly but also indirectly through increased mistrust. The direct flow of competitive orientation to ineffective and escalatory behaviors is drawn directly from Deutsch's theorizing, whereas the inclusion of contentious tactics is reflective of the more recent work of Pruitt and Rubin (1986).

7. *Ethnocentrism increases perceptual and cognitive biases, which escalate conflict.* The perceptual distortions and selectivities that feed destructive intergroup conflict are documented in Chapters 3 and 7. This principle serves as the primary link between the orientation of ethnocentrism and the individual-level processes of perceptual and cognitive biases, which in turn feed back into the intergroup level through their effect on intergroup behavior (i.e., communication and interaction). The effect of these biases can be particularly escalatory and destructive when the individuals in question are representatives as opposed to simply members of their groups. Although not articulated as a primary principle, it is expected that these biases will also affect the problem-solving competence of the group (e.g., Allison, 1971).

8. *Ethnocentrism decreases problem-solving competence and increases constituent pressure, which escalates conflict.* This principle links the intergroup level to the group level and back again. The ethnocentric reaction, through increased solidarity, loyalty, and cohesion, leads to the development and enforcement of more rigid and restrictive group norms regarding approaches to and interaction with the out-group. These processes have been well documented in the work of Sherif and Blake and Mouton, among others, and have been extended through more contemporary research, as discussed in Chapter 4. Ethnocentric biases distort group problem solving away from the open, systematic, and comprehensive process that it needs to be for optimal effectiveness. In intergroup conflict, such processes also bear down specifically through the influence that the constituency of group members direct toward their representatives who engage in direct intergroup interaction. The concept of constituent pressure captures this phenomenon. The effect of constituent pressure is to further inhibit productive communication and coordination and to support the use of contentious behaviors directed toward the other group's representatives. These forms of interaction feed the escalatory spiral at the intergroup level.

9. *Intergroup conflict initially increases group cohesion and affects the social organization of the group in competitive directions.* While not shown in Figure 5-2, this principle further links the intergroup interaction to group processes. The functional effect of conflict on group cohesiveness is stressed in the work of Coser (1956), identified in RCT, and supported by later research (Dion, 1979). The possible effects on organization, particularly status and the qualities of chosen leaders, are directly reflective of the studies of Sherif and Blake and Mouton. The ultimate effect on cohesion and other characteristics, such as satisfaction with leadership, will depend on the outcome of the conflict in relation to the goals of the group. As demonstrated by Sherif as well as Blake and Mouton, winning results in increased cohesion and satisfaction, whereas losing leads to group disintegration and dissatisfaction. These considerations lead to the final principle at the intergroup level.

10. *Outcome satisfaction in intergroup conflict is positively related to group cohesion, satisfaction with group and leader, and self-esteem of group members.* The positive effects of outcome satisfaction on group variables has received more attention and support than the connection to individual self-esteem. However, the prediction of increased self-esteem following positive outcomes follows clearly from the

tenets of social identity theory and the observations of Sherif, and Blake and Mouton. A positive social identity, which is supportive of self-esteem, is based on favorable comparisons with other groups. Thus, membership in a group that is satisfied with its performance and outcomes in intergroup conflict should contribute to increased self-esteem of the individuals involved.

Principles at the Group Level

Group variables are seen primarily as contributing to intergroup processes. Principles containing group variables are scattered throughout the conflict literature, with Sherif being perhaps the main source and group solidarity being the primary concept of interest. Thus, principles at this level often relate one side of ethnocentrism (the in-group side) to other variables. Group solidarity means not only the sense of "we-ness" or identity that the group provides its members, but also the elements of in-group loyalty and glorification that characterize ethnocentrism. Two other variables figure prominently in group-level principles: the antecedent variable of cohesion and the process variable of problem-solving competence. The order of principles will move from those emphasizing antecedent variables to orientations and then to processes.

11. *Group identity and group cohesion are positively and reciprocally related to ethnocentrism.* This principle indicates that the degree of group identity and the level of group cohesion that are in existence before intergroup awareness or interaction will have a subsequent effect on the development of ethnocentric attitudes. The basis for this is partly found in social identity theory in that the need for positive intergroup comparisons to support a positive social identity leads to intergroup discrimination. Once the intergroup conflict is fueled by other variables (primarily competitive orientation and perceived threat) influence flows in the other direction. Increased ethnocentrism heightens in-group identity and cohesion. This part of the principle comes from the ideas of Coser, the work of Sherif, and subsequent research on the relationship between cohesion and intergroup conflict (e.g., Dion, 1979).

12. *Increased in-group solidarity results in overestimation of in-group achievements and underestimation of out-group achievements.* This principle flows directly from the theorizing and results of Sherif, and Blake and Mouton, and is supported by further research (e.g., Hinkle & Schopler, 1979). It states that the in-group side of ethnocentrism leads to perceptual biases in favor of the in-group in judging products and outcomes that the group is responsible for. With regard to the underestimation of out-group achievements, more recent research is equivocal (M.B. Brewer, 1979), and this part of the principle requires further investigation.

13. *Group cohesion is positively related to constituent pressure on representatives during intergroup conflict.* Cohesion in the small group literature generally refers to the degree of attraction that members have toward the group and the degree to which they are motivated to remain in the group. Cohesion is generally seen as increasing normative pressures in the group—members are more receptive to influence and conformity to group norms is greater (see Chapter 4). Thus, in intergroup conflict,

Principles or Laws of Interaction 103

it is expected that more cohesive groups will successfully exert greater pressure on leaders and representatives to adhere to the wishes of the group when interacting with out-group representatives. The pressure for conformity will tend to be in the escalative direction in line with the competitive and ethnocentric orientations of the group.

14. *Increased cohesion fosters concurrence seeking, which leads to ineffective problem solving.* The work of Janis (1982) has demonstrated through retrospective analysis the relationship between heightened cohesion and poor decision making. The reduced quality of the problem-solving process occurs through a number of concurrence-seeking behaviors that are captured by the term *groupthink*. Critical judgment and the expression of alternative opinions and minority positions are stifled by direct and subtle conformity pressures, thus creating an illusion of unanimity. Contrary evidence to a developing decision is rationalized or denied and the leader is protected from criticism. The group's problem-solving capacity to adequately develop and evaluate a range of alternative solutions is therefore attenuated.

15. *Inadequate problem solving and competitive constituent pressure result in ineffective intergroup interaction.* It follows from Principle 14 that reduced in-group competence will negatively affect intergroup communication, interaction, and dispute resolution. The processes of groupthink lead to restricted and escalatory alternatives being fed into the intergroup interaction. The biased and competitive nature of the alternatives developed feeds directly into the use of contentious tactics, which are bolstered by competitive constituent pressure on representatives. Thus, poor in-group functioning heightens escalation in intergroup conflict.

Principles at the Individual Level

Principles involving individual variables will take the form of relationships in which individual antecedents, orientations, or processes affect group or intergroup variables. Again, the development of principles is highly selective, attempting to give priority to relationships that are seen as primary rather than secondary in the development and escalation of intergroup conflict. In the interests of parsimony, principles will link one individual-level variable with more than one group-level or intergroup-level variable. When propositions are drawn from these principles, it will be appropriate to restrict them to two variables at a time.

16. *Self-esteem is positively related to group identity and cohesion, and negatively related to perceived threat and ethnocentrism.* This principle partly comes from social identity theory which holds that group membership relates to social identity and self-esteem. The link between self-esteem and group cohesion is based on the rationale, with some supporting research, that attraction to oneself is related to one's attraction to a social unit of which one is a member. The first part of this principle by itself may be of little consequence for intergroup relations. However, as increased group identity and cohesion subsequently affect intergroup orientations, such as ethnocentrism, the contribution of self-esteem may be worthy of recognition. The second part of this principle does not dispute that real threat, as drawn from RCT, is the primary basis of perceived threat, as used in the eclectic model. However,

perceived threat is likely to be affected by many other variables in ways that increase or decrease its level in relation to real threat. Self-esteem is one individual antecedent that has been postulated to affect perceived threat and increased ethnocentrism. A person with low self-esteem is seen as vulnerable and likely to overestimate the level of threat from another group, whereas the individual with high self-esteem will possess greater confidence in perceiving and meeting the threat realistically. Again, the effect of self-esteem on ethnocentrism is seen as flowing indirectly, this time through the group-level orientation of perceived threat.

17. *Authoritarianism is positively related to perceived threat and to ethnocentrism.* Authoritarianism, according to the original authors (Adorno et al., 1950), is a complex antecedent variable consisting of a number of components, including submission to authority, destructiveness and cynicism, and superstition and stereotypy, and is based on a variety of psychodynamic processes and structures. Later theorizing and research have also cast authoritarianism as a multiple concept (e.g., Altemeyer 1981). Thus, it may relate to a range of group and intergroup orientations and processes. However, its use in the eclectic model is restricted to two primary relationships. First, authoritarianism is seen as increasing perceived threat through the operation of projection, which casts undesirable and threatening characteristics upon the outgroup and through the existence of a weak ego that clings to the in-group and is threatened by others. Similar and related processes link authoritarianism to ethnocentrism, thus fueling both in-group solidarity and out-group derogation.

18. *Need for dominance is positively related to a competitive, controlling personal style.* This first principle on personal motivation, classed as an individual orientation, links the need for dominance or power to individual processes as expressed by personal style. The latter concept is seen as important in two areas: the style or approach one takes to managing conflict and the leadership style one prefers in a group setting. In the former area, it is postulated that individuals with a high need for power will tend to approach conflict with a competitive, win–lose orientation. This assertion is supported by some research at the interpersonal level (e.g., Haythorn & Altman, 1967). In the second area, the need for power is linked to a directive or autocratic leadership style that could also negatively affect intergroup interaction through decreased problem-solving competence. The development of appropriate propositions and hypotheses is necessary to articulate and test these relationships.

19. *Need for achievement is positively related to a participative and collaborative personal style.* In contrast to a high need for power, the need for achievement demands that the individual work well with others in order to accomplish group and intergroup goals. Thus, with regard to group functioning, achievement motivation should foster a democratic and cooperative approach, thus improving problem-solving competence. At the intergroup level, need for achievement is expected to engender a collaborative stance which will partly be expressed through effective communication and productive dispute resolution. Bell and Blakeney (1977), for example, found that a confrontive, or problem-solving, approach to intergroup conflict was related to the need for achievement as assessed by a standardized measure of personality.

20. *A controlling and competitive personal style contributes to inadequate problem-solving competence and to ineffective communication, contentious tactics, and counterproductive intergroup dispute resolution.* This principle suggests connections among a number of variables not so much on the basis of previous research, which is limited, as on logical connections between similar behaviors at different levels. The main theme is that a competitive and antagonistic approach to human relations will be expressed consistently at the interpersonal, group, and intergroup levels, usually with negative effects. Pruitt and Rubin (1986) present an analysis based on a variety of research that is generally supportive of the negative effects (i.e., the counterproductive nature) of a competitive, contending strategy of attempting to handle conflict. As with other complex principles, this one would need to be broken down into a series of propositions for empirical testing.

Boundaries of the Model

In theory building, boundaries specify the limits within which the theoretical model is purported to hold (Dubin, 1976). Boundaries are generally invariate but may be different for different system states, thus becoming part of the defining characteristics of various states. Boundaries may be established logically or empirically, and on the basis of internal or external criteria (Dubin, 1969). In initial model building, as is the case here, most boundaries relate to internal criteria; that is, they are established by the characteristics of the units and the limits of the principles. Furthermore, most boundaries are created logically; that is, given the units and principles of the model, certain things must be true and others must be false. As a model is tested, empirical criteria for establishing or modifying boundaries may enter; that is, measured values of units should be within the specified limits of probability and principles should hold in the stated directions. External criteria come in when the model cannot account for obtained results and a new variable or law must be introduced, thus creating new boundaries. Finally, some boundaries are established by logically setting the space over which the model is seen as holding. In total, boundaries determine the *domain* of the model, that is, the theoretical territory over which one can make truth statements based on the model.

With regard to the eclectic model of conflict, it is possible to specify a number of different types of boundaries in relation to the major elements of the model to which they apply. Some boundaries are very general, relating to the overall nature of the model and the phenomena to which it is relevant, that is, the theoretical space it occupies. Some boundaries apply to the type of individuals, some to the characteristics of the groups, and some to the nature of the intergroup relationship. Finally, other boundaries will help define the model in terms of the basic dimensions and characteristics of intergroup conflict. These various types of boundaries and the differences among them will be elaborated and clarified in this section.

The general area of study in which the model is located is that of intergroup relations. Sherif (1966) has provided a definition of a group and of intergroup relations that has been widely acknowledged in the literature:

> Our claim is the study of relations between groups and intergroup attitudes of their respective members. We therefore must consider both the properties of the groups themselves and the consequences of membership on individuals. Otherwise, whatever we are studying, we are not studying intergroup problems....
> Abstracting the minimum essential properties characterizing actual groups, we attained a definition of groups of any description. The definition bears repeating here: a *group* is a social unit that consists of a number of individuals (1) who, at a given time, stand in status and role relationships with one another, stabilized in some degree, and (2) who possess, explicitly or implicitly, a set of norms or values regulating the behavior of individual members, at least in matters of consequence to the group.
> *Intergroup relations* refer to relations between groups thus defined. Intergroup attitude (such as prejudice) and intergroup behavior (such as discriminatory practice) refer to the attitude revealed and the behavior manifested by members of groups collectively or individually. The distinguishing characteristic of an intergroup attitude or behavior is its relationship to membership in a social unit. This relationship has to made explicit in research on the problems. (p. 62)

The eclectic model is therefore restricted to the attitudes and behaviors of members of groups in relation to members of another group. It is the existence of group membership and the relations between groups that are the limiting parameters or general boundaries within which the model operates. However, the model is not a general theory of intergroup relations but only of intergroup conflict. The model exists within the field of intergroup relations but is not coincident with it, being only a subset of the field. The model applies to instances of intergroup relations in which the basic definition of intergroup conflict is met—that is, a social situation in which perceived incompatibility of goals, interests, values, motives, or needs occur between two groups who hold antagonistic attitudes toward each other and attempt to control each other. Thus, the model does not deal with many other important questions in the field of intergroup relations, such as the initial development of relations or the attitudes and behavior of intergroup cooperation.

The boundaries of the model that relate to individuals are straightforward and few. The individuals engaged in intergroup conflict either as members or representatives of the groups involved are seen as normal and well-adjusted in both the personal and social sense. The model is not designed to deal with abnormal individuals, such as psychopaths or social deviants, who ascribe to no organized collectivity. There are times, of course, that such individuals have involvement and influence in situations of intergroup conflict, but other models are required to deal with these instances. It is assumed that the model has some degree of applicability to individuals from different cultural, political, and economic backgrounds, but the degree of this generalizability is an empirical question for cross-cultural research. As with the work of Sherif, it is expected that the broad processes and outcomes of intergroup conflict have some amount of universality in relation to human social groups and their relationships. The replication of Sherif's (1966) basic findings in a number of different cultural contexts is a laudable approach that merits following with respect to the eclectic model.

The boundaries that relate to groups assume a definition of group as a collectivity of persons who interact with and influence each other, are in status and role relationships with each other, and share a set of values and norms underlying and regulating their behavior. This definition is drawn from a combination of those offered by Shaw (1981) and Sherif (1966). Beyond the definition, one boundary requires that the group have some minimal sense of identity, that members identify with it as a meaningful social category that has relevance to their behavior in relation to other groups. Thus, the group is both a membership group and a reference group to which the individual refers his or her attitudes and behavior for purposes of social comparison. Another boundary requires that the group have developed some minimal degree of cohesion so that members are attracted to the group and have a sense of loyalty to it in contrast to other groups. These characteristics must be complemented by an additional boundary that requires the group to have adequate decision-making and problem-solving capacities so that it can function both internally and in relation to other groups.

Finally, on the mundane matter of size of group, the proposed boundary is actually a wide range. Groups to be covered by the eclectic model may range from a small number of individuals to a large collectivity. It is important to note, however, that even in the case of large collectivities, the intergroup relations are handled by a small number of members, usually in the form of decision-making groups. Thus, the eclectic model is seen as encompassing the essential processes and outcomes of intergroup conflict exhibited by a wide variety of groups, from small laboratory groups of three or four individuals, to departments within organizations, to ethnic groups in communities, and finally to nations in the global context. The units of the model that would enter in with larger and more complex groups would of course be greater in number and sophistication, but with this important qualification the basic principles of the model are seen as holding across the entire gamut of intergroup conflict.

With respect to boundaries relating to the intergroup relationship, the model applies to only two groups at a time. Relationships between any one group and a number of other groups could be considered sequentially, but not simultaneously, within the model. This is a considerable limitation on the model because the behavior of one group toward another is often influenced by the presence or behavior of a third group that has some interest in the relationship in question. Some of this influence may be accounted for indirectly through its effect on variables relating to the groups in question, such as their level of mistrust, but direct influence cannot be studied unless the third group is included in the model. Another boundary is established by seeing the model as only relevant to groups that exist within adequate proximity to each other to be able to engage in significant interaction. Intergroup relationships that involve minimal contact for the groups in question are not of interest. Proximity and interaction are important in that they establish the potential for interdependence, another boundary criterion for the model. Groups that are interdependent have a meaningful stake in the relationship. In addition, interdependence is often synonymous with a mixed-motive (i.e., competitive/cooperative) relationship, which is seen to underlie intergroup conflict. Finally, the model applies to intergroup relationships between groups of approximately equal power. This is a considerable limitation of the model. In terms of classifications of social conflict, such as that offered by Dahrendorf (1961, cited in Angell, 1965), the model does not include superordinate versus subordinate, or whole versus part, conflict. This is a very significant boundary because it leaves out numerous intergroup relationships between majority and minority groups where conflict appears nonexistent or is being suppressed. When the power relation has shifted to the point where the minority group is in a position to meaningfully challenge the majority, then the model is seen as relevant. Thus, the model is applicable to manifest, but not latent, intergroup conflict. In that way, the model is seen as overlapping with the later stages of intergroup relations specified by developmental theories, particularly the five-stage model developed by D.M. Taylor and McKirnan (1984). In sum, with respect to the intergroup level, the domain of the eclectic model encompasses conflict between two relatively equal power groups interacting within an interdependent, mixed-motive relationship.

Finally, certain boundaries of the model can be specified in relation to the basic dimensions of social conflict, as articulated primarily by Stagner (1967). With regard to size, the model is relevant to conflicts of varying size (i.e., the number of people involved, as indicated above) in allowing both very small and very large groups to be included. In terms of duration, the model applies to either very short or very long time frames, but is particularly useful during conflict episodes of intense interaction or periods of escalation. This boundary relates to the intensity of the conflict as well. The model will be rendered applicable to both low intensity and high intensity conflicts by specifying two respective system states as well as propositions that predict change between the states (see the next section). In relation to the dimension of regulation or institutionalization, the model is restricted to conflicts that evidence minimal regulation and that are therefore susceptible to uncontrolled escalation. A breakdown in regulation would also shift the conflict in question into the domain of the model. Stagner (1967) also specifies a realistic–neurotic dimension, and as presaged in the preceding discussion of conflict, the model is regarded as applicable to conflicts that are a mixture of objective and subjective elements. In terms of power discrepancy, the model is bounded by a focus on conflict between groups with a limited discrepancy, in that they are more or less equal. In terms of majority/minority group relations, this means that the minority has gained sufficient power to begin challenging the rule of the majority. Thus, total and absolute power may still be moderately different, but the weaker party has gained enough influence so that the majority must now take its demands seriously. Finally, in relation to the characteristics of the issues (number, complexity, interdependence), as discussed by Deutsch (1973), the model is open to a wide range. Most intergroup conflicts of note do involve a variety of complex issues, and any adequate model needs to take account of this reality. In sum, consideration of the basic dimensions of conflict provides some limitations on the domain of the model, but by and large it remains a middle range theory of considerable scope.

System States of the Model

System states are conditions of the system in which all units take on distinctive values or ranges of values that persist over some period of time (Dubin, 1969, 1976). This means that the model may exhibit a number of conditions or regions within its

System States of the Model

boundaries that are not identical. The transitions from state to state and the recurrence of states within the model can thus provide for a dynamic flow that can account for crucial aspects of social reality. Specifically, this feature of system states allows for the asking of important analytical questions. What are the conditions under which a given system state will persist through time? What are the critical values of variables that when exceeded cause one system state to change to another? How can we predict the patterning in the succession of system states? The final element of system states that deserves attention is the designation of certain units (termed *state coordinates*) that determine the characteristics of the state and provide its distinctive name. These units serve as the primary identifiers of the system state in comparison to other states in the model.

In the eclectic model of intergroup conflict, two system states are posited with two forms of transition between them. The pivotal variable, or state coordinate, is conflict intensity defined both as the psychological investment of the parties in the conflict and the objective difference between winning and losing. The two system states are low intensity conflict and high intensity conflict and the two forms of transition are escalation and de-escalation (See Figure 5-3). The regions occupied by the system states and the transitions fall within the boundaries delineated above and within these are central to the general field of intergroup relations. The following description will attempt to characterize the two system states in terms of variables of the model that have already been specified. The transitions of escalation and de-escalation are best captured by a series of propositions based on sequential laws, some of which are articulated above in principles at the intergroup level. Each system state will be described in terms of primary sources of conflict, individual behavior, group process, intergroup relationship, and the appropriate form of settlement with regard to specific disputes in the conflict. In addition, variables that are regarded as indicators of intensity will be described in terms of their characteristic ranges of value for the system state in question.

The system state of low intensity conflict is identified by the intensity indicators of low to moderate ethnocentrism, low to moderate threat, low mistrust, and a small number of issues. The primary sources of low intensity conflict are to be found in differences of interest (resource or position scarcity) and of values. These differences may be substantial and significant to the parties, but the parties do not see their basic needs for identity or security threatened nor do they perceive and approach the conflict as a power struggle for their very existence. In terms of individual behavior, the representatives of the groups who interact over the conflict exhibit a moderately flexible style and only limited perceptual and cognitive biases toward each other and their respective groups. In low intensity conflict, group functioning addressed to intergroup relations shows moderate cohesion and adequate, relatively undistorted problem-solving competence. Constituent pressure on representatives is moderate, as opposed to severe and highly constraining. The intergroup relationship involves a mixed competitive/cooperative orientation, with each party seeing costs and benefits in the relationship and being willing to give and take. This orientation is paralleled by adequate communication and interaction and satisfactory, although difficult and challenging, dispute resolution. Finally, the settlement

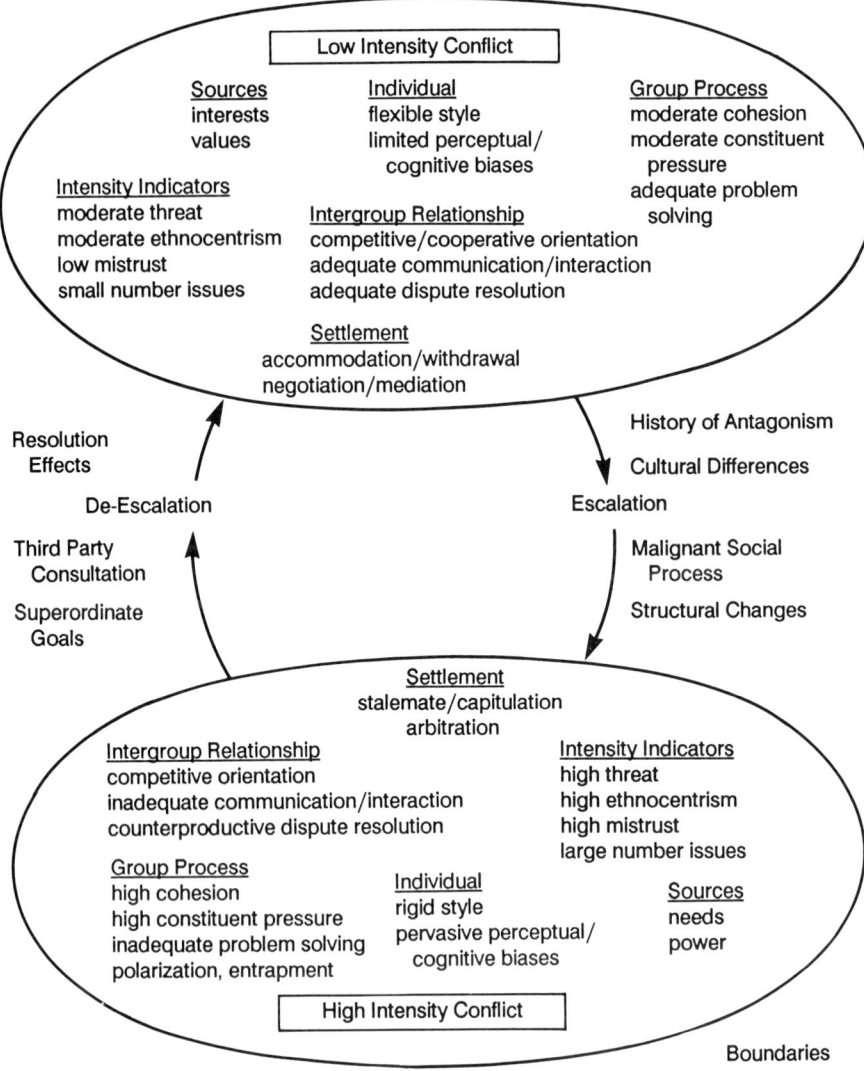

Figure 5-3. System state of the eclectic model.

of specific disputes between the parties is successfully handled by negotiation or mediation acceptable to the parties. Although such outcomes and the general state of low intensity conflict may seem acceptable, it is important to point out that integrative solutions of high mutual benefit are not obtained and that in general the benefits of the intergroup relationship could be significantly improved through a more cooperative and less competitive orientation. The essential and most significant characteristic of low intensity conflict is that it can all too easily be shifted toward high intensity conflict.

System States of the Model

Through the process of escalation, the low intensity system state is transformed to high intensity conflict. The move to escalation is made more likely by the existence of cultural differences and/or a history of antagonism in the relationship. The process of escalation will not be spelled out here, but generally follows that identified in the literature, particularly the malignant social process recently described by Deutsch (1983). The escalation process also draws on elements of the conflict spiral and structural change models as described by Pruitt and Rubin (1986). Propositions drawn from these sources and related principles of the model that deal with escalation will be illustrated later. These propositions will involve strategic predictions that have particular significance for the model, especially its dynamic quality.

The system state of high intensity conflict is indicated by high mutual threat, high ethnocentrism, high mistrust, and a large number of issues. The primary sources are the denial and frustration of basic needs and the struggle for power. To some recognizable degree, both groups perceive that their inexorable needs for identity, recognition, security, and self-determination are being threatened or thwarted by the other. This fundamental threat requires that they mobilize every available form of influence in order to acquire or maintain the satisfaction of the needs that are nonnegotiable. It is therefore understandable that high intensity conflicts are usually protracted and apparently insoluble (Azar & Burton, 1986). Individual processes characteristic of high intensity conflict include a rigid personal style and pervasive perceptual and cognitive biases. Intergroup attitudes become particularly ethnocentric and intransigent. At the group level, there is high cohesion with a detrimental effect on problem-solving competence through processes such as groupthink. In addition, there is high constituent pressure on representatives to the point that their ability to interact effectively with the other party is severely restrained. Positions become polarized and the parties are vulnerable to entrapment in which they become increasingly committed to costly and destructive courses of action (Brockner & Rubin, 1985). The intergroup relationship is based on a mutual orientation in which competition greatly outweighs cooperation. Inadequate communication and interaction are complemented by counterproductive and largely unsuccessful dispute resolution. It is therefore not unexpected that the conflict remains at a stalemate with capitulation and arbitration being the most common forms of settlement.

The process of de-escalation transforms the high intensity, protracted conflict to a low intensity conflict that is capable of management and open to further improvement in terms of the overall intergroup relationship. De-escalation has received inadequate theoretical, empirical, and practical attention in the general field of conflict resolution (Kriesberg, 1982). Therefore, there is little to be said about it and a great need to develop and test propositions that are relevant to successful de-escalation. The process of de-escalation is to some degree the reverse of escalation, but there is a great need to spell out propositions that will aid detailed understanding and serve as a basis for ameliorative interventions. At least three general approaches to de-escalation have been proposed by social scientists. The first is the imposition or mutual discovery of *superordinate goals* as championed by Sherif (1966). The second is *Graduated Reciprocation in Tension-reduction* (GRIT) as articulated by Osgood (1962) and complemented by the proposal of Etzioni (1962) on gradualism (see Chapter 8). The third is the problem-solving approach pioneered by Blake,

Shepard, and Mouton (1964), Burton (1969), Doob (1970), and Kelman (1972), and captured in a general model of *third party consultation* by Fisher (1972) (see Chapters 8 and 9). Each of these approaches is seen as influencing some or most of the variables in the model in ways that move their range of values toward those characteristic of the low intensity system state. The challenge for theory building in this area is to articulate principles and propositions that indicate how the various interventions influence the relevant variables in the direction of de-escalation and ultimate transformation. This would constitute a *theory of understanding* that would underlie and support the further development of *theories of practice* designed to bring about de-escalation.

Propositions of the Model

Propositions are truth statements or the logical consequences of a theoretical model, derived through the process of deduction from laws or principles. Whereas the law states in general terms what the relationship between units is, the proposition states what the predicted values of the units will be. Propositions are therefore predictions about the model in operation. Dubin (1969) distinguishes three types of propositions: (a) propositions about the value of a unit as revealed by the values of other units, (b) predictions about the continuity of a system state, and (c) predictions about the oscillation of system states. Because propositions predicting one value of a unit from one value of another are both trivial and infinite, Dubin recommends forming strategic propositions that predict in one statement the linear relationship between two variables and that give the limiting values for a unit. In the interests of parsimony, only strategic propositions are tested. It should be noted that strategic propositions are expressed in terms very similar to principles.

In terms of the eclectic model, two kinds of propositions would seem to be appropriate. The first are relational, focusing on the positive or negative relationship between the values of two units. The second are sequential in the same sense that Dubin speaks of sequential laws: predicting the relationship between the values of two variables over time. Such a prediction does not imply the inference that the first variable is causally related to the second, although some of the principles and propositions of the eclectic model will posit both a temporal and a causal relationship. Relational propositions can be developed to link variables in ways that will hold for both system states of the model, although the range of values covered will be different for the two system states. Sequential propositions are applicable to the processes of escalation and de-escalation that capture the transitions between the system states.

No attempt will be made at this point to list all or even most of the propositions that can be derived from the principles of the model. However, illustrative propositions of both relational and sequential types will be provided. It should be noted that most of the principles of the model, although logically consistent, are rather complex in that they involve more than two units or variables. The intention was to state the total number of principles with as much parsimony and organization as possible. However, this approach dictates that more than one strategic proposition can be

Propositions of the Model   113

derived from one principle. In the odd case, some of these propositions may seem to be in opposition to each other, that is, they may hold in different situations or may each account for some of the variability in the relationship, the different amounts of which are determined empirically. Thus, empirical testing is the approach by which the strength and applicability of competing propositions or factors is determined, thereby leading to the subsequent refinement of the model.

Relational propositions derived from the model can be separated into two categories, depending upon the manner in which they would need to be tested. The first, and smaller, category includes propositions that would need to be tested over a number of intergroup conflicts because they involve categorical values that either occur or do not occur. For example, Principle 1 states that real conflict of interest, values, needs, or power causes intergroup conflict. Propositions derived from this principle would need to be tested through case analyses of a wide range of intergroup conflicts. Each would need to be examined to determine which sources were present at the onset of the conflict. The results of the analysis would be used to test a number of propositions such as the following:

1. Competing economic interests are positively related to the onset of intergroup conflict.
2. Incompatible values are positively related to the onset of intergroup conflict.
3. Frustration of a basic need for identity is positively related to the onset of intergroup conflict.

Comparative analyses could be used to determine the relative strength of the propositions either in particular kinds of intergroup conflict or in general.

The second type of relational proposition is that which states the relationship between two variables in a continuous fashion. Typically, the relationships will be assumed to be linear and within limits to be established by the selection of empirical indicators and the collection of values on the indicators. A good number of the principles of the eclectic model lend themselves to the derivation of relational propositions, particularly at the individual and group levels. For example:

1. Self-esteem is positively related to group cohesion.
2. Authoritarianism is positively related to perceived threat.
3. Group identity is positively related to ethnocentrism.

These general relational propositions are strategic in that they encompass an infinite number of values of the variables in question, at least in theory. In practice, the values are limited by the use of certain empirical indicators and the ranges they cover. These example propositions are also drawn directly from the related principles, and in that way, the testing of the propositions will reflect directly back on the principles. As the model is elaborated and extended, it is expected that propositions will be developed and tested that are farther removed from the basic principles of the model.

The largest number of propositions derived from the principles of the model would appear to be sequential. That is because *the model gives prominence to the process of escalation*, which involves the transition from the system state of low intensity conflict to that of high intensity conflict.

These propositions are relational but are also temporal and must be tested over time, with the measurement of the second variable occurring at an appropriate lag point after that of the first. These propositions should also be tested over a reasonable number of intergroup conflicts rather than within one conflict. For example:

1. Perceived threat increases ethnocentrism.
2. Ethnocentrism increases constituent pressure on representatives.
3. Intergroup conflict increases group cohesion.
4. Competitive orientation increases ineffective communication.
5. Perceived threat increases contentious tactics.

Propositions that relate to the process of de-escalation are also sequential in nature and relate to the system state transition from high to low intensity conflict. However, the sources on which the eclectic model is based are close to being silent on the question of conflict resolution. One exception is a principle of Realistic Group Conflict Theory, based on the work of Sherif, which states that intergroup conflict and mutual ethnocentric hostility can only be removed by superordinate common goals or shared threats. The challenge for the eclectic model is to develop propositions of de-escalation based on the principles of development and escalation in reverse. The point has been well articulated by Osgood (1962) and others that the de-escalation of conflict requires a process of reversing all of the sequences and relations that escalated the conflict in the first place. The point has also been well made that the intervention of an impartial third-party catalyst is often required to initiate and sustain the process of de-escalation (e.g., Deutsch, 1973; Fisher, 1972) (see Chapter 9). In addition, the general field of intergroup relations has brought forward propositions for the general improvement of relations, such as the facilitative conditions of intergroup contact (e.g., Amir, 1976; Cook, 1970), which hold promise for the more specific process of intergroup conflict resolution (see Chapter 8). Therefore, there exists to some degree a knowledge base from which to develop propositions that extend the eclectic model in order to deal with system change from high to low intensity conflict. Most of these propositions would again be sequential, involving both relational and temporal considerations. For example:

1. Equal status contact facilitates intergroup cooperation.
2. Cooperative intergroup interaction reduces competitive orientation.
3. Attainment of common goals reduces ethnocentrism.
4. Reduced ethnocentrism decreases perceived threat.

It is important to note that the eclectic model and the propositions that could be developed to describe de-escalation do not assume that intergroup conflict can be eliminated, either in general or in the vast majority of specific instances. In line with the basic tenets of RCT, real differences are seen to underlie intergroup conflict. Thus, the objective of de-escalation is to bring about the system state transition to low intensity conflict wherein the substantive issues in the conflict can be managed effectively through acceptable mechanisms of dispute resolution such as negotiation. Where resolution as such can occur is in the changed relationship between the parties such that disputes are handled in an adequately cooperative and respectful manner and within which the parties' basic needs for identity and security are not threatened. The challenge is to develop and test valid propositions of de-escalation that can be used as the basis for ameliorative procedures and interventions. In short, what is required is a science and practice of conflict resolution. The development of the eclectic model is seen as a step in this direction.

Conclusion

The model of intergroup conflict is seen as both eclectic and essential: eclectic in that it is drawn from a variety of sources; essential in that it attempts to capture the essence of intergroup conflict. It is also a model of both the process and structure of intergroup conflict (cf., Thomas, 1976). It focuses on the dynamics of conflict while at the same time attempting to understand how underlying conditions shape conflict behavior. The eclectic model attempts to provide an integrative framework for both classic and contemporary contributions that have never been connected all at the same time. It does so by adopting a temporal flow and a multiple levels of analysis approach, which it must be noted, is limited in complexity at the "top end." That is, further organizational realities of collectivities and the complexity of the wider social environment are not adequately represented. This is only one of a number of major limitations.

The boundaries specify many of the considerable limitations of the model. It is not coterminous with a more general theory of intergroup relations, nor even a theory of intergroup conflict. Intergroup relations and conflict involving majorities and minorities are not handled by the model until a point of some power parity is reached. The wider contexts of communal relations, political realities, and external influence are not encompassed in the model. The processes of de-escalation, regulation, or institutionalization are underrepresented or ignored. Much of the ongoing, everyday interaction among interdependent groups is outside the scope of the model. Thus, the model is seen as only partly informing the wider field of intergroup relations and the broader reality of intergroup conflict.

Nonetheless, through its eclectic and essential nature, the model provides both a useful summarization and a stimulating juncture for further theoretical and empirical work. The variables and principles are seen as representing the core of intergroup conflict in a manner that is open to empirical assessment. The characteristics of the model require that this assessment involve longitudinal, multilevel research, thus proposing a new and more powerful reality for the social-psychological study of intergroup conflict.

Chapter 6

The Intergroup Conflict Simulation

Peter R. Grant, Ronald J. Fisher, Donald G. Hall, and Loraleigh Keashly

An eclectic model of intergroup conflict presents a multilevel, interactive, process-orientated, longitudinal picture of the development, escalation, and resolution of intergroup conflict. As such, the model is congruent with a general call in social psychology for the development of middle range theories that integrate variables from different levels of analysis (Fisher, 1982). In McGuire's (1973, 1979) terms, there is a need for "miniature systems theories" specifying the relationships among a variety of theoretically important variables. Particularly in the field of intergroup conflict, there is a clear need for integrating existing independent theories into a comprehensive systems theory having both descriptive and predictive power (Thomas, 1976; Sherif & Sherif, 1979). However, once such a need is identified, a related deficiency immediately becomes apparent: the social sciences and social psychology in particular have failed to develop the required research methodologies to test and refine such models!

In social psychology, the field experiments of Sherif and the management training workshops of Blake and Mouton (see Chapter 2) come the closest to a methodology that could test a middle level systems theory of intergroup conflict. Unfortunately, these studies only suggest that relationships exist among certain variables, and do not provide an empirical test of a model derived from theory. The lack of complete methodological control inherent in the case study approach used by these researchers makes it difficult to ascertain the causal relationships among variables and to rule out competing explanations for observed effects. Thus, the high external validity of the field experiments is offset by limited internal validity. In contrast, much contemporary research on conflict in social psychology errs in the opposite direction. High internal validity is gained by utilizing simple paradigms, such as the Prisoner's Dilemma game, the minimal group paradigm or interpersonal bargaining situations, and by varying only one or two independent variables in any one experiment. Much of this research has been criticized because it does not incorporate essential dynamics at the group and intergroup levels. Many such studies examine only interpersonal interaction and yet extrapolate to the intergroup level – a strategy that leaves much to be desired (Stephenson, 1981). Finally, it is difficult if not impossible to piece together the results of hundreds of separate studies into an integrated, coherent theory of conflict (Pruitt & Kimmel, 1977).

Thus, both the requirements of theory development and the deficiencies of past research drive one toward a methodology wherein intergroup conflict can be studied in a holistic and longitudinal fashion. This methodology must allow for the systematic and controlled development and observation of real intergroup conflict, in which a range of important variables are allowed to co-vary. If these variables are repeatedly assessed, their relationships can be studied as the conflict develops, providing insight into the escalation of conflict as a dynamic process. Potentially, such a procedure can have adequate internal validity and external validity.

These considerations led the authors of this chapter toward the development of a simulation in order to study the processes and outcomes of intergroup conflict (Fisher & Grant, 1985; Hall, 1986; Hall, Fisher & Grant, 1986). After consulting several sources, we defined a simulation as *an operating analog carried out under controlled conditions to represent the essential processes and outcomes of a set of phenomena selected on the basis of theory*. In particular, a *strategic simulation*, was developed in which conflict is created by imposing a situation of scarce resources over which the parties attempt to negotiate their differences. Klimoski (1978) distinguishes this type of simulation from an enactment simulation in which individuals from groups with existing differences work toward agreement, and from a role play simulation in which participants enact roles created to ensure group differences. In a situation involving intergroup conflict, an enactment simulation can involve intense value differences that are methodologically and ethically difficult to deal with in a controlled situation, whereas a role play simulation can create expectations and behaviors that are exaggerated and artificial, thus compromising external validity. A strategic simulation based on real differences, and allowing for unrealistic aspects to operate as well, would appear to yield an optimal balance of internal and external validity. This paradigm provides for face-to-face interaction within and between groups in a realistic and flexible fashion, but within manageable limits of time, numbers, space, and cost.

Beyond this basic rationale, there are a number of requirements that a strategic simulation needs to meet in order to have adequate internal and external validity. It must allow for the natural co-varying of selected variables over time with repeated measurement, so that causal relationships can be examined without the experimental manipulation of independent variables. To mirror the full reality of intergroup conflict, the simulation must meaningfully create new groups, which are then assisted to develop identity, cohesion, competence, loyalty, trust, norms, and role differentiation. The groups must work to create a valued product over which they have a sense of ownership. The products of the two groups need to be mutually exclusive, thus creating a real conflict of interest through a combination of economic and value differences which can be further exacerbated through power tactics involving the use of tangible threat. The groups should perceive themselves to be in a real conflict and should experience a moderate to high degree of perceived threat from each other. In line with common strategies of conflict management in the real world, the groups should have the opportunity to engage in negotiations involving group representatives who have been chosen by and are under constituent pressure from their respective groups. Negotiations should allow for a range of cooperative and competitive behaviors and should occur within the constraints of typical rules and reasonable time limits. The negotiations should allow for a continuing escalation of the conflict through contentious tactics and the threatened withholding of valued resources. The goal structure of the conflict should permit a range of distributive or integrative outcomes expressed through deadlock, capitulation, compromise, or creative resolution. Finally, it is essential that the outcome be quantifiable with a high degree of precision.

With these considerations in mind, Hall (1986), in consultation with the other authors, developed the initial design and materials for a comprehensive simulation, herein referred to as the *Intergroup Conflict Simulation* (ICS). The overall design of the ICS involves moving two groups simultaneously through the stages of group development, intergroup competition, the emergence of conflict, and intergroup negotiation leading to resolution of the conflict. As part of the group development phase, the two groups separately develop their positions on the utilization of valued resources. The resources exist within a land development task for which the groups design separate development plans to support a future community. The groups are then placed in conflict by the necessity of having to share the land and the resources. Negotiation by representatives is provided as the process by which decisions are made that satisfy the needs of both groups and resolve the conflict. The simulation ends with debriefing and analysis of the experience by the researchers and the participants. The design of the ICS allows for the measurement and tracking of variables from three levels of analysis: individual, group, and intergroup. All sessions of the simulation are videotaped, thus creating a complete archival record of group and intergroup behavior to complement the self-report measures completed by the participants.

Following development and pilot work, the initial design of the ICS was run eight times. Analysis of key indicators signaled the need for certain modifications, both in the simulation design and in some of the measurement procedures. With these changes in place, the ICS was run a further 16 times and the results were used to assess the final design. In addition, a third party intervention component was added to the negotiation sessions in order to assess the comparative effectiveness of mediation versus third party consultation. This chapter will describe the development and refinement of the initial design and the testing of the final design. The results relevant to third-party intervention are reported in Chapter 9.

Development of the Initial ICS Design

A combination of theoretical and practical considerations led to the actual design of the initial simulation. Simply put, it was necessary to create a set of constraints and activities that would meet the objective of producing intergroup conflict within reasonable boundaries of time and resources. The outcome was a 10-hour simulation consisting of five 2-hour sessions held over approximately a 2-week period. The participants were male undergraduates and were randomly assigned, taking their class time schedules into account, to one of two 5-person groups. An overview of the sessions will be provided before describing the instructions, materials, and activities of the simulation.

Overview of the ICS

The overview of the initial ICS design is presented in Table 6-1. In Session I, the two groups meet simultaneously in different rooms and without knowledge of each other. The session involves briefing the participants on the nature and demands of the simulation and the administration of a questionnaire package measuring individual characteristics. The participants sign a consent form and the researcher emphasizes the importance of being able to attend all sessions. Session II is devoted to activities designed to accelerate group development. Members of each group are separately led through a series of structured exercises drawn from the field of human relations training by a researcher. Thus, it is necessary that the researchers who

Table 6-1. Intergroup Conflict Simulation: Initial Design Overview

Session I	Potential participants telephoned (prior to session).
	Recruited participants meet in two groups ($n = 5$).
	Orientation and briefing.
	Informed consent.
	Individual-level measures (60 min).
Session II	Group development activities (70 min).
	Who am I?
	Experiences in groups.
	Ideal group norms.
	Land development, Part 1 (30 min).
	Group-level measures (10 min).
Session III	Land development, Parts 2, 3, and 4 (60 min).
	Increasingly threatening information about out-group.
	Information about ensuing negotiation.
	Selection of "Chief Negotiator" and "Group Leader."
	Strategy planning.
	Group- and intergroup-level measures (15 min).
Session IV	Continued strategy planning.
	Preparation of opening statement.
	Introduction of land use proposal task.
	Negotiation intervals 1–3 (75 min).
	Group- and intergroup-level measures (15 min).
Session V	Continued strategy planning.
	Negotiation intervals 4–6 (75 min).
	Group, intergroup and postconflict measures (15 min).
	Debriefing.

Development of the Initial ICS Design

lead the groups be selected in part on the basis of their expertise in human relations training. The structured experiences are designed to enhance familiarity, trust, cohesion, loyalty, and the development of group norms. In the latter part of Session II, the groups receive the first of several parts of the main decision-making task concerning the development and division of land tracts. This session, as with all subsequent sessions in the initial design, ends with the administration of questionnaires measuring group and intergroup variables. In Session III, work on the land development task continues, culminating in a final product for each group, that is, the group members' proposal for the division of the land tracts between themselves and the other group. Information upon which the two groups act independently leads them to choose different and opposed land divisions. Throughout Session III, participants receive information about the existence of the other group. Late in the session, participants are informed of the conflict between the groups in that only one final decision on how the land is to be divided will be accepted. Thus, the two groups are placed in a conflict of interest over scarce resources. The groups are instructed that this conflict will be resolved through negotiation with the other group. In Sessions IV and V, negotiations between chosen representatives takes place in a separate room. This interaction is controlled by procedural rules and time boundaries. Groups are given payoff matrices, which indicate the points they will receive for various possible divisions of the land tracts. Between negotiation sessions, representatives are given the opportunity to caucus with their groups. At the conclusion of negotiations, total points are awarded according to the final agreement. If a decision cannot be reached, arbitration is imposed by the researchers. Session IV concludes with debriefing the participants. In addition, participants complete a final set of individual and group measures.

The Simulation Procedure

Participants were recruited from introductory psychology courses to take part in a "group dynamics" research project. Depending upon availability, five to six subjects were assigned to each of two groups, which met simultaneously. Due to attrition, final group n's ranged from 3 to 6 with a mode of 4. Rooms used for the two groups were counterbalanced over runs of the simulation. Identical procedures were followed for both groups with the only differences being in the information reports for the land development task, the instructions regarding which half of the land tracts the group was to receive the development rights to, and the payoff matrices, which represented the value each group placed on each land tract. These differences are explained below. After a briefing of the simulation requirements in Session I, subjects indicated their availability to attend subsequent sessions and completed a consent form. The individual-level questionnaire items were then completed with no formal interaction among group members.

Session II was devoted to the development of familiarity and group cohesion and identity. Researchers served as facilitators of the discussion in order to obtain balanced participation and to ensure that each group exercise took no more than the time it was allotted. Following the script provided to the researchers, the

Table 6-2. Group Development Activities

Exercise	Description	Duration of exercise
"Who am I?"	Members shared where they were from, their current interests, and the reasons for their participation in the project.	10 min
Experiences in groups, Part 1	Individually, members reflected upon a negative and a positive experience they had in a group. These experiences were then shared with the other members.	20 min
Experiences in groups, Part 2	Members verbally completed and discussed the following sentence stems: When I first enter a group I feel . . . , In a group, one of my strengths is . . . , In a group, I usually try to have people think I am . . . , To me, trust in a group is a matter of . . . , In this group, I feel	15 min
Building effective groups	Individually, members generated a list of characteristics of an effective problem-solving team and the ideals for how their present group should operate. Members each shared their lists and common themes were recorded on newsprint by the researcher. Brief discussion was encouraged throughout. Group members reread this list at the beginning of Session II.	20 min

participants engaged in a number of exercises designed to accelerate group development (see Table 6-2).

The "Who am I?" exercise involved the sharing of information among group members in order to increase their familiarity with each other. The "Experiences in groups" exercise was composed of two parts. In the first, the participants shared both a negative and a positive experience that they had had in a group. In the second part, the members in turn verbally completed incomplete sentence stems that invited them to talk about their orientations toward working in groups. In the "Building effective groups" exercise, the members were asked to generate a list of five characteristics they believed made an effective problem-solving team. Following this, the members discussed the importance of each item and related it to how they would like their group to ideally operate. This produced a list of group norms, or standards for behavior, that the members shared. The ideal group norms were recorded on newsprint and were referred to at the beginning of the next session. Typical characteristics generated included such items as support for each other, freedom for members to state opinions, flexibility, dedication to group goals, cooperation, the importance of organization, equality among the members, and respect for variety of knowledge

Development of the Initial ICS Design   123

and experiences. In general, the norms that were generated reflected many of the characteristics suggested in the group dynamics literature as being important for effective task groups (see, for example, Napier & Gershenfeld, 1985). Throughout these group development exercises, the role of the researcher was to facilitate discussion and to provide rationale and detailed instructions to the participants.

The main decision-making task for the two groups involved a land development project in which information was provided on the renewable and nonrenewable resources on five tracts of land. In the last part of Session II, this task was initiated by giving each group a map and information reports describing 10 different resources and their development potential. The locations of the resources were referenced on the map with symbols. The groups were randomly assigned to receive differing, although not contradictory, information about five of the resources. For one group this information led them in the direction of taking a conservationist, or renewable resource, approach to developing the land, involving such activities as fishing, tourism, farming, and recreation. For the other group, the information was more in line with a nonrenewable resource approach to development, including activities such as mining, smelting, and petroleum extraction. The map with the five tracts indicated is shown in Figure 6-1, with the information reports given in Table 6-3.

Part 1 of the Land Development Task required the groups to reach a group decision about the importance of the resources found on the map before information on the location of the five tracts was provided. Then the groups were asked to rank order the 10 resources and to make a few notes about their rationale. This decision ended Session II.

In Session III, the remaining parts of the land development task were completed. These concerned the location and division of the tracts and their ranking in terms of importance for the group's development plan. Prior to beginning work, the researcher reviewed the norms that the group had produced as guidelines for its functioning. In addition, at this point the groups first learned about the existence of the other group that was working on the land development task. In Part 2 of the Land Development Task, the researcher provided the coordinates for the five tracts that had been set aside for development and the groups marked these on their maps. The groups were then told that they would receive development rights for only one half of each tract and that they were to propose a division for each tract so that their group would receive the "best" half. The groups were told to assume that as the tracts were developed, a community would establish itself and they therefore needed to consider the future needs of the residents. In Part 3, detailed rules were provided for how the tracts would be divided and the groups received differing instructions on which half of the tract they would receive. One group received either the west half or the south half of the tracts, whereas the other received either the east or the north half. These instructions generally resulted in diametrically opposed dividing lines, because the groups tended to go after the same section of each tract, albeit for different reasons. The typical dividing lines are shown in Figure 6-1, wherein the half of the tract that each group received is indicated by the number 1 or 2 adjacent to their respective dividing line. Thus, the value orientation provided to the groups combined with a situation of resource scarcity to produce a set of differences over which

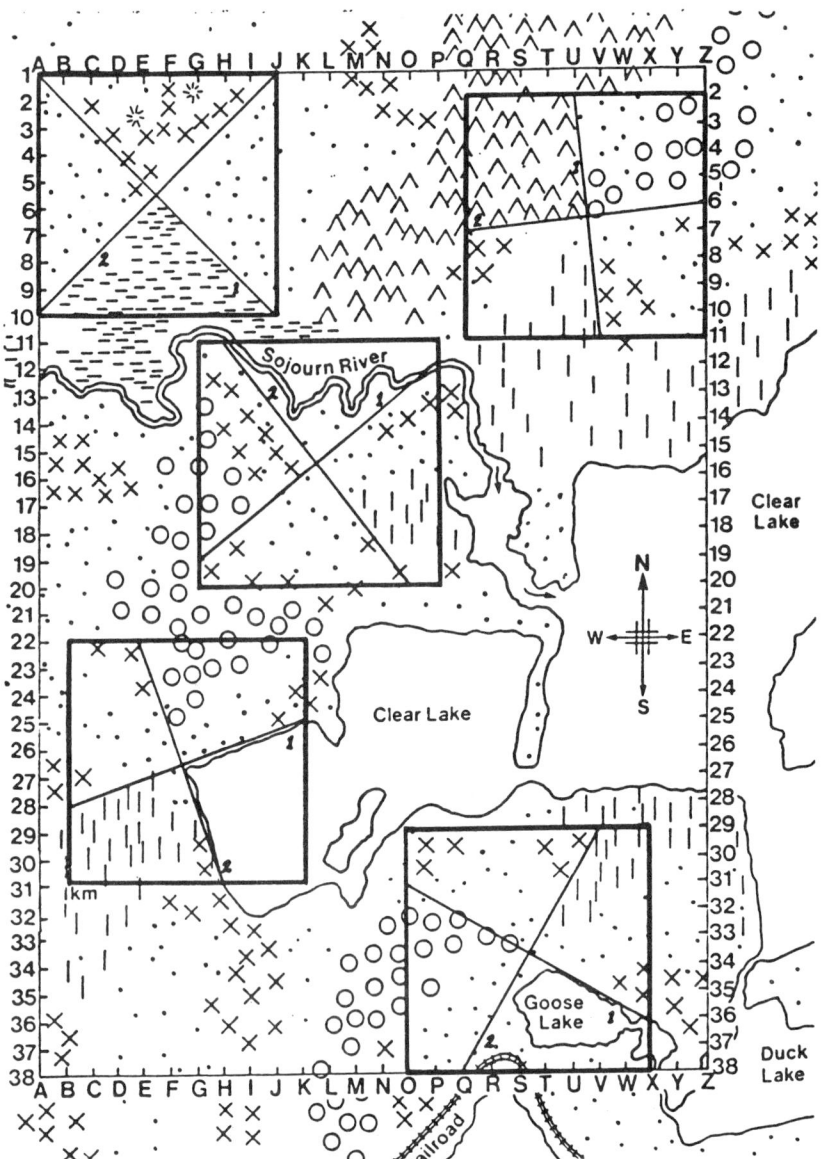

Figure 6-1. Map, tracts and dividing lines for the ICS.

Development of the Initial ICS Design 125

Table 6-3. Information Reports for the Groups

Group 1

Great Hills	The Great Hills are notable because of their beauty and their potential for a hiking-skiing resort center. Surveys show that these hills could be developed to attract tourists from other parts of Canada. In fact, estimates suggest that a tourist industry worth several hundred thousand dollars per year could be developed.
"Rich" Land	Among other things, there is excellent rich farm land in the northwest area of the map. This scenic flatland, with its spectacular sunsets, is a natural agriculture area. Estimates suggest that many families could develop highly profitable vegetable farms, which would provide a continuing supply of fresh produce for the community.
Clear Lake	Clear Lake is one of the best fishing lakes in Canada. In fact, estimates suggest that, with relatively little effort, an approximately 3 to 4 million dollar per year fishery could be established on its shores. Such an industry could employ hundreds. Clear Lake is a deep lake, and is also unpolluted – a fact which contributes to its quality as a fishing lake.
Sojourn River	The Sojourn River, in addition to being one of the most beautiful waterways for hundreds of miles, is an ideal place (in fact the only *feasible* place) for fish hatcheries. Estimates suggest that a series of small hatcheries, spaced at least ½ km apart, could *increase* Clear Lake's fishing industry profits by at least 1 million dollars per year.
Goose Lake	The southeast area of the map is interesting because of its small, waterfowl lake: Goose Lake. This would be a good place for a local campground, where naturalists and nature lovers could enjoy the scenery and the huge variety of waterfowl that roost there every summer.
Great Hills	The Great Hills have been surveyed and have been found to contain abundant iron ore. It has been established that an approximately 5 million dollars per year mining industry could fairly easily be established there. Such an industry could employ hundreds. The Great Hills have ore in virtually their entire area. Although the reserves would eventually be depleted, there is enough ore, if properly mined, to keep a mining operation viable for many decades.
"Rich" Land	Among other things, a small limited lifetime oil deposit has been located in the "rich" land in the northwest area of the map. Even after drilling costs, wells there could produce enough, estimates suggest, to establish a profitable oil industry, which would provide many jobs. It is flat, thus transporting oil from the site would be fairly economical.

Table 6-3. *Continued*

Clear Lake	Clear Lake, with its abundant supply of water, is an excellent location for an iron ore smelter. While the smelter could be set up elsewhere, building the refinery on the shores of Clear Lake, estimates suggest, sould *save* several hundred thousand dollars per year in costs. Furthermore, a longer shoreline (up to about 2 km) would mean larger savings.

Group 2

The Railroad	Just barely within the southern border of the map runs the main east-west freight train line. Estimates suggest that by building a freight yard along the tract, mining profits could be *increased* by about 1 million dollars per year through more efficient transportation of refined iron ore from the Great Hills. Note: Iron ore is too heavy to be reasonably transported by truck. Thus rail is the preferred method. In fact a profitable center for shipping a variety of goods to and from the region is quite feasible. If the yard could not be built directly on the track, some costs could still be saved, depending upon the distance the track is from the main line and the amount of new connecting track needed.
Sojourn River	The Sojourn River is too shallow for any shipping, or industrial use. It is, however, a pleasant and scenic river which could provide a useful recreation outlet.

Groups 1 and 2

Scenic Land	Much of the land shown on the map is scenic, and potentially suitable as park land for recreational use. This land is lightly forested, with occasional, small freshwater ponds. It is grassy, hilly and pleasant, though not very fertile. An abundance of small wildlife exists in these areas.
Forests	Spreading out from the shores of Clear Lake is excellent forest land. Properly managed, this land could be used to generate a small, profitable, family-run forestry business and/or a wildlife sanctuary. It is a pleasant and useful area, marked by its rolling hills.
Grazing Land	In certain areas, there is land which, experts report, would provide for good ranching, and probably support several families.
Gold Deposits	Though not large, and potentially unprofitable for years to come, there are gold deposits in the wasteland of the northwest. These are deep and probably small. Depending on the gold market in the future, these deposits *could* make some entrepreneurs quite wealthy some day.
Waste Land	The parts of the map marked as wasteland are rocky, unfarmable, unusable and unscenic. They may not even be solid enough to build a road on. Government regulations prohibit the dumping of waste on this land.

Development of the Initial ICS Design 127

they now had to negotiate. After dividing the tracts, the participants were told that the other group working on the task was proposing divisions as well and that the other group would receive the opposite half of each land tract. As Part 4 of the Land Development Task, the tracts were rank ordered in terms of the importance to the group's development plan. In Part 5, the groups were told that in the next session they would negotiate an agreement with the other group as to how each of the five tracts would ultimately be divided. The researcher then presented the rules for negotiation and read them to the group (see Table 6-4). The groups were also informed that the other group was proposing divisions quite different from their own. The groups were told (under rule 6) which tract they had the power to disallow any development on. This provided each group with a tangible threat that it could use against the other: the ability to essentially remove a tract from the negotiation table. This tract was always the second most important tract to the other group as determined by the earlier rankings of tracts. Groups then chose a chief negotiator, a group leader, and a group name, thus establishing elements of group structure and identity. Finally, the group was given time to plan a strategy for the first negotiation session.

Prior to Session IV, the researchers used payoff matrices (developed from Erikson, Holmes, Frey, Walker, & Thibaut, 1974) to prepare a value sheet for each group (see Table 6-5). In constructing the value sheet, column 1, containing the highest points, was matched to the land tract that the group valued the most, column 2 was matched to the next most valued tract, and so on. Within the columns, the highest points were matched to the group's proposed division, whereas the lowest points were matched to the other group's proposed division. Points in between were then matched sequentially to all the possible boundary lines in between. This procedure resulted in a value sheet, which indicated the possible divisions for each tract and their corresponding point values. The closer each group got to its original dividing line in the negotiations, the greater the points it received from the payoff matrix as shown on its value sheet.

At the beginning of Session IV, the groups were provided with the value sheet and given time to firm up their negotiating strategy. They were also asked to finalize an opening statement, which the chief negotiator read at the beginning of negotiations. Following this strategy planning, each researcher then led the chief negotiator to a third room for the first negotiation interval. This interval began with a brief explanation of the role of the researchers as referees, and the negotiators were then left on their own to begin the interaction. The researchers only intervened if negotiation rules were violated. Negotiators could end an interval early, in which case they would have more time to caucus with their groups. Following each 15-min negotiation interval, there was a minimum 10-min in-group strategy session during which the negotiators met with their respective groups. In Session IV, there were three 25-min negotiation interval/strategy-session time periods. While negotiations were taking place, the remaining members of the group continued their strategy planning and worked on their land use proposal. To provide motivation, the land use proposals were allotted up to an additional 25 points on top of the values obtained through the negotiations.

Table 6-4. Negotiation Rules

1. Negotiations are to be carried out for 75 min during Session IV and 75 min during Session V. At the end of this time, the negotiations will be considered over.

2. The groups have two tasks for the negotiation. One is to complete the NEGOTIATION ANSWER SHEET. This will be supplied; it is basically identical to the earlier Part 3 Answer Sheet; however, in this case, *both groups must agree* on one and only one dividing line for each tract. This is to be completed and signed by the negotiators and their groups in *duplicate* (i.e., such that each group ends up with a copy signed by all). The second task is to complete, within your own group (i.e., independently of the other group) the LAND USE PROPOSAL.

3. Your group will receive points based on the final agreement between your group and the other group. You should strive to achieve as many points as possible. You will receive a VALUE SHEET at the beginning of Session IV which shows the points you will receive for the various possible dividing lines in each tract. (The Value Sheet will be compiled based in part on your earlier work—particularly your rankings of the importance of the tracts. Essentially, you will get the most points for an agreement which is closest to *your* original proposal.) You will also receive up to *25 additional points* based on the Simulation Coordinator's objective assessment of your LAND USE PROPOSAL. Points will be awarded for "creative land use which enhances community life." Assessments will be made in the areas of (1) work opportunities, (2) leisure opportunities, (3) co-existence with the natural environment, (4) present and projected full use of resources, and (5) realistic attention to the needs and wishes of the other development group. Points will be assessed on the basis of your own group's proposal and will not be affected by the proposal of the other group.

4. If, at the finish of the negotiations, the NEGOTIATION ANSWER SHEET is not *completely* filled out (i.e., a decision for *each* tract), and signed, the Researchers will divide *all five* tracts (including any the groups may have agreed on). This will be done through traditional *Arbitration*. The researchers will examine your group's LAND USE PROPOSAL, and that of the other group. They will also examine your group's initial proposal for the division of each tract (i.e., ANSWER SHEET 3) and your ranking of the tracts (i.e., ANSWER SHEET 4), and those of the other group. The researchers will then decide on divisions for each tract, and divide a *total* of 420 points between the two groups. Each group will receive no more than 220 and no less than 200 points.

5. You were informed earlier that your group is to receive the "west" ("east") half of tracts A, C, and E, and the "south" ("north") half of tracts B and D. This remains true for the boundary lines you negotiate with the other group. The other group receives the "east" ("west") half of tracts A, C, and E and the "north" ("south") half of tracts B and D.

6. For tract ___ only, your group has the power in these negotiations to disallow *any* development of the tract—by the other group or your group. If you choose to exercise this power (and you may do so at any time during the negotiations) indiciate this by crossing tract ___ off the NEGOTIATION ANSWER SHEET before signing it and handing it in to the researchers.

7. Only *one* member from your group will meet with only *one* member of the other group. He will be designated "Chief Negotiator."

8. All discourse between the Chief Negotiators will take place in a *separate* room. Your group will remain in your room in order to plan your strategy.

Development of the Initial ICS Design 129

Table 6-4. *Continued*

9. Your group will also designate a "Leader" who is to *chair* the strategy sessions, *including* those in which the Chief Negotiator is present. (The roles of the Chief Negotiator and Leader will be explained later.)

10. The Negotiation Period in each of Sessions IV and V will last 75 min. This time is to be used by the group members to plan their negotiation strategy. During this time, the Chief Negotiators will meet in a separate room for a total of three intervals of up to 15 min each. After 15 min, or sooner if the Chief Negotiators wish, Chief Negotiators are to return to their own groups to report, and to join the strategy session, for 10 min (or more if the Negotiation Interval ended early). There will be a total of three 25-min intervals, up to 15 min of which may be used to negotiate, the remainder being used for your group to meet as a whole. The Researchers will keep track of the time.

11. All group members, including the Chief Negotiator and Leader, will receive pencils and note paper on which they should make any and all notes pertaining to the negotiations. The Chief Negotiator may take notes, and any other materials he wishes, in with him to the negotiation room.

12. Prior to the first Negotiation Interval, you are to write an Opening Statement, which your Chief Negotiator will read to the other group's Chief Negotiator. You will receive more instructions about the Opening Statement at the beginning of Session IV.

Session V involved the conclusion of negotiations with three more negotiation intervals interspersed with caucus sessions. The session began with a 10-min strategy planning time. The groups were instructed to complete their land use proposal and at the conclusion of negotiations to sign the negotiation answer sheet if the settlement was agreeable to them. This answer sheet had a place to indicate the agreed-upon dividing lines for each tract and required the signatures of the chief negotiators, leaders, and group members. The negotiation answer sheets were exchanged for signing by both groups. As the final questionnaire package was being completed, the researchers calculated the outcome scores based on the final agreement, and added 20 additional points for the land use proposal. The outcome scores were revealed to the groups, which then finished the part of their questionnaire which dealt with reactions to the outcome. A debriefing session then followed in which the researcher talked to the groups about the purpose of the project as a study of intergroup conflict and negotiation. Participant questions were answered and the researcher indicated that a summary of the research would be mailed out to participants individually.

The Measurement Package

The variables selected and the measures utilized were chosen on the basis of both theoretical relevance and past research. As shown in Table 6-6, the measures can be grouped according to level of analysis. At the same time, the majority of the measures were based on individual self-reports of the participants. As with most

Table 6-5. Payoff Matrices for the ICS[a]

Matrix for N.E. group				
1	2	3	4	5
120	90	60	30	30
107	86	56	24	29
93	81	50	17	28
78	77	46	11	28
66	72	38	6	27
54	64	36	2	25
47	55	24	− 1	24
38	47	16	− 5	22
29	38	9	− 7	21
20	30	0	−10	20

Matrix for S.W. group				
1	2	3	4	5
105	80	70	50	25
96	74	64	45	23
86	64	57	41	23
78	56	52	36	21
69	47	46	30	20
57	39	42	22	18
46	34	39	13	17
32	28	35	6	17
19	25	32	− 3	16
5	20	30	−10	15

Column 1 is matched to group's first choice in Land Development, Part 4. Column 2 is matched to group's second choice, etc. Highest points in columns are matched to in-group's respective *proposed* divisions. Lowest points are matched to the out-group's *proposed* divisions. Points in between are matched to the possible boundary lines in between. In cases where there are more than 10 possible divisions: for 11, duplicate bottom number for "correct" groups (according to the design of the map), and top numbers for "incorrect" groups. For 12, duplicate top and bottom numbers for all groups. For 13, add mean of fifth and sixth numbers to middle for all groups. For 14, add mean of fourth and fifth numbers for correct groups, and sixth and seventh numbers for incorrect groups, etc. In cases of less than 10 possible divisions: delete bottom numbers for correct groups, and top number for incorrect groups, until, in the case of incorrect groups only, remaining top number is going to be equal to or less than top number of next lower ranked tract. In such a case, delete from bottom.

[a] Adapted from Erikson et al. (1974, p. 297, Table 2). Copyright 1974 by the American Psychological Association. Reprinted by permission of the publisher.

research on social systems—for example, organizations—theorizing was carried out at a number of levels of analysis even though the level of measurement is typically that of the individual (Katz & Kahn, 1978). At the individual level, a number of variables were assessed in Session I. Conflict management style or mode was assessed using the Thomas–Kilmann Conflict Mode Instrument (Thomas & Kilmann, 1974), which provides scores on the respondent's predisposition to avoid, accommodate, compromise, compete, and collaborate. Leadership style was measured using the scale developed by Fiedler (1967) to assess controlling and participative styles in relation to his contingency model. Individual self-esteem was measured using the

Table 6-6. Measures of Variables Grouped by Level of Analysis

Measure	Session	Item characteristics[a]
Individual level		
Conflict management style	I	30 FC
Leadership style	I	18 BA, 8 pt. RS
Self-esteem 1	I	10, 4 pt. LS
Self-esteem 2	II, III, IV, V	10, 7 pt. RS
Authoritarianism	I	30, 6 pt. LS
Personality characteristics:		
Achievement	I	20 TF
Affiliation	I	20 TF
Autonomy	I	20 TF
Dominance	I	20 TF
Rigidity	I	20 TF
Social recognition	I	20 TF
Group level		
Identity	II, III, IV, V	2, 7 pt. RS
Cohesion	II, III, IV, V	25, 7 pt. LS
Competence	II, III, IV, V	1, 7 pt. LS
Norm development	II, III	List of norms
Trust	II, III, IV, V	1, 7 pt. LS
Atmosphere and satisfaction	II, III, IV, V	14, 7 pt. RS
Constituent pressure	III, IV	4, 7 pt. RS
Sanction of negotiator	III	Behavioral measure
Intergroup level		
Out-group liking	III, IV, V	2, 7 pt. RS
Out-group trust	III, IV, V	2, 7 pt. RS
In-group loyalty	II, III, IV, V	10, 7 pt. LS
Out-group derogation	III, IV, V	10, 7 pt. LS
In-group attitudes	III, IV, V	17, 7 pt. RS
Out-group attitudes	III, IV, V	17, 7 pt. RS
In-group stereotype dimensions	II, III, IV, V	18, 7 pt. SD
Out-group stereotype dimensions	III, IV, V	18, 7 pt. SD
In-group cooperativeness	III, IV, V	2, 7 pt. RS
Out-group cooperativeness	III, IV, V	2, 7 pt. RS
In-group blame	III, IV, V	3, 7 pt. RS
Out-group blame	III, IV, V	3, 7 pt. RS
In-group/out-group similarity	III, IV, V	1, 7 pt. RS
Perceptions of collaboration	IV, V	1, 7 pt. RS
Perceived threat	III, IV, V	1, 7 pt. RS
Anger/frustration	III, IV, V	2, 7 pt. RS
Negotiation progress	IV, V	6, 7 pt. RS
Joint payoff	V	Actual/potential
Satisfaction with outcome	V	1, 7 pt. RS
Commitment to outcome	V	3, 7 pt. RS
Satisfaction working together	V	2, 7 pt. RS

[a] Note: BA = Bipolar Adjectives; LS = Likert Scale; SD = Semantic Differential Scale; FC = Forced Choice; RS = Rating Scale; TF = True, False.

scale developed by Rosenberg (1965). The measure of authoritarianism was a modified and modernized version of the original F scale (Adorno et al., 1950) developed and refined by Altemeyer (1981). Finally, a number of typical personality characteristics were assessed using scales developed by Jackson (1970) as part of the *Jackson Personality Inventory*. These included scales for the measurement of the needs for achievement, affiliation, autonomy, dominance, rigidity, and social recognition. Although it would be desirable to include a number of other measures of individual-level characteristics, the necessity to keep the measurement package at a reasonable length precluded the inclusion of additional measures.

At the group level, a number of variables relating to group development and functioning were assessed at the end of the in-group phase, during the intergroup phase, and at the end of the simulation, that is, in Sessions II, III, IV, and V. Measures of group development included a 4-item cohesion scale (Grant, 1980), as well as a lengthier measure of group cohesion based on items from Pfeiffer and Jones (1974). In order to assess group identity, a 2-item scale developed by McCann (1985) was used. This is a measure of the extent to which group members associate with the goals and values of their group. Trust in the group was measured by a single rating scale. Norm development was not measured directly but can be assessed through the videotapes of Sessions II and III. Finally, atmosphere and satisfaction with the group as a whole, as well as satisfaction with particular meetings, was assessed using a collection of single-item ratings scales (Brilhart, 1982). Constituent pressure as perceived by the group members and as received by the negotiator were both assessed using 4-item scales. The latter was a measure of the extent to which the negotiators felt that they would represent the wishes of their group and would follow the group's negotiation strategy. In addition, a behavioral measure of sanction of negotiator was available, in that groups were given an opportunity to remove their negotiator and replace him with another group member.

At the intergroup level, a variety of measures of various perceptions and attitudes toward the other group and the relationship were obtained. Degree of liking and trust for the out-group and the other chief negotiator were measured by single, 7-point rating scales. Attitudes toward both the in-group and the out-group in terms of a general evaluation was measured using 17 semantic differential scales (Grant, 1986, 1987; Peabody, 1967). By subtracting the in-group score from the out-group score, an evaluative bias in favor of the in-group or the out-group can be observed. In addition, a descriptive measure of the out-group was observed by following the procedure developed by Peabody, which used three sets of six semantic differential scales that measure the same descriptive content but are counterbalanced in terms of evaluation. This approach gives a measure of in-group and out-group stereotypes. More specific attitudinal dimensions were assessed by using a measure of in-group loyalty and glorification and a measure of out-group hostility and derogation developed by Fisher (1968). A number of other measures of the intergroup relationship were developed using rating scales (Grant, 1980; Hall, 1986). In-group blame and out-group blame were each measured using three rating scales, whereas similarity between the groups was assessed by a single rating scale. An assessment of the perceived competitiveness–cooperativeness of one's own group and of the other group was measured by four 7-point rating scales. The difference between ratings for one's own group versus the other group produced a measure of the similarity between the groups on this dimension. The perception of the degree of collaboration between the groups in the negotiations was directly assessed with a single rating scale. Finally, two items assessed the degree of satisfaction with the manner in which the two groups worked together.

With regard to outcomes of the negotiations, the primary measure of joint payoff was determined using the payoff matrices. The use of the matrices made it possible to calculate the points achieved by each group in the negotiated outcome. Outcome scores were converted to a proportion that indicated the degree to which the groups approached the total number of possible points that could be achieved through a completely collaborative or integrative settlement. The subjective assessment of the outcome was measured in a number of different ways. Satisfaction with outcome, commitment to the outcome, involvement in determining the outcome, and responsibility for the outcome were measured by separate rating scales after the groups were informed of their point totals. A behavioral measure of outcome satisfaction was also provided in that the groups could request an appeal of the settlement.

In addition to the measures completed by the participants, the simulation was videotaped, thus making it possible to apply various coding schemes both to group interaction and to the negotiations. Process analysis schemes relevant to negotiator behavior have been used in both the initial and later runs of the simulation. These schemes are described in Hall (1986) and Keashly (1988).

The Testing and Refining of the Initial ICS Design

The initial design of the simulation was run 8 times, comprising 16 groups and a total of 69 participants. For measures of group development and conflict intensity, individual scores were averaged across group members to create group-level scores. Quantitative analyses were performed on the questionnaire responses, whereas qualitative impressions were formed from the information gathered from the experimental materials and the researchers' records. Experimental materials included answer sheets from the various exercises and tasks, as well as written notes on negotiation strategies, land use proposals, and so on.

Group development was assessed using measures of cohesion, identity, atmosphere, loyalty, and attitude. Cohesion was measured using a combined scale from items provided by Pfeiffer and Jones (1974) and items used by Grant (1980) in laboratory experiments on intergroup conflict. Item analysis based on individual data from this first series of runs ($N = 69$) of the simulation indicated that 22 of these items formed a reliable scale at each of the three measurement points, with alpha coefficients ranging from .94 to .96.

Group identity was measured by the two items included in the overall measurement package described earlier. Item analysis indicated that this scale has sufficient reliability, with an alpha coefficient of .64 to .77. Group atmosphere was assessed using 14 items taken from Brilhart (1982), which cover a number of areas related to

Table 6-7. Mean Scores on Group Development Measures (First Series)

Dependent variables	Measurement time[a]				p
	After group development	Prior to negotiations	After first negotiation	End of simulation	
Cohesion	5.60	5.68	5.68	5.74	ns
Identity	5.24	5.48	5.45	5.50	ns
Atmosphere	5.73ab	5.64a	5.62a	5.84b	.01
Loyalty	3.28a	3.97b	3.83b	3.81b	.001
Attitude	5.50	5.43	5.35	5.50	ns

[a] Note: Scores on these scales range from 1 to 7, with a high number indicating a high degree of group cohesion, identity, loyalty, atmosphere, and a positive attitude toward the group. Significance levels refer to the results of one way, repeated measures analyses of variance. Means with different subscripts are significantly different ($p < .05$, Neuman-Keuls). ($N = 16$.)

group discussion such as freedom to speak, level of trust, frequency of misunderstandings, and satisfaction with the discussion. Item analysis indicated that these items formed a highly reliable scale at the three measurement points, with alpha coefficients ranging from .87 to .91. Loyalty toward the in-group, which is an important indicator of ethnocentrism, was measured using items developed by Fisher (1968). A 9-item scale was developed that showed acceptable internal consistency, with alpha coefficients ranging from .65 to .77. Finally, the participants' overall attitudes toward their own group was measured using a 17-item semantic differential scale. In the first series of runs, this scale evidenced alpha coefficients of .85 to .91.

Table 6-7 presents the mean scores on the group development measures at the four assessment points. Repeated measures analysis of variance indicated the group cohesion, identity, and attitude toward the in-group, which were strong and positive at all measurement points, did not change over the course of the simulation. Group atmosphere did change during the simulation and was most positive just after the group development exercises and at the end of the simulation: $F(3,39) = 5.15, p < .01$. As might be expected, the groups seemed to experience the most strain just before and during the negotiations. In contrast, facing the strain of negotiations after the group development exercises significantly increased in-group loyalty; $F(3,39) = 15.83, p < .001$. In absolute terms, the scores on these measures are moderate to high, indicating that acceptable levels of group development were in evidence following the group development activities.

The observations of the researchers also indicated group development took place during Session II. Typically, a group would transform from five strangers into a familiar and cohesive unit ready to take on the approaching task. Generally, then, these results suggest that acceptable levels of group development were obtained as a result of the activities in Session II, and that these levels were maintained throughout the simulation. However, the results did indicate a need for earlier measurements interspersed among the group development activities in order to track this development process more directly.

Table 6-8. Mean Scores on Perceived Threat Measures (First Series)

Dependent variables	Measurement time[a]				p
	After group development	Prior to negotiations	After first negotiation	End of simulation	
Perceived threat	n/a	3.38	3.44	3.16	ns
Anger/frustration	1.89a	2.09ab	2.30b	2.19ab	.05

[a] Note: Scores on these scales range from 1 to 7, with higher numbers indicating greater perceived threat and anger/frustration ($N = 16$).

Turning to other aspects of group development, an agreed-upon normative style was brought about through the exercise on building effective groups, which, as indicated above, generally resulted in a list of positive group norms. In addition, the validity of the role differentiation procedures was quantitatively examined by correlating the assigned role of negotiator or nonnegotiator with certain individual characteristics that were expected. Being chosen as negotiator was found to correlate positively with competition scores from the Thomas Killman Conflict Mode instrument ($r = .31, p < .01, n = 69$), and negatively with accommodation and compromise ($r = -.31, p < .01, r = -.27, p < .05, n = 69$). These results indicate that groups are generally choosing chief negotiators who have a more competitive style. This finding is congruent with previous comments on the characteristics of group members selected as negotiators (Blake & Mouton, 1961; Thomas, 1976).

The intensity of the conflict generated by the simulation was partly assessed by examining levels of perceived out-group threat and feelings of anger and frustration over the sessions (see Table 6-8). The results showed that perceived threat remained stable through the simulation. The grand mean indicated a mild degree of threat, which was not as high as desired or anticipated (3.32 on a 7-point scale, where 1 was labeled *not at all threatened* and 7 *very threatened*). In contrast, although feelings of anger and frustration were low, they did increase significantly over the course of the simulation, reaching a maximum halfway through the negotiations at the end of session 4: $F(3,39) = 3.37, p < .05$. Again, however, these feelings were very mild and lower than desired.

On the qualitative side, the strategy planning worksheets were examined for indicators of feelings of threat due to the other group or for plans of threatening actions. Typically, these sheets contained instructions to the negotiators in the form of brief comments on each tract. At some points, instructions about actual negotiating tactics were given and these provided some information on the extent to which the groups felt threatened. These comments included such phrases as "pressure them on tract B," "bluff," "veto Goose Lake," and so on. Researchers also observed participants to make threatening comments about the other group and the other negotiator on some occasions. Example comments include seeing the other negotiator as "intimidating," "blowing the other negotiator away," and "'nuking' the other group." However, in negotiations, these types of comments did not tend to be made directly

Table 6-9. Means, Standard Deviations, and Ranges of Group and Joint Outcome Scores

Score[a]	M	SD	Range
Group outcome ($N = 16$)	0.96	0.09	0.84–1.18
Joint outcome ($N = 8$)	0.97	0.06	0.84–1.06

[a] Note: Outcome score is actual score received, divided by potential score.

to the other negotiator. In summary, it appears that most of the participants had a sense of being in a team competition with the other group and engaged in mildly threatening behavior. By and large, they did not feel that the other group threatened their own group to any great degree and they only felt mildly angry and frustrated.

In terms of outcomes, seven of the eight groups reached a settlement in the initial runs of the simulation. The group and joint outcome scores were examined in terms of means, standard deviations, and ranges in order to assess their adequacy. Table 6-9 shows these scores expressed in terms of proportion of points from the payoff matrices that the groups obtained in relation to the total obtainable points. Based on previous research using these payoff matrices, the expected range for joint outcomes was approximately .85 to 1.0. Group outcomes were expected to vary more (.75 to 1.20), because some groups would receive more than the points they would get for a "fair" solution at the expense of the points received by the other group. Table 6-9 indicates that the ranges obtained were similar to those expected, with the exception that the low end on the group outcome is somewhat higher than might be expected, and the range is therefore more restricted. Nonetheless, the observations of the researchers indicated that high outcomes were relatively easy to obtain. Again, the simulation appeared to be a competition between the two teams that did not involve much intergroup conflict.

In conclusion, the initial runs of the ICS indicated that the design was working moderately well. The group development aspect of the simulation appeared adequate, as did the overall operation of the design. However, the intensity of the conflict appeared to be relatively low. Thus, a number of changes were recommended for the final design in order to increase the intensity of the conflict.

Testing the Final ICS Design

For the second series of runs, the following modifications were incorporated:

1. Additional payment for participation was tied to outcome points in order to enhance participant investment in the conflict and feelings of out-group threat.
2. Press releases developed by the groups during negotiations were added to facilitate the dissemination of threatening intergroup messages and thus increase perceived threat.
3. In-group cohesion and perceived threat were measured more frequently, and new items were added to more sensitively measure perceived threat.

Testing the Final ICS Design   137

4. Each group was given the power to unilaterally set the dividing line on one tract (the other group's second most valued tract) in order to increase the level of available threat. (Previously, each group could only remove this tract from the negotiating table.)

In addition, the design was changed to incorporate a session in which different third-party interventions were introduced and their effects assessed. This was accomplished by combining the group development activities with the completion of the individual measurement package in the first session.

The design overview of the second series of runs of the simulation is presented in Table 6-10. The major components of the simulation were the same as in the first series of runs. The major procedural changes involved moving the group development activities to Session I and including the third-party interventions in Session IV. Time for the group development activities in Session I was made possible by spreading the completion of the individual-level measurement package over the first three sessions, if required. The sessions were again 2 hours in length and typically scheduled 2 days apart, so that a complete run of the simulation took approximately 2 weeks. Informing the groups about each other's existence now began in Session II within the land development task. The sequencing of events and provision of information remained the same. In addition to a land use proposal, groups now also had the task of developing press releases in the in-group session of each negotiation interval. The introduction of the third party began in Session IV when the researchers first introduced the idea of "activities" that were related to the upcoming negotiations. Following the completion of the third negotiation interval and the group and intergroup measures, the third party was introduced to the group as a skilled intermediary who would help the groups with negotiations. The third-party intervention consisted of either traditional mediation activities or a more innovative third party consultation design. These interventions and their effects are described in Chapter 9. Both interventions were designed to enhance the process and outcomes of the final three negotiation intervals. In the fifth and final session, the main addition to the design was the awarding of bonus money that the groups earned in relation to their point total. A group could earn up to $50.00 for points achieved above the level of a simple compromise. Measurement and debriefing were the same as in the initial ICS design. The final design of the ICS was run 16 times involving 32 groups, with a modal size of 4, for a total of 135 participants.

In order to assess the functioning of the final ICS design, particular attention was directed to measures of group development and conflict intensity taken at three key points during a simulation. These points were immediately following the group development exercises in Session I, just before the negotiation interval in Session III, and just prior to the third-party intervention in Session IV (i.e., following the third negotiation interval).

Group development was assessed using the same measures of cohesion, identity, atmosphere, loyalty, and attitude as in the initial runs. Individual data from this second series of runs ($N = 135$) confirmed the high degree of internal consistency of the cohesion measure with alpha coefficients ranging from .94 to .97. In addition,

Table 6-10. ICS Final Design Overview

Session I	Potential participants phoned (prior to session).
	Recruited participants meet in two groups ($n = 5$).
	Orientation and briefing.
	Informed consent.
	Group development activities.
	Group level measures.
	Individual level measures.
Session II	Land development, Parts 1, 2, 3, and 4.
	Increasingly threatening information re: other group.
	Information about ensuing negotiations.
	Selection of "Chief Negotiator" and "Group Leader."
	Negotiation strategy planning.
	Individual-level measures.[a]
Session III	Continued negotiation strategy planning.
	Preparation of opening statement.
	Introduction of land use proposal task and press releases.
	Group and intergroup measures.
	Negotiation intervals 1 and 2.
	Negotiation planning.
	Individual-level measures.[a]
Session IV	Continued negotiation planning.
	Reference to upcoming third-party session.
	Negotiation interval 3.
	Group and intergroup measures.
	Introduce third party.
	Timing and ability measures.
	Third-party intervention.
	Third-party measures.
	Intergroup measures.
Session V	Intergroup measures.
	Continued negotiation planning.
	Negotiation intervals 4, 5, and 6.
	Group, intergroup and postconflict measures.
	Debriefing.

[a] If not completed in earlier session.

a 5-item short form of the scale was also administered prior to each of the group development exercises in Session I. This was done in order to track the development of group cohesion during the first session. Scale analysis indicated that this briefer measure was highly reliable with alpha coefficients on the first series of runs ranging from .83 to .90, and in the second series from .90 to .92. In addition, the short form correlates very highly with the complete scale ($r = .90$ to .94). Item analysis on the individual data from these runs also confirmed that the other group develop-

Table 6-11. Mean Scores on Group Development Measures (Second Series)

Dependent variables	Measurement time[a]			p
	After group development	Prior to negotiations	After first negotiation	
Cohesion	5.30a	5.54b	5.58b	.001
Identity	4.91a	5.48b	5.32b	.001
Atmosphere	5.48	5.48	5.57	ns
Loyalty	3.32a	4.03b	3.90c	.001
Attitude	5.27	5.27	5.27	ns

[a] Note: Scores on the scales range from 1 to 7, with a high number indicating a high degree of group cohesion, identity, loyalty, atmosphere, and a positive attitude toward the group. Significance levels refer to the results of one way, repeated measures analyses of variance. Means with different subscripts are significantly different ($p < .05$, Neuman-Keuls). ($N = 32$.)

ment scales had acceptable to high reliabilities (Cronbach's alpha equaled .52 to .68 for group identity, .87 to .91 for group atmosphere, .63 to .71 for in-group loyalty, and .87 to .93 for in-group attitudes).

The level of intergroup conflict was partly assessed using a 3-item measure of perceived threat, which was administered in Sessions II through IV. The scale consisted of the direct rating of out-group threat used in the first series of runs and two additional items developed to be more sensitive but less direct measures of perceived threat (concern with active interference of the in-group's plans by the other group, and the likelihood of this interference taking place). This scale of three items showed acceptable internal consistency with alpha coefficients ranging from .62 to .70. Again, the 2-item semantic differential scale developed by Grant (1980) was used to assess the degree to which the subjects felt angry and frustrated during the negotiations (alpha = .79 to .81).

The analysis of the results pertinent to group development indicated that the design of the simulation was even more successful in achieving its purpose in the second series of runs. Table 6-11 presents the mean scores on the group development measures at the three assessment points. Repeated measures analysis of variance using the group as the unit of analysis indicated that in these runs group cohesion and identity increased significantly from after the group development exercises to prior to negotiations and to after the first three negotiation intervals: $F(2,62) = 11.10, p < .001$; $F(2,62) = 10.51, p < .001$; and $F(2,62) = 84.00, p < .001$, respectively. In addition, scores on the short form of the cohesion scale that was administered three times before, during, and after the group development activities provide more direct evidence that these activities are linked to the initial development of cohesion. These results demonstrate that group cohesion increased significantly from prior to the first exercise ($M = 5.07$) to the end of the first session ($M = 5.69$): $F(5,155) = 31.12, p < .001$.

As before, group loyalty increased in the period following the group development exercises but prior to negotiations. However, it declined significantly during the

Table 6-12. Mean Scores on Perceived Threat Measures (Second Series)

Measurement time	Dependent variables[a]	
	Perceived threat	Anger/frustration
End of Session I	n/a	2.02a
First reference to out-group	2.92a	n/a
First reference to dividing tracts	3.73b	n/a
First reference to negotiations	4.58c	n/a
After negotiation rules	5.20d	n/a
Just before negotiations	5.20d	2.35b
After first three negotiation intervals	4.93cd	2.67c

[a] Note: Scores on these scales range from 1 to 7, with a high number indicating a high level of perceived threat or more anger/frustration. Repeated measures analyses of variance on these measures is significant (Perceived Threat: $F(5,155) = 52.61, p < .001$; Anger/Frustration: $F(2,62) = 15.37, p < .001$). Means with different subscripts are significantly different ($p < .05$, Neuman-Keuls). ($N = 32$.)

first half of the negotiations, although it was still significantly higher than after the group development activities. Group atmosphere did not decline prior to or halfway through the negotiations as it did in the first series of runs, but remained unchanged. In addition, in-group attitudes were very positive and also did not change throughout the simulation.

By and large, these results indicate that refinements to the simulation created even greater involvement than before. In particular, it was pleasing to note that group cohesion and group identity continued to strengthen as the groups worked on the land development task, suggesting that it had been made more involving for the simulation participants. As before, the researchers noted that the participants developed group norms in Session I and achieved role differentiation by selecting a leader and a chief negotiator. Thus, overall, the results indicate that the participants became members of well-established groups during the first three sessions of the simulation. The conclusion is that they were, therefore, in a position to address the intergroup conflict as a cohesive group during the negotiations.

With regard to the intensity of intergroup conflict, Table 6-12 presents the means for the indices of out-group threat and the feelings of anger and frustration. The repeated measures analysis of variance performed on the perceived threat measure was highly significant, indicating that threat increased systematically from the first reference to the out-group, through the first reference to negotiations, and finally to just before negotiations: $F(5,155) = 52.61, p < .001$. This level was maintained until after the first three negotiation intervals. In absolute terms, perceived threat moved from moderately low to moderately high during the first three and one-half sessions of the simulation. With regard to feelings of anger and frustration, these increased significantly from the end of the first session to just before negotiations and then again to the point after the first three negotiation intervals: $F(2,62) = 15.37, p < .001$. These results indicate that the subjects are experiencing an increasingly competitive intergroup relationship in which they feel increasingly threatened and become increasingly angry and frustrated with the intergroup relationship as expressed through the negotiations. Additional evidence suggests that the conflict was taken in increasingly serious terms following the first three negotiations intervals. At this point, perceived threat was strongly correlated with more negative out-group attitudes ($r = .52, p < .001$), as compared to just prior to negotiations when this relationship was nonsignificant ($r = .13$, ns). In addition, at the end of the first three negotiation intervals, perceived threat was also significantly related to greater blame, distrust, and dislike of the out-group ($r = .43, p < .01; r = .46, p < .01, r = .39, p < .05$, respectively). Taken together, these results indicate that the intergroup conflict in the simulation was a moderate but not highly escalated one. However, within the realistic and ethical limitations of a laboratory simulation, the degree of intensity is deemed to be adequate for the testing of relationships among variables. In addition, an adequate degree of intensity has been produced so that the potential ameliorative effects of third-party interventions can be assessed.

Conclusion

The analyses presented above, particularly with regard to the final design, indicate that the Intergroup Conflict Simulation has potential merit as a methodology for studying the process and outcomes of conflict between two groups. The adequacy of the simulation can be assessed in terms of group development and the intensity of the conflict. In terms of group development, results from the initial design demonstrated that moderately high levels of cohesion and identity were achieved rapidly and maintained throughout the simulation. The analysis from the second series of runs further indicated that group cohesion, identity, and loyalty increased significantly over the first three sessions of the simulation, and that these moderately high levels of group development were maintained throughout the remainder of the sessions. As an additional indicator of the effectiveness of the group development activities, the brief measure of cohesion used in the second series of runs demonstrated rapid and significant increases throughout the first session. Then, as indicated by the lengthier measure of cohesion, these gains were maintained up to the point of starting negotiations. In contrast to cohesion, identity, and loyalty, the measures of atmosphere and attitude showed moderately high levels immediately after the group development activities and evidenced no further increases. This lack of increase could be due to the initially high levels, that is, a ceiling effect, or it could be that these characteristics develop more rapidly than the qualities of cohesion, identity, and loyalty. In any event, the results from the two series of runs allowed for the conclusion that the group development activities, in conjunction with the teamwork on the land development task, result in groups that are adequately developed to meet the requirements of the simulation design.

With regard to the intensity of the conflict, the important indicators of perceived threat and anger and frustration showed that the intensity of the conflict was too low in the first series of runs. Consequently, modifications were made to the simulation design to increase intensity and to gain a more sensitive measure of perceived threat.

With these modifications in place, the results indicated that perceived threat increased dramatically from the first reference to the out-group, through the land development task, to preparation for negotiations. These moderately high levels of perceived threat were then maintained throughout the negotiations. From the beginning to the end of negotiations, it makes sense that there was no further increase in perceived threat, because the groups were by and large dealing constructively with the conflict through the negotiation process. In the second series of runs, the intensity of the conflict was also shown by the significantly increasing levels of anger and frustration from the first session to before and after the first three negotiation intervals. Thus, while perceived threat was maintained, anger and frustration was increasing up to the midpoint of negotiations. It is likely that this pattern of reactions is typical of intergroup conflicts in the real world that are managed through the negotiation process. Therefore, in terms of both group development and conflict intensity, the ICS appears to evidence adequate external validity.

The design of the simulation has a number of limitations in terms of the types of intergroup conflict to which it is relevant. However, the range of applicability could be increased by changing certain parameters to create a variety of intergroup conflict situations. For example, a more intense conflict of interest could be produced by adjusting the payoff matrices so that the difference between "winning" and "losing" is increased. It is anticipated that such adjustments would be represented by higher levels on relevant indicators, such as perceived threat, and would allow for the study of more extreme escalatory processes in areas such as perceptual distortion, competitive constituent pressure, and contentious tactics in negotiations. Another area for potential modification would be to adjust the power differential between the groups, so that relevance to majority–minority relations would be attained. Many of the most intractable conflicts in the world involve majority–minority relations in which the minority has reached the point of consciousness and power to challenge the majority. This adaptation could easily be achieved through the manipulation of each group's ability to threaten the other. For example, one group could be given the power to unilaterally determine the division on more than one of the land tracts. The effects of this power imbalance on both the process and outcomes of the conflict could then be monitored through the measurement package and the videotaping.

In conclusion, the final design of the Intergroup Conflict Simulation meets the rationale and requirements specified in the introduction, and has the potential for modification in the direction of even greater applicability to many real world conflicts. Thus, the simulation appears to capture the essence of intergroup conflict in a manageable and observable fashion. The final design evidences an uncommon fusion of adequate amounts of internal and external validity, and therefore has potential value as a methodological alternative for the continuing study of intergroup conflict.

Chapter 7

International Conflict: The Question of Survival

The field of international relations has shown an abiding interest in intergroup conflict among states and/or factions, particularly as expressed in the violence of war (e.g, Wright, 1965a). Conflict is a pervasive and permanent, even inherent, feature of world politics, because it may be the inevitable consequence of interactions among groups who live in an anarchy (Matthews, Rubinoff, & Stein, 1984). More specifically, competing demands for scarce resources in a world of inequality and disorder guarantee that conflict will remain at the center of the study of international relations (Fox, 1984). However, how conflict is conceptualized and what methods are recommended to address it have varied considerably over the history of the international relations discipline. Such differences exist to the present day and provide for varying degrees of receptivity to social-psychological concepts and methods.

Banks (1984, 1986) has charted the development of the discipline of international relations and the evolution of theories and paradigms within it. His particular concern is how different developments within the discipline have provided varying contexts for the study of conflict and for the practice of conflict management. The classical heritage of the discipline provided a set of concepts centered on the sovereign state, which used force to maintain discipline internally and force to maintain security externally. The sovereignty of states involved a moral claim to legitimate rights for ownership and control, which were honored between states through reciprocal recognition. Thus, concepts such as national interest, legitimate self-defense, and deterrence became the mainstays of thinking about international relations. However, this conception of a relatively stable and efficient system was disrupted by the massive irrationality of World War I, one effect of which was the growth of the international relations discipline in universities.

Between the world wars, liberalism came to dominate mainstream thinking with an emphasis on self-determination, the rule of law, reconciliation, and disarmament. However, liberalism failed, and in fact never intended, to transform the international system, because liberalism continued to rely on the use of force as the ultimate arbiter. The harsh realities of the failure of the League of Nations and the outbreak of World War II ended the reign of liberalism and heralded a retrenchment to traditional thinking in the form of realism and power politics. The use of force and the threat of aggression in the form of deterrence were seen as acceptable and necessary mechanisms to maintain vital interests and a balance of power, that is, to deal with disputes. Conflict was seen as inevitable—because the world system is essentially an anarchy—but controllable through the direct use of power. Realism became intermixed with superpower ideology, particularly in the United States; liberal, and even moreso radical, thinking was ignored.

In the 1960s and 1970s, the "behavioral revolution" swept through the discipline, emphasizing empiricist methodologies with the purpose of creating an objective science of world politics. This created considerable receptivity to the other social sciences in terms of both concepts and methods. In addition, the behaviorist movement exposed some of the simplicity of realism by proposing that states were not the only actors in the international system and power was not the only motivating force. The behaviorists' concentration on specific questions moved the field toward fragmentation into specialties without general theory, yet at the same time toward an eclectic mainstream.

Concurrently, the discipline began to debate the merits of competing paradigms, most notably, realism, structuralism, and pluralism. Although the realist paradigm has come under attack, many in the discipline are reluctant to embrace structuralism, which has maintained a radical minority position for decades. At the same time, for pluralism to become the mainstream paradigm, a number of significant challenges must be met. Rather than states being seen as the single set of actors in global society, multiple sets—including ethnic communities, business firms, and political parties—would need to be addressed. Attempting to understand the values of all of these groups would require a shift in emphasis from national security to human needs. In addition, conflict should be approached not through the realists' forced suppression or aggression but as a condition that requires diagnosis and resolution. Security can be attained through integration and not threat of force. The pluralist alternative has been appropriately labeled the *world society paradigm*, as conceived and developed in the work of Burton (1965, 1968, 1972) and his colleagues (e.g., Mitchell, 1981a).

One positive effect of the behaviorist revolution and the growth of pluralism is the increased receptivity of the international relations discipline to input from the other social sciences, notably psychology and social psychology. The face of the discipline has been changed, particularly by work on perceptual and cognitive processes, on the dynamics of decision making at both the individual and group levels, and on communication and negotiation. On a broader scale, the discipline is now more accepting of a general behavioral science approach to the study of war and peace. According to Kelman (1985), the central assumptions of this approach are that war and peace (a) are forms of human behavior that can therefore be understood at several levels of analysis using general principles for studying behavior, (b) can be studied scientifically using the array of methodologies that social science provides, and (c) must be viewed from a systems perspective in the context of the global or regional system rather than viewed by focusing on state actors. This approach contrasts quite sharply with much prebehaviorist work, which tended, in the classical or realist mode, to be descriptive, historical, and at times normative. Thus, the behavioral approach has become an accepted way of working in international relations and has fostered the interdisciplinary nature of the enterprise now reinforced by pluralism.

As part of the behavioral approach, contributions from social psychology have had significant influences on the international relations discipline. These effects have come within the interdisciplinary study of international behavior – in which social-psychological concepts and methods have played an integral part, as proposed by Kelman (1965), rather than through the development of an independent social psychology of international relations. The social-psychological approach attempts to explain international behavior by starting at the level of interaction among states and applying concepts that help explain the processes and outcomes of that interaction (Fisher, 1982). Special emphasis is given to how international actors perceive, think, communicate, negotiate, and make policy decisions in concert with other actors and within the constraints of the national and international systems. Recent and continuing areas of research interest include international images, group and intergroup processes in decision making and negotiation, the personality of leaders, public opinion studies, and the development and advocacy of policy implications (Oskamp, 1985).

Kelman (1985) identifies three broad lines of investigation that comprise the behavioral science study of war and peace, each of which has benefited from social-psychological input. First, there is the systematic study of macroprocesses of interaction among nations, as exemplified by the work of Russett (1972) and Singer (1979). This work has benefited from the development of sophisticated quantitative methodologies in social science in general, including social psychology. Second, there is the study of microprocesses of national and international behavior, which has drawn considerably on social-psychological concepts and methods. This line includes research on perception and images (e.g., Jervis, 1976; White, 1984), crisis decision making (e.g., Holsti, 1979; Janis, 1982), attitudes on foreign policy and international relations (e.g., Tetlock & McGuire, 1985), negotiation processes (e.g., Pruitt, 1981), and the analysis of deterrence as a strategy of influence (e.g., Jervis, Lebow, & Stein, 1985). Third, there is the conceptualization and development of alternative approaches to international security, that is nonmilitary methods of conflict management. Included here is work on nonviolent action (see Stephenson, 1982), various forms of unofficial, or "track two," diplomacy (e.g., McDonald & Bendahmane, 1987), and various types of third-party intervention (e.g., Rubin, 1981), including mediation (e.g., Touval & Zartman, 1985) and problem-solving workshops (e.g., Kelman, 1972; Kelman & Cohen, 1976, 1986). Each of these areas has benefited from social-psychological contributions, especially the development of problem-solving workshops, which is intrinsically a social-psychological methodology (see Chapter 8).

Thus, the evolution of the international relations discipline and the acceptance of the behavioral science approach within it provide a supportive context for the continuing input and development of social-psychological concepts and methods. In relation to the eclectic model of intergroup conflict presented in Chapter 5, the leading edges of development are seen primarily in the category of processes, with antecedents receiving some attention. More specifically, profitable foci include (a) perceptual and cognitive biases, as represented in the work on international images, (b) problem-solving competence, as represented by the model of groupthink (discussed in Chapter 4); (c) communication, particularly as it occurs through the articulations of decision makers, and (d) interaction and dispute resolution, as represented in the process of negotiation. In terms of antecedents, the diagnosis of international conflict in terms of basic human needs in an area of growing potential, while the aspect of cultural differences as they affect both conflict escalation and resolution cries out for greater attention. Finally, the process of de-escalation in international conflict is a crucial and yet underdeveloped area of study to which social psychologists could make significant contributions. These considerations provide a rationale for the contents of this chapter, which will be illustrated where appropriate with consistent reference to the central relationship of contemporary international relations: the superpower rivalry between the Soviet Union and the United States.

The Sources of International Conflict

The complexity of intergroup conflict is most fully expressed at the level of international relations, wherein variables from all levels of analysis have relevance to conflict between national groups. In terms of the eclectic model, the most important causative variables are to be found at the group and intergroup levels and in the category of antecedents. In particular, real conflicts of interest in terms of resources, values, needs, and power must be considered as they are expressed within the context of national and international politics. At the group level, the variables of cohesion and identity gain relevance as they are expressed in the phenomenon of nationalism.

In a pioneering contribution of enduring significance, D. Katz (1965) discusses the forms and processes of nationalism, as intertwined with sources of international conflict, and appropriate conflict resolution strategies. In particular, Katz identifies three types of conflict: (a) economic, which is due to competing motives for scarce resources, (b) power, in which each party wishes to maximize its influence, and (c) value, which involves incompatibilities in ideology, religion, or way of life (see Chapter 2). These types are linked to nationalism as it drives interaction among states. Nationalism is defined as the ideology of the nation state, or in other words, an integrated set of values and attitudes that reflects and sustains the major functions of the state: internal integration, maximization of the input–output ratio, and survival against external enemies. Of specific relevance to the causation of international conflict is the maximization dynamic by which the national system pushes toward realizing more of its basic character. This results in expansionistic tendencies which bring the nation state into competition with others for scarce resources, markets, or territory, thus creating economic conflict. However, the maximization dynamic also involves an ideological expression in which the justification of a nationalistic ideology fuels international conflict. Also of relevance is the component of nationalism, which Katz identifies as *statism*, that is, the proposition that the state has supreme authority to protect national sovereignty. This doctrine is a potential source of incompatibility, as states put forward their own value systems as superior, thus creating value conflict. Finally, Katz identifies power conflict as the most general form of international conflict, which makes sense because nation-states are primarily systems for dealing with power relationships. However, power is not only a strategy for economic or ideological maximization, but is also a source of international conflict in its own right. Finally, through the concept of nationalism, Katz links the individual-level variable of self-concept through group identity to the level of the nation-state in an integrated and consistent fashion.

The continuing validity of D. Katz's (1965) typology and analysis is evident in a review of contributions of the behavioral sciences to the study of international conflict by Smith (1979). The reality of economic sources continues to be evident in a global structure in which there is unequal distribution of resources and in which scarcity means competition. Whether competition is translated into conflict depends on a number of factors, not the least of which is the presence of relative deprivation (see D.M. Taylor & Moghaddam, 1987). At its base, the inequitable distribution of resources is immense, and the situation is further exacerbated by tension and intervention between the Eastern and Western blocs. Power conflict in international relations is typically revealed by an examination of the political processes through which conflict is waged (Smith, 1979). In terms of interaction among states, political processes are represented through international diplomacy and negotiation. Although economic and political factors appear to be the major preconditions of international conflict, Smith maintains that the human element cannot be overlooked. Thus social-psychological models linking the individual to the international system are essential in order to explain international conflict. D. Katz's (1965) linking of the different forms of nationalism to appropriate strategies of conflict resolution is an excellent example of the social-psychological approach.

Our understanding of the sources of international conflict has recently been expanded by the analyses of political scientists John Burton (1979) and Edward Azar (1983). Their approach to understanding international conflict is inherently social-psychological, because it links the needs of the individual through the identity group to the existence of international conflict. Azar provides a description of the characteristics of protracted social conflict, that is, ongoing, intense, and seemingly unresolvable conflict. The source of such conflict is not to be found in the traditional areas of economics or power, but rather in the denial of those elements necessary to the development of all people, and whose pursuit is therefore a compelling need. These basic and universal needs include security, distinctive identity, social recognition of identity, and effective participation in determining development requirements. Protracted social conflicts also include the enduring features of economic and technological underdevelopment as well as unintegrated social and political systems. Thus, structural inequality and protracted social conflict are inherently linked through a set of complex relationships (Azar & Farah, 1981). Multiethnic and communal cleavages are combined with underdevelopment and distributive injustice to provide for the irrepressible nature of deep-rooted, protracted conflict. It follows that the most useful unit of analysis in protracted conflict is that of the identity group, whether based on racial, religious, ethnic, cultural, or other grounds. It is through the identity group that the expression of compelling human needs is brought forward. Protracted social conflicts arise when identity groups perceive that they are being victimized through a denial of their identity and an absence of security and political participation. Thus, protracted conflicts are not resolvable by centralized structures that deny or ignore the basic needs of the various identity groups. Decentralized structures are required that will serve the needs of identity groups through local control, while providing for functional relations among communities.

The theoretical and practical work of John Burton is now coming to be based on a conception of universal human needs. While cognizant of Maslow and other classic needs theorists, Burton places particular emphasis on the conceptualizing of sociologist Paul Sites (1973), who maintains that individuals and groups will pursue all means possible to satisfy basic needs, constrained only by an overriding need to maintain valued relationships. In particular, Burton (1979) emphasizes the needs for consistency, security, recognition, and distributive justice. The linking of distributive injustice with underdevelopment, and thereby to class conflict, provides a richer meaning to Galtung's (1969) concept of structural violence (Burton, 1985a). In a search for the universal and fundamental needs that underlie protracted or deep-rooted conflict, Burton has turned to the more contemporary work of needs theorists (see Lederer, 1980). Burton contends that if one can identify a set of human needs that must be satisfied for societies to reach their goals, then heretofore subjective concepts like justice and democracy can be defined in terms of basic needs fulfillment. Furthermore, the existence of universal and inexorable human needs would point to the necessity of a conflict resolution process that would take such needs into account. In short, it would be necessary to substitute the approach of analytical problem solving for elite decision making (Burton, 1988a). This conclusion is based on the assumption that the power of individuals and groups to resist coercion and work toward satisfying basic needs is greater than the power of authorities. Burton maintains that in many contemporary protracted conflicts, the power of identity groups is greater than that of the political authorities. Thus, it should be possible within the context of needs theory to define situations in which force and coercion cannot be effective, even at great cost (Burton, 1988b).

A current difficulty with a needs theory approach, however, is reaching consensus on a common list of basic needs and demonstrating empirically that these in fact explain a considerable amount of human behavior, particularly in situations of intergroup conflict. An additional difficulty is that needs theory generally makes positive assumptions about the basic motives of human behavior, building on the influence of Maslow, who was looking for the positive side of human motivation in contrast to the negative side espoused by the Freudians. It is possible that there exist human needs that in fact fuel intergroup conflict, such as a need for aggression. In addition, some of the basic human needs, which are initially seen as positive, may in fact fuel the escalation of intergroup conflict when their expression is exaggerated. For example, the need for identity, which is included in many lists of basic needs, often gains expression through the social identity of the ethnic group, which at the same time may fuel ethnocentrism. Thus, group identity is combined with a sense of in-group solidarity, the dark side of which is derogation and hostility toward out-groups. It is therefore clear that a great deal more clarification of needs theory in relation to conflict escalation and resolution is required. However, enough reasoned analysis exits to include needs as an antecedent of international conflict along with the more traditionally recognized sources of economics, values, and power. In particular, the needs for security, identity, recognition, and participation would seem to be supported by a great deal of theorizing and research in the social psychology of intergroup relations. The basic need for freedom as identified by Bay (1958) and by Galtung (1980) may be an important addition. It is also essential to keep in mind, as Galtung maintains, that even though the meeting of basic needs is necessary to functioning as a human being in a social context, the problem of needs and their satisfaction is a profoundly political question. In this sense, consideration of basic needs and their priorities will be at the heart of conflict and development in international relations for a long time to come.

The search for a universal set of human needs must not be allowed to take the emphasis away from another very important antecedent identified in the eclectic model, that of cultural differences. When the emphasis is on basic needs that are universal, inexorable, and non-negotiable, it is easy to forget that differences in cultural identities may be one of the primary influences on the development and escalation of international conflict. This is true in part because individual identity and group identity are strongly expressed through the existence of a culture. At the national level, D. Katz (1965) identifies cultural identity as one of three components of nationalistic ideology. Cultural identity is seen as reflecting the unique heritage and way of life of the people that is contrasted with the identity of other cultures. Research in social psychology, including that using the minimal group paradigm to study social identity, indicates that the existence of cultural differences will immediately lead to discrimination in favor of the in-group. In addition, the existence of differences will fuel the perception of threat between groups and thereby heighten ethnocentrism. In combination with the history of antagonism common in protracted conflict, cultural differences will also drive the competitive orientation, thus heightening perceived threat and ethnocentrism. Thus, the aversion for those who are different, which includes a sense of mistrust, is seen as a central element in the development of many international conflicts. Unfortunately, the field is generally deficient in its coverage of the processes fueled by cultural differences. There have, of course, been many useful studies on the effects of cross-national contact, for example, de Sola Pool (1965) and Brislin (1981). However, the majority of this work relates to interaction on a citizen-to-citizen basis in a variety of travel and exchange programs (see Fisher, 1982, Chapter 12, for a summary). However, the more pressing requirement is to gain a sense of how cultural differences affect the perceptions, images, and behavior of decision makers who are directly involved in conflict processes.

Perception, Cognition, and Images

There is considerable body of knowledge in experimental and social psychology that indicates the fallibility of human perception (see Chapter 3 and Fisher, 1982, Chapter 2). In perceiving the world, there is a degree of selectivity and distortion. We create a filtering process to deal with the confusing complexity of the world, and we tend to see what we expect or want to see, and in that way are prone to assimilate incoming information to existing beliefs. Impressions, once formed, are strong determinants of the evaluation of additional information through influences such as the halo effect. We tend to form and maintain attitudes that are functional for us in terms of meeting our various needs. A great deal of perception and cognition appears to be governed by the principle of cognitive consistency, by which we strive to maintain congruence among our beliefs, feelings, and behavior. Given that all these processes are part of human social behavior in general, it is not surprising that their impact on intergroup and international conflict has aroused considerable interest.

Although earlier comments on perceptual processes in international relations exist, a comprehensive and ground-breaking treatment is offered by political scientist Robert Jervis (1976). Although appropriately critical of work in psychology, especially with respect to limitations in external validity, Jervis is nonetheless successful in applying a variety of concepts in a historical and contemporary analysis of real world events. A fundamental finding is that cognitive consistency, although useful in ordering information, becomes irrational when it selects or distorts the acquisition of new information. Thus, decision makers are seen to assimilate incoming information in ways that are consistent with preexisting beliefs and to engage in cognitive distortion in order to reach closure. Irrational consistency is demonstrated by decision makers who favor a particular policy, coming to believe that it is supported by many logically independent reasons. Thus, belief systems often come to display overkill as more and more pieces of information are selected to support a particular position, regardless of their logical interconnections. In the extreme, decision makers gain psychological harmony at the price of neglecting conflicts among their own values. Concurrently, irrational consistency may result in a policy that fails to reach any goals because it tries to reach too many that are logically contradictory. In terms of assimilation, the processes fostering cognitive consistency influence decision makers to fit new information into preexisting beliefs and to perceive in line with their expectations. Individuals often preserve their images by simply ignoring or distorting contradictory information. Categorization is also an important process in that the label placed on an idea will influence how it is seen and determine its later relevance to decision making. The influence of preexisting beliefs is typically compounded because of the decision maker's failure to recognize their impact. Thus, decision makers become overly confident of their views, inappropriately exclude alternatives, and thereby reach premature closure. Jervis concludes that decision makers are typically faced with ambiguous and confusing evidence, and thereby will often draw inferences that are incorrect. In order to minimize misperception, the decision maker should attempt to examine the world through a variety of possible perspectives. In particular, an attempt to see the world the way the adversary sees it would help interpret the other's behavior and construct one's own behavior so that others will draw the desired conclusions. Ideas about corrective action are important because these types of perceptual and cognitive biases not only limit the effectiveness of decision making, but tend to fuel the escalation of conflict.

Following the work of Jervis and others, there has been significant growth in perceptual and cognitive research on foreign policy. Tetlock and McGuire (1985) contend that researchers using different methodologies are arriving at very similar conclusions. Although the theoretical analyses are quite varied, two central assumptions guide this endeavor: very heavy information processing demands are put upon policy makers, who like all human beings have a limited capacity to process information; therefore, they resort to strategies of simplification to handle the complexity, uncertainty, and painful tradeoffs. Thus, the primary research objective is to understand the cognitive strategies that policy makers use to construct and maintain their simplified images. Tetlock and McGuire identity two such strategies: a reliance on cognitive structures that provide frameworks to which new information is assimilated, and a reliance on low effort heuristics, such as satisficing, that allow policy makers to decide with speed and confidence. Regardless of the concepts used to describe belief systems, it appears that decision makers are "cognitive misers" who are unwilling or unable to carry out demanding information processing tasks. A number of social-psychological concepts and principles affect this process. Examples include the fundamental attribution error in which the observer overestimates the importance of internal or personal causes of behavior to the detriment of external causes, and analogical reasoning in which individuals categorize and analyze new problems in terms of familiar ones. Thus, Tetlock and McGuire conclude that a cumulative body of knowledge on cognitive processes in policy making is developing that offers promising avenues for further exploration.

A key concept in the social-psychological analysis of international relations is that of image, that is, the organized representation of a social object in a person's cognitive system (Kelman, 1965). The concept of image is particularly useful because it captures the basic attitudes that different nationalities hold of themselves and others. Although images could be simply equated with stereotypes, it is more useful to regard images as attitudes. This more complex view sees image as composed of cognitive attributes about the object or group, an affective component that involves liking or disliking, and an action or behavioral component that consists of appropriate responses to the object (Scott, 1965). Images are seen as formed and shaped by many forces, including personality characteristics, socialization, international interaction, and by events at large. Once formed, images are powerful determinants of the ways in which international actors perceive the intentions and actions of others, and thereby how they make policy decisions bearing on conflict escalation and resolution.

One useful extension of the concept of image is that of mirror image, a term introduced by Bronfenbrenner (1961) in the context of American–Soviet relations. Through conversations with Soviet citizens in combination with his experience as an American, Bronfenbrenner came to the realization that the Soviets' distorted view of the United States is very similar to the negative that many Americans hold of Russia. In short, both sides saw the other as the aggressors, with a government that exploits and deludes the people, and with a majority of the people not sympathetic to the government. Thus, each side sees the other as not to be trusted and as advancing policies that verge on madness. This reciprocal distortion is especially disturbing because it demonstrates the power of misperception in building and maintaining unrealistic images. Once formed, these images also have a powerful influence on behavior toward the other party in the form of self-fulfilling prophecies.

The concept of image has also played a central role in the social-psychological analyses of major conflicts provided by the work of Ralph White (1966, 1970). White's work focuses on perceptual processes and the distortions of reality that feed escalation. He lists a number of major forms of misperception, three of which relate directly to the images of self and other that are held by the major decision makers. These include the diabolical enemy image, the virile self-image, and the moral self-image. In addition, the major processes of misperception include selective inattention, the absence of empathy, and military overconfidence. White uses these major forms of misperception to analyze the dynamics of World War I, World War II, and the Vietnam War. In addition, he has produced similar analyses of misperception in the Arab–Israeli conflict (White, 1977) and the Cold War between the superpowers (White, 1965). The latter work sees the American–Soviet negative mirror image as being developed and maintained by selective inattention, slanted interpretation, paranoid suspicion, and other forms of perceptual and cognitive distortion.

White's most recent treatment of the superpower conflict, entitled *Fearful Warriors* (1984), is especially deserving of attention. In analyzing the present situation, White once again brings forward the paradox of unwanted war in which all people and all nations in the world favor peace and hate war and yet prepare for war. It is perplexing that fear of the ultimate tragedy, nuclear annihilation, is not a greater motivator toward peace. However, in making the decisions that lead to war, decision makers do not proceed because they want war, but for other psychological reasons. Thus, White attempts to provide a concrete picture of the processes by which individuals who sincerely want peace favor policies and make decisions that lead to war without that desire or intention. As an initial approach to analyzing the superpower conflict, White calls for Americans to develop "realistic empathy" of the Soviets' point of view. The evidence indicates that Soviet decision makers are motivated primarily by a strong underlying sense of insecurity rather than a determination to conquer the world. Thus, when the United States seeks to contain Soviet power, the Soviets fear this as encirclement by their enemies. In addition, much Soviet behavior can be interpreted as basically defensive rather than offensive. Given Russian experience in the past, particularly in World War II, it is easy to see why the protection of the motherland, Rodina, is of the highest priority to the Soviets. The Soviet arms buildup, like the American, appears to be primarily based on the need for defense and security. In fact, the strongest Soviet intention appears to be to avoid another large war. Thus, Soviet intentions and initiatives as feared by Americans are not regarded as realistic or likely. These include an invasion of Western Europe, a nuclear first strike, or an intensification of aggression in the

Third World. More plausible scenarios for the outbreak of war are predicated not on the assumption that the Soviets wish world domination, but on the assumption that they are primarily driven by "defensively motivated aggression," which is much more important than power motivated aggression in the relationship between the superpowers. Although concentrating on psychological factors in the escalation of international conflict, White does not rule out the significance of nonpsychological factors. He identifies national sovereignty, an ambiguous equality of military power that fuels an intense military competition, a strong power surrounded by weaker ones, and a central nation that is not yet accepted as an equal. However, these structural elements simply provide the context in which the major psychological factors operate. These include war-promoting motives, motivated errors of perception, and unmotivated cognitive errors, following the distinction made by Jervis (1976).

In terms of war-promoting motives, *exaggerated fear* and *macho pride* stand out as driving forces toward aggression. This is not to deny that realistic war-preventing fear exists and is the basis for a strategy of reasonable deterrence. White contends that most recent conflicts, including both world wars and the superpower rivalry, involve situations where exaggerated fear leads to defensively motivated aggression. In the superpower rivalry, exaggerated fear has fueled the arms race to the point of an irrational overkill capacity on both sides. Macho pride is seen as a particular form of pride defined as undue satisfaction from, or an undue craving for, an image of one's own group as powerful, prestigious, tough, and courageous. Macho pride and exaggerated fear are not opposites, but often occur together and are mutually reinforcing. In the superpower conflict, macho pride is represented by the United States' determination to remain the number one power in the world, whereas the Soviet Union maintains the belief that history is on its side and that its way of life will eventually dominate. The emotions of anger, hate, and aggression in the psychological sense are also considered to be important in that they tend to distort perceptual and cognitive functioning. However, they are not seen as motivators in the way that exaggerated fear and macho pride are.

The motivated errors of perception are covered in White's earlier work and are applied with considerable insight to the current United States–Soviet conflict. Motives combine with perceptions to produce behavior, and White considers perceptions more important than motives in causing conflict behavior. This is because perceptions are much more varied—for example, among "hawks" and "doves" in the West—than motives, all of which tend to be supportive of peace. Thus, variability in perceptions is more important in determining variability in attitudes and behavior. White identifies five types of motivated misperceptions that are due mainly to the operation of subconscious motives, including anxiety and the need for self-esteem. The *diabolical enemy image* involves a perception of the adversary as a monster-like enemy embodying evil. There is an excitement to conflict, and the more evil and powerful the enemy, then the greater the virility and righteousness of the hero. In the United States–Soviet conflict, Americans see the Soviets as aggressors, whereas the Soviet image of the United States stresses imperialism. The *moral self-image* is fueled by a nearly universal tendency to think well of one's own group in comparison with others. Thus, the people of the Soviet Union perceive themselves as innocent, as do people in the United States, in regard to the superpower rivalry. Furthermore, Americans identify with the positives of democracy and freedom, whereas the Soviet system stresses socialist equality and liberation movements in the developing (and oppressed) world. The *pro-us illusion* involves a tendency to perceive others as more friendly to one's own country than they actually are. Thus, for example, in attempting to maintain the borders of the free world, the United States underestimated the tenacity of the North Vietnamese. In a similar vein, the Soviet Union has been surprised by the resistance in Afghanistan. In both cases, the superpowers maintained that the majority of people were receptive to their interventions. The perceptual error of *military overconfidence* has been a factor in the causation of numerous wars and is relevant to the behavior of the superpowers. Thus, the United States supported the Bay of Pigs invasion and the Soviet Union intervened confidently in Afghanistan. *Overlapping territorial self-images* help to explain why a number of geographic locations in the world have been the source of an incredible amount of conflict. This situation occurs where there is a zone of overlap between one people's territorial image of itself and that of another. The identity of each group is linked to the possession of territory, the ownership of which is in dispute. White maintains that such territory is perceived as part of the "national self" of the people. There is also a strong link with macho pride. In the United States–Soviet conflict, these territorial self-images are not merely national, but involve large groups of nations, that is, the free world and the socialist community. Thus, the United States feels justified in intervening in locations such as Korea and Vietnam, and the Soviet Union perceives its intervention in Afghanistan as legitimate. Finally, White sees *selective inattention* as the chief process by which all of the motivated errors are maintained. Through this process, subconscious motives influence a person's thought process and picture of the world. A number of defense mechanisms operate through the process of selective inattention. Thus, for example, projection appears to be the rule and self-blame the rare exception in international affairs. Resistance to ideas that are not part of modal thinking is also one of the forces fueling selective inattention. Through the mechanisms of resistance, repression, rationalization, projection, and compensation, selective inattention is a powerful form of subconsciously motivated exclusion.

Unmotivated cognitive errors are forms of misperception that cannot be attributed to subconscious motivational influences. White identifies six such forms of misperception. The *influence of preexisting beliefs* on present perception is given prominence. This includes the effects of well-established images, particularly the "good guys–bad guys" picture of the political world that is held by mutual antagonists. Given that most new events are ambiguous and open to varying interpretations, the expectations created by preexisting beliefs determine how the new information will be perceived and interpreted. One specific problem in the superpower rivalry is that each side persists in holding *prenuclear beliefs* and behaves as if it lived in a nonnuclear world. These beliefs include outdated assumptions about the importance of national sovereignty and about deterrence as the primary means for preventing war. *Blurred distinctions and the spread of attribution* are also a form of unmotivated misperception. When the political world is divided between good guys and bad guys, distinctions within the bad guys are blurred and the attribution of evil spreads throughout that entire part of the world. Thus, American conservatives blur the distinctions among socialists, communists, and liberals. The *injured-innocence mechanism* occurs when each nation believes itself innocent of any aggressive intention, and therefore infers that an arms buildup by its opponent must have an aggressive purpose. This is linked with the process of *universalization*, in which people universalize their own subjective perceptions as being objective realities that should be seen in the same way by others. Another misperception involves the *credulous acceptance of propaganda*, in which evil and powerful elements on the other side are seen as deliberately duping the mass of its people, inducing them to accept a distorted view of the world that motivates preparation for war. Analysts in both the United States and the Soviet Union contend that the power elite in the other country has biased the thinking of the masses through the skillful use of propaganda. Finally, the *extrapolation of a trend* is a frequent tendency of assuming that existing trends will continue into the future. Thus, many Americans, seeing the Soviet Union reaching parity in nuclear strength, predict that this trend will continue beyond parity, and they therefore support increased buildup on the American side.

In comparison to these powerful forms of misperception, White contends that ideological and economic factors are of minor consequence in the superpower rivalry. He draws this conclusion from his analysis of both world wars and the current United States–Soviet conflict, in which the source is seen primarily as a combination of exaggerated fear, macho pride, and anger. The contending ideologies are seen as mainly rationalizations of these underlying motives. Similarly, economic motives are seen as almost irrelevant, because each side has vast and varied resources at its disposal. Thus, White gives preeminence to perceptual and cognitive factors, not simply as processes in the development and escalation of conflict, but as underlying sources. This is in contrast to the eclectic model of intergroup conflict, which sees ideological or value differences as well as economic and power sources as important in the etiology of the superpower rivalry (see Chapter 5). One connection between the two models comes through the source of basic needs, in which psychological motives such as self-esteem fuel societal needs for identity and recognition that in part cause the conflict. In this way, war-promoting motives, particularly macho pride, come into play. However, in general, the motives and misperceptions identified by both White and Jervis appear to fit more appropriately in the category of perceptual and cognitive biases in the eclectic model that fuel escalation. These biases are driven to some degree by the perception of threat, the competitive orientation, and the influence of ethnocentrism. Once in operation, these perceptual and cognitive biases impinge upon the problem-solving competence of decision-making elites, as captured by the model of groupthink (see Chapter 4). Furthermore, such biases distort the processes of communication and interaction between the antagonists, making it extremely difficult to move in a cooperative direction in terms of dispute resolution. This is not to deny the importance of motives, such as fear and pride, in the etiology of intergroup conflict, but is to reassert that realistic group conflict theory has more to say about causation than do psychological, and especially psychodynamic, factors. Thus, the importance of perceptual and cognitive biases is acknowledged, but in a different location than that proposed by White. Nonetheless, his analysis of major conflicts in recent history, including the United States–Soviet rivalry, is an extremely valuable contribution to the social-psychological understanding of intergroup and international conflict.

Communication and Interaction

The processes of perception and cognition blend almost imperceptibly into those of communication and interaction in the social-psychological study of international relations (Fisher, 1982). Misperceptions and images of international actors shape the style and content of communicative acts and, in turn, are revealed by those same acts. Thus, the manner by which decision makers communicate and interact is usually consistent with their perceptions and images.

One important line of investigation in studying international communication has been initiated by Suedfeld and his colleagues through the development of a measure to assess the *integrative complexity* of communicative acts (Suedfeld & Tetlock, 1977; Suedfeld, Tetlock, & Raminez, 1977). The concept and measurement of integrative complexity was initially based on early work measuring the degree of cognitive complexity in personality functioning (Harvey, Hunt, & Schroder, 1961). These investigators studied the complexity of operating rules that individuals used to analyze incoming information and to make decisions. The assessment looks at two important dimensions: differentiation, which relates to the number of dimensions that are used in interpreting information, and integration, which relates to the degree and nature of connections among differentiated characteristics. Differentiation is therefore a prerequisite for integration. Tetlock (1988) provides a historical discussion of how these two dimensions have been combined in the measurement of integrative complexity, moving from seeing the concept as a dispositional trait at the individual level to an interactionist view in which numerous situational variables serve as additional determinants. Methodologically, the measure of integrative complexity has moved from an individual measure involving sentence completion to the content analysis of a wide range of archival documents, including speeches, letters, diaries, diplomatic communications, transcripts of meetings, policy statements, and interviews. Low scores reflect limited awareness of different ways of viewing problems and reliance on rigid decision-making rules; moderate scores are indicative of awareness of different ways of viewing problems (differentiation), with no awareness of the relationships between elements (integration). High scores reflect both awareness of different perspectives and of the relationships among them.

In the initial work on international communication, Suedfeld and Tetlock (1977) compared speeches and diplomatic notes from international crises that led to war with communications from crises that were resolved peacefully. In the crisis situations that moved to war, integrative complexity was not only lower, but also showed a decreasing trend as the crises moved toward climax. In other words, decision makers appeared to become more and more simplistic and rigid in their positions. To further test the hypothesis that crises leading to war are signaled by decreasing complexity, Suedfeld, Tetlock, and Raminez (1977) studied the integrative complexity of communications over 30 years of the Arab–Israeli conflict as represented in speeches at the United Nations. Integrative complexity dropped dramatically during every one of the years in which war occurred between Israel and its Arab neighbors. Thus, in a continuing hostile confrontation, it appears that low levels of integrative complexity are signals of impending outbreaks of violence.

The study of integrative complexity in international communication has been extended by Tetlock to the conflict between the superpowers (Tetlock, 1985, 1988). In a comprehensive piece of work, Tetlock (1985) has tested a number of hypotheses that relate the integrative complexity of foreign policy rhetoric to the actual foreign policy behavior of the United States and the Soviet Union. The extensive data source consists of official foreign policy statements between 1945 and 1983, drawn from such authoritative sources as the *Department of State Bulletin* and the *Current Digest of the Soviet Press*. From an initial population of approximately 20,000 words of policy statements for each country in a year, a random selection of 10 paragraph-sized statements was taken for each quarter-year period. Levels of integrative complexity for each quarter year were studied over time in relation to major foreign policy initiatives, including military or political interventions, major American–Soviet agreements, the integrative complexity of policy statements in earlier periods, and leadership transitions. For the Soviet Union, there were significant decreases in integrative complexity immediately before and during major competitive policy initiatives, such as military or political interventions. In contrast, there were significant increases in Soviet complexity immediately before and at the same time as the reaching of successful agreements in negotiation. In addition, levels of integrative complexity in Soviet statements were a positive function of the levels in immediately preceding quarters. Finally, Soviet complexity was different during different leadership periods. Moreover, the complexity of American foreign policy statements was found to influence the complexity of Soviet statements issued in the same quarter year. In other words, a reciprocity effect emerged. With respect to the American data, the analysis showed decreases in integrative complexity coincidental with major American interventions, as well as decreases before major agreements, which turned to increases in the same period as the agreements. Furthermore, there were significant downturns in American complexity at the same time as major Soviet interventions abroad. American complexity was also a positive function of complexity in the immediately preceding quarter year and was found to change with different administrations. For example, the Kennedy, Johnson, and Nixon administrations showed greater integrative complexity than the Truman or Reagan administrations. American complexity was also found to be related to Soviet complexity in the previous quarter year, thus demonstrating a lagged reciprocity effect. Overall, the most important similarity in the American and Soviet data was the relationship between integrative complexity and competitive versus coordinative policy initiatives, that is, interventions versus agreements.

Tetlock (1985, 1988) points out that the association between integrative complexity and foreign policy behavior can be interpreted in one of two ways: in information processing terms or in political impression management terms. According to the former, policy statements are actual indicators of how key policy makers see the relationship between the two countries. Changes in integrative complexity may occur as a result of individual variations, such as the emergence of new leaders with different cognitive styles, or situational variations, such as crisis-induced stress or the adoption of new styles of decision making. Regardless of the source, shifts in cognitive style are very important in that they shape the assessment of how to deal with conflict between the two countries. Policy makers who think with low integrative complexity, that is, in simple, black-and-white terms, tend to be suspicious of coordinative solutions and resort to pressure tactics to coerce concessions from the other party. In contrast, policy makers who think in complex terms will make active efforts to see the conflict from the perspective of the other side and will look for ways to integrate different perspectives into proposals that satisfy the needs of both parties. According to the second interpretation, focusing on impression management, foreign policy statements are not indicators of true perceptions, but are actually designed and intended to manipulate varied target audiences in desired ways. The intent would be to create particular impressions of being conciliatory, tough, or whatever for important domestic and international audiences. Thus, integrative complexity of communications is not a determinant of a competitive or coordinative strategy, but is in fact a manifestation of it. For example, in the American data there was an unexpected downturn in integrative complexity two quarter-year periods before major agreements. Through an impression management interpretation, these downward shifts could be designed to convince Americans that the administration is trying to strike a tough bargain with the Soviets as well as to convince the Soviet Union that there are limits to American willingness to make concessions. There is of course no way of choosing between the two interpretations without knowing the true intentions of the policy makers. Nonetheless, the significance of Tetlock's work lies in the strong and multifaceted relationship between communication and interaction in international relations. It appears that there is much to be learned from the study of communicative acts in relation to the foreign policy behavior of decision makers. The occurrence of reciprocity in the integrative complexity of policy statements is particularly revealing in that it indicates some degree of sensitivity to the behavior of the other party. Thus, one side or the other may have some influence in moving the relationship to either lower or higher levels of complexity in communication. Tetlock's results suggest that moving to higher levels of integrative complexity in communication would have beneficial effects on the interaction between the parties in terms of negotiation and, possibly, in terms of nonintervention. In particular, higher levels of integrative complexity might augur well for successful dispute resolution and ultimate de-escalation of the conflict.

Communication is one form of interaction between parties engaged in conflict, and is complemented by a variety of other behaviors within that context. In international conflict, a primary concern in interaction between nations has focused on the phenomenon of escalation. Many theorists maintain that conflict has a definite predisposition to escalate, that is, as indicated in the system states of the eclectic model, to become more intense and hostile, to include more issues, and to involve more powerful attempts at control (see Chapter 5). In combination with perceived threat and mistrust in the context of a competitive and ethnocentric orientation, it is not surprising that interaction between the parties moves conflict in the direction of escalation. Selected and distorted perception complements a competitive and cautious approach to the other party. Through a sense of mistrust, each party attributes negative intentions to the other and engages in threats that are designed to control the other party but that simply lead to counterthreats and escalation. A good deal of the reality of conflict escalation is captured by the malignant social process described by Deutsch (1983) outlined in Chapter 2. In the field of international relations, political scientists Quincy Wright (1965b) and J. David Singer (1970) have offered useful descriptions of conflict escalation.

Conflict theorists in both social psychology and international relations have come to identify two major models of interaction and escalation in international conflict. These are the deterrence, or aggressor–defender, model and the conflict spiral model (e.g. Jervis, 1976; Pruitt & Rubin, 1986; Tetlock, 1983). Pruitt and Rubin also add a third model, which they believe has been underemphasized: the structural change model. The deterrence model is based on the common strategy of nations to develop military power to protect their national sovereignty and security, maintain internal control, and prevent or resist outside aggression (Fisher, 1982). At its base, deterrence involves the threat of force as a response to prevent the potential use of aggression by an adversary (Morgan, 1983). Although the basic tenets of deterrence are simple, the field has been developed as a very complex study in military and political science (Dedring, 1976). Thus, deterrence theory is described as a sophisticated rational exercise calculating what weapons are necessary to support what threat with what punishment as a reaction to what attack. This aura of logical and technological complexity overlies the simple essence of deterrence, that is, manipulation via threat, which is an exceedingly primitive approach to social relationships (Morgan, 1983). It involves the resort to threat and punishment that human beings are predisposed to use with children, animals, criminals, and others who are seen to only understand force and violence. There are increasing indications that in dealing with all kinds of supposed deviant behavior, deterrence is breaking down on a global scale (Burton, 1979, 1985a). Nonetheless, the deterrence model retains considerable appeal in the field of international relations, where the potential costs of aggression are very high. According to Jervis (1976), the central argument of the deterrence model is that great dangers arise if an aggressor believes that powers maintaining the status quo are weak either in capability or in resolve. Thus, the aggressor begins interaction with small tests of the opponent's strength, and if there is retreat, the aggressor is encouraged to escalate to more aggressive intrusions. Therefore, it is essential that the powers who are challenged display both the willingness and the ability to wage war, even in disputes over minor issues. Cast in terms of the aggressor–defender model, the deterrence approach sees one party (the aggressor) as having goals that place it in conflict with the other party (the defender). From this basis, Pruitt and Rubin (1986) content that the aggressor begins with low level contentious tactics, and if these are not successful in reaching the desired goal, the aggressor moves to heavier tactics, thus escalating the conflict. The defender simply reacts to these efforts, escalating responses to the same levels as the aggressor's tactics.

Deterrence theory is often put forward as captured in the Roman dictum, "If you want peace, prepare for war." However, both rational analysis and empirical research in international relations are coming to support the more accurate admonition, "If you prepare for war, you get war." An analysis of 2,000 years of international relations history by Naroll, Bullough, and Naroll (1974) found that military preparedness was typically practiced as a form of deterrence, but in the long run, the preparation for war through arms races made war more, rather than less, probable. Similarly, a quantitative analysis by Wallace (1979) indicated that international disputes preceded by an arms race, fueled by policies of mutual deterrence, were much more likely to lead to war than disputes with no arms race. More recently, a number of political scientists have produced historical analyses that severely question the rationality of deterrence theory as well as its effectiveness in preventing war (Jervis, Lebow, & Stein, 1985; Lebow & Stein, 1987). These analyses indicate that, in practicing deterrence theory, both challengers and defenders behave in ways that are contradictory to the model, make serious misjudgments, and bring about the very behavior they are seeking to prevent. It is clear that the principles and prescriptions of the deterrence model as a form of international interaction are being seriously questioned.

Part of the failure of the deterrence model is captured in the related model of the conflict spiral, first articulated by political scientists and social psychologists in the early 1960s (North, Brody, & Holsti, 1964; Osgood, 1962). These analyses indicated that, in crisis situations, decision makers who perceive threats from another country are likely to respond with a threat or hostile action, thus confirming the other party's belief that its initial perception was justified, and resulting in further threats. Pruitt and Rubin (1986) describe the conflict spiral as resulting from a vicious circle of action and reaction in which one party's contentious tactics encourage a contentious response from the other, which contributes to further contentious behavior from the first party and moves the interaction to a higher level of hostile behavior. The link between the deterrence and spiral models is that mutual deterrence initiates and feeds the conflict spiral. Thus, it is ironic that an approach designed to limit conflict (deterrence) appears to increase both its likelihood and its ultimate intensity. In Jervis' (1976) analysis, states seeking to defend themselves get both too much and too little: too much because they gain the ability to carry out aggression, but too little because others who are threatened will increase their own capacity, thus reducing the first nation's security. This creates the so-called "security dilemma," in which the unintended or undesired consequences of defensive actions actually result in less security.

The viability and utility of the deterrence model hinges on the use of threat, which in the eclectic model is seen as a core element in the development and escalation of intergroup conflict. Perceived threat, in conjunction with a competitive orientation, tends to fuel the ethnocentric reaction and related mistrust of the adversary. The difficulty with threats is that they are typically responded to in ways that further aggravate the situation. The threat communicates that the initiators sees the receiver as untrustworthy and hostile, and through the self-fulfilling prophecy may in fact lead the adversary to behave in a hostile manner. However, the use of threats is a complex process, and can have positive outcomes under certain conditions (Milburn, 1977; Lockhart, 1973). Complexity is partly induced because the parties to a conflict will emphasize different elements of the threat in their perceptions. The threatening side is most aware of the demands, that is, what the threat is supposed to accomplish. In contrast, the receiving party is likely to be more aware of the dangers and costs that are threatened. The strength of the threat is also a complex matter in terms of the reaction of the receiving party. Weak threats, which lack credibility, may only produce hostility with no desired change in behavior. On the other hand, very strong threats may be seen as general statements of intent; that is, the threatening party intends to engage in aggression regardless of what the threatened party does. Thus, effective threats require both credibility and contingency. The receiver must believe that the threat is real and that the reaction will indeed affect the threatening party. In that way, threat can be useful in communicating the seriousness of the situation between parties. The difficulty is that the threat will often be perceived in very different terms than it is intended, and the outcome will be to feed the conflict spiral rather than de-escalate or terminate the dispute.

Tetlock (1983) has captured the deterrence and conflict spiral models in the form of images held by policy makers, thus providing another way of linking perceptual and cognitive processes with behavioral interaction in terms of policy initiatives and reactions. In particular, Tetlock focuses on the long-standing debate in the United States over United States–Soviet relations. The basic argument is that foreign policy is not the simple product of rational calculations, but depends a great deal on the image that the policy maker holds. Tetlock contends that:

> Policy-makers see the world "through a glass darkly"–through the simplified images they have created of the international scene. Policy-makers may behave rationally, but only within the context of their subjective representations of reality (the principle of bounded rationality). To predict foreign policy, one must understand how key decision-makers construct simplified images of reality and, for this purpose, one must draw upon basic principles of cognitive, social and personality functioning. (p. 68)

Thus, what one sees as a rational policy depends on which of the two images one believes best captures American–Soviet relations. The images are based on fundamentally different assumptions about international relations in general and about the policies that will bring peace. Following the deterrence image leads to the general implication that the United States must convince the Soviet Union that the United States possesses adequate second-strike nuclear forces to inflict unacceptably large losses on the Soviet Union. A weakening of either the will or the capacity to maintain a strong nuclear deterrent is seen as resulting in destabilization of the international system. Thus, for example, agreeing to a nuclear freeze would actually make nuclear war more likely in the minds of those who hold the deterrence image. The deterrence approach assumes a real difference of interest in which mutual fear maintains stability. In contrast, the conflict spiral image proposes that mutual fear destabilizes international relations and leads to an exaggeration of incompatibility. Within the context of the anarchic nature of the international system and the security dilemma, nations in competition have difficulty discovering the potentially cooperative side of their relationship. The link between the two images is that the conflict spiral is the result of both nations' policy makers holding to the deterrence image. However, the two images result in very different policy implications. The deterrence image leads decision makers to build up military strength and to appear willing to risk all-out war in order to deter aggression. In contrast, the conflict spiral image prescribes an emphasis on peaceful objectives and a statement of willingness to de-escalate the arms race. The deterrence image leads policy makers to stand firm and to use pressure tactics, whereas the conflict spiral image recommends collaboration in the search for mutually acceptable solutions. Tetlock points out that the key difference separating the advocates of the two images and policy implications is their perception of trust in the Soviet Union's interest in achieving an integrative solution. Thus, the question of which image is more valid depends on the assessment or attribution of the Soviet Union's intentions. If the Soviet Union is determined to achieve world domination through expansion, the deterrence model may be justified. If the Soviet Union is in a defensive position, attempting to gain security by assisting pro-Soviet governments, then the spiral image holds true. Unfortunately, social-psychological research cannot help resolve this controversy, but it can and has pointed toward a variety of concerns regarding the validity of images held by policy makers, as indicated in the previous section.

Finally, Pruitt and Rubin (1986) bring forward the structural change model, which they see as implied in the writings of Burton (1962) and others. This model states that the interaction of conflict produces residues in the form of changes in the parties that encourage further contentious behavior and inhibit efforts at resolution. Thus, conflict produces structural changes that feed further escalatory interaction. Structural changes have been hypothesized at three levels of analysis: the psychological, the group, and the community. Psychological residues include, for example, negative perceptions and attitudes of the adversary, such as the diabolical enemy image. At the group level, psychological reactions tend to become collective norms and to support goals calling for the defeat of the adversary, as opposed to searching for collaborative solutions. The emergence of more aggressive or militant leadership is another example of a structural change at the group level. Finally, structural changes at the level of the broader community include polarization, in which other parties join the conflict.

Pruitt and Rubin (1986) point out that the three models are not mutually exclusive. Each one helps explain certain aspects of escalation. The aggressor–defender model leads into the conflict spiral model through mutual deterrence, whereas the structural change model adds the element of escalatory residues. Thus, the structural change model could serve as a framework within which a comprehensive model of international conflict could be developed. Such a model would have a high degree of commonality with the eclectic model presented in Chapter 5. This underscores the assumption that international conflict is a form of intergroup conflict, which differs mainly in terms of increased complexity at higher levels of analysis and the potential costs of destructive interaction.

The Social Psychology of International Negotiation

The traditional and most common form of attempting to manage conflict in international relations is that of diplomatic negotiation. A wide variety of issues involving territory, trading arrangements, environmental concerns, fishing rights, economic cooperation, and arms control have traditionally been handled through this conflict management process (see Winham, 1977). It is important to point out, however, that negotiation is not appropriate to all conflicts, whether at the international level or elsewhere (Rubin, 1983). Values or beliefs that are deeply held are simply not negotiable because there is no room for concession making, a core process in negotiation. However, arrangements for groups to exist and relate to each other in the face of deeply held value conflicts would be amenable to negotiation. In general, disputes involving economic sources are more amenable to negotiation than those involving value, need, or power differences.

International negotiation has been studied from a variety of perspectives. Case study observations and general descriptions have provided detailed and concrete accounts of the process and substance of negotiation (e.g., Ikle, 1964; Lall, 1966). Game theorists have attempted to reduce negotiation to essential elements that can be represented mathematically (e.g., Fouraker & Siegel, 1963). Political scientists are increasingly turning their attention to both single and comparative case analyses of particular negotiations in an attempt to derive general principles (e.g., Kriesberg, 1988). In conjunction with these various methodological approaches, negotiation can also be conceived of in a number of different ways. For example, negotiation can be seen as a learning process, a psychological process, a joint decision-making process, or a process of dual responsiveness (see Zartman, 1977).

Within the study of international negotiation, the social-psychological approach has made a particular contribution by emphasizing the process and conditions of negotiation as they affect outcomes. While relying primarily on empirical data from experiments and simulations, social psychologists have attempted to develop generic models that capture the major elements of negotiation (Druckman, 1973, 1977, 1983; Druckman & Mahoney, 1977; Pruitt, 1981; Rubin, 1983; Rubin & Brown, 1975; Sawyer & Guetzkow, 1965).

Sawyer and Guetzkow (1965) have developed a social-psychological model of international negotiation that has served both as a foundation and a stimulus for further theorizing and research. They define negotiation as a process through which two parties interact to develop agreements that guide and regulate their future behavior, and they divide their model into antecedent, concurrent, and consequent conditions (see Figure 7-1). The model thus has a temporal flow with variables from different levels of analysis being mixed within the different components. The focus is clearly on the negotiation process as it is affected by a variety of factors. A fun-

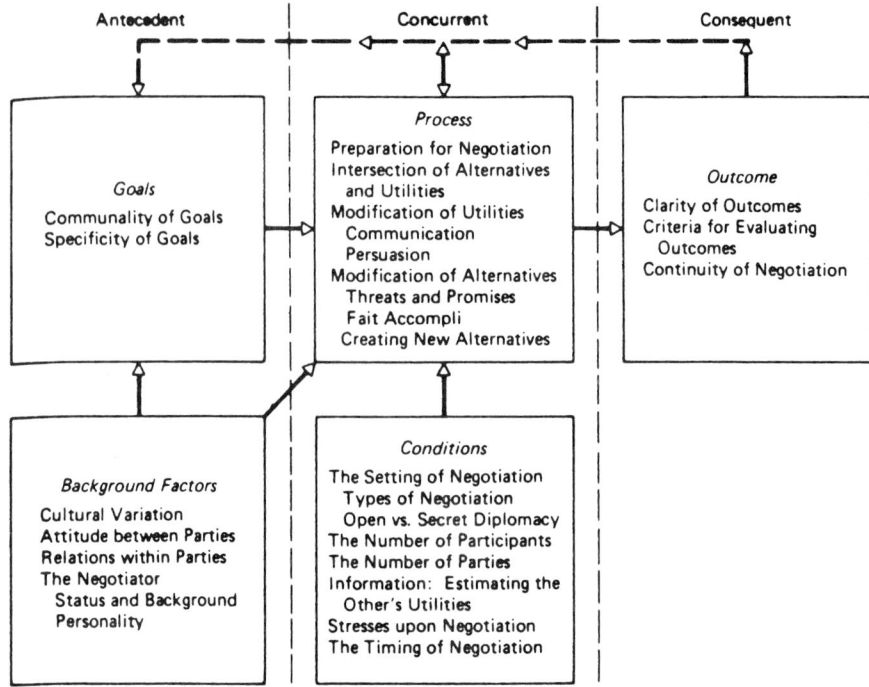

Figure 7-1. A model of international negotiation. Negotiation involves: (1) antecedent or existing conditions including the negotiator's goals and background; (2) concurrent or contemporary conditions, which influence the process or ongoing behaviors of negotiation; and (3) consequent conditions, which are the outcomes produced by negotiation. Source: Sawyer & Guetzkow (1965). Illustration from *International Behavior: A Social-Psychological Analysis*, edited by Herbert D. Kelman, copyright © 1965 by Holt, Rinehart and Winston, Inc., reprinted by permission of the publisher.

damental assumption is made that international conflict typically results from objective differences between the parties, but that social-psychological factors, such as misperception and misunderstanding, can aggravate existing conflicts and attempted processes of resolution, including negotiation. Thus, the model provides a useful starting point for the study of international negotiation.

Druckman (1973) uses the Sawyer and Guetzkow (1965) model to organize and discuss research up to the time of his review. In particular, Druckman brings forward some 70 propositions based on a variety of research results. Propositions with varying degrees of support are stated, specifically, those based on initial findings versus those based on replicated findings. Example propositions, following the flow of the model, include the following:

> The more competitive the parties, the more exacerbated the conflict and the longer the negotiations. (p. 14)

The Social Psychology of International Negotiation 165

> The more resolutions obtained on "smaller" issues, the more likely will parties be able to negotiate their differences on the broader issues which have served to sustain long-term hostilities. (p. 18)
>
> Negotiations are facilitated to the extent that parties engage in prenegotiation communication that avoids intensive strategy preparation (i.e., detailed planning for postures). (p. 24)
>
> The more information exchanged between the parties, during negotiations, the easier it is to reach an agreement. (p. 28)
>
> Bilateral use of commitment tactics is likely to lead to deadlock in negotiations. (p. 33)
>
> Differences between nations on cognitive presuppositions or linguistic structure are less likely to impede negotiations when opposing contestants have received training on the concepts of the contrasting culture. (p. 37)
>
> The larger the potential discrepancy in outcomes perceived by the parties, the more difficult it is to attain a resolution. (p. 42)
>
> Competitiveness which results from the norms of the negotiation situation is enhanced by the presence of an audience during deliberations. (p. 47)
>
> In international negotiations, competitive advantage is regarded as being more important that ideology or policy positions (i.e., negotiators more likely to compromise their ideological positions than to forfeit their competitive advantage when these factors conflict. (p. 50)
>
> The higher the tension, the less capable negotiators are of evaluating information and of making the final discriminations that are necessary in order to achieve a satisfactory agreement. (p. 57)
>
> The fewer cultural and cognitive differences between national representatives made salient in the negotiations, the easier it will be to resolve a conflict of interest. (p. 62)

These illustrative propositions demonstrate the kinds of hypotheses that have been generated and tested by social-psychological research on the negotiation process. The model provides a useful framework for organizing these propositions into a manageable and meaningful format. Druckman concludes that although there have been important substantive and methodological gains, it is difficult to see a progressive trend toward an integrated theory of negotiation. That is, international negotiation can be examined from several different perspectives. Furthermore, Druckman notes that the social-psychological approach and its products up to that time, ignore the impact of broader contextual variables.

Druckman and Mahoney (1977) add further elaboration and substantiation to elements of the Sawyer and Guetzkow (1965) model by combining results of laboratory and field investigations. International negotiation is seen sequentially as a social process that includes formulation of positions, attempts to resolve differences, and an outcome that has ramifications for the wider global system. Thus, three questions are of primary importance: (a) how negotiators arrive at initial positions, (b) what factors affect the negotiating process, and (c) what the consequences of outcomes are for future relations. In terms of the development of negotiating positions, two competing views can be discerned: one asserts that negotiating positions can be predicted from the national attributes of the nations involved, and the other believes that positions develop from an internal policy-making process that sees nations as complex organizations. Interestingly, both approaches emphasize domestic factors, rather than the policy preferences of a small elite, as the major determinant of negotiating postures. In discussing the process of negotiating, Druckman and Mahoney (1977) cover three major elements. First, preparatory meetings are convened in order to define issues, set ground rules, and arrange conditions for the negotiating sessions. Various tactics are then used by the negotiator, who is in a boundary role position, in order to achieve a settlement that is acceptable both to the other party and to the negotiator's constituency. Finally, a variety of factors interfere with the negotiating process, including cultural differences, misattribution of intentions, and various stresses, such as time pressure. In relation to consequences, it is becoming increasingly accepted that relations between nations cannot be described on a single continuum ranging from cooperation to conflict, but that both these dimensions are necessary to capture reality. Thus, agreements that reduce conflict may not necessarily increase the level of cooperation, for example. From these considerations, Druckman and Mahoney conclude that insights into understanding international negotiation will be produced only by moving between levels of analysis and weaving together a variety of data sources into a "mosaic of influences."

In contrast to much previous work on the social psychology of international negotiation, Druckman (1983) makes a strong case for expanding the analysis to take into account a variety of contextual factors. Context refers to the processes and structure of the broader systems in which negotiation takes place. Thus, Druckman emphasizes the reciprocal interplay between negotiator behavior and context, and categorizes variables into four broad areas: social-psychological, bureaucratic, structural, and contextual. An example of a social-psychological variable is that of cultural differences wherein variations in tradition or ideology can affect negotiating style. An illustrative bureaucratic variable is that of team composition in which the different agencies represented on the team engage in internal bargaining, which can effect negotiating positions. An important structural variable is that of relative power between the parties, which affects their bargaining power, for example, the degree to which one side can afford to deadlock rather than make a small concession. Finally, contextual variables include external events, such as changes in the domestic environment, which can bring about shifts in negotiating behavior.

In adding further to the complexity of the analysis, Druckman (1983) also discusses the importance of stages, turning points, and impasses or crises. Although a number of authors have proposed various stages in the process of negotiation, Druckman points out that the stage concept is speculative due to limited empirical evidence. He distills previous work down to a model comprising five stages of negotiation with concurrent benchmarks for each. Progression from one stage to the next is coincident with turning points, whereas stalemates at each stage are accompanied by impasses or crises. Turning points are seen as breakthroughs that build momentum toward a final agreement. The first stage in the model is the agenda debate, and the benchmark is agreement on the agenda. The turning point occurs when the parties agree that negotiation is realistic; that is, they come to see that their expectations are within a manageable range. The turning point might be signaled by a mutual declaration of principles moving to an agreement on the agenda for negotiations. The second stage of negotiation is the search for a formula, with the benchmark being the acceptance of a formula by both parties. The turning point is signaled by the creation and agreement on the formula, which provides a framework on which negotiations may proceed. Once this is done, it is necessary for the parties to flesh out the issues in the third stage of negotiation. Each party must estimate the range of concessions that may be necessary to reach agreement and acknowledge a commitment to pursue negotiations to a final agreement. Details are deduced from the framework, and a benchmark is reached when the issues have been rendered negotiable. The fourth stage then involves the bargaining process covering the identified issues to arrive at a mutually acceptable concession exchange, which is the benchmark at the end of the stage. The turning point that is required at this stage is for each party to adjust its expectations toward what is needed to actually get an agreement. This is the essence of the bargaining process and, like the other turning points, typically occurs after a period of little or no progress. Once an acceptable concession exchange has occurred, the parties are in a position to search for the implementing details, which constitutes the fifth stage of negotiation. When this search is successful, the benchmark is the ultimate outcome of negotiation in the form of a treaty or other document of agreement. The sequence described in Druckman's stage model emphasizes the need for progression through the stages if negotiation is to be successful. In that sense it is both a descriptive model of actual negotiations and a prescriptive model that provides guidelines for successful negotiation. The model is also a development one – negotiations must progress from one stage to the next or an impasse and ultimately failure will occur. Druckman (1986) uses the stage model to profitably analyze the negotiations on military bases between the United States and Spain.

Druckman's stage sequence is prescriptive in that it describes activities of negotiators that are useful for moving negotiations forward. In a more explicit vein, a number of other social psychologists have proposed strategies and tactics for successful negotiation, particularly for achieving integrative solutions (Pruitt 1986; Pruitt & Rubin, 1986; Rubin, 1983). Rubin (1983) emphasizes the fundamental point that negotiation is a situation of interdependence that requires the parties moving toward a common center. One approach and negotiator skill that is useful in promoting effective negotiation is sensitivity to the other party, at least to a moderate degree. In addition to helping negotiators distinguish the difference between what the other party says and what it really means, sensitivity enables negotiators to anticipate and evaluate how the other party responds to offers. Concurrently, negotiators should follow a strategy of supporting the other party's sense of competence. This is because negotiators prefer to see their concessions not as signs of weakness but of their willingness to negotiate from a position of strength and choice. A strategy of avoiding commitments to intransigence is also useful. Too often, negotiators commit to rigid positions, assuming that this will potentially cost the other party so much that it will yield its position. Unfortunately, this assumption is often wrong, and negotiators are better advised to follow a strategy of flexibility.

Pruitt (1986) puts forward methods for achieving integrative agreements, that is, ones that reconcile the parties' interests and yield high joint benefits. Integrative agreements usually emerge out of creative problem solving on the substantive issues at stake. Five strategies are proposed that lead to five types of integrative solutions. First, *expanding the pie* is useful in conflicts involving a resource shortage where, in fact, the available resources can be increased. This approach is useful when the parties find each other's proposals inherently acceptable but reject them because they involve foregone opportunities. If increasing the pie overcomes these costs, then settlement is assured. In the second strategy, that of *nonspecific compensation*, one party gets what it wants while the other receives payment in some unrelated coin. The party whose demands are granted provides compensation to the other, often in the form of promises of later benefits. The third approach to integrative solutions is that of *log rolling*, in which each party concedes on lower priority issues that are of higher priority to the other. Thus, each party gains on only some of its demands, but on those that are most important for a settlement. Parties need to develop an understanding of each other's priorities and need to look for creative combinations that will yield an integrative settlement. The fourth approach is that of *cost cutting*, in which one party gets what it wants while the other party's costs are eliminated or reduced. Cost cutting is often in the form of specific compensation, in which the party that concedes is compensated. Thus, parties need to share information about the costs of various alternatives and to search for ways to reduce these costs. The final strategy is *bridging*, in which neither party gains its initial demands, but in which a new option is created that satisfies the most important underlying interests. Thus, an analysis of interests underlying the parties' positions is required so that issues may be reformulated. Interests are seen as the hidden concerns that underlie preferences, whereas issues are the concrete matters under discussion. Once interests are understood, it may be possible to create alternatives that were not initially perceived as possible or relevant. For each of these approaches to integrative solutions, Pruitt provides a number of refocusing questions to help choose the best approach. In addition, a number of suggestions are provided to facilitate the general process of creative problem solving. These include asking whether there really is a conflict of interest, analyzing each party's interests and setting reasonably high aspirations with firmness, seeking a way to reconcile the aspirations of both parties, and lowering aspirations and searching for more alternatives if necessary. Overall, a strategy of being firm but conciliatory is recommended as lighting the road to integrative solutions.

In conclusion, the social-psychological study of international negotiation increases our understanding of some of the core processes and yields some valuable prescriptions for practitioners that are paralleled by other commentators (e.g., Fisher & Ury, 1981). However, much social-psychological work is limited both conceptualy and empirically. As Druckman (1973) points out, Sawyer and Guezkow's (1965) model de-emphasizes system level processes and contextual factors in favor of perceptual, situational, and background variables. In contrast, Druckman (1983) would prefer to see the wider context as an important element of the social-psychological study of international negotiation. Empirically, the most distinguishing aspect of the social-psychological approach is the high reliance on experimental laboratory methodology. Proponents of this methodology hold that it will result in the identification of essential variables and their relationships within the process of negotiation. Not surprisingly, the limitations of the laboratory method, especially in terms of what we would now call external validity, were soon noted by critics (e.g., J.D. Singer & Ray, 1966). Numerous important dimensions can be identified in which laboratory experiments differ from the more complex decision-making arena of world politics. At the same time, some analyses have indicated that social-psychological models such as Sawyer and Guetzkow's can be used to characterize both laboratory work and real world negotiations (e.g., Bonham, 1971). Druckman (1983) acknowledges that most social-psychological contributions have involved analyses of interpersonal or small group interaction, and that the failure to take account of context creates problems for generalization. Thus, a paradox exists in which a large and sophisticated literature on the bargaining process is contrasted with few attempts to apply the findings to complex negotiations. Part of the problem is that the predominant conceptualization in the social psychology of international negotiation has remained that of the bargaining process, while the prevailing methodology has remained laboratory experimentation. According to Druckman:

> International negotiation is not simply bargaining as we observe in bartered exchanges, in bilateral monopoly in collective bargaining, or in limited markets.... Bargaining is one element in a complex environment of domestic and international politics: Other process occur: Negotiators are debaters, they are problem solvers, they are responsive to bureaucratic interests, they are managers of information and structures, and they are game players intent on keeping their constituents in the game without allowing them to limit the range of options that could lead eventually to an acceptable agreement. (p. 53)

In addition, Druckman (1983) identifies restrictive assumptions from game theory that underlie the experimental study of negotiation. It is assumed, for example, that each side has complete information about the other's value system and that all messages are completely understood. The context of international negotiation both erodes these simplistic assumptions and adds many other considerations. For example, international negotiators seem rarely to move into the gradual convergence toward a compromise because there is no single issue at stake, but rather a variety of issues that are difficult to compare. Furthermore, much international negotiation has side effects that are beyond the particular issues at stake and may serve various aims beyond the stated goals. Nations may wish simply to perpetuate the negotiation forum in order to have continuing contact for pursuing other interests. Such considerations lead Druckman to conclude that:

> The bargaining-theory approach assumes that bargaining is the essence of negotiation, that preferences are generally stable, that the purpose of negotiation is to achieve a mutually satisfactory agreement, and that the bargaining dynamic is not subject to contextual influences.... International negotiation is a more complex form of social interaction than that depicted by bargaining theorists: more extended in time, more parties, embedded in the broader context of international politics, more dynamic in the sense of changing preferences, more communication problems due to cultural differences, and more subtle incentives than those ostensibly apparent to the outside observer. (p. 55)

These conclusions lead to the necessity of a broad interdisciplinary approach to studying international negotiation in which social-psychological concepts and methods play a part. Concurrently, a combination of methodological strategies are useful for studying negotiation. In addition to the laboratory approach of bringing critical aspects under study in a precise manner, it is important to superimpose general dimensions upon case studies of negotiation in the real world. Moving between the laboratory and case studies in a complementary fashion should also be combined with the task of model building. Thus, the experimental work on the bargaining process needs to be integrated both methodologically and conceptually into a broader conception of the reality of international negotiation. In that way, the social-psychological approach can not only yield insights on the process of negotiation, but may eventually produce prescriptions that have utility for practitioners.

The De-Escalation of International Conflict

A considerable amount of attention in the social scientific study of conflict and, specifically, international conflict has focused on the process of escalation by which conflict increases in intensity. As indicated in Chapter 5, escalation is the process by which a change in the system states of the eclectic model takes place, that is, from a low intensity system state to a high intensity one. Various social-psychological descriptions—such as the malignant social process, the spiral model, and the structural model—describe the characteristics and effects of escalation.

Unfortunately, the process of de-escalation has received much less attention in the social science literature, especially as it is applied to international conflict (Kriesberg, 1982, 1987). This contrasts with reality, in which conflicts often move toward states of decreased tension after persisting at high levels of hostility. In a sense, however, the process of de-escalation has been indirectly studied through the discussion of a wide variety of strategies for conflict resolution, all of which involve assumptions about it. De-escalation is seen essentially as the reverse of the process of escalation. Therefore, if escalation is defined in a simple manner—for example, as the "controlled and specified application of sanctions in a fashion of increasing magnitude over time"—then de-escalation is defined as the same process but with a *decreasing* magnitude over time (Bonoma, 1975). When escalation is seen as a more complex subjective and objective process, as in the eclectic model, then de-escalation must be cast in similar terms. Comprehensive and detailed descriptions of this process tend not to be available in the social science literature.

A number of schemes and strategies have been offered for the resolution of international conflict. These various options usually involve differing degrees of de-escalation. D. Katz (1965), for example, outlines several methods for dealing with international conflict. The use of force and deterrence is a common approach that usually keeps the conflict at the same level of intensity, or, as noted above, often escalates it. Conflict denial is another strategy that is not likely to either escalate or de-escalate the conflict. Conflict restriction, such as in limited war, has the effect of controlling escalation, but not of inducing de-escalation. Nonviolence and ideological conversion has seen little use at the international level; however, the mutual trust that nonviolence emphasizes is one important basis of international agreements. The common strategies of bargaining and compromise at the international level are typical procedures of attempted de-escalation. This of course requires some degree of change from a strategy of deterrence to one of negotiation, a shift which is difficult to induce in highly escalated conflicts. Finally, problem solving and creative integration is a direct approach to de-escalating and resolving international conflict, but is most notable through its absence of application.

It is apparent that some strategies of conflict management foster de-escalation whereas others maintain the status quo. In addition, some approaches, such as negotiation, may require some de-escalation before they can be effectively instituted. Thus, a key question is: How may international conflicts be de-escalated in a manner that not only reduces the risk of violent confrontation but paves the way for negotiation on substantive issues? Two specific social-psychological contributions addressing this question include the problem-solving workshop and Graduated Reciprocation in Tension-reduction (GRIT) (see Chapter 8). The focus of this section is to discuss de-escalation as a broad process within the context of international interaction, and to consider overall strategies that may foster de-escalation over escalation or continuing stalemate.

Kriesberg (1982) maintains that a number of important conditions must arise in order for de-escalation to become a serious option in international conflict. In a situation of continuing hostility and stalemate, the high costs of continuing the conflict need to gain greater visibility in the eyes of the antagonists. At the same time, the stalemate clearly communicates that the current methods for dealing with the conflict are unsuccessful. Thus, parties become disheartened with the prospect of continuing the conflict and may begin to reevaluate the initial goals over which the conflict began—the "sour grapes" phenomenon. In addition, it becomes clear that continuing the conflict, and certainly escalating it, will be even more costly. Thus, leaders, who have already established ties with each other though conflict interaction, may look for mutually acceptable means to de-escalate and yet save face. There may also be changes in political alignments that affect the degree of support for continuation versus de-escalation. The emergence of a constituency and leadership in favor of moderation can hasten a shift to de-escalation. These types of conditions increase the probability that one or both parties will make moves toward de-escalation. Therefore, Kriesberg (1987) maintains that de-escalation moves emerge not from crises or wars but from an ongoing antagonism, the costs of which become increasingly salient. Because de-escalation moves may lead to long-lasting mutual accommodation when they are well-managed, it is important to understand the reasons for their success or failure. In particular, attention must be given to the differential effectiveness of various combinations of coercive and noncoercive moves in reducing tensions. Whereas some theorists support primarily the use of concessions and conciliatory gestures, others stress coercive inducements that increase the costs for the other party of not de-escalating the conflict.

Also of importance is the stage of de-escalation in which the moves are brought forward. Specifically, de-escalation efforts may have differential efficacy depending on whether the parties are initiating de-escalation or are already in a situation of negotiation. Through analyzing the two cases of United States–Soviet and Arab–Israeli relations, Kriesberg (1987) concludes that neither unilateral concessions nor coercive threats were effective in the initiation of de-escalation or negotiation. It appears that combining coercive and noncoercive inducements may be more effective, although using these strategies simultaneously may induce confusion in the other party. The most effective sequence is to follow a coercive action with a conciliatory gesture, thus demonstrating resolve at the same time as a wish to de-escalate. For the moves to be successful, a number of elements in the international context and the domestic political situation need to be supportive of de-escalation. Otherwise, the strategies will fail regardless of their nature and sequence. When parties have actually moved into the negotiation stage, different considerations regarding de-escalatory moves arise. Kriesberg's analysis of cases indicates that negotiation accompanied by coercion typically fails to culminate in an agreement. In contrast, when significant benefits in the future are promised during negotiations, the probability of agreement increases. Similarly, conciliatory actions taken during negotiations also have a beneficial effect. It is clear that once negotiations are underway, conciliatory moves are less risky and more likely to be acceptable to the negotiators' constituencies, because there is more likelihood of reciprocation. In addition, positive incentives to the adversary may increase mutual dependence, thus facilitating integrative bargaining. In conclusion, Kriesberg (1987) suggests that the oft-proposed "tit-for-tat" strategy appears to be an effective combination of firmness and conciliation (see Chapter 8). If the sequencing of coercive and noncoercive inducements is handled skillfully, it will convey firmness about goals but flexibility about means, and this appears to be the best way to achieve settlement.

Kriesberg (1984) provides a broader context for understanding the process of de-escalation by developing an interactive paradigm, which considers both multiple actors and multiple processes in international relations. It is noted that, due in large part to their complexity, major conflicts do not readily de-escalate, but often persist and at times escalate into extensive violence. Nonetheless, the failure of a completely coercive approach often underlies the move toward noncoercive strategies. At the same time, efforts to de-escalate seldom move quickly and smoothly toward the desired reduction in hostility. De-escalation moves are often not reciprocated, and even if they are, mutual de-escalation can easily be disrupted. In a multiple actor and mutual process context, de-escalation is usually the result of many converging factors in which no single set of determinants is paramount. Finally, de-escalation is not equivalent to resolution in the sense that the conflict disappears. Often, only the conflict's relative importance shifts, and further changes in the international

The De-Escalation of International Conflict

	Options of nation A		
Options of nation B	Action rewarding to B	No action	Action penalizing to B
Action rewarding to A	5 Compromise 5' A	2 Unilateral advantage to A 8 B	1 Exploitation of B by A 9 C
No action	7 Unilateral advantage to B 3 D	4 No change in situation (stalemate) 4 E	3 B hurt but does not retaliate 7 F
Action penalizing to A	9 Exploitation of A by B 1 G	8 A hurt but does not retaliate 2 H	6 Fight 6 I

Figure 7-2. Options and outcomes in an international dispute. The number in the lower left-hand corner of each cell represents the rank order preference of nation B for this outcome. The number in the upper-right corner of each cell represents the rank order preference of nation A. The number 1 is the highest preference. Source: Patchen (1988). Reprinted with permission.

context or domestic politics may in fact bring it back into focus with a resulting escalation to former intensity. Thus, many protracted conflicts take on a cyclical nature, moving through periods of de-escalation and escalation. However, the central importance of de-escalation is that it can create conditions within which resolution is possible. It is in this light that understanding de-escalation, and the strategies and behaviors that encourage it, is essential to resolving international conflict.

The understanding of de-escalation must be developed within a broader framework of international conflict. Such a framework has recently been offered by Patchen (1988), who draws on social-psychological and games theory approaches to provide a systematic analysis of conflict behavior. Conflict and cooperation between two interdependent parties is seen as a process of strategic interaction in which each party exercises options, that, in combination with the actions of the other party, produce predictable outcomes (see Figure 7-2). For example, if both nations in a conflict choose actions that are rewarding to the other party, compromise is the outcome, whereas if each nation chooses actions that penalize the other party, the outcomes will be a fight. The situation is of course not so simple, especially at the outset of a conflict, because the nature of the strategic situation in terms of options, actions, and preferences is not clear to the parties. Therefore, Patchen's treatment looks at different patterns of preferences, as well as different perceptions of the situation, that affect the choices that nations make. This leads into a consideration of decision making regarding the choices among options and the effectiveness of different strategies in terms of de-escalation and resolution. Within these categories, Patchen integrates results from games research and case studies of international conflict to yield a number of conclusions and prescriptions. His suggestions for dispute resolution are similar to those emerging from the study of the more limited interaction in negotiation; they also demonstrate congruence with the ideas offered by Kriesberg. In terms of overall strategies, it appears that those that rely primarily on either coercion or cooperation have serious limitations. The former tends to lead to escalation and war, and the latter tends to result in exploitation by the adversary. Combined strategies, especially those that begin with coercion and move toward conciliatory behavior, appear the most effective in inducing cooperative actions from an adversary. However, within this generalization, the most effective combined strategies are those in which one's own actions are made contingent upon the actions of the adversary. Thus, the so-called "tit-for-tat," or reciprocity, approach is generally successful in bringing about mutual cooperation. In addition, the reciprocation of competitive moves should "undermatch" the other party's competitive action, because overmatching leads to escalation. The prescribed strategy is to de-escalate conflict while demonstrating that one cannot be exploited. This reasoning applies, for example, to the current relationship between the Soviet Union and the United States, in which neither side can realistically expect to dominate the other. The first concern is avoiding escalation of the conflict to the point of nuclear catastrophe, while at the same time engaging in ideological and economic competition. Patchen (1988) suggests that in this relationship the conditions exist for the successful use of a combined strategy of firmness and cooperation. Furthermore, the use of reciprocity in combination with a program of unilateral initiatives to get out of competitive deadlock should be effective in moving toward mutual cooperation. These assertions for eliciting cooperation from an adversary are supported by results from games research, computer simulations and the analysis of interactions between conflicting nations (see also Patchen, 1987). Thus, Patchen (1988) concludes:

> The basic message that underlies many of the specific conclusions presented in this book is that a successful policy—one that maintains the essential interests of one's own side while avoiding war—is one that combines both a measure of firmness and a measure of flexibility, both a willingness to vigorously resist coercion by an adversary and a willingness to reciprocate and sometimes to initiate concessions. By words and especially by deeds, it is important to show the adversary that one will not be exploited by also that one is ready to cooperate. The adversary should be convinced that he has little to gain by coercion and much to gain by cooperation. (p. 342)

The analysis provided by White (1984) for de-escalation in the superpower rivalry bears a strong resemblance to the ideas of both Kriesberg and Patchen. Before providing his own prescription, White discusses and dismisses three common but unpromising approaches to de-escalation and peace. An approach of military superiority without any reduction in tension is based on the diabolical enemy image and is not only unrealistic but potentially disastrous. The approach of a balance of power without tension reduction is at variance with historical analyses, which indicate that major wars occur more often in situations of escalated parity. On the other hand, a strategy that would call for arms reduction agreements without any reduction in tension has been found simply not to work when one looks at the continual failure to reach such agreements. White's alternative is elegant in terms of being both simple and powerful: In order to bring about de-escalation and prevent nuclear war, each side should pursue a combined strategy of minimal deterrence and drastic tension reduction. The idea of minimal deterrence is based on the concept of sufficiency rather than parity. It is also based on the assumption that the primary motives of both superpowers in trying to achieve superiority are in fact defensive rather than offensive. In concrete terms, minimal deterrence could be established, with each side maintaining 10 or fewer nuclear armed submarines along with the present level of conventional forces. Such a level could, of course, only be reached in conjunction with drastic tension reduction. Drawing on the work of Osgood (1962), as well as Deutsch (1983), White suggests the initiation of a constructive circular process to de-escalate the conflict. In the context of intergroup conflict, tension is seen as a blend of anger and fear involving a vicious and escalating cycle of hostile interaction and a black-and-white picture that distorts reality. One difficulty in de-escalating tension is that once a hostile interaction is established with deep suspicion and a power approach on both sides, any conciliatory moves are seen as signs of weakness and are exploited—thus the case for minimal deterrence at the same time as moves to reduce tension are initiated. The initiatives in tension reduction need to be drastic at this point because of the advanced state of the malignant process and because any minor moves would be denied or ignored. Thus, the initiatives need to be significant, genuine, well-explained, and sustained. White concludes that the right kind of deterrence is quite compatible with the right kind of tension reduction, and that in fact each reinforces the other in the movement toward de-escalation.

The prescription of minimal deterrence with drastic tension reduction is compatible with other analyses offered by White in terms of preventing nuclear war (1985) and in developing a positive approach to peace (1988). In describing the positive approach, White (1988) indicates realistic means toward peace that are inherently attractive and morally unobjectionable. Positive approaches include the drastic reduction of nuclear weapons, including the total elimination of first-strike capability; the cultivation of realistic empathy and global consciousness; the humanization of the diabolical enemy image; the drastic reduction of fear appeals; and the cultivation of realistic hope. These positive actions should be used in combination with some negative actions that communicate firmness and maintain minimal deterrence. Such actions include the retention of adequate conventional strength and approximately 5% of nuclear weapons capacity, realistic criticism of the Soviet Union, the occasional use of fear appeals, and the guarding against unrealistic hope.

White (1988) thus links the basic strategy of his approach to the activities of both decision makers and citizens in the United States. All of these actions can be seen as moving in the direction of de-escalation of the superpower conflict to a level of greater manageability and relative safety.

In a comparable manner, Deutsch (1983) offers some suggestions for de-escalating conflicts that have reached the dangerous point of potential mutual destruction through the malignant social process of escalation. Although he applies his thinking to the superpower relationship, the prescriptions are applicable in general form to any situation of escalated and protracted international conflict. The first initiative is to take steps to simply reduce the danger of the current situation. Specific steps in the superpower rivalry include an agreement on a "no-first-use policy" on nuclear weapons, to be followed by negotiations to reduce both nuclear and conventional armaments. Furthermore, both the United States and the Soviet Union should renounce the "launch-on-warning policy" and move toward a verifiable freeze, followed by a reduction of nuclear weapons to a level of approximately 300 on each side. Coincidentally, the United States should initiate a Graduated Reciprocation in Tension-reduction (GRIT) program as initially outlined by Osgood (1962). These specific moves, however, are unlikely to occur unless there is a simultaneous undoing of the malignant social process. First, it is essential to heighten consciousness of how crazy the malignant social process really is and to increase awareness of its very real dangers and enormous economic costs. Second, it is important to focus on the underlying dynamics of the process and to realize that old approaches to defense are not appropriate to the new situation brought about by the deployment of nuclear weapons. At the same time, because both superpowers take a competitive orientation to their relationship, it is important to develop fair rules for competition so that escalation and stalemate at a high level of tension are replaced by a less escalated situation. By and large, these rules would require that the superpowers not involve other nations of the world in their destructive rivalry. Ideally, the superpowers could then move beyond fair competition to the development of a cooperative framework. This would require the provision of varied and repeated opportunities for mutually beneficial interactions. Unfortunately, many see cooperation as the same as appeasement. In contrast, Deutsch (1983) offers the approach of firmness and friendliness in which cooperation plays an important role. His general conclusion, then, is highly similar to those of Kriesberg, Patchen, and White, which propose a combined strategy of firmness and conciliation as being most effective in de-escalating international conflict, specifically the potential nuclear holocaust between the Soviet Union and the United States.

Chapter 8

Social-Psychological Approaches for Resolving Intergroup and International Conflict

The problem of destructive intergroup and international conflict can be seen as the most significant issue confronting humankind, particularly in the nuclear age. The immediate question for all disciplines, including social psychology, is what unique contribution each might make to the nonviolent and constructive resolution of such conflict. As noted in Chapter 2, social psychology can be largely characterized as the study of intergroup relations and, directly or indirectly within that context, of intergroup conflict. Unfortunately, as also noted, social-psychological studies have tended to rely strongly upon concepts and methods at the individual or interpersonal levels of analysis, thus ignoring group, intergroup, and higher level variables. A similar concern is voiced by D.M. Taylor and Moghaddam (1987) in their integrative treatment of theories of intergroup relations that have a social-psychological orientation. These authors note the individualistic approach of much social-psychological work, with a consequent disregard of societal factors and a lack of relevance to collectivities such as ethnic groups. All of the theories discussed involve psychological processes at the level of individuals. Some theories, such as equity theory and relative deprivation theory, remain predominately at the individual level of analysis, while others, such as social identity theory and the 5-stage model of intergroup relations (D.M. Taylor & McKirnan, 1984), blend individual-level concepts with group-level concepts to explain the nature of intergroup relations.

Given these limitations, what is the unique orientation and emphasis of the social-psychological approach to understanding and resolving intergroup and international conflict? At the broader level of intergroup relations, D.M. Taylor and Moghaddam (1987) maintain that the "unique perspective of social psychology in the intergroup context is that the perceptions, motivations, feelings, and overt actions of individuals are studied to identify how they influence, and are affected by, relations between groups" (p. 3). With regard to intergroup conflict, the seminal work of Deutsch (1973), reviewed in Chapter 2, similarly emphasizes the phenomenology of conflict in that parties interact with reference to their motives, perceptions, cognition, and expectations of each other. Deutsch's analysis also goes beyond the individual level in noting the importance of subsystems within the parties and the social environment and in holding to the general law of reciprocity regardless of the level of the conflict. In distinguishing competitive versus cooperative relationships, and in describing the malignant social process of escalation, Deutsch further emphasizes the importance of perceptions, attitudes, orientations, and communication between the parties. Similarly, in a more recent, yet selective, treatment of the social psychology of intergroup conflict, Stroebe, Kruglanski, Bar-Tal, and Hewstone (1988) include examples of work on cognitive processes, social identity, and interaction between the parties, such as negotiation and intergroup contact. Thus, the consensus appears to have developed over time that a social-psychological approach to intergroup conflict will emphasize individual-level variables like perceptions, cognitions, expectations, and attitudes as they intertwine with group concepts, such as identity and norms, in influencing intergroup communication and interaction within a societal or global context. The eclectic model of intergroup conflict presented in Chapter 5 is an attempt to capture these types of variables and the essence of their relationships. The implication of this consensus is that a social-psychological approach to de-escalating and resolving intergroup conflict will emphasize changes in perceptions and attitudes, will be cognizant of essential elements such as group identity and the norm of reciprocity, and will look for mechanisms of communication and interaction that will help shift the underlying relationship from competition to cooperation.

Largely using a basis of humanistic values, social psychologists have articulated the conditions and principles by which different groups should be able to interrelate effectively in the societal and international context (Fisher, 1982). These principles generally emphasize the importance of each group having sufficient autonomy, identity, and power to enter into an interdependent relationship in a secure, meaningful, and respectful fashion (Fisher, 1988). For example, in discussing race relations in the United States, Pettigrew (1971) relates group autonomy to the dichotomy of living separately or together. With little autonomy, separation produces a minority ghetto, whereas living together results in mere desegregation with continuing prejudice and discrimination. With adequate autonomy, separation results in racial isolation with power (and probably continuing intergroup conflict), whereas living together produces true integration, that is, interdependence, institutional integration, and cross-group friendship. For race relations to move in the direction of true integration, social psychologists generally propose a mixed enrichment and integration strategy in which minority group development and self-determination is enhanced, while at the same time meaningful interdependence is established. The societal or international context in which this is most likely to occur is one of democratic pluralism and multiculturalism. In terms of political structure, some form of federation among ethnically different regions is compatible with true integration. The key concept in establishing these types of relationships may be that of group identity, as discussed in social identity theory (see Chapter 2) and as identified in the eclectic model (see Chapter 5). Furthermore, identity emerges as a common factor in most expressions of needs theory that attempt to articulate the compelling and universal needs of human beings that must be met for satisfactory individual and social development (see Lederer, 1980). In Chapter 7, on international conflict, the sources of protracted disputes were seen to lie in the continuing frustration of basic needs including those for security, freedom, identity, recognition of identity, and participation in identifying developmental requirements. Thus, the critical unit of analysis in protracted communal and international conflict may very well be that of the identity group, through which the expression of basic needs is articulated. The manner in which identity groups might effectively interrelate within a multicultural context thus becomes of paramount importance in developing approaches to resolving intergroup and international conflict.

Numerous countries and regions in the world today struggle with the issue of multiethnicity, that is, the necessity of meeting the basic needs of different identity groups. Differences among identity groups may be along ethnic, cultural, religious, racial, and class lines, or, as is often the case, some combination of these dimensions. Many states are turning to programs and policies of multiculturalism in order to deal effectively with these types of group differences, that is, in order to prevent or reduce intergroup conflict and to enhance the cultural quality of life for their citizens. For example, in the early 1970s, the government of Canada initiated policy and program developments in multiculturalism, sparked by the need to place French–English bilingualism in a wider and more acceptable context. A social-psychological analysis of this policy is provided by Berry (1984), who sees an explicit assumption that group development toward a collective sense of confidence will lead to ethnic tolerance among different groups. Based on this, the policy seeks to build intergroup harmony by offering programs that develop ethnic groups as vital communities and that encourage interaction and sharing among groups within a national context. The four major elements of the policy are therefore: own group maintenance and development, other group acceptance and tolerance, intergroup contact and sharing, and the learning of the two official languages to foster full participation at the national level. The policy thus actively encourages different groups to maintain their unique cultural identity while at the same time accepting and interrelating with other groups in the manner of true integration. Available research, although limited, generally indicates that the policy is congruent with the preferences and attitudes of the populace and that intergroup contact under appropriate conditions is a positive and useful experience. On the practical side, the government continues to commit considerable resources to multicultural programs and has recently enacted new legislation to strengthen its commitment to constructive intergroup relations within the national context.

The unique focus and the underlying principles of intergroup relations embodied in the social-psychological approach are seen as providing a potentially powerful analysis and overall strategy for the de-escalation and resolution of intergroup and international conflict. Founded on the humanistic value base, which calls for respecting the dignity and identity of all peoples, this approach sets the tone for a certain form of intergroup relations encompassing interdependence and true integration within national contexts. Similar relationships are prescribed across national boundaries within an environment of pluralistic internationalism. Rather than being idealistic, this approach is seen as both realistic and necessary, given its basis in universal and compelling human needs, and in group and intergroup processes that are fundamental elements of the human social experience. The challenging question, however, is how to translate this basic approach into strategies and activities that will actually de-escalate and resolve intergroup conflict in the preferred directions. Four avenues will be explored in this chapter. First, theory and research on the so-called facilitative conditions of intergroup contact will be reviewed in order to see how interaction between members of groups in conflict might lead to increased understanding and acceptance. Second, different approaches to managing conflict developed mainly in organizational settings will be analyzed in terms of their general applicability to intergroup conflict. Third, the broad strategy of Graduated Reciprocation in Tension-reduction (GRIT) will be examined for its utility, particularly in de-escalating international conflict. Fourth, and finally, the potential of the problem-solving workshop, based largely on social-psychological theory and practice, will be explored as a promising social technology for the resolution of intergroup conflict. The overarching consideration throughout is the question of how destructive intergroup and international conflict can be de-escalated and resolved toward the type of relationship envisaged by the concepts of multiculturalism and internationalism.

The Facilitative Conditions of Intergroup Contact

Well-meaning proponents of improved intergroup and international relations often look for ways to bring members of conflicting groups together on the assumption that contact will increase understanding and foster de-escalation. Unfortunately, the true picture is not so simple—interaction between members of conflicting groups may have negative, neutral, or positive outcomes depending on a host of factors. This realization has led social psychologists to search for the conditions under which intergroup contact does lead to increased understanding and decreased prejudice—the so-called facilitative conditions, which make up the contact hypothesis. According to Stephan and Brigham (1985), the contact hypothesis has always been at the heart of the study of intergroup relations; this is particularly true in the United States, where relations between black (and more recently Hispanic) and white Americans has held center stage for decades. In this context, a variety of studies from the field and the laboratory have formed the basis for a number of reviews that have articulated roughly comparable lists of the facilitative conditions of positive intergroup contact (e.g., Amir, 1969, 1976; Allport, 1954; Cook, 1970; Simpson & Yinger, 1972). Allport's classic work on the nature of prejudice still offers one of the most succinct statements of the contact hypothesis:

> Prejudice may be reduced by equal status contact between majority and minority groups in the pursuit of common goals. The effect is greatly enhanced if this contact is sanctioned by institutional supports (i.e., by law, custom, or local atmosphere), and provided it is of a sort that leads to the perception of common interests and common humanity between members of the two groups. (p. 281)

Allport's conclusions can be combined with the work of others, particularly Cook, to yield a fairly well-accepted list of the facilitative conditions (Fisher, 1982):

1. A high *acquaintance potential* by which the contact situation offers the opportunity for the participants to get to know one another as persons and not simply stereotypical members of the other group. This requires interaction that is informal, personal, and intimate as opposed to formal and impersonal.
2. *Equal status contact* in which the interaction is on a co-equal basis as opposed to the common minority group member's experience of being less than equal. Higher status on the part of minority group members is also deemed to be facilitative.
3. *Social norms*, including institutional supports that set expectations for friendly, respectful, and trusting interaction. This includes formal prescriptions and sanctions as well as informal customs and preferences.
4. A *cooperative task and reward structure*, which involves participants in functionally important activities directed toward common goals. This creates a cooperative atmosphere that is pleasant and rewarding in addition to the tangible benefits of cooperation.
5. The *characteristics of individual participants*, including moderate to high competence and mild to moderate prejudice. The competence of minority group members is particularly important in confronting the typical majority stereotype of incompetence, whereas majority group members who are less intense in their prejudice will be open enough to take in new information and to experience positive attitude change.

The contact hypothesis thus helps explain why some situations of intergroup interaction lead to positive outcomes while others do not. It has generally been supported by research covering a variety of settings and using a range of methodologies (M.B. Brewer & Kramer, 1985; Hewstone & Brown, 1986a; Stephan & Brigham, 1985). According to Stephan and Brigham, initial field studies in the United States in settings such as housing projects, the military, and industry were used by the early theorists to develop the contact hypothesis. Subsequent research followed three approaches. Laboratory studies have been useful in assessing the various conditions and in affirming that intergroup cooperation resulting in successful outcomes could improve intergroup relations (Cook, 1970, 1984; Stephan, 1985). Structured field studies have reinforced the importance of cooperation and have also indicated the significant role of status and institutional supports (Cohen, 1984; Slavin, 1985). Related empirical studies of school desegregation in the United States have generally not yielded positive results (St. John, 1975; Stephan, 1978), but such contact has often violated the facilitative conditions (Cook, 1979). Subsequent research continues to demonstrate the importance of the facilitative conditions as a determinant of the outcomes of intergroup contact (M.B. Brewer & Kramer, 1985; Stephan & Brigham, 1985).

The contact hypothesis thus provides a surface explanation of why cooperative, equal status, person-to-person interaction results in positive attitude change, whereas contact under conditions of inequality, competition, tension, and frustration does not. However, a more fundamental explanation is to be found through the concept of *intergroup anxiety* as discussed by Stephan and Stephan (1985). These authors propose a model that places intergroup anxiety, that is, anxiety stemming from contact with outgroup members, in a central position between its antecedents and consequences in situations of intergroup conflict. The anxiety itself is rooted in fear of negative psychological or behavioral consequences for the individual and fear of negative evaluations by either peers or out-group members. Antecedent conditions that affect anxiety include prior intergroup relations, intergroup cognitions (e.g., knowledge, stereotypes, ethnocentrism), and situational factors. The latter category includes at least two variables that relate to the facilitative conditions of the contact hypothesis: type of interdependence (cooperative or competitive) and relative status. These conditions, along with others such as the amount of structure and the degree of intimacy, are seen as affecting the level of intergroup anxiety during contact, which in turn leads to a number of behavioral, cognitive, and affective consequences. High levels of intergroup anxiety tend to amplify normative responses (particularly avoidance), cause both cognitive and motivational biases in information processing, intensify self-awareness, and lead to heightened emotional reactions and polarized evaluations. Thus, the model explains why intergroup contact in the absence of the facilitative conditions leads to negative attitudinal and behavioral outcomes. Moreover, the model provides a broader perspective and a more fundamental explanation of intergroup contact by linking a wide range of variables through the central construct of intergroup anxiety. One important implication is that situations of intergroup contact should be designed not just with the facilitative conditions in mind but with sensitivity to the full range of variables that affect intergroup anxiety.

A supportive yet constructively critical analysis of the contact hypothesis has been recently offered by Hewstone and Brown (1986b). These authors contend that intergroup contact embodying the facilitative conditions can improve relations, and their edited collection offers several relevant studies from different settings and countries, thus complementing the large amount of research done in the United States. However, they also build a strong case for saying that the traditional contact hypothesis is too narrow and has a number of limitations. The most significant of these is the failure to distinguish the interpersonal and intergroup levels of analysis in developing the theoretical basis for the hypothesis. The primary explanation for the positive effects of contact as articulated by Cook (1970) and extended by Pettigrew (1971) is to be found in theories about interpersonal attraction, particularly that of Newcomb (1961). Interpersonal attraction is seen to be primarily based in similarity of attitudes, and the assumption is made that intergroup contact along the lines of the facilitative conditions allows the participants to share a wider range of values and beliefs and to see that their attitudes are indeed more similar than they previously realized. Thus, the perception of increased similarity of attitudes leads to increased attraction to members of the other group, which fosters continuing positive interaction, which eventually improves the intergroup relationship. Unfortunately, the causal chain is likely to be much more complex. Hewstone and Brown (1986b) reiterate the crucial question first raised by Allport (1954) as to whether the contact is perceived in terms of intergroup relations or not. If individuals are interacting in terms of their personal identity rather than their social identity, a distinction made by Turner (1982) between the interpersonal and intergroup levels, then any changes in attraction or attitudes will be restricted to the particular individuals from the other group involved in the interaction rather than the group in general. Moreover, intergroup behavior is not likely to be affected by interpersonal relations, but by intergroup variables such as status, power, and material interdependence. Thus, Hewstone and Brown (1986b) conclude: "Unless the contact can be characterized as intergroup (i.e., between individuals as group representatives or qua group members), any such positive outcomes will be primarily cosmetic, in the sense that they will leave divisive and conflictual intergroup relations unchanged" (p. 16). A related limitation is the lack of generalization of attitude change to the groups in general, a concern identified especially by Cook, who noted that positive attitude change toward out-group participants in the contact situation may not be accompanied by attitude change toward the out-group as a whole. Cook's answer is to add a supplementary influence in the form of peer group support for nondiscriminatory behavior to the contact situation. Hewstone and Brown's prescription is that favorable contact with an out-group member must be clearly defined as an intergroup encounter, thus reinforcing previous recommendations that the out-group participants need to be seen as typical and representative members of their groups so that generalization of attitudes will take place.

The limitations of the traditional contact hypothesis are perhaps not surprising when one considers the post-World War II, American context in which it arose. According to Pettigrew (1986), the basic idea that contact would be beneficial was founded on three assumptions of the American human relations movement: (a) the fundamental problem of intergroup conflict is individual prejudice, (b) prejudice is largely a psychological problem rooted in gross ignorance about out-groups, and (c) the remedy is education to change attitudes, which will in turn alter behavior. Accordingly, the movement stimulated a variety of intergroup contacts that provided the settings for many of the initial studies of the contact hypothesis. Pettigrew maintains that the broad consensus that emerged from this early work remains at the core of the contact hypothesis and that the best of this work anticipated many of the later criticisms and qualifications. At the same time, approximately four decades of social research have now provided the following counterpoints to the assumptions of the human relations movement: (a) institutional discrimination is at the core of the problem of intergroup conflict rather than individual prejudice, which while important is not fundamental; (b) prejudice is also based in a variety of cognitive processes involving misperception and stereotyping and is embedded in the culture of society; and (c) education is a woefully insufficient remedy in contrast to institutional change requiring new intergroup behavior to reshape intergroup attitudes. Pettigrew also points out that the black American situation, which defines one pole of the relationship on which so much research has been conducted, is unique in the world and therefore only amenable to very limited generalization. It is therefore very valuable to see the American research complemented and extended by contemporary studies from Israel, West Germany, Northern Ireland, Quebec, South Africa, and great Britain (See Hewstone & Brown, 1986a).

Some of the practical limitations of the contact hypothesis can be overcome by the addition of augmenting factors, four of which are discussed by Hewstone and Brown

(1986b). These include the use of superordinate goals to reinforce the positive effects of contact, intergroup cooperation to increase communication and trust, crosscutting social categories to reduce polarization, and manipulating expectation states to achieve perceived equal status prior to interaction. Some of these factors, such as cooperation, actually overlap with the facilitative conditions themselves, while at the same time they may serve a reinforcing function prior to or after the intergroup contact.

The concept of superordinate goal goes back to the camp studies by Sherif and his colleagues (see Chapter 2) in which a series of common goals that could only be achieved through intergroup cooperation were instituted by the experimenters to de-escalate the conflict. Sherif (1966) maintains that superordinate goals exist in any intergroup conflict and can be identified through open communication and productive confrontation between the parties. The social-psychological literature on conflict is generally receptive to the idea of superordinate goals, but assessments of their potential effectiveness in de-escalating conflict vary. Diab (1970), for example, provides a cross-cultural replication of Sherif's results and argues in a later work (Diab, 1978) that superordinate goals produced by intergroup conflict are a necessary prerequisite for the implementation of measures to reduce intergroup hostility. Superordinate goals exist in the form of threats to the status quo by which dominant groups come to realize that peaceful measures for dealing with the intergroup conflict must be instituted. However, as noted by Condor and Brown (1988), the formulation of superordinate goals within the context of an unequal power conflict may simply seek to subordinate the interests of minority groups to the "superordinate" goal of national unity or whatever. In any event, Hewstone and Brown (1986b) cite a number of critics of Sherif's work who point out that when the superordinate goals were finally introduced in the camp studies, the intergroup conflict had virtually run its course. The further reduction of the conflict may have been due to the creation of a new combined group in place of the two conflicting groups and not to the effect of the superordinate goals. In addition, the transitory nature of the camp groups presents a more malleable situation than the long-standing differences and opposing identities that exist in protracted social conflict in the real world. Within organizational settings, Blake, Shepard, and Mouton (1964) also raise questions about the efficacy of superordinate goals. They point out that superordinate goals in the form of threat from a common enemy may induce cooperation between conflicting factions, but only until the enemy is dealt with and the threat removed. At that point, the old differences reemerge and the conflict returns to its previous level of hostility. Blake, Shepard, and Mouton also maintain that superordinate goals that are imposed by higher management can actually lead to an intensification of intergroup competition and conflict because each group attempts to protect its own operations and expects the other to make the greatest contribution to the attainment of the superordinate goal. In a somewhat related vein, Hewstone and Brown (1986b) discuss more recent experimental work that indicates that superordinate goals may be effective when the groups involved have clearly differentiated roles or tasks rather than similar ones in achieving their shared objectives. Thus, the condition of intergroup distinctiveness may be important. In sum, the role that superordinate goals may play as a form of functional cooperation in intergroup contact and the de-escalation of intergroup conflict awaits further clarification before Sherif's original proposition can be adequately evaluated.

Based on all these various considerations, Hewstone and Brown (1986b) propose a new theoretical framework (see Figure 8-1) that addresses the limitations previously identified and that also considers the role of cognitive factors in intergroup contact. Their framework is clearly situated at the intergroup rather than interpersonal level and assumes that groups will maintain their social identity while establishing mutual intergroup differentiation, recognizing both similarities and differences as well as superiorities and inferiorities. This is consistent with Taylor and Simard's (1979) proposition that groups may hold socially desirable stereotypes of each other while maintaining their cultural distinctiveness. Thus, Hewstone and Brown's (1986b) framework is cognizant of wider social factors and calls for intergroup interaction in which out-group participants are seen as typical, thereby allowing for a focus on both similarities and differences, and leading to positive attitude change that is generalized to other members of the outgroup.

What, then, are the implications of theory and research on intergroup contact for the de-escalation and resolution of intergroup and international conflict? In the conceptual vein, it is clear that we need both a "theory of practice" and a "theory of understanding." The initial facilitative conditions inform a theory of practice because they provide indications of how to design situations of intergroup contact for positive attitude change. The model of intergroup anxiety presented by Stephan and Stephan (1985) and the broader framework provided by Hewstone and Brown (1986b) contribute toward a theory of understanding in that they help explain underlying principles such as how wider social factors affect intergroup anxiety and how cognitive processes mediate the outcomes of contact. Ideally of course, practice is based on theoretical understanding so that situations of contact can be designed whenever possible to take into account the range of variables that will affect intergroup anxiety and the eventual outcomes. In this process, it is essential to assure that contact is perceived to be at the intergroup level and that both similarities and differences are acknowledged. It is also essential to realize that most contact in situations of intergroup and international conflict involves cultural differences. Thus, as Brislin (1978) points out, it is important to understand the social-psychological processes involved in intercultural relations and to design contact programs for increasing cultural awareness with these in mind. Based on relevant theory and research, Brislin (1981) and others have been developing specific practice guidelines for increasing the effectiveness of intercultural interaction. These guidelines, together with the facilitative conditions within an adequately broad theoretical framework, should be considered when arranging all forms of intergroup contact, whether through tourism, exchange programs, development activities, recreational programs, or social interaction and whether in educational, workplace, or residential settings. This implication is especially important in designing programs that have the objectives of changing attitudes in a more realistic and thereby positive direction and of building more cooperative orientations to the relationship with the ultimate goal of de-escalating and resolving the intergroup conflict. Thus, the approach of

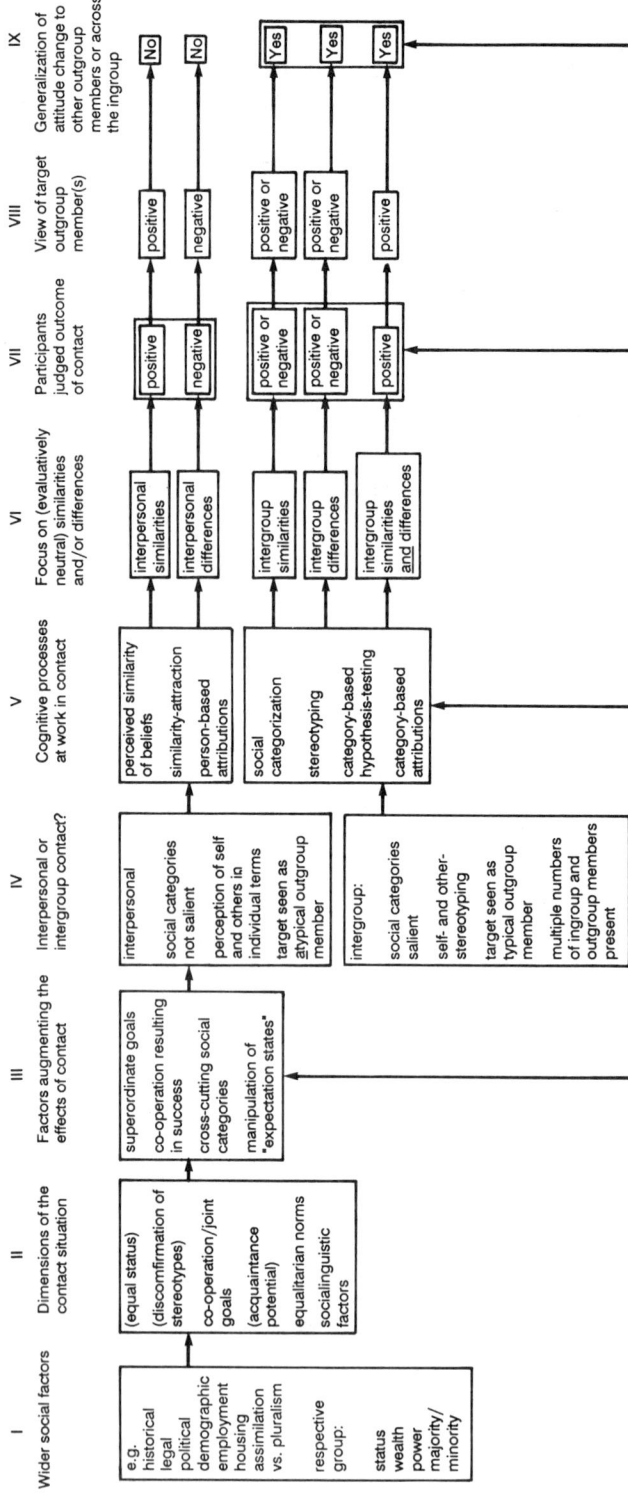

Figure 8-1. A model of intergroup contact: Hewstone and Brown (1986b). Reprinted with permission.

problem-solving workshops (to be discussed later), which brings together informal representatives of groups engaged in destructive conflict, needs to be highly cognizant of the facilitative conditions and related considerations. In terms of the eclectic model described in Chapter 5, these elements can affect the quality of intergroup interaction in ways that will facilitate de-escalation and dispute resolution.

Approaches to Managing and Resolving Conflict

How a party approaches conflict depends initially on the assumptions made regarding the basic nature of conflict, in particular, the degree to which it is seen as an objective or subjective phenomenon. Objective assumptions see conflict as rooted in real differences of interest, usually involving scarce resources such as territory. These differences exist irrespective of the perceptions, attitudes, values, etc. of the parties, and can only be managed through some division of the resources, whether through compromise or "winner take all." A subjective approach to conflict does not deny real differences of interest but holds that perceptions, preferences, evaluations, etc., especially over a period of time, render conflict a subjective phenomenon (Mitchell, 1981b). Thus, it is the parties' orientations to the objective difference that determine whether a conflict exists at any point in time (Burton, 1972). This is not to deny the potential importance of so-called latent conflict, especially that based on inequality, which parties may not be conscious of or concerned about and which may become manifest at some future point. In addition, there are a number of more specific arguments against a purely objectivist view of conflict (Mitchell, 1981b): Conflict may be over values that are not in short supply; through collaboration the amount of the valued commodity may be increased; increased awareness of the cost of continued conflict or of the importance of other goals may reduce the relative value of the disputed goal; and a redefinition of the situation may transform it into one where both parties gain. As stated earlier, social psychologists generally see conflict as an interplay among objective and subjective factors, and place emphasis on the process of how the conflict develops, escalates, and is managed or resolved. Whereas objectivists maintain that conflict can only be managed in the sense of compromise or continuing negotiation, social psychologists join with other subjectivists in holding that many conflicts are amenable to resolution, in the sense that mutually acceptable and beneficial outcomes can be found that will be self-sustaining in the long run. Furthermore, a fundamental point of the social-psychological analysis is that the approach adopted toward a conflict will in part determine the process and outcomes that accrue. Through mechanisms such as the norm of reciprocity and the self-fulfilling prophecy, the approach, strategies, and behavior of the parties will affect both the nature and the intensity of the conflict. Therefore, it is extremely important to develop the widest possible picture of alternative approaches for dealing with conflict and their typical effects on both process and outcomes.

In working to understand alternative approaches, social psychologists and others first determined the importance of competitive versus cooperative orientations,

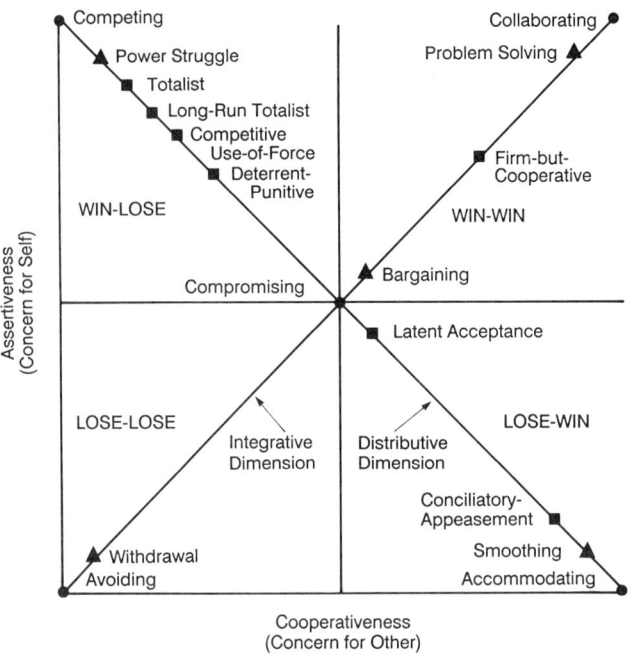

- ● Interpersonal styles after Blake & Mouton (1964) and Thomas (1976).
- ▲ Intergroup approaches after Blake, Shepard, & Mouton (1964).
- ■ Inter-nation strategies after Kaplowitz (1984).

Figure 8-2. A two-dimensional model of conflict management. After Blake and Mouton (1964) and Thomas (1976). Reprinted with permission by John Wiley & Sons, Inc.

such as those highlighted in the work of Deutsch (see Chapter 2). However, an extremely important realization occurred, first in the work of Blake and Mouton (1964) on managerial behavior, that two dimensions were required to adequately describe conflict approaches or styles. As extended by Thomas (1976), these two dimensions are (a) assertiveness or concern for self and (b) cooperativeness or concern for other. Assuming that these dimensions are independent, placing them at right angles produces a two-dimensional space in which a variety of approaches to handling conflict can be placed (see Figure 8-2). After identifying basic approaches that correspond to the quadrants of the space, typologies of styles at the interpersonal, intergroup, and international levels will be described with reference to Figure 8-2.

Combinations of low and high assertiveness with low and high cooperativeness produce four basic approaches to conflict which are labeled in the respective quadrants as win–lose, lose–lose, lose–win, and win–win, following the terminology of Blake, Shepard, and Mouton (1964) and Filley (1975). The win–lose approach is based on objectivist assumptions about the "fixed-pie" nature of scarce, disputed resources. Because what one party gains the other loses, the appropriate behavior is to defeat the other party at all costs, thereby gaining full acquisition of the desired resource. This behavior is typically accompanied by the full range of ethnocentric attitudes and justifications, and usually leads to victory for one party and defeat for the other or to a stalemate of continual tension. The lose–lose approach assumes at the low end that avoidance of conflict is more desirable than confrontation, and at the high end, that compromising for half a loaf is the best possible or least risky outcome. This results in behaviors such as ignoring differences, withdrawing from the scene, or agreeing to the simplest of compromises without exploring integrative alternatives. In common with the win–lose approach, there is usually a strong we–they distinction and little potential of improving the relationship through dealing with the conflict. The lose–win approach is essentially the flip side of the win–lose orientation and is based on the same assumptions about conflict. However, for whatever reasons, one party chooses to accede to the demands of the other. The emphasis may be on a quick solution that limits the damage to the relationship that open and sustained warfare might bring. The win–win approach is based on subjectivist assumptions about the malleability and tractability of conflict. The conflict is perceived as a mutual problem to be approached through conscious, systematic, joint problem solving. Thus, the needs and constraints of both parties must be examined in detail with the hope that alternative and creative outcomes can be found. Attitudes of respect and trust, as opposed to ethnocentrism, are useful in facilitating solutions that also work to improve the wider relationship between the parties.

At the interpersonal level, the two-dimensional space yields a model comprising five conflict management styles at the four corners and at the center point (Blake & Mouton, 1964; Thomas, 1976; Thomas & Kilmann, 1974). Competing is highly assertive but uncooperative, and involves one party pursuing its interests potentially at the complete expense of the other. Avoiding is low on both assertiveness and cooperativeness and indicates a lack of significant interest in the concerns of either party. Accommodating is high on cooperativeness but low on assertiveness wherein one party sacrifices its interests in order to satisfy those of the other. Compromising is intermediate on both dimensions and entails a search for an acceptable yet expedient solution. Collaborating, which is high on both dimensions, demonstrates a concern for the self and a concern for the other and is directed toward the goal of mutual satisfaction of interests. The two-dimensional space also lends itself to the depiction of two other dimensions that are very important in conflict resolution: the distributive and integrative ones (Thomas, 1976). The former runs from the competing position to the accommodating one and indicates the division of resources and satisfaction between the two parties; thus it relates to the win–lose nature of conflict. The integrative dimension runs from the avoiding corner to the collaborative one and represents the total extent of resources and satisfaction available to both parties; thus it relates to the win–win element of conflict. Hence, nonextreme approaches to conflict handling can be placed on these dimensions within the space to indicate the degree to which they foster distribution or integration in addition to

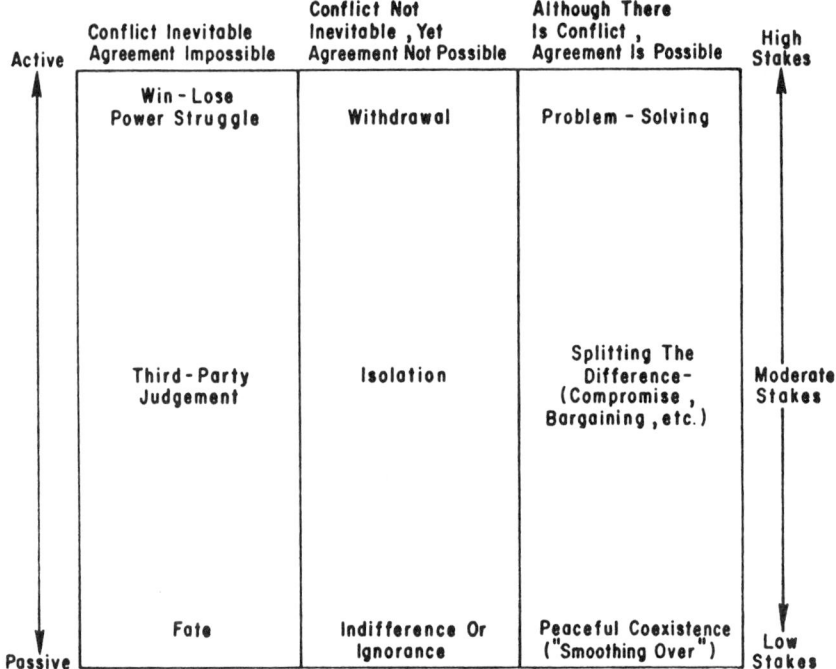

Figure 8-3. A framework for understanding intergroup conflict: Blake, Shepard, and Mouton (1964). Reprinted with permission.

assertiveness and cooperation. Research on the two-dimensional model of conflict generally supports its validity, links with some success different personality motives to particular styles, and demonstrates the positive effects of collaborating in interpersonal relations (see, for example, Burke, 1970; Kilmann & Thomas, 1977; Ruble & Thomas, 1976). In addition, work at the interpersonal level is potentially useful at higher levels because it is conceptually instructive and yields results on process and outcomes, the generalizability of which deserves to be tested.

At the intergroup level, the classic work of Blake, Shepard, and Mouton (1964) on intergroup conflict in industry still stands as an elegant exposition of the alternative approaches that are typically used for handling conflict between interdependent groups in a social system. Drawing on their combined research and consulting experience, these social psychologists developed a framework for understanding intergroup conflict based on the assumptions that the parties make in regard to disagreements (see Figure 8-3). When the parties assume that disagreement is inevitable and permanent, and therefore that agreement is impossible, it follows that the dispute must be resolved totally in favor of one party or the other. If the stakes are high, the approach of the parties will be to engage in a win–lose power struggle to the point where one party capitulates. With moderate stakes, the parties may turn to a third party for an arbitrated judgment; when the stakes are low they may decide not to determine the outcome and simply wait for fate to intervene in some fashion. These approaches also vary on an active–passive dimension as shown in Figure 8-3. If the parties assume that disagreement is not inevitable, but that neither is agreement possible, they perceive that conflict can be avoided because interdependence is not necessary. Thus, depending on the stakes, one or both of the parties may withdraw from the scene, maintain indifference regarding the dispute, or isolate itself from the relationship. In the third and final situation, the parties assume that although there is conflict, agreement is possible and therefore interdependence is to be maintained. Therefore, a way to resolve the dispute must be found. With low stakes, the parties are likely to smooth the difference over, for example, by making reference to broad common goals and downplaying the issue. With moderate stakes, the parties are likely to enter into bargaining to reach a compromise that meets both parties' needs to an acceptable degree. However, with high stakes compromise will not be acceptable, and the parties will be attracted to genuine problem solving to find a creative resolution of the fundamental points of difference. Again, these different approaches can also be placed meaningfully on the active–passive dimension. Most of the approaches identified by Blake, Shepard, and Mouton (1964) lend themselves to depiction on the two-dimensional space in Figure 8-2. Arbitration and fate options are not depicted, because they involve outside parties; neither are isolation and indifference, because they are equivalent to withdrawal in terms of the underlying dimensions of assertiveness and cooperativeness. That leaves five of the approaches at the intergroup level, all of which correspond quite closely to those at the interpersonal level, thus indicating their general applicability within interdependent social relationships.

At the international level, Kaplowitz (1984) presents a comprehensive analysis of different conflict strategies and their reciprocal effects in terms of how the attitudes and behaviors of each party affect the other. He regards his analysis as psychopolitical in reference to how psychological, social-psychological, and cultural factors influence political behavior. He notes that although an interactionist approach to international conflict has been suggested by social psychologists such as Deutsch (1973) and Kelman (1965), the vast majority of relevant studies involve laboratory games rather than systematic studies of actual internation interaction. However, based on the few that do exist, as well as on other treatments, Kaplowitz is able to develop an initial theory that links the various strategies to the parties' beliefs about conflict, their self-images, and their perceptions of each other (see Table 8-1). It is then possible to examine the reciprocal interaction effects of the different strategies under differing conditions of power distribution between the parties.

Kaplowitz (1984) defines conflict orientations as "dispositions to achieve particular aims and to act in particular ways toward adversaries," whereas conflict strategies are "the plans and actions designed to achieve these aims" (p. 375). National self-images and perceptions of enemies, which are relatively stable and often common to leaders and elites, are seen to determine conflict orientations, which in interaction with situational variables give rise to conflict strategies. The influence of the strategy on the adversary depends on how it affects the adversary's self-image and perceptions of the enemy, as well as on the adversary's gains and losses. Within this

Table 8-1. International Conflict Strategies, Images, Beliefs, and Outcomes

Strategies/ orientations	Self-Images	Perceptions of the enemy	The nature of IR	Beliefs about conflict				Conflict outcomes
				Sources of conflict	Likelihood of military conflict	Value of military conflict	
Totalism	Highly grandiose manifest, and negative underlying	Highly negative	Extremely conflictual	Unalterable	Inevitable	Valuable	Only total victory acceptable
Long-run totalism	Grandiose manifest, and negative underlying	Highly negative[a]	Highly conflictual	Unalterable	Inevitable	Ultimately valuable	Ultimately, only total victory acceptable
Latent acceptance of the enemy	Negative	Highly negative to negative[b]	Mixed; emphasis on conflictual	Unalterable	Inevitable	Mixed; emphasis on valuable	Manifest—same as above; Latent—same as below
Competitive use-of-force	Positive or ambivalent	Negative	Mixed; emphasis on conflictual	Mixed; emphasis on unalterable	Highly probable	Mixed; emphasis on valuable	Zero-sum—what one wins, the other loses
Deterrent-punitive	Positive or ambivalent	Negative	Mixed; emphasis on conflictual	Mixed; emphasis on unalterable	Mixed; somewhat probable; can be avoided	Mixed; valuable and destructive	Mixed; emphasis on zero-sum
Firm-but-cooperative	Positive or ambivalent	Mixed; positive and negative	Mixed; harmonious and conflictual	Mixed; emphasis on alterable	Mixed; likely can be avoided	Mixed; emphasis on destructive	Mixed; emphasis on mutual interests
Conciliatory-appeasement	Negative or ambivalent	Emphasis on positive	Harmonious	Alterable	Avoidable	Totally destructive	Mutual and convergent interests

[a] With belief that it cannot be defeated in short-run.
[b] With expectation that it cannot be totally defeated.
Source: Kaplowitz (1984). Reprinted with permission.

context, Kaplowitz defines seven conflict strategies and their reciprocal effects in various combinations. The *totalist strategy* aims for a complete victory with regard to basic issues and therefore is directed toward the total elimination or subordination of the other party. The means to achieve this are almost exclusively negative, that is, the use of threats and punishments. An important variation is the *long-run totalist strategy*, in which the aims are approached gradually and interim agreements to consolidate specific advances are acceptable. Total victory remains the ultimate goal, even though it must be approached in stages. The *competitive-use-of-force* and *deterrent-punitive strategies* are both aimed at maximizing gains regardless of losses to the other party, but are not locked into a need for total victory. In the former, the goal is to win as much as possible, whereas in the latter, the emphasis is on preventing the adversary from taking all that it can. Both strategies attempt to demand or force certain behaviors through the use of threats and coercion. Within that context, negotiation may be used to consolidate gains or stabilize balances. The *firm-but-cooperative strategy* aims to achieve mutually satisfying resolutions by according some measure of legitimacy to the adversary's claims and assuming this may eventually be reciprocated. Attempts are made to elicit rather than to force change in the adversary's behavior, and the emphasis is on promises and rewards while at the same time the capability for negative sanctions in maintained. This not only communicates the possibilities for cooperation, but also the potential costs of belligerence. The *conciliatory strategy* emphasizes the satisfaction of the other party and the downplaying or ignoring of own needs. Positive means of influence, in the form of promises and rewards, are used to the exclusion of negative sanctions. A final strategy, which is somewhat subtle, is the *latent acceptance of enemies strategy*, which involves a denial of anything less than total victory but which shows evidence of expecting the enemy cannot be defeated and of resignation to some form of coexistence. This occurs when one party becomes convinced of the other's staying power. However, the means of influence continue to emphasize threats and punishments because the possibility of cooperation and compromise is not openly acknowledged.

Having delineated a variety of strategies for approaching international conflict, Kaplowitz (1984) next considers the reciprocal interaction effects when different combinations of strategies are paired together. He presents hypotheses for all pairings of strategies with three different variations depending on the relative power of the parties. Concern here will be restricted to the situation of equal power, which is the most likely to lead to escalation and destructive outcomes. Also, not all combinations will be considered, but only those that have the most important implications for international relations in general.

A pairing of totalist strategies leads understandably to a mutually reinforcing escalation, as predicted by general conflict theory. Furthermore, Kaplowitz contends that such actors often are pleased with evidence of totalism on the other side because it adds to the legitimacy of their own approach! Mutual totalism feeds each party's sense of self-righteousness, determination, and ruthlessness, thus adding to the intransigence of the conflict. Parties that adopt a totalist or long-run totalist strategy are, of course, the most difficult and dangerous actors in international affairs. The key question is therefore how to respond to such actors in ways that might eventually influence their behavior in positive directions, that is, away from totalism to some degree of compromise and cooperation. The answer seems to lie in the application of the competitive-use-of-force and deterrent-punitive strategies. When paired with the totalist strategy, both of these strategies have the potential effect of moving the totalist strategy toward a long-run totalist strategy, and the long-run totalist strategy toward one of latent acceptance. These outcomes may not be ideal, but are at least steps in the right direction, that is, toward de-escalation and the eventual building of cooperative relationships. At the same time, the effect on the more cooperative party (using the competitive or deterrent strategy) is to reinforce its approach or, in some cases, to move a deterrent-punitive strategy toward a competitive-use-of-force one. Kaplowitz thus concludes that traditional strategies of competition and deterrence are the most useful in dealing with totalist adversaries. A firm-but-cooperative strategy in response to totalism or long-run totalism is predicted to lead to an intensification of these strategies because the totalist adversary is likely to interpret any cooperation as a sign of weakness. It is interesting to note that Kaplowitz's prediction in this regard appears to be contradictory to those of some other theorists, such as Patchen (1988), White (1984), and Deutsch (1983), who put greater faith in a firm-but-cooperative approach (see Chapter 7). One must also ask how many totalist actors there actually are in the world today and raise the related possibility that misperceptions of an adversary as totalist are to be expected, as are the self-fulfilling prophecies to which they can give rise. In any event, the perplexing difficulty of attempting to deal with a genuinely totalist adversary cannot be denied. A response of using a conciliatory strategy does not fare well in Kaplowitz's analysis either, because it tends to reinforce totalism even more than the firm-but-cooperative strategy. Furthermore, this combination tends to pull the conciliatory party in the direction of a deterrent-punitive strategy. A similar outcome accrues when the conciliatory strategy is paired with the latent strategy, that is, the latent party tends to move toward long-run totalism while the conciliatory party shifts toward deterrence or a firm-but-cooperative strategy. In the pairings of competitive and deterrent strategies with each other, the predicted escalatory effects are similar to those embodied in general conflict theory. Such confrontations are mutually reinforcing and fragile over the long run, as indicated, for example, by data showing that arms races generally tend to be associated with the outbreak of war rather than the maintenance of peace (see Chapter 7). In contrast, a firm-but-cooperative strategy in response to a competitive or deterrent one is predicted to have salutary effects and to lead to conflict resolution, according to Kaplowitz's analysis. This strategy has the potential of moving both the competitive or deterrent strategies toward a firm-but-cooperative one, because the cooperative element has the effect of easing the concerns regarding security held by the other party, while at the same time their disposition toward aggression is dissuaded. Kaplowitz suggests that this combination is particularly important because it provides a way of emerging out of the deterrence dilemma over the long run, a point more or less echoed by Patchen (1988) and others (see Chapter 7).

Kaplowitz (1984) thus provides a useful analysis that shows some complementarily to discussions of approaches to conflict at the intergroup and interpersonal levels. One interesting comparison, however, is that the international strategies are predominantly placed on the distributive dimension in Figure 8-2. The implication is that the international scene tends to evidence more variations in win–lose approaches based on the fixed-pie assumption, with perhaps less attention to possibilities on the integrative dimension. This is countered by the observation that negotiation, always with the chance of integrative solutions, is a very common method of conflict management at the international level. Also, the absence of an identified lose–lose approach may simply indicate that it is relatively difficult to withdraw, isolate, or otherwise avoid conflict in global interaction. Nonetheless, the predominance of win–lose approaches is mirrored by the emphasis on contentious tactics at the international level and is indicative of the normative supremacy of power politics in both theory and practice. This use of negative sanctions, particularly threats and punishments, in attempts to compel or deter the adversary is much more frequent in Kaplowitz's framework than is the use of positive influencers such as promises and rewards. The latter would be increased by the more frequent use of integrative strategies such as the firm-but-cooperative strategy. It is possible that this development will be encouraged by the adoption of a *contingency approach* to dealing with conflict at the international and intergroup levels, similar to that which is increasingly being advocated at the interpersonal level (Thomas & Kilmann, 1974; Taft, 1987). While basically supportive of collaboration, the contingency approach suggests that the conflict management style adopted should depend on the characteristics of the situation as well as the priorities of the initiating party. Thus, for example, when the issue is seen as minor, but the other party is highly concerned, accommodation is the style of choice. When the issue is moderate and a quick, expedient solution is required, compromise makes most sense. Sharply differing value positions that are not amenable to integration may be shifted toward peaceful coexistence through compromise and accommodation. The contingency approach is further extended through the idea of *sequencing* conflict styles, that is, initiating or responding with one style until certain effects are obtained or a lack of success is evident, and then continuing the interaction with another style. Thus, for example, a competing stance may need to be met with a competing stance before collaboration can then be effective in moving toward win–win outcomes. These types of appealing possibilities are highlighted in Kaplowitz's discussion when he concludes that the design of internation strategies should be shaped to particular types of adversaries and when he suggests that an actor may employ various combinations of strategies in sequence.

These considerations illustrate the general need to inject greater complexity and flexibility into the discussion and development of approaches to managing conflict at the intergroup and international levels. A social-psychological analysis has much to offer such developments because it inherently adopts an interactionist perspective, within which reciprocity is seen as a key element. These points will become clearer in the following sections on Graduated Reciprocation in Tension-reduction and on problem-solving workshops — two social-psychological methods for the de-escalation and resolution of intergroup and international conflict.

The GRIT Strategy for De-Escalating Conflict

In the early 1960s, psychologist Charles Osgood (1962) and sociologist Amitai Etzioni (1962) independently brought forward proposals for the systematic de-escalation of the intense and dangerous conflict between the superpowers. Etzioni's plan was termed "gradualism," whereas Osgood's was entitled "Graduated Reciprocation in Tension-reduction," also referred to as "Graduated and Reciprocated Initiatives in Tension-reduction" and commonly referred to as GRIT, an acronym Osgood liked because it indicated that it takes greater courage and resolve to be conciliatory in an intense conflict than it does to be continuously belligerent. These plans were proposed as alternatives to the politically unacceptable one of unilateral disarmament, and assumed that because the arms race had built up little by little over many years, a systematic, step-by-step process would be required to throw it into reverse, so to speak. The goal of GRIT is to reduce tension and mistrust while maintaining an adequate deterrent, to the point where negotiation and other conflict resolution methods will have a greater chance of success. The major components of the GRIT strategy are simple and straightforward (Fisher, 1982). A series of unilateral moves to reduce tension are planned and announced, and made open to international verification. These steps are graduated from lower risk moves to those that are more significant and risky. At some specified point, however, the moves must result in some form of reciprocation by the adversary in order for them to continue. The initiatives are clearly communicated and the adversary is given ample time to reciprocate. At the same time, an adequate deterrent is maintained so that the initiating party is not overly vulnerable. Evidence for the potential utility of GRIT comes from the real world of international diplomacy, from a simulation of international conflict, and from experiments using laboratory games. While each of these sources provides encouraging support for GRIT, the paucity of data and the limitations of the methodology require a sense of cautious optimism.

The clearest real-world example of attempted implementation of GRIT is the so-called Kennedy Experiment described by Etzioni (1967). In June of 1963, President John Kennedy gave his "strategy of peace" speech, in which he called attention to the danger of nuclear war, took a conciliatory tone toward the Soviet Union, and asked the American people to reexamine their cold war attitudes and to support policies that encouraged genuine peace. He also announced a unilateral reduction in tension and an American halt to nuclear tests in the atmosphere, and indicated that the United States would not resume testing unless another country did so first. The Soviet Union reciprocated immediately, publishing Kennedy's speech in *Izvestia* and agreeing to the United States' request to send United Nations observers to war-torn Yemen, a move they had previously blocked. The next American initiative was to agree to restore full recognition of the Hungarian delegation at the United Nations. Two days after Kennedy's speech, the Soviet leader, Nikita Khrushchev, welcomed the initiative and announced that the production of strategic bombers had been stopped. Shortly thereafter, the Soviets agreed to the implementation of the "hot line" and announced the continued abeyance of atmospheric nuclear tests, leading to the signing of the test ban treaty, which had been stalled for some time. For its part, the United States approved the first sales of wheat to the Soviet Union and agreed to the opening of new consulates in both countries. Additional overtures for mutual cooperation, such as joint space efforts, were made by both sides, but unfortunately the overall peace initiative ended in late 1963. A number of reasons for this have been identified, including the influence of American domestic politics, with its ethnocentric concern about being soft on communism; the escalation of the Vietnam War; and the tragic assassination of John Kennedy in November. Nonetheless, there was a significant, if fleeting, reduction in tension between the superpowers and the GRIT strategy can be seen as receiving some validation from the experience. However, as Etzioni (1967) points out, the implementation was not entirely a full and genuine instance of GRIT: The United States was far ahead of the Soviet Union in atmospheric testing, the Soviet bombers were close to being discontinued, and because of regulatory barriers the eventual sale of wheat was only a fraction of that approved. Thus, a number of the moves were lower risk than might appear at first, and the rhetoric of some appears to have outdistanced the ultimate reality.

Unfortunately, there are only piecemeal and limited instances of other diplomatic activity that might be construed as compatible with the GRIT strategy. For example, in 1979, the Soviet leader, Leonid Brezhnev, brought forward a proposal for the reduction of Soviet forces in Eastern Europe, including the gradual pullback of troops and tanks and a cut in the number of nuclear missiles (Osgood, 1979). The moves carried the condition that there would be no increase in NATO forces, and the expectation of further reciprocation was communicated. However, the United States and its NATO allies did not respond and the initiative died. Interestingly enough, the reality of such moves has now reemerged in late 1988 with Mikhail Gorbachev's announcement of unilateral and significant reductions in Soviet conventional forces in Eastern Europe, coupled with an indication that Western responses in some form would be welcomed. This initiative, like the earlier one, follows the Soviet approach of gradualism, termed "mutual example," and may have the effects of replicating the reduction of tension that occurred during the Kennedy experiment and of providing further real-world support for GRIT. From an American perspective, a useful illustration of how GRIT might be implemented in the current context of American-Soviet relations is provided by Granberg (1978). His prescription includes a detailed series of conciliatory moves, which, with some updating, provide a concrete sense of how the strategy could be used to hopefully begin de-escalation of the superpower rivalry.

The support for GRIT based on conflict simulations is about as meager as its implementations in the real world. In fact, there appears to be only one clear and comprehensive assessment through simulation—that provided by Crow (1963) using the Inter-Nation Simulation created by Guetzkow and his colleagues (1963). The Inter-Nation Simulation is a complex analog of international relations in which participants, often graduate students, play the leading decision makers of countries engaging in the essential business of global politics. The simulation usually runs over 12 to 15 sessions in excess of 1 hour each, with each country being represented by three decision makers who have available certain resources with which to produce economic and military values through interaction with other countries' decision makers. The production of values has consequences for standard of living and national security, which in turn have consequences for orderly change or revolution, including the retention or loss of office for the decision makers. The simulation utilized by Crow involved 13 sessions in which a confederate serving as the main decision maker of a major country moved to maintain a hostile status quo and to escalate conflict between two blocs of countries over the first 7 sessions. This was accomplished by building up military capability and solidifying an alliance with a friendly country to the point of supplying it with nuclear capability. These activities resulted in an increasing tension level, as assessed by participant perceptions of the likelihood of war, the degree of trust among nations, etc., which accelerated sharply with the move toward nuclear proliferation. At this point, the confederate decision maker introduced GRIT, following the steps outlined by Osgood (1962) with appropriate adaptation to the Inter-Nation Simulation. The immediate response of the primary adversary was one of suspicion and continued hostility, but the moves were eventually reciprocated and the tension level dropped to its lowest level by the end of the simulation. Crow emphasizes the dramatic nature of this turnaround in relations as well as the utility of the Inter-Nation Simulation for studying strategic doctrines. Given this convincing demonstration, it is unfortunate that little further work has been done using simulations to assess GRIT. The Intergroup Conflict Simulation described in Chapter 6 would have some utility in this regard, with the potential limitations that its complexity and intensity may not be high enough to provide an adequate test.

Most of the evidence for the efficacy of GRIT comes from studies utilizing laboratory games, especially the Prisoner's Dilemma—a mixed-motive game involving two players in simultaneous choices of competition or cooperation over a number of trials. Although this methodology embodies very limited external validity, it does provide for studies breaking the GRIT strategy down into various components to see which have the predicted effects within this highly simplified and yet essential representation of two-party conflict. Lindskold (1986), after providing an overview of the strategy and the nonexperimental evidence, presents the experimental support for GRIT, much of which has been produced by himself and his colleagues (e.g., Lindskold, 1978, 1979; Lindskold & Collins, 1978; Lindskold & Finch, 1981; Lindskold, Walters, & Koutsourais, 1983). Lindskold's (1986) treatment is organized by breaking the GRIT strategy down into its components and then discussing the experimental evidence supporting each point. What follows is a brief summary of his analysis.

1. A general statement of intention to reduce tension is used to set the atmosphere and to indicate the advantages of reciprocating. Numerous studies demonstrate that cooperative instructions to game players increase the rate of cooperative moves. More specifically, studies by Lindskold and his colleagues have shown that messages between players signaling conciliatory intentions, particularly those not requiring

prior commitment, tend to increase cooperation. Lindskold concludes that conciliatory intentions should be shared in advance and linked to mutual benefits for maximum effect.

2. Each unilateral initiative is announced in advance and identified as part of the general strategy. Many studies using the Prisoner's Dilemma indicate that increased communication increases cooperation. (In fact, with completely open communication, the game breaks down entirely as players cooperate for maximum mutual benefit.) In relation to GRIT, Lindskold's initial work indicated that it is more effective to announce explicitly each conciliatory move, especially after having made the general announcement of intent. However, a later study by Lindskold, Han, and Betz (1986) lends even more support to the opening announcement as both necessary and sufficient, whereas specific announcements added nothing to GRIT's effectiveness, at least within the simple context of the Prisoner's Dilemma.

3. Each announcement invites reciprocation in some form. Although there is little direct experimental evidence for this component, indications are that there is a fine line between inviting reciprocation and attempting to control the adversary by stating expectations or norms of interaction. Particularly in the hostile and suspicious environment of escalated conflict, the possibility of inducing psychological reactance is very real.

4. Initiatives need to be carried out as announced without any requirement of reciprocation. This attempt to build an image of credibility has been shown to be important in numerous studies wherein the consistency of the initiator's follow-through affected the proportion of cooperative responses. Thus, cooperation can be increased in a mixed-motive situation of characteristic of much real-world conflict.

5. Initiatives must be continued for some time in the absence of reciprocation. This component is necessary to build credibility and to increase the influence on the adversary to reciprocate. The studies varying initiator credibility yield indirect evidence, whereas principles of person perception and attribution theory provide conceptual support. However, direct evidence, such as that provided in the simulation study noted earlier, is necessary to better assess this component.

6. Initiatives should be unambiguous and open to verification. The second part of this double-barreled component has received some support from experimental studies, whereas the first part has not been tested, but is perhaps self-evident. Openness to inspection, especially when voluntary, appears to build trust and lead to more cooperative and mutually beneficial outcomes.

7. Initiatives need to involve risk and be vulnerable to exploitation, but they must not reduce the capacity for nuclear retaliation.

8. Because nuclear attack is unlikely, conventional capacity to respond to hostile acts must also be maintained. These two components relate to the maintenance of an adequate deterrent in the GRIT strategy, which appears to be most effective in relationships of relatively equal power. Experimental results generally indicate that a power imbalance reduces cooperation. Furthermore, a strong party has been shown to exploit a GRIT strategy, although a weak party is as responsive as one of equal power. In terms of initiation, a strong party is more successful in gaining reciprocation than a party of equal strength. In terms of retaliation, that is, meeting a subse-

quent competitive response with competition, the GRIT strategy is again most effective in equal power relationships. It appears that a willingness to maintain an adequate and credible deterrent may be an important element of GRIT.

9. Subsequent initiatives should match or be slightly more risky than the reciprocation of the adversary. Unfortunately, it is difficult to know what an exact match is, given the perceptual and usually self-serving biases that creep into such judgments. Nonetheless, a GRIT strategy involving more cooperative moves, and therefore risk, has been demonstrated to induce greater cooperation than a simple reciprocity strategy. More direct tests of this component, however, await the development and use of more complex paradigms in which degree of risk can be varied precisely and systematically.

10. Initiatives should be diversified in type of action and geographical location in order to provide variety and flexibility of moves to both the initiator and the reciprocator. This also means that the initiator should not make a number of moves in the same area, thus inducing too much vulnerability. However, the simplicity of laboratory games does not offer a variety of moves to the players and thereby proscribes the testing of this component.

Unfortunately, the simplicity of the Prisoner's Dilemma and other laboratory games raises another serious question about their utility in evaluating GRIT, and that is its proposed applicability to intense conflicts, which the games have limitations representing. Lindskold (1986) points out that intensifying conflict in games appears to make threats rather than conciliatory moves more likely. In addition, there is some evidence that GRIT becomes less effective when intensity is increased by simply adjusting the payoff matrix to reward competition more and cooperation less. In contrast, other evidence indicates that GRIT continues to work when intensity is increased through a longer history of competition before initiation. In addition, subsequent research by Lindskold, Betz, and Walters (1986) has found that GRIT maintains its effectiveness when intensity is manipulated in other ways, for example by being totally noncooperative or using threats, insults, or challenges prior to initiation. Thus, within the confines of the Prisoner's Dilemma, GRIT appears to be a highly robust strategy that does maintain its impact over varying levels of conflict intensity. Lindskold, Betz, and Walters conclude that a competitive climate (or a cooperative one) can be quickly altered if one party begins behaving in ways that are contradictory to that climate. This conclusion adds an optimistic corollary to Deutsch's crude law of social relations (see Chapter 2), which in general emphasizes the difficulty of changing a competitive atmosphere once it has been established.

Part of the reason for the effectiveness of GRIT is that it involves and builds on the norm and strategy of reciprocity, which by itself has been demonstrated to be successful in inducing cooperation in both laboratory games and real-world interaction between nations. Using the Prisoner's Dilemma, Axelrod (1980, 1984) has consistently demonstrated that a reciprocating, or tit-for-tat, strategy, which cooperates on the first move and then matches what the other did on the previous move, is the most effective among a considerable number of strategies, some of which are quite sophisticated. In their analysis of (20) serious international disputes, Leng and Wheeler (1979) found that reciprocating was more effective than bullying, appeasing, or trial and error in avoiding a diplomatic defeat without having to go to war. The reciprocating strategy, which Leng and Wheeler characterize as *firm-but-fair* overlaps considerably with Kaplowitz's firm-but-cooperative strategy noted above, except that actors employing the latter do not respond negatively to every act of belligerence. In this terminology, GRIT may be characterized as cooperative-but-firm in that the initiator may persist in cooperative moves for some time before reacting to exploitation, that is, retaliating. Thus, the initiative is not surrendered to the adversary as it is in the tit-for-tat strategy, where the player's move is always contingent upon the other's previous move. It would thus appear that GRIT builds upon the power of the norm of reciprocity, but adds to it by going the extra mile toward cooperation. In a direct comparison using the Prisoner's Dilemma, Han and Lindskold (1985) found that GRIT with communication of intentions resulted in increased cooperation as compared to a tit-for-tat strategy with or without communication. With GRIT, reciprocity is capitalized upon to the maximum degree in pulling for cooperation, while at the same time the power to reciprocate competitive moves (to retaliate) is not relinquished. This delicate balancing and sequencing most likely underlies the effectiveness of GRIT.

The primary difficulty with GRIT is that it's conceptual rationale comes mainly from the levels of individual psychology and interpersonal relations. Osgood's (1962) formulation stressed the perceptual biases and distortions, the negative effects of stress and anxiety, and the rigidity and stereotypy of cognitive processes in intense conflict—all of which needed to be overcome by GRIT in the move toward de-escalation. Lindskold's (1978) interpretation is based on social-psychological principles dealing with person perception, trust, and social influence. In addition to confronting existing images, GRIT promotes trust through open communication and benevolent action, and works partly because it serves the self-interests of both parties. The rewarding responses of GRIT are predicted to increase the mutual attraction of the parties, as posited by principles of interpersonal attraction. In addition, GRIT draws on the norms of equity and reciprocity in that cooperation is reciprocated and competition is provided equivalent retaliation. All of these interpretations make good sense, but unfortunately, they say very little about the group, intergroup, organizational, societal, or international levels of analysis. Lindskold and his colleagues have demonstrated that small, three-person groups are as responsive to the GRIT strategy in the Prisoner's Dilemma as are individuals (Lindskold & Collins, 1978), and that a single conciliatory individual in a group with two competitive or neutral partners is unable to induce cooperation. The simulation study by Crow (1963) provides somewhat of a counterpoint in that the confederate decision maker was able to introduce GRIT in the face of ignorance and, one would expect, some resistance on the part of the other two members of this group. Unfortunately, neither of these methodologies, especially the Prisoner's Dilemma, can come close to capturing the complex reality faced by decision makers in the real world. The subtle pressures of groupthink, the history of ethnocentric antagonism, the complex web of bureaucratic interests and priorities, the press of domestic politics, and the multiple, intertwined, and shifting agendas of the global anarchy all would work to affect the initiation and the reciprocation of GRIT. Thus the current, limited rationale for GRIT needs to be complemented by theoretical support at higher levels of analysis and by practical considerations derived from operating in the systems in question—those of intergroup and international relations. Parenthetically, it should also be noted that there are few, if any, studies or descriptions of GRIT being implemented at the intergroup level in community or organizational settings. Thus, there is a considerable gap between the experimental research at the interpersonal level and the historical content analyses at the international level. The true potential of GRIT can therefore only be assessed through much more work, particularly with a range of intergroup conflicts in a variety of settings.

Regardless of limitations in both theory and research, it is still legitimate to concur with Lindskold's (1986) conclusions that GRIT is a persuasive proposal with supportive evidence that open and consistent conciliation can lead to cooperative relations. Similar conclusions are voiced in a review by Newcombe (1982), who sees GRIT as especially applicable to the transition toward disarmament. It appears that the strategy is most effective with opponents of equal power and that all or most of the components need to be implemented as prescribed. When successful, GRIT is a unilateral mechanism for reducing tension and increasing trust, that is, for de-escalating conflict and creating a cooperative atmosphere. It is at this point that bilateral methods of conflict resolution may be successfully instituted. These could include negotiation on substantive issues (see Chapter 7), or the initiation of problem-solving workshops as described in the following section.

Problem-Solving Workshops for Improving Intergroup Relations

Work on the facilitative conditions of intergroup contact in the United States has often gone hand in hand with the development and implementation of a variety of community programs to reduce prejudice and discrimination (e.g., Dean & Rosen, 1955). Based on their developing knowledge in small group discussion, training, and problem-solving methods, social psychologists moved to apply these concepts and techniques to the intergroup level with the objectives of increasing understanding and positive action among members of conflicting groups, that is, primarily the white, Protestant American majority and various racial and religious minorities. The classic prototype of this approach is a 2-week workshop that was organized by Kurt Lewin and his colleagues to help community leaders from a variety of groups develop ideas and skills for improving intergroup relations (R. Lippitt, 1949). This workshop also turned out to be the forerunner of the human relations training movement in the United States as the after-hours discussions of the trainers came to involve participants and led to the discovery and development of the sensitivity training, or "T group," that is, a group that learns about interpersonal and group dynamics by analyzing its own interaction. The core experience of the workshop involved participants in small, ethnically mixed groups (the most represented minorities being black and Jewish Americans) in which they identified and diagnosed typical intergroup problems and tried out role playing, psychodrama, and reality practice to deal with the problems. An extensive evaluation of the workshop indicated that participants developed a broader view of intergroup problems and increased motivation and skill level for dealing with them. Subsequently, they reported increased participation in intergroup relations work in their communities and application of the methods acquired in the workshop. Following the development of sensitivity training, this social technology was also adapted to focus on intergroup relations within ethnically mixed groups (e.g., Cobbs, 1972; Lakin, Lomranz, & Lieberman, 1969).

A second early approach to improving intergroup relations followed a more traditional, didactic methodology, using lectures, discussions, and extracurricular activities in an attempt to change intergroup attitudes among ethnically mixed participants (Levinson, 1954; Levinson & Shermerhorn, 1951). These workshops involved predominantly white, middle-class American professionals along with other participants from a variety of ethnic, racial, and religious backgrounds in an attempt to improve attitudes and impart useful knowledge and skills relevant to intergroup relations. Evaluations based mainly on measures of personality and attitudes indicated that participants did become less prejudiced and more egalitarian as a result of their experience. However, although these changes are to be valued, it must be emphasized that, like the gains reported by R. Lippitt (1949), they were necessarily and primarily at the individual level rather than the level of intergroup relations. Thus, although it is important to know that such workshops can improve the individual attitudes and strategies of community leaders, this is a far cry from dealing directly with the issues that are at the root of intergroup conflict. But what these early workshops did, apart from their immediate value, was to help lay the base for the direct application of the small group problem-solving method to the resolution of intergroup conflict. Social psychologists working in organizational settings were at the forefront of these developments. These connections make sense because intergroup conflict in organizations, such as union–management strife, often involves the same kind of stereotyping, hostility, and ineffective communication and interaction as ethnic conflict (Stagner, 1967).

Based on the pioneering field studies of intergroup conflict by Sherif, as well as on their own replications with adult American managers (see Chapter 2), Blake, Mouton, and their colleagues developed intergroup problem-solving methods for dealing with conflict in industrial and business settings (Blake, Mouton, & Sloma, 1965; Blake, Shepard, & Mouton, 1964). Extending the general work on group problem solving (see Chapter 4), intergroup problem solving involves both groups in the steps of defining and reviewing the problem, developing and debating a range of alternatives, searching for and evaluating potential solutions, and weighing and choosing from the final set of solutions. In addition, these scholar/practitioners extended human relations training and process consulting to focus directly on dysfunctional intergroup relationships, including headquarters–field relationships, interdepartmental relationships, union–management relationships, and old–new companies in a merger. The overall goal of these interventions is to change a hostile, win–lose orientation to a cooperative, win–win one. A number of activities, or exercises, within a workshop format were designed to accomplish this objective of breaking down old attitudes and behaviors and replacing them with new, more functional ones. These include a procedure for the development and exchange of intergroup images, wherein each group develops a working picture of its view of itself as well as of the other group. These images are then shared in joint discussion with the clarification of similarities and differences, thus leading to increased understanding of some of the symptoms and dynamics of the conflict. Another procedure involves the joint identification of issues that are critical to the relationship. These activities result in a mutual diagnosis of the conflict, and flow logically into developing action plans that help move the relationship in constructive directions. These types of interventions at the intergroup level have now become commonplace in the wider practice of organization development in the United States and elsewhere (e.g., Alderfer, 1977; Burke, 1974; French & Bell, 1984). They have also been applied with some success to the more challenging situation of interracial and other conflicts in community settings (e.g., Bell, Cleveland, Hanson, & O'Connell, 1969). More recently, Blake and Mouton (1984) have encapsulated their intergroup problem-solving technology into an Interface Conflict-Solving Model, which can be used by groups in conflict to identify and eliminate underlying causes and to restore their relationship based on trust and respect. The model involves six steps: (1) developing an optimal model of interface effectiveness by both groups working separately, (2) consolidating the optimal model through joint discussion, (3) describing the actual, present relationship with each group working separately, (4) consolidating the actual relationship into a joint picture, (5) planning for change in operational terms jointly agreed to by both groups, and (6) follow-up review and replanning if necessary. Blake and Mouton contend that the model works because it focuses at the group and intergroup levels of analysis; it provides a comparison between the ideal and actual relationships, which frees thinking and identifies concrete actions; it places responsibility for success on the adversaries themselves; and it leads to the direct resolution of disagreements. The model is illustrated and substantiated using examples drawn from three decades of work in a variety of organizational settings in which both external consultants and internal managers have served as the design administrators for the execution of the model. All in all, the work of Blake and Mouton serves as a very powerful paradigm for the development and implementation of innovative and creative methods for resolving destructive intergroup conflict. The fact that their practice work is firmly rooted in social-psychological theory and research on intergroup conflict is even more commendable.

A parallel and independent line of development in intergroup problem solving has been pioneered at the international level by political scientist John Burton. Initially terming his approach *controlled communication*, Burton has arranged problem-solving discussions involving informal representatives from countries and factions engaged in violent conflict with a panel of social scientists serving as impartial facilitators (Burton, 1969). The panel works to establish a nonthreatening, problem-solving atmosphere in which the participants can jointly examine their perceptions, analyze the interaction between their respective parties, and explore ways of resolving the conflict and establishing wider common interests. An attempt is made to establish effective communication among the representatives, which Burton sees as central to resolving the conflict. In addition, the role of the panel members is to use their knowledge of conflict processes to assist the representatives in diagnosing the conflict and searching for alternative solutions. Burton's method has been applied with varying degrees of success to a number of international and factional disputes (Burton, 1969, 1985a, 1985b). Recent descriptions by Burton (1987a, 1987b) emphasize the problem-solving, conflict analysis, and resolution nature of the method as a form of "track two diplomacy." Within that context, Burton stresses the importance of engaging the parties in an analysis of needs, values, and interests in order to understand the causes of the conflict and to develop potential solutions. Thus, this later rationale places more emphasis on universal human needs such as identity and recognition (see Chapter 7) and less on problematic processes of interaction such as misperception and miscommunication. The thrust of the problem-solving workshop is therefore to provide the parties with an analytical framework leading to the realization that they are actually pursuing common goals through adversarial tactics and to assist them in developing cooperative options to resolve the conflict. The evolution and application of Burton's method has made a creative and seminal contribution to the visibility and legitimacy of the problem-solving approach to resolving intergroup and international conflict.

The work of psychologist Leonard Doob and his associates has brought methods of human relations training to bear directly on intergroup and international conflict. His initial efforts focused on applying sensitivity training supplemented by other techniques to the border conflict in the Horn of Africa among Ethiopia, Somalia, and Kenya (Doob, 1970). Participation in two mixed T groups was followed by workshop discussion of substantive issues and solutions proposed by the groups. Although there was improved communication and favorable attitude change, the total workshop was unable to reach consensus on solutions to the conflict. Focusing on the conflict in Northern Ireland, Doob and his associates arranged a workshop involving influential grassroots leaders from the Catholic and Protestant communities of Belfast (Doob & Foltz, 1973). The objectives were to establish a degree of mutual trust and to develop plans for improving intergroup relations in the community setting. The first phase of the workshop followed the Tavistock model of group training, using an autocratic, distant, and unstructured leadership style that places almost total responsibility for learning about group process on the participants. Participants interacted in mixed religious groups and also took part in total workshop meetings. In the second phase, small mixed groups focusing on applications met concurrently with sensitivity training groups in which unstructured discussion of interpersonal interaction and group functioning was facilitated by a supportive yet nondirective leader. This experience was followed by opportunities to plan "back-home" activities and to engage in skill practice necessary to implement the plans. Evaluation of the workshop indicated useful learning about group and intergroup processes and increased awareness of the other group. Also, a number of plans for community development projects were developed. Follow-up interviews 10 months later determined that participants continued to experience increased personal and organizational effectiveness (Doob & Foltz, 1974). In addition, a follow-up workshop elicited generally positive evaluations from participants (Doob & Foltz, 1975).

However, two of the co-workers involved in the organization and implementation of the initial workshop became critical of its goals and effects (Boehringer, Zeruolis, Bayley, & Boehringer, 1974). A rejoinder by Doob, Foltz, and the group trainers (Alevy et al., 1974) helps to clarify the misunderstandings that occurred around intentions and strategies, but this interchange indicates the difficulty of applying group training methods developed in other contexts and for other purposes to the analysis of intense intergroup conflict. Nonetheless, generally positive effects did occur and the learnings gained about how to approach situations of intense conflict are useful. Doob and his associates are to be commended for their willingness to openly share their experiences in a concrete fashion and to openly debate the issues that work in this area gives rise to. Doob (1981) maintains that the workshop approach remains promising and indicates the importance of distinguishing between problem-solving and process-promoting goals. Workshops with the former goal are directed toward discovering possible solutions to the conflict, whereas those having the latter goal provide participants with concepts and skills that will be useful back home and may be relevant to mitigating the conflict. In this light, the workshop on conflict in the Horn of Africa was a problem-solving initiative, whereas the workshop on Northern Ireland was a process-promoting initiative. These are useful distinctions to help understand the problem-solving approach and the strengths and limitations of its different variants.

The early work of Burton and Doob has been compared and contrasted by social psychologist Herbert Kelman (1972) in developing his initial statement of the concept of the problem-solving workshop. Kelman introduced the term to indicate the utilization of workshop (i.e, participatory, experiential, etc.) techniques and to emphasize the focus on problem solving rather than personal growth or sensitivity training. Kelman identified the unique strength of the approach as providing a novel context for communication that is impossible in public, formal settings, and he foresaw the primary limitation of workshops as the question of "transfer," that is, how any changes or solutions can be fed back into the policy-making process. Kelman's conclusion, now generally shared, is that ideal participants are "influentials" who can impact policy, but are not required to make it or carry it out, thus removing the rigidity and restrictions that go with formal office. Based on this conceptual analysis, Kelman and Cohen (1976, 1986) have developed a rationale for an interactional approach to international conflict resolution that uses problem-solving workshops as the central method. Their approach assumes that social interaction among antagonists is a necessary condition for resolution; consequently the workshop method engages participants in a detailed analysis of the conflict and promotes a collaborative, problem-solving process. This is largely done through the facilitative role of social scientists, serving as a special kind of third party, who work to establish new norms of interaction emphasizing respectful, task-orientated analysis rather than legalistic debate or hostile accusation. Furthermore, the facilitators use process interventions to improve communication and problem solving and content observations tnat contribute ideas and theories on the conflict and the interaction of participants. Thus, it is hoped that the participants can set aside their prejudices and hostilities and begin the search for mutually acceptable solutions. In terms of application, Kelman and his colleagues have focused on the Middle East, particularly the conflict between the Israelis and the Palestinians. A prototype workshop (held in 1971) is described by Cohen, Kelman, Miller, and Smith (1977) in which Palestinian and Israeli nationals living in the United States were able to produce a joint statement on the legitimacy of Palestinian nationalism. Subsequently, Kelman has organized and facilitated numerous workshops on the Israeli–Palestinian conflict involving both preinfluentials (usually graduate students living in the United States) and influentials (usually present and former officials, parliamentarians, and policy advisors). Concurrently, he has increasingly turned his attention to the ways in which problem-solving workshops can identify the psychological prerequisites for mutual acceptance and create the conditions for negotiations between Palestinians and Israelis (Kelman, 1978). Thus, in line with earlier statements (Kelman, 1972; Kelman & Cohen, 1976), he has come to see problem-solving workshops as a central element of the prenegotiation process that helps to move the parties to the bargaining table (Fisher, 1989; Kelman, 1982). Problem-solving workshops facilitate the emergence of new ideas, the development of trust, the sharing of perspectives and concerns, and the exploration of solutions and action steps to break the impasse. Thus, problem-solving workshops can be seen in a broader sense as a linkage mechanism between the facilitative conditions of intergroup contact (which they embody) and the process of effective negotiation as described in Chapter 7. The work of Herbert Kelman has been at the forefront in both developing the problem-solving approach and linking it to the wider reality of resolving intergroup and international conflict.

The problem-solving workshop represents a unique amalgam of principles and practices drawn largely from the fields of social psychology and international relations. The design of such workshops needs to be based directly or indirectly on principles relating to the facilitative conditions of intergroup contact so that intergroup anxiety is kept at a low to moderate level to maximize receptivity and learning. The administrative arrangements, especially the selection of participants, need to be carried out with an understanding of the practices and norms of international affairs and with sensitivity to the realities of the particular conflict. The implementation of a workshop is a creative combination of principles of human relations training with the norms and atmosphere of an academic seminar. Understanding the dynamics of group interaction, the processes of attitude change, and the complexity of intergroup conflict enable the facilitators to enact their challenging role effectively. Conceptual inputs for the workshop need to be drawn from a very wide range of concepts and theories of human social behavior and intergroup and international relations. By and large, the facilitators are working to create an environment in which the parties can move to a cooperative, or win–win, approach to their conflict through mutual analysis and problem solving. The problem-solving workshop as a method for the resolution of intergroup and international conflict is gaining increasing recognition and acceptance. Its essence is fairly well-understood and its rationale continues to be developed and articulated by scholars of international relations (e.g., de Reuck, 1974, 1983; Groom, 1986). This rationale from a social-psychological perspective will be explored in Chapter 9, which will cast the problem-solving workshop as a form of third party consultation—a method for the study and resolution of conflict (Fisher, 1972, 1983). A comparison between third party consultation and other forms of third-party intervention, such as mediation, will also be presented.

Conclusion

Social-psychological approaches to understanding and resolving conflict place emphasis on how individual and group processes intertwine to affect intergroup communication and interaction. Therefore, these approaches take a phenomenological stance in concert with a subjectivist position that sees changes required at numerous levels for the de-escalation and resolution of intense conflict. The wider study of intergroup relations in social psychology provides useful ideas for understanding and dealing with intergroup conflict. These include the facilitative conditions of intergroup contact and principles for positive intergroup relations in community settings and the societal context. In particular, social-psychological thinking stresses the importance of all groups being able to develop and maintain their unique identity within a framework of multiculturalism and political federalism where appropriate.

The social-psychological analysis also provides for a wider consideration of styles or approaches for managing conflict. The application of the two-dimensional model combining cooperativeness and assertiveness yields a commonality of styles across levels. Within this context, the international level shows a preponderance of win–lose, or distributive, approaches. This could be due to the necessity of a cautious stance within an anarchic and complex situation, or it could indicate that international relations has yet to catch up to other levels, such as the organizational level, in terms of its capacity to deal flexibly and creatively with potentially destructive conflict.

On the optimistic side, evidence from a variety of sources, including games research, simulation studies, and historical analyses, supports the firm-but-cooperative approach as the most effective unilateral way of de-escalating conflict and achieving a positive relationship. This strategy is further extended by GRIT to a cooperative-but-firm orientation that appears to have considerable merit, but that needs further testing in the real world. In terms of third-party methods, problem-solving workshops for resolving protracted conflict hold much promise. This approach builds on the facilitative conditions and is one form of intergroup contact between selected influentials that is specifically directed toward improving the relationship through joint problem solving.

A primary difficulty with all of the social-psychological approaches is that their espoused rationale is predominantly at the individual and interpersonal levels of analysis. Although these considerations form part of their unique appeal, they nonetheless downplay or ignore the importance of contextual factors. Work at the organizational level shows good sensitivity to specific contextual factors related to intergroup conflict, but the same cannot often be said of work at the communal and international levels. Thus, the development of more sophisticated rationales is essential. This will then flow through to more adequate operationalizations in terms of practice so that the ultimate utility of these methods can be better evaluated. The ongoing integration of social-psychological approaches into various social systems in an interdisciplinary fashion is therefore prescribed.

Chapter 9

Third Party Consultation as a Method of Intergroup and International Conflict Resolution

Ronald J. Fisher and Loraleigh Keashly[1]

The ubiquitous phenomenon of intergroup conflict has a built-in tendency to escalate, as indicated in the eclectic model and as substantiated by a host of research results documented in the preceding chapters. Human limitations and fallibilities in perception and cognition lend themselves to misperceptions, cognitive errors, and self-fulfilling expectations that feed the conflict spiral of mistrust, threat, and counterthreat. The competitive and ethnocentric tendencies of cohesive and threatened groups feed decision making and constituent pressure that support contentious and escalatory tactics. For purposes of either defense or aggression, win–lose approaches to handling conflict are often reciprocated as conflicts move to new and ever more destructive levels of intensity. As indicated in the high intensity system state of the eclectic model, the parties become locked into inadequate communication and interaction, and counterproductive dispute resolution. At this point, parties are usually unable and unwilling to search seriously and effectively for alternative means to de-escalate and resolve their conflict. Even if one party does consider a unilateral move toward cooperation, it is immediately constrained by fear of exploitation, which, given the situation, is not unrealistic. If both parties attempt cooperative moves, existing perceptions and entrenched styles of interaction fueled by suspicion and hostility make it difficult if not impossible to maintain de-escalation. It is for these reasons that the intervention of a third party is often necessary to initiate de-escalation and mutual interaction toward resolution in situations of intense intergroup and international conflict.

Although the history of third-party intervention is as old as that of conflict itself, it is only recently that social scientists have turned their attention to a systematic understanding of third party roles and effectiveness (Rubin, 1980; Wall, 1981; Walton, 1969; Young, 1967). There is, of course, a wide range of roles that third parties may effectively fill, and these lead into a number of distinguishable approaches.

---

[1]The authors contributed equally to this chapter and the order of names does not indicate senior or junior author status.

Deutsch (1973) enumerates several possible roles, including those of helping the parties identify the issues in the conflict, providing favorable conditions for confronting the issues, removing blocks and distortions in communication, helping establish norms for rational interaction, helping determine possible solutions, and helping to make a workable agreement. In terms of overall strategies or approaches of third-party intervention, there is no agreed-upon typology, and even the labeling and definitions of particular methods will vary from treatment to treatment. For purposes of this chapter, four types of third-party intervention will be identified and distinguished: mediation, arbitration, and consultation.

Conciliation involves a trusted third party providing an informal communication link between the parties in the hope of identifying the major issues, lowering tensions, and helping them move toward direct interaction, (i.e., negotiation). This form of intervention usually casts the third party as a "go-between" who carries messages and encourages de-escalation, but does not inject ideas on alternatives for settling the dispute. *Mediation* (called conciliation in some contexts) involves the intervention of a skilled intermediary who facilitates a negotiated settlement to the dispute on a set of specific substantive issues. The mediator usually combines individual meetings involving each parties' representatives with joint negotiating sessions and uses reasoning, persuasion, the control of information, and the suggestion of alternatives to help the antagonists find a workable agreement. *Arbitration* involves a third-party judgment by an accepted authority that is arrived at by considering the merits of the opposing positions and by imposing a settlement that is deemed to be fair. This is, of course, the third-party approach largely adopted by the legal and judicial systems of various jurisdictions, and is typically used when mediation fails. *Consultation* (also referred to as problem solving) is a newer, innovative form of intervention in which a skilled and impartial third party attempts to facilitate creative problem solving through communication and analysis aided by social-scientific knowledge of conflict. An attempt is made to confront the underlying issues in the conflict so that the relationship between the parties can be shifted in a cooperative direction, thus rendering the settlement of substantive issues more likely.

What distinguishes these four approaches initially are the assumptions that they make about the nature of conflict, that is, whether they take an objectivist or subjectivist position as discussed in Chapter 8 (see Burton, 1982; Mitchell, 1981b; Silbey & Merry, 1986). Consultation assumes that conflict exists both in incompatible realities and in the subjective elements of perception, communication, and interaction. Thus, an analysis and reevaluation of such elements may lead to increased understanding and cooperation that will support creative and integrative solutions to substantive issues. In contrast, conciliation, mediation, and arbitration place much more emphasis on the objective aspects of conflict, that is, the incompatible goals and positions. Although these methods are cognizant of subjective elements, they attempt to work around such relationship issues in the search for an acceptable settlement (Brett, Goldberg, & Ury, 1980; Folberg & Taylor, 1984; Prein, 1984). Thus, they accept a distributive and competitive orientation to conflict and concentrate on achieving a compromise settlement by eliciting or enforcing concessions from the parties (Burton, 1969, 1984; Filley, 1978; Wall, 1981).

This brief comparison suggests that different third party approaches view different elements as crucial in de-escalating and resolving a conflict. They will therefore adopt different strategies and techniques and look for different outcomes of intervention. The comparison also suggests that different methods may be more appropriate to different types and levels of conflict. As the system states of the eclectic model indicate, low intensity conflict based mainly on competing resource interests may be amenable to mediation, whereas an escalated, high intensity resource conflict involving a power struggle may require arbitration. Furthermore, a high intensity conflict based on the denial and frustration of basic needs may only be amenable to creative problem solving through consultation. These types of considerations are important not simply because the application of an inappropriate intervention will not work, but because it may in fact make the situation worse. Rubin (1980), for example, in reviewing experimental evidence on the effectiveness of third party intervention, concludes:

> It appears that certain tried and true techniques of third-party intervention, such as the introduction of communication between the parties, the recommendation that the disputants consider multiple issues as a package, and the use of such issue identification procedures as role reversal, facilitate concession making and agreement only when conflict is relatively low in amount or intensity. When conflict is intense, these very techniques may prove ineffectual and may even exacerbate the conflict. (p. 385)

It is therefore extremely important that would-be third parties, whether invited in by the parties or mandated by some external authority, proceed with a great deal of caution in addressing intense conflicts. It is also essential that our collective understanding of the differences, relative applicability, and potential complementarity of different third party approaches be increased substantially.

The primary concern of this book is the understanding and resolution of intense and protracted intergroup and international conflict. Thus, the focus of this chapter is on third-party intervention that is appropriate to such conflicts. The emphasis is therefore on consultation as a unique and innovative third party method for the study and resolution of high intensity conflict. A descriptive model of consultation will be presented and the largely social-psychological rationale of the method will be described. In order to better understand consultation and its relation to other third-party methods, an initial taxonomy of third-party intervention will be developed. A detailed and rigorous comparison of consultation and mediation within the context of the Intergroup Conflict Simulation (see Chapter 6) will also be described. Finally, a contingency approach to third party intervention will be suggested as a way of capitalizing on the relative strengths of the different methods and of maximizing their potential complementarity.

Third Party Consultation

The pioneering initiatives on problem-solving workshops described in Chapter 8 laid part of the groundwork for the development of an initial model of *third party consultation* (Fisher, 1972), using the term coined by Walton (1969) to label his work on interpersonal peacemaking between corporate executives. In addition to Walton's conceptualization, the model drew primarily from the contributions of Blake, Shepard, and Mouton (1964), Burton (1969), and Doob (1970). The term itself was chosen to emphasize that these and related initiatives are in large part distinguished by the unique and essential role enacted by the third party, typically a team of social scientist/practitioners with specialized knowledge in conflict processes and expertise in human relations skills for facilitating confrontation. The interventions subsumed by the model have typically involved small group problem-solving discussions organized by impartial third party consultants with objectives ranging from individual attitude change for participants, through the generation of creative solutions to the conflict, to anticipated improvements in the wider relationship between the parties. The model is based on the assumption that problem solving can most effectively be initiated in protracted conflict through the assistance of a skilled and trusted intermediary working with informal yet influential representatives of the parties.

A revised version of the initial model is presented in Figure 9-1, in which each circle represents a major component of the method (Fisher, 1976). The components were chosen to represent and emphasize the identity, strategies, and behavior of the impartial and skilled third party who enters directly into the arena of conflict in a facilitative and diagnostic manner, hoping to aid the antagonists to analyze and deal with the underlying attitudes and basic issues in their relationship. The major components are common to a wide range of problem-solving and related interventions and are designed to specify the requisites of the effective practice of third party consultation.

The third party *identity* specifies that the consultant be a skilled and knowledgeable scientist/practitioner whose background, attitudes, and behavior engender impartiality and whose understanding and expertise enable the facilitation of productive confrontation, that is, the open and direct discussion of the contentious perceptions, attitudes, and issues separating the parties. Thus, the third party should have a high degree of skill in human relations, including interpersonal, small group, and intergroup functioning, in consultation as a form of professional practice, and in problem solving as a systematic social process. On the content side, the consultant should have moderate knowledge of the parties and their conflict, but not such a high degree of knowledge that it tends to support predefined perceptions. In addition, the third party should have low external control over the parties so that they are free to explore their relationship, but high internal control over the consultation situation in order to manage the discussions toward productive confrontation. Given this complex set of demanding requirements, it is easy to see why most interventions have involved a team of social scientist/practitioners whose combined identities adequately form this component.

An adequate third party identity lays the basis for a *helping relationship* with each of the parties that involves trust, respect, and understanding, thus serving as a prerequisite for confrontation and problem solving between the parties. The consulting relationship is a special form of helping relationship in which the clients, that is, the parties and their representatives, maintain the power to use or not use the

Third Party Consultation

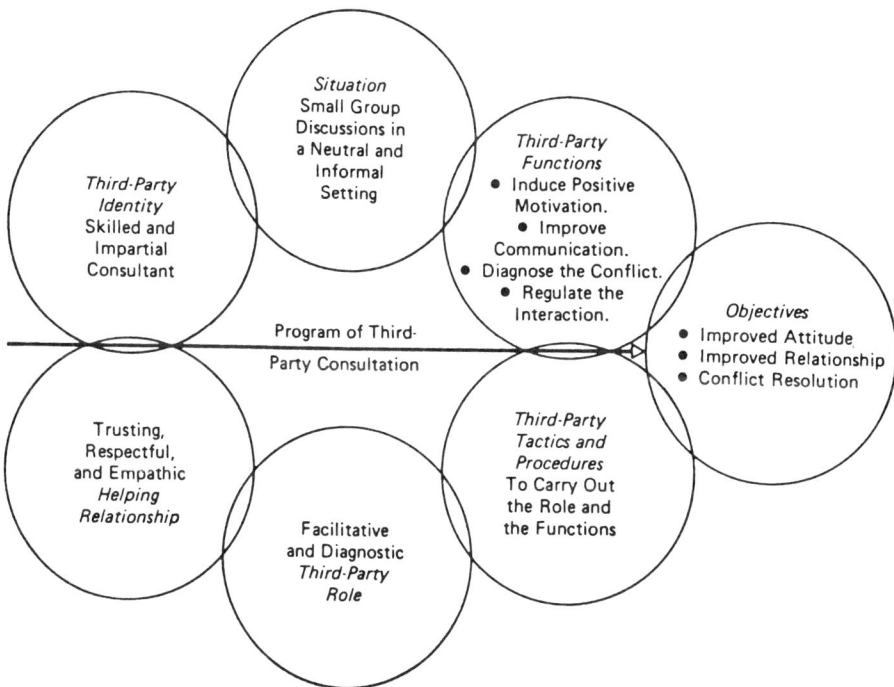

Figure 9-1. A model of third party consultation. Fisher 1976. Copyright 1976 by the American Psychological Association. Reprinted by permission of the author.

consultant's services as they see fit. All of the professional and ethical requirements of a consulting relationship are thus encumbent upon the third party. The *situation* refers to the essential social and physical arrangements by which the consultant organizes a series of informal and flexible small group, problem-solving discussions in a neutral and informal setting. The face-to-face, flexible interaction of the discussions, akin to an academic seminar, are a hallmark of the method. The rationale is to provide a context that is supportive of productive confrontation. The third party *role* is the appropriate pattern of behavior for the consultant, and is basically facilitative and diagnostic, using the skills and knowledge necessary for conflict analysis and confrontation. In addition, the role is nonevaluative and noncoercive so that the parties will express themselves openly and make their decisions freely. Thus, the role is also nondirective over solutions or outcomes, but does maintain control over the process of the discussions. The initial model (Fisher, 1972) also considered the identity and role of the participants, who at a minimum are interested and typical members of their respective groups and at a maximum are informal yet appointed and influential representatives.

The driving forces of the method are captured in the third party *functions*, which are the core strategies for instituting the systematic process of effective problem solving. These include inducing and maintaining mutual positive motivation for problem solving, improving the openness and accuracy of communication, diagnosing the issues and processes of the conflict, and regulating the interaction among the participants. The functions are operationalized through specific behavioral *tactics* (e.g., paraphrasing a participant's statement) and more general *procedures*, or exercises (e.g., the development and exchange of group images). Fisher (1972) provides further description and illustration of functions, tactics, and procedures, all of which are designed to create and maintain the conditions necessary for productive confrontation and effective joint problem solving. These components need to be combined with a range of supportive activities, such as preliminary interviews and follow-up evaluations, in order to mount a program of consultation that will reach the specified *objectives*. These include more veridical, complex, and favorable attitudes toward the other party, an improved relationship which has shifted from a destructive, win–lose orientation to a collaborative, problem-solving one, and resolution of the conflict involving innovative solutions freely and mutually agreed upon that will be self-sustaining until conditions change. In addition, the uniqueness of third party consultation is underscored by the objective of studying and learning about conflict, for the participants, but more importantly, for the consultants and other scientist/practitioners who can use this increased knowledge in future work.

Following its initial development, the model was applied and evaluated through interventions in the community, organizational, and international spheres. Fisher and White (1976a; 1976b) used the model as a guide in arranging problem-solving discussions between various groups representing a neighborhood schism between public housing tenants and private home owners in a small Canadian community. One of the programs followed some of the systematic procedures of image exchange and so on developed by Blake and his associates (see Chapter 8) and involved a rigorous evaluation based on intergroup attitude measures from preinterviews and postinterviews within a control group design. The assessment indicated increased positiveness and complexity of attitudes, but no change in behavioral orientations to improve the relationship. At the same time, a number of participants became more involved in community development activities in the neighborhood.

Organizational consulting work by the author, dealing with intergroup relationships, has often been guided by the model of third party consultation. For example, in one case involving the management team of a large department in a city government, an initial diagnosis indicated interface problems between the executive and management levels as well as among the four divisions making up the department. Again, systematic procedures were used to develop mutually acceptable lists of the issues in each relationship, and intergroup problem-solving techniques were used to confront, diagnose, and resolve the issues to the satisfaction of the different parties.

In the international sphere, the model was used to plan and implement a pilot workshop on the India–Pakistan conflict by involving nationals of the two countries living in Canada (Fisher, 1980). The third party team consisted of the author, with skills in human relations and conflict resolution, and an international student advisor, with understanding of the cultural similarities and differences of the parties. A series of single and joint discussions followed the Blake, Shepard, and Mouton (1964) approach of developing and exchanging various perceptions, that is, the present relationship, the national images, the ideal relationship, the major issues,

Table 9-1. Third Party Functions and Tactics Over the Course of a Workshop

Function and Tactic	Observed Percentage of Total Acts				All Meetings
	Meeting 1	Meeting 2	Meeting 3	Meeting 4	
Inducing positive motivation					
Encouraging problem solving	5.7	6.7	3.6	1.1	4.5
Supporting participants	40.3	19.2	37.8	28.6	30.8
Maintaining optimum tension	2.2	3.0	1.0	8.2	3.5
Balancing situational power	1.5	3.7	1.3	0.0	1.8
Total	49.7	32.6	43.7	37.9	40.6
Improving communication					
Eliciting information	9.5	16.6	12.0	6.0	11.4
Paraphrasing, empathizing	3.2	1.0	3.3	0.5	2.0
Translating, clarifying	8.5	18.6	23.0	14.2	16.2
Summarizing	2.7	3.4	6.5	1.9	3.6
Total	23.9	39.6	44.8	22.6	33.2
Diagnosing the conflict					
Injecting information	5.5	11.5	4.6	34.9	13.6
Processing and feedback	0.2	0.4	0.3	0.8	0.4
Stimulating self-diagnosis	2.5	1.8	1.8	0.5	1.7
Total	8.2	13.7	6.7	36.2	15.7
Regulating the interaction					
Pacing the phases	4.5	1.6	1.0	0.0	1.8
Initiating-monitoring agenda	12.7	8.9	2.8	3.3	7.1
Controlling disruptive interaction	1.0	3.6	1.0	0.0	1.6
Total	18.2	14.1	4.8	3.3	10.5

Source: Journal of Social Psychology, 112 MA, page 202, 1980. Reprinted with permission of the Helen Dwight Reid Educational Foundation. Published by Heldref Publications, 400 Albemarle St., N.W., Washington, D.C. 20016. Copyright © 1980.

and the potential solutions to the conflict. Case study analysis and postworkshop interviews indicted that the model was successfully implemented and that there were beneficial effects on the attitudes of participants. This study is also unique in its attempt to monitor the process of the workshop in terms of problem solving and third party interventions. Tape recordings of the sessions were coded using Bales' Interaction Process Analysis, a well-accepted technique for the content analysis of small group discussion. The results showed that the joint sessions in the workshop followed the same patterns of interaction over time as other types of problem-solving discussions, thus supporting the validity of the model in this regard. In addition, a coding scheme was developed based on the functions and tactics described in the model (see Table 9-1). Content analysis of the third party's behavior in the four joint meetings yielded results that make sense in relation to the model and the problem-solving process. Inducing problem-solving motivation was the most prominent function, particularly at the beginning of the workshop, when it was essential to get the process moving. Improving communication was also prominent throughout the workshop and peaked in the middle sessions, when the greatest amount of exchange occurred between the parties. Diagnosing the conflict became more frequent later in the workshop, when motivation and communication had been established and the consultants could then provide ideas about conflict that would further aid the parties' analysis. Regulating the interaction was more frequent at the beginning and declined throughout the workshop as the participants adjusted to the atmosphere and norms of the workshop. All in all, these results support the validity of the model as capturing the essential flow of third party consultation.

A review covering more that 35 published illustrations of intergroup and international conflict resolution that can be subsumed by the model is provided by Fisher (1983). As with the earlier review (Fisher, 1972), it is apparent that although a variety of approaches use different labels and emphasize different aspects, there is considerably more similarity than variability among them. Thus, it makes sense to talk about a generic model to which different variations can be compared. For example, some interventions take more of a laboratory learning approach inspired by human relations training, whereas others follow more strictly the mold of problem-solving discussions. The assessment of interventions at the organizational, community, and international levels generally yields positive results in terms of increased understanding and improved attitudes and relationships, but is unfortunately based largely on case study impressions. There is, therefore, a need for evaluations of greater rigor and sophistication. On the conceptual side, existing theories or models such as the present one are primarily descriptive and implicitly prescriptive, but require much more specification and elaboration in terms of underlying dynamics in order to fully support practice interventions. Therefore, there is a great need for further theory development fueled by the comprehensive assessment of a wide variety of applications. In moving this agenda forward to the development of an effective social technology of intergroup and international conflict resolution, the continued involvement of scientist/practitioners will be essential.

The Social-Psychological Rationale of Third Party Consultation

Given that third party consultation is a small group, problem-solving method for individual attitude change and the creation of alternatives, it is not surprising that its rationale is primarily to be found in concepts and theories from social psychology. This field is concerned with how the behavior of individuals is influenced by and, in turn, influences the actions of others in a social environment (Fisher, 1982). Thus, topics of prime concern include attitude formation and change; the links between perception, cognition, and behavior; social influence; role behavior; small group dynamics; organizational functioning; and intergroup relations—all areas, among others, that relate to third party consultation. Thus, in attempting to address the question as to why consultation should work, attention is initially given to a range of social-psychological theorizing. Subsequently, attention will need to be given to conceptual input from disciplines that relate more directly to the social system in which the conflict is occurring and the consultation takes place. For example, if the conflict is between departments in a corporation, concepts from organizational psychology and organizational behavior would be necessary in order to tailor the general rationale to that setting; if international conflict is the focus, then the discipline of international relations has much to offer for understanding how consultation needs to be instituted in order to be successful. Therefore, it is useful to think of a general rationale for the method along with some number of specific or more refined rationales that would adapt interventions to the particular conflict and system in question. The attempt will be made here to spell out an initial general rationale that underlies all applications of the method.

A general statement on the rationale of the problem-solving workshop is provided by Kelman and Cohen (1986), who see crucial differences between this and other approaches to promote communication between conflicting parties.

> What is unique about the problem-solving workshop is that it represents a systematic effort to utilize social-psychological principles in achieving a specific set of effects, both within the communication situation itself and within the larger conflict system. Social-psychological principles enter into the formulation of the structure, the process, and the content of the problem-solving workshop: The structure is based on analysis of the place of the workshop within the larger social system in which the conflict takes place. The process is designed to create the conditions conducive to establishing and maintaining certain patterns of social interaction and to utilize the ongoing interactions themselves as raw materials for gaining greater understanding of the dynamics of the conflict. The content focuses to a considerable degree on social-psychological analyses of collective experiences and processes, such as mutual perceptions and images, national self-images and national identity, sources and forms of nationalist ideology, interaction processes conducive to the escalation of conflict, and structural changes conducive to its perpetuation. (p. 340)

Within this broad context, concepts from a number of levels of analysis are useful in understanding how third party consultation or problem solving works toward its objectives. What follows is a selective treatment from theorizing at the individual, interpersonal, group, intergroup, and international levels that would appear to have relevance to the rationale of consultation. References will not be provided because most of the principles and theories can be found in general social psychology texts, especially ones that take a multilevel, applied approach to the discipline (see Fisher, 1982).

At the level of individuals, the concept of attitude and the process of attitude change have relevance to third party consultation because the method is in part directed toward changing the intergroup attitudes of the participants in more veridical and positive directions. The concept of attitude is usually defined as an individual's tendency to evaluate and respond to a social object in a consistently favorable or unfavorable way, and is often seen as comprised of a cognitive, an affective, and a behavioral component. The objectives of consultation include attitude change toward a more realistic cognitive component, a more positive affective component, and a more cooperative behavioral orientation. It is assumed that face-to-face interaction is necessary in order to break down rigid and simplified stereotypes and to provide direct information about the other group on which attitude change can be based. It is therefore crucial, as in any form of intergroup contact (see Chapter 8), that participants see each other as typical members of their respective groups so that any attitude change will generalize beyond the consultation experience. This may mean that some negative elements of attitudes will be confirmed or indeed created, but the development of positive aspects should also occur, leading to a more balanced picture as the overall outcome. Although it is a simple hypothesis, research indicates that providing information on either or both similarities and differences between conflicting groups tends to reduce prejudice and stereotyping (Stephan & Stephan, 1984). It is further assumed that positive changes in attitudes will subsequently affect the perceptions, cognitions, and behaviors that characterize the relationship between the parties, at least for participants in consultation and those whom they may influence in the situation back home. Predicted changes would include reduced selectivity and distortion in perception, increased flexibility and complexity in cognition, and a wider range of acceptable behavioral options in relation to the other party. Groom (1986), for example, indicates that parties must come to realize that their definition of the situation may need to be revised in some respects and that they may have misunderstood the perceptions of the other. It is also hoped that self-fulfilling prophecies might be counteracted in the workshop by focusing on such interaction as it occurs, and that the results of such confrontation would generalize beyond the consultation situation. Whether these kinds of changes would occur depends on a host of factors in the participants' wider social environment and is informed by a number of other conceptualizations, including cognitive consistency, attribution theory, and the functional theory of attitudes as well as processes of social influence. Thus, a variety of ideas is available to explain why consultation should have beneficial effects at the level of the individuals involved in an intense and protracted conflict.

At the level of interpersonal relations, the interaction among participants in consultation allows certain processes to occur that may have beneficial effects. The sharing of ideas about the conflict and the other party involves a considerable amount of self-disclosure in a manner that is typically absent in the wider interaction between the parties. Mutual and respectful self-disclosure supported by the third party role and functions is predicted to lead to greater understanding and trust among the participants. Furthermore, the opportunity to share similarities (as well as differences) is predicted to lead to an increased sense of attraction between participants that should increase receptivity to the ideas of the other party and support attitude change. Note that this principle is also the primary (and limited) rationale of the initial contact hypothesis (see Chapter 8). The more open and accurate communication that consultation endeavors to create allows the participants to see each other's intentions more clearly and to then more critically evaluate their own interpretations and reactions. This can lead to a much greater degree of congruence in the communication process as compared to the breakdowns and barriers characteristic of intense conflict. It also leads to an increase in the level of trust between the participants, which is a key element in any process of de-escalation, as indicated in the rationale of GRIT (see Chapter 8). In addition, the norm of reciprocity predicts that as each party shares its views in a relatively respectful and objective fashion, the other feels an obligation to do the same. Such a mutual and rewarding interaction would be predicted by exchange theory to become self-supporting and to lead in the direction of beneficial outcomes identified in the model, particularly a more cooperative orientation to the relationship. At the level of roles, which is a half step above that of interpersonal relations, consultation can be seen as influencing the participants away from an argumentative, bargaining stance and toward one of problem solving (Fisher, 1972). De Reuck (1983) describes this intended role shift as divesting the participants of their inhibitions as adversaries and offering them alternative roles as conflict analysts and then as partners in problem solving. Thus, a number of principles converge to influence the participants away from the traditional orientations of debate or negotiation and toward behavior that is congruent with the problem solving mode of consultation.

At the level of group processes, a number of theories and concepts indicate that the small, informal nature of interaction in consultation should create a climate conducive to positive attitude and behavioral changes. Theories of group development predict that the atmosphere and agenda that consultation provides should lead the parties through a number of stages to the creation of a new social reality, albeit a temporary one. De Reuck (1983) discerns three phases that consultation groups go through. In the first, the parties are still constrained by the norms of their groups and avoid direct communication with each other by talking at or through the third party. In the second phase, the parties engage in the analysis of the conflict and begin to exchange messages with each other. In the third phase, the parties join with the third party in forming an integrated group, albeit a fragile one, and collaborating in joint problem solving. Thus, the new social reality involves a shared approach in jointly analyzing the conflict as a mutual problem. A new set of group norms develop that support behaviors typically proscribed in the wider relationship. The norms are in part those of an academic seminar with no fixed agenda, exploration of topics, empirical examination of statements, and respect for the views of others (Groom, 1986). In terms of social process, consultation blends human relations training with small group problem solving. Meetings are not simply sensitivity sessions, as noted by Kelman (1972), although the increased openness and flexibility of interaction do parallel the norms of a T group. Social structure is added to consultation by an adherence to the task and process requirements of the systematic problem-solving sequence, and external content is added by focusing directly on the real-world conflict and not simply on the interaction of the participants, as in a sensitivity training session. Thus, the consultant facilitates movement of the discussions through problem identification and diagnosis to the creation and selection of alternatives that might assist in de-escalation. The existence of a situation in which the participants are functioning as a single group helps to assure that a mutual, collaborative approach will accrue to some degree. De Reuck (1983) notes that each party is first influenced to see itself as a member of a group in conjunction with the third party, and the parties then come to consider members of the opposing party as members of the group as well. Hence, consultation capitalizes on a number of influential elements of group dynamics to create a unique and potentially useful forum in which participants may explore innovative paths out of their mutual dilemma.

At the intergroup level, the contact hypothesis and the facilitative conditions of intergroup contact provide the primary rationale for consultation. As discussed in Chapter 8, it is essential that the interaction be perceived as being at the intergroup rather than the interpersonal level and concurrently that the other participants be seen as representative members of their group. If this is the case, then a high degree of acquaintance potential will help to break down barriers and stereotypes in ways that will generalize to the wider intergroup relationship. Equal status interaction is essential to respectful and productive dialogue and can be fostered by the third party according a high and equal degree of recognition to all participants. The social norms of the interaction, as noted above, are initially set by the third party, and are designed to engage participants in an open, friendly, and trusting exchange. In addition, some degree of institutional support from the decision makers of the two parties is important for the participants on both sides to take the discussions seriously and to engage in them with a sense of confidence and legitimacy. The involvement of participants in a cooperative task and reward structure will tend to build a collaborative atmosphere that will support problem-solving behavior and positive attitude change. The parties will begin by cooperating with the third party in the conflict analysis and will move through a process of transfer to cooperating with each other in conflict resolution through problem solving, an immediately rewarding experience (de Reuck, 1983). Finally, the characteristics of individual participants need to be considered in invitations to consultation sessions. Participants need to be generally competent, secure, and not so extreme in attitudes that any change is unlikely. At the same time, as Kelman (1972) has argued, the full range of positions, including extreme ones, needs to be represented in a program of consultation so that realistic outcomes acceptable to all constituencies are ultimately developed. The dynamic underlying intergroup contact is intergroup anxiety (see Chapter 8), and it is generally accepted that moderate anxiety is conducive to learning. The demands of the consultation situation would generally be expected to lead to high levels of intergroup anxiety, and the task of the consultant is to operationalize the facilitative conditions in the design and implementation of the sessions so that anxiety is moderated and the potential for learning is maximized.

At the international level, social psychologists have emphasized the importance of nationalism, or the ideology of the state, as it affects interactions between individuals from different countries (see Chapter 7). Nationalism involves a favorable attitude toward one's country and a predisposition to support its interests in international relations. Advanced in a competitive fashion, nationalism works against international cooperation in general and collaborative approaches to conflict resolution in particular. The state is seen as having supreme authority to protect and advance the national interest in opposition to the interests of other nations. Often, nationalism is linked to a sense of cultural identity that embodies the unique history and way of life of the people who constitute the majority of the population. This element can be expressed as ethnocentrism, in which the predominant national ethnic group is seen as superior to others, thus fueling communal as well as international conflict. This collection of sentiments must become part of the conflict analysis in consultation if its effects on the behavior between parties is to be understood. Thus, many of the procedures employed encourage participants to jointly examine their national images and ideologies in order to gain a sense of how these factors influence policy development within nations and interaction between nations. This analysis is essential for moving toward the objectives of consultation.

This brief overview indicates that there is an extensive and compelling rationale for the potential efficacy of third party consultation, at least in terms of the workshop experience itself. As noted in Chapter 8, the transfer of outcomes to the wider relationship remains a key issue, and an additional rationale needs to be developed, with the assistance of other social scientists, as to how the method might facilitate conflict resolution at the system level. A related task is to develop an understanding of how third party consultation might be used in conjunction with other methods of conflict management and de-escalation to move toward ultimate resolution. The contingency model of third party intervention to be discussed below partly addresses this agenda.

Toward a Taxonomy of Third Party Intervention

The development of a taxonomy of third party intervention is a challenging undertaking for a number of reasons. First, the number of third party roles is quite large and appears to be increasing with the advent of hybrid roles such as mediator–arbitrator (e.g., McGillicuddy, Welton, & Pruitt, 1987) or mediator–adviser (Brett & Goldberg, 1983). In addition, the strategies subsumed under a particular label are often quite varied. For example, arbitration encompasses such procedures as final offer versus conventional arbitration, interest arbitration, and rights arbitration, to name a few (e.g., Anderson, 1981; Grigsby & Bigoness, 1982; Hameed & Sen, 1987). These realities partly indicate the myriad of approaches that fall under the rubric of third party intervention and that pose a considerable challenge for any systematic development of theory. In addition, there is a tendency to assign third party intervention to the realm of art as opposed to science (Shapiro, Drieghe, & Brett, 1985). This does not permit systematic study of third party intervention directed at identifying dimensions of commonality and divergence. Contrary to the expressed concern, systematic study does not deny the influence of an individual third party's style and skill. For example, Kolb's (1983) participant observation study of federal and state mediators revealed systematic differences in approach between the two and yet acknowledged individual variability among the mediators themselves. Systematic study has important implications for understanding the "blooming, buzzing confusion" of intervention approaches, the development of a contingency approach to third party interventions, and, within that, the effective application of third party strategies.

The development of a taxonomy of third party interventions involves a consideration of different types of third party methods, which are at least initially distinguished by the label applied to them. The basis of a taxonomy is formed by selecting approaches that are described differently, and systematically comparing them to identify dimensions of difference and similarity. From the brief definitions provided earlier, conciliation, consultation, mediation, and arbitration appear to be sufficiently familiar and different to be useful anchors in this development. It is assumed that the variability between each of these approaches is greater than the variability within each.

Important sources of information in this endeavor are works on procedural taxonomies (e.g., Bercovitch, 1985; Lippitt & Lippitt, 1986; Sheppard, 1984) and on models of specific third party approaches (e.g., Fisher, 1972, 1983). Initially, Fisher and Keashly (1988) utilized the *model of third party consultation* to distinguish between consultation and mediation in terms of the role, identity, functions, and tactics of the third party; type and focus of interventions; problem-solving orientation; and objectives. Although this work clarified some of the confusion regarding these two approaches, some of the dimensions of the model overlap, indicating that there are broader dimensions that capture the distinctions among methods. In addition, the large number of dimensions made the analysis less than efficient for categorizing other approaches. In reviewing the model, the components continually echo three main dimensions of third party control: (a) control over the process, (b) control over the content, and (c) control over the outcome of the interaction between disputants.

Briefly, *process control* refers to third party influence on the way in which disputants interact during the resolution effort (e.g,. how information is shared, rules of conduct or interaction). *Content control* relates to third party influence on the issues dealt with during the interaction (e.g., what concerns are dealt with, what information is shared). *Outcome control* refers to the influence of the third party in determining the outcome or settlement (e.g,. suggestions made, information on other settlements). These themes were particularly salient when mediation and consultation were compared with respect to the problem-solving orientation and activity level of the third party. Sheppard (1984) has also identified, albeit by a different route, the importance of process and content control as they relate to the stage of conflict resolution. Outcome control is identified with his last stage of conflict resolution, labeled reconciliation, in which the third party hands down the decision.

Sheppard's (1984) taxonomy is currently the most developed framework and could be used to initially distinguish between the four approaches. However, the inclusion of consultation as an anchor in this comparison points to other important areas in need of development. For example, all four approaches utilize process control during the problem definition stage, but they differ in the degree and form of that control. All four approaches establish particular rules of control and order for the communication process, but they differ in how this is achieved. Parties under arbitration present their cases to the third party often in the form of written briefs and not directly to each other. Mediation and conciliation often involve separating the parties while the third party functions as a channel of communication that can be closed and opened at its discretion. In consultation, parties are brought together in face-to-face discussions and the third party facilitates the communication process to ensure accuracy and openness. Thus, the approaches also differ in the extent of interparty contact. Such differences are not captured in Sheppard's (1984) classification scheme, and yet they are important to the overall experience and impact of the intervention on the conflict resolution process and, hence, the outcome.

It is therefore important to include an assessment of the degree of third party control in any taxonomy. One way to capture this aspect is to examine the balance of third party versus the other parties' control over process and content. While Sheppard (1984) acknowledges this balance as implicit in the definition of third party control, he does not pursue it. Lippitt and Lippitt (1986) utilize the term *directiveness* to capture this balance of power. As anchor points, negotiation would be seen as completely under the control of the disputants, whereas arbitration, in which parties deal only with and through the third party, who renders a binding decision, would be seen as completely under the control of the third party. This dimension of balance of third party/disputants' control will be incorporated in the initial taxonomy for distinguishing conciliation, consultation, mediation, and arbitration.

Another fundamental distinction is the nature of the issues focused on for discussion and resolution. It is generally accepted that substantive and relationship issues are typically involved in conflict to varying degrees. Consultation differs from the other three approaches in that the interparty relationship is the central focus of the problem-solving process. These differential foci would be expected to influence the nature of process control, that is, how it is operationalized. For example, while arbitration, mediation, and conciliation acknowledge the role of relationship issues such as misperception, miscommunication, and hostile feelings, the third party's tactics focus on diffusing them as opposed to dealing with them as key elements in the conflict. Thus, process techniques, such as role reversal and sharing of interparty perceptions, would be characteristic of consultation but not of the other three.

A classification scheme incorporating these dimensions of control permits an initial and yet detailed comparison and discrimination of the four third party approaches. Such detail is necessary to allow the effective matching of intervention approach to specific conflicts. Consistent with an emphasis on conflict resolution as a problem-solving process (Fisher & Keashly, 1988; Pruitt & Rubin, 1986; Sheppard, 1984), the problem-solving sequence will be used to identify the process and content control by the third party at each stage. Some comment will also be made on the sources of third party influence as another dimension for comparison among the approaches.

The goal of substantive agreement in mediation, arbitration, and conciliation reflects an acceptance of the objective nature of social conflict. In mediation and conciliation, participants work to develop a mutually satisfactory solution to a substantive problem such as wages, land, child custody, etc. (Folberg & Taylor, 1984; Wall, 1981; Webb, 1979). Arbitration seeks to bring about a satisfactory substantive solution as well, but the decision is rendered by the third party. Although consultation acknowledges the need to resolve substantive issues, the improvement of the

Table 9-2. An Initial Taxonomy of Third Party Intervention: Third Party Control Across Stages of Problem Solving

Stage	Control	Type of Intervention			
		Conciliation	Consultation	Mediation	Arbitration
Definition/ diagnosis	Process	Moderate	Moderate	Moderate-high	High
	Content	Low	Low-moderate	Moderate-high	Moderate-high
Solution generation	Process	Low	Moderate	Moderate-high	High
	Content	Low	Low	Moderate	Moderate
Solution evaluation/ selection	Process	Low	Low	Moderate	High
	Content	Low	Low	Moderate-high	High
Solution implementation	Process	Moderate	—	Moderate	High
	Content	Moderate	—	Moderate	High
Solution evaluation	Process	—	—	—	High
	Content	—	—	—	High
Outcome Control		Low	Low	Moderate	High
Sources of Influence					
Expert		No	Process	Substantive	Substantive
Referent		Yes	Yes	Yes	Yes
Legitimate		No	No	No	Yes
Reward		No	No	Sometimes	Yes
Coercive		No	No	Sometimes	Yes
Information		No	No	Yes	Yes

relationship is viewed as a necessary prerequisite (Blake, Shepard, & Mouton, 1964; Burton, 1969; Fisher, 1983). Parties focus their joint problem-solving efforts on issues in their relationship, laying the groundwork for settlement.

An examination of the nature of third party involvement in the problem-solving sequence illustrates further the differences among these approaches. Although the number of steps in problem-solving schemes varies, there are typically five basic phases to the sequence (see Likert & Likert, 1978; Morris & Sashkin, 1976): (a) problem definition and diagnosis, (b) problem–solution generation, (c) solution evaluation and selection, (d) solution implementation, and (e) evaluation of the product and the process. The activities of the different third party approaches on the dimensions of process and content control can be distinguished in relation to the stages of problem-solving, thus yielding an initial taxonomy of third party intervention (see Table 9-2).

The initial problem definition and diagnosis phase involves gathering and integrating information in an effort to identify and clarify the issues in dispute. While all four types of third parties are active in this phase, their involvement is qualitatively different. In arbitration, the third party gathers information from the parties' presentations of positions and their responses to questions. The definition of the issues in dispute is based on a synthesis of this information by the third party. According to Wall (1981), the mediator takes on the role of information gatherer, relying on his or her own experience, the parties' interpretations, and the current state of other disputes in the area (Douglas, 1962; Kolb, 1985). The mediator then lays out his or her perceptions and interpretations of the issues to the parties. This process of information gathering and synthesis emphasizes the key role and responsibility of the mediator in deciding, or at least prioritizing, the issues to be mediated. The conciliator takes a less active role in problem definition than the mediator by ensuring clear communication through clarifying parties' messages and transmitting them to one another (Webb, 1979). The conciliator does not make decisions about what the key issues are, except by summarizing overlapping themes. Similarly, the consultant focuses on the development of open and accurate communication as opposed to selectively passing on information. The parties are actively encouraged to gather the information themselves regarding their conflict. The third party facilitates this by having participants share their perceptions of the issues and of the other party, and by encouraging them to focus on the developing interaction. The consultant provides ideas and models about social conflict, group dynamics, and intergroup processes to help participants understand their behavior and, hence, their conflict (Burton, 1969; Fisher, 1972; Kelman & Cohen, 1976). The emphasis is on the central role of the participants in analyzing and defining their conflict as a mutual problem. Thus, although the level of process control in problem definition is moderate to high in all approaches, it is of a different nature and degree.

With respect to the content of the problems identified, the mediator and, to some degree, the arbitrator are quite influential, relying on their expertise in the substantive area of conflict. The consultant's influence is less evident yet still present in the introduction of theoretical information to facilitate understanding of the interparty interaction. The conciliator tends to manifest little influence over the content of the interchanges, and functions primarily as a facilitator of communication. Thus, content control varies considerably over the four approaches.

In the second and third phases of problem solving, the generation, evaluation, and selection of alternatives in consultation and conciliation are carried out by the participants themselves. Neither third party puts forward specific solutions or proposals—the conciliator does not because of the emphasis in the role as go-between and the consultant does not because of the belief that the resolution of the conflict must come from the parties. In contrast, the mediator does not simply facilitate the interaction during these phases but actively enters in as a participant by providing proposals and backing them up with knowledge of and experience in the substantive area (Kolb, 1985; Wall, 1981). The mediator also places limits on the range of alternatives by informing participants of the solutions attained in related situations, that is, what is reasonable (Douglas, 1962; Kressel, 1972). Thus, while the mediator does not choose the solution, he or she has a strong influence through the control of interparty contact and the coordination of successive approximations to the ultimate solution deemed to be appropriate. In arbitration, the third party does choose the solution, within certain variations. Some forms involve parties putting forward solutions from which the third party can choose one or the other (final offer arbitration); other forms involve the arbitrator choosing a compromise point (Anderson, 1981; Grigsby & Bigoness, 1982). Thus, parties are involved in limited solution generation, but evaluation and selection are under the strict control of the arbitrator. Thus, both the mediator and the arbitrator continue to manifest significant control over the content of discussions at these stages, which is not the case for the conciliator or the consultant.

With regard to the fourth and fifth phases—solution implementation and evaluation—typically only the arbitration intervention manifests control in that there may be penalties for failure to comply with the decision rendered. The role of the other third parties is virtually nonexistent at this stage. However, the mediator (and the conciliator to some degree), unlike the consultant, can play an active role in "selling" the proposal to the constituencies of the parties. The mediator does so through direct statements as well as by taking on some of the responsibility for the agreement (Wall, 1981). The third party consultant may be involved in follow-up activities that aid the future interaction of the parties (Fisher, 1972).

With regard to the level of involvement of the third party, the arbitrator maintains a high level of process and content control throughout all phases of the problem-solving process. The mediator remains actively involved in the content and process of the interaction across the first four phases of problem-solving by maintaining control over information flow and the generation of appropriate alternatives (Sheppard, 1984). Even in the solution implementation phase, the mediator is often actively involved in gaining acceptance of the solution from the constituents. The consultant is quite active relative to participants in the initial problem definition phase, for example, improving communication and facilitating the discussion of viewpoints and the analysis of the conflict. In the latter phases, the consultant is primarily supportive and generally less active. Finally, the conciliator's activity, which is primarily focused on facilitating the communication of parties' positions, tends to continue at this low level up to and including alternative selection.

The dimension of outcome control was briefly introduced and deserves some discussion. The dichotomous definition of outcome control as whether or not the third party hands down a final decision or solution does not capture the range of influence a third party has on the nature of the solution. Examination of the mediation process has found evidence to suggest that mediators select their tactics on the basis of the type of outcome they wish to achieve, whether it is compromise, advisor opinion, or one side withdrawing (Shapiro et al., 1985). Thus, while mediators do not actually render the decision, they appear to deliberately influence its nature through control over the process and content of the disputants' interaction (Carnevale, 1986). Thus, outcome control should not be defined as whether or not the third party makes the final decision, but rather as degree of influence as effected by third party control over the process and content of the interaction. Given this definition, the arbitrator has high control, the mediator has moderately high control, and the consultant and conciliator have low control over the content of the outcome (see Table 9-2).

The source of influence upon which each type of third party draws is also consistent with the degree and type of control it utilizes (Sheppard, 1984) (See Table 9-2). The arbitrator is identified as a legitimate authority whose decision is binding. The other third parties do not often hold such recognized positions and thus rely on other sources of power. Expertise in the substantive area of the dispute is a key source of influence for the mediator, and the conciliator to a lesser degree. In the case of international mediation, control over present and future rewards and the ability to punish noncompliance provide the mediator with "muscle" in achieving settlement (e.g., Rubin, 1981). Referent power is another basis of influence when parties recognize the professional qualifications and affiliations of the mediator and conciliator (see Kolb, 1983). Control over information shared is another source of influence for the mediator. In contrast, the consultant's influence stems from perceived expertise in the areas of human relations, group and intergroup processes, and conflict theory. Also, because the consultation intervention has been a relatively informal and voluntary process, often at the instigation of the third party, referent power is an important source of influence here.

A procedural taxonomy of third party intervention not only provides a common framework within which to conceptualize different approaches, but also has implications for the development of a contingency approach to intervention for the effective application of third party methods. In this discussion, the dimensions of process and content control have been highlighted and refined by introducing the importance of the degree of third party versus disputant control on each of these dimensions. In addition, the nature of issues (substantive and relationship) focused on during the problem-solving process has been introduced as an important dimension of comparison. These refinements are a result of including third party consultation, which could not be accurately categorized using other procedural taxonomies such as that of Sheppard (1984).

Although the proposed taxonomy permits finer distinctions among the four approaches, it is still somewhat imprecise in that it turns on determining the balance of third party/disputant control over content, process, and outcome, This balance, although conceptually useful, may be difficult to assess in practice. Furthermore, the taxonomy needs to be extended to include other developing forms of third party intervention, particularly those of a hybrid nature. Nonetheless, the initial taxonomy provides a useful basis for the development of a contingency approach to third party intervention encompassing the methods of conciliation, consultation, mediation, and arbitration.

Comparing Consultation and Mediation Using the ICS

The initial taxonomy of third party intervention presents some clear distinctions between consultation and mediation, which are the two methods of most interest within a social-psychological approach to conflict resolution. In addition, the development of the Intergroup Conflict Simulation (ICS), as described in Chapter 6, presents a unique opportunity to test some of these distinctions in a rigorous and valid manner. Furthermore, the development of the taxonomy and the creation of the ICS make it possible to address two serious contemporary problems — one conceptual and one empirical — in the social-psychological study of third party intervention.

The conceptual problem that has developed in the past several years is a blurring of the distinctions between the innovative problem-solving approaches captured by third party consultation and the more traditional method of mediation (Fisher & Keashly, 1988). An instructive example is provided by a recent special issue of the *Journal of Social Issues* on mediation, in which the editors reference the work of problem-solving strategists such as Blake, Shepard, and Mouton (1964), Burton (1969), Doob (1970), and Kelman and Cohen (1979) as illustrations of mediation (Pruitt & Kressel, 1985). Similarly, reviews of problem-solving workshops and third party consultation by Hill (1982) and Fisher (1983) are identified as reviews of mediation rather than consultation. Each of the authors cited has in fact taken great pains to clarify and justify consultation as distinct from mediation, and the inclusion of these approaches under the rubric of mediation ignores these differences and thereby downplays the unique significance of consultation. This is particularly true in the areas of industrial and international conflict where mediation has a long history, is relatively well-articulated, and therefore stands in clear contrast to consultation. In developing areas such as community and environmental mediation, the boundaries are perhaps less clear, as some of this work appears to blend mediation and consultation. However, many of these applications are at the interpersonal level rather than the intergroup, and emerging descriptions follow a predominantly traditional style of mediation (e.g., Moore, 1986). Thus, it is clear that greater care needs to be taken to distinguish different forms of third party intervention. As these differences are delineated, it will be possible to see the unique strengths and limitations of each method. Subsequently, their special applicability as well as their potential complementarity can be explored.

The empirical problem is that very few studies have explored the differences between consultation and mediation, and those that have generally suffer from severe limitations, primarily in external validity. Simple laboratory analogs of conflict, usually involving interpersonal bargaining, have served as the context for limited third party interventions operationalized in very narrow terms. Mediation, for example, has been operationalized simply as nonbinding suggestion from an outside party (e.g., Bigoness, 1976), whereas consultation has been operationalized as teaching parties how to paraphrase (e.g., Bartenuk, Benton, & Keys, 1975). These interventions are often delivered in a one-shot fashion through the researcher without a third party actually being present (e.g., Bigoness, 1976; Johnson & Tullar, 1972). Furthermore, the assessment of third party impact focuses almost exclusively on qualities of the substantive outcome such as amount of or time to settlement. Evaluations of substantive outcome in terms of satisfaction and fairness, and more importantly, subjective outcomes such as changes in perceptions and attitudes have largely been ignored. Thus, key differences between mediation and consultation in terms of attitude and relationship dimensions have not been investigated. Documentation of differential impact in these areas is necessary to lend support to the conceptual distinctions that are being made.

To address these issues, the ICS was used to assess and compare the outcomes achieved by consultation versus mediation (Keashly, 1988; Keashly, Fisher, & Grant, 1989). Given the conceptual distinctions between the two methods, it was hypothesized that mediation would result in faster agreements, but that consultation would lead to higher joint outcomes and greater satisfaction with the settlement. In regard to subjective outcomes, consultation was predicted to result in more positive intergroup perceptions and attitudes and a more satisfying and collaborative relationship. In order to test these hypotheses, consultation and mediation interventions were introduced into the ICS in Session IV midway through the six negotiation intervals (see Chapter 6 for details). The 16 simulation runs following the final ICS design were randomly assigned to receive either a consultation or mediation intervention up to an equal total of 8 each.

The third party intervenors were two male graduate students in applied social psychology with training and experience in group dynamics and intergroup relations. Two third parties were used to deal with the possible interaction of personal style with intervention. Each third party intervened in half of the consultation runs and half of the mediation runs, and post hoc analysis indicated that the respective interventions were implemented similarly by the two. The third party interventions were designed to capture the characteristic flow of each approach through direct interactions with the participants. At the end of the third negotiation interval, groups were informed of the upcoming intervention of a third party who would help them look at the progress of negotiations and help them to get what they wanted. The interventions were matched for length (60 min) and overall agenda in that the groups were given an initial task, the third party provided conceptual input, and the implications of the intervention for subsequent negotiations were considered. The consultation intervention involved a combination of individual and joint meetings with the two groups. Working separately with the groups, the consultant facilitated a discussion exercise in which each group identified its perceptions of negotiations and of the present relationship between the groups. A joint meeting was then held in which the groups presented and clarified their perceptions. After the consultant provided conceptual input on intergroup conflict and its escalation, the groups jointly identified the characteristics of an ideal relationship and the implications of these for negotiations. The mediation intervention involved separate meetings of the groups, as is typical in the real world. Initially, the groups identified their perceptions of the main issues and of the other group's positions. The third party examined the two sets of perceptions and reported to each group on the similarities and differences in positions as well as the potential points of movement in negotiations. After the mediator provided conceptual input on negotiation as a process of mutual concession making, the groups were asked to reconsider their positions and to develop their next proposal for negotiations.

In order to assess the impact of the interventions, a number of the measures at the intergroup level, described in Chapter 6 were utilized. Substantive outcome measures included joint payoff, as determined from the point matrices, and time to settlement. Subjective evaluations of outcome were measured by ratings of satisfaction with, fairness of, and commitment to the outcome. Subjective outcomes were gauged using ratings of out-group liking and trust, and the semantic differential measure of out-group attitude. Perceptions of the intergroup relationship were assessed using a set of semantic differential scales (e.g., pleasant–unpleasant, trusting–suspicious, caring–indifferent), combined ratings of the cooperativeness/competitiveness of their own group and the other group, a rating of the degree of collaboration during negotiations, and a rating of satisfaction with how the two groups were working together. The measures of the subjective outcomes were taken prior to and after the third party intervention and at the end of negotiations. Thus, the impact of the interventions was directly assessed and any effects of settlement could be ascertained.

The results indicated that consultation and mediation did not differ with regard to their impact on substantive outcomes but did produce very different effects on perceptual and attitudinal variables. There were no differences on joint payoff or time to settlement and both consultation and mediation groups were equally satisfied with and committed to the outcome and perceived it as equally fair. However, in terms of perceptions of the other group, groups exposed to the consultation intervention expressed greater liking and trust toward the other group after the intervention, and this effect held until postnegotiation (see Table 9-3). Mediation groups showed no increase on these dimensions and were significantly lower on them at postintervention and postnegotiation than consultation groups. Similarly, consultation groups developed more positive attitudes toward the other group over time as compared to mediation groups, and these effects continued through to the end of negotiations. On perceptions of the intergroup relationship, consultation groups showed increased positiveness, both over time and in comparison to mediation

Table 9-3. Means of Perceptions and Attitudes Toward the Other Group

Measures	Time of Measurement		
	Pre-TPI	Post-TPI	Post-NEG
Liking			
Mediation	3.89a	3.98a	3.99a
Consultation	3.96a	4.66b	4.87b
Trust			
Mediation	3.40a	3.37a	3.65a
Consultation	3.15a	4.27b	4.89b
Attitude[a]			
Mediation	61.05a	61.02a	59.37a
Consultation	61.80a	53.02b	49.88b

[a] Note: Lower scores on the attitude measure indicate more positive attitudes; Means with different subscripts are significantly different ($p < .05$).

Table 9-4. Means of Measures of Perceptions of Intergroup Relationship[a]

Measures	Time of Measurement		
	Pre-TPI	Post-TPI	Post-NEG
Relationship			
Mediation	57.99a	58.06a	61.95a
Consultation	54.33a	62.25b	71.95b
Cooperativeness			
Mediation	3.58a	3.71a	3.72a
Consultation	3.34a	3.74a	4.68b
Collaboration			
Mediation	4.50a	4.43a	5.05a
Consultation	4.22a	4.83b	5.75c
Satisfaction			
Mediation	4.92a	4.70a	5.17a
Consultation	4.63a	5.18b	6.03c

[a] Note: Means with different subscripts are significantly different ($p < .05$).

groups (see Table 9-4). On the semantic differential measure, consultation groups demonstrated a more positive evaluation of the relationship following the intervention and at the end of negotiations. On the combined measure of perceived cooperativeness, consultation groups exhibited higher ratings than mediation groups at postnegotiation, although not at postintervention. On the ratings of collaboration during negotiations and satisfaction with working together, consultation groups showed significantly higher scores following the intervention and again at the end of negotiations. This indicates that the completion of negotiations may have some positive effects on the relationship in conjunction with that provided by the consultation intervention. Most importantly, in all cases, the consultation intervention produced more positive effects than the mediation intervention on the subjective measures of perceptions and attitudes.

These results using the ICS are the first to provide a rigorous and yet moderately complex comparison between the third party methods of mediation and consultation. On substantive issues, one interpretation is that consultation is equally effective with mediation even in a situation of negotiation, which is typically seen as more amenable to mediation. However, it is possible that given the moderate intensity of the simulation, any intervention or even no intervention might have been equally effective or ineffective, because the groups were perhaps handling the negotiations adequately on their own. Thus, no firm conclusions should be drawn on substantive outcomes. However, in relation to subjective outcomes, the superiority of consultation is clearly demonstrated in the more positive perceptions and attitudes toward the other group and the intergroup relationship. These results also contradict the assumption typically made by proponents of mediation that a successful settlement of substantive issues will lead to improvements in subjective aspects of the relationship. In contrast, it was the consultation intervention that consistently led to such changes on a variety of dimensions and these held to the point of settlement, thus auguring positively for the future of the relationship as well. These outcomes are clearly supportive of the rationale of third party consultation, in that the results predicted by theory are those that obtain. In addition, the conceptual distinction between consultation and mediation described in the initial taxonomy of third party intervention is supported. Given that, the results also indirectly indicate the potential complementarity of mediation and consultation, and encourage their application within a contingency approach to third party intervention in intense intergroup conflict, as discussed in the next section.

A Contingency Approach to Third Party Intervention

Conceptualizing conflict as a mixture of objective and subjective elements that escalates and de-escalates over time is compatible with the realization that different third party interventions may be most appropriate and effective at different stages of a conflict. If conflict is seen predominantly as an objective phenomenon based on resource scarcity and thus inherent in the structure of the situation, then third party approaches that facilitate or require a compromise are considered relevant. If subjective elements such as misperception, miscommunication, and the differential valuing of real interests are accepted, then third party strategies that aid the search for collaborative outcomes are seen as appropriate. Thus, the beliefs held about the fundamental nature of conflict by the parties (and the third party) will have a strong effect on what approaches are regarded as realistic (Beres & Schmidt, 1982; Burton, 1987a; Mitchell, 1981b). The initial taxonomy of third party intervention provides a starting point by distinguishing different interventions on which a contingency approach can be built.

The acceptance of an objective/subjective mix in conflict is usually complemented by the realization that subjective elements increase and take on greater importance as conflict escalates. In general, the assumption is made that conflict is a dynamic interplay of structural and social-psychological elements that vary in their influence at different points throughout the course of escalation and de-escalation. It is also assumed that for resolution to occur all these various elements must be acknowledged and dealt with at some point (R. Fisher, 1986). Because third party interventions vary in the emphases they give to objective versus subjective elements, the possibility of matching the intervention to the level of escalation becomes feasible. In addition, it also becomes conceivable to enter into the sequencing and coordinating of interventions to de-escalate and resolve the conflict beginning at any particular stage. This acknowledges that no one intervention strategy should be expected to deal with all or even most aspects of a conflict. Given that third party interventions in real world conflicts are seldom if ever coordinated (Ury, 1987), the potential of a contingency approach for the more effective handling of conflict may be considerable.

Table 9-5. Stages of Conflict Escalation

Stage	Dimensions of the Conflict			
	Communication/ interaction	Perceptions/ relationship	Issues	Outcome/ management
I	Discussion/debate	Accurate/trust, respect commitment	Interests	Joint gain/mutual decision
II	Less direct/deeds, not words	Stereotypes/ other still important	Relationship	Compromise/ negotiation
III	Little direct/ threats	Good vs. evil/ distrust, lack of respect	Basic needs	Win–lose/ defensive competition
IV	Nonexistent/direct attacks	Other non-human/ hopeless	Survival	Lose–lose/ destruction

In order to develop a contingency and sequencing approach, it is necessary to identify the characteristics of conflict that can be used as cues for the implementation of a particular strategy. In this regard, the stage of escalation of a conflict has been identified as a critical cue for the selection of the appropriate strategy (Glasl, 1982; Prein, 1984; Wright, 1965b). Glasl presents a model of escalation based mainly on organizational conflict that distinguishes nine stages defined by changes in overt behavior, patterns of interaction, perceptions, and attitudes. These stages are then combined into three main phases based on significant shifts in beliefs and interaction. Different third party interventions are connected to the stages and phases, thus providing the most comprehensive statement of a contingency approach to date. Prein also presents a contingency approach for third party intervention in organizational conflict that describes the conditions and indications that favor mediation or consultation as the strategy of choice. Wright's model is drawn from escalation in international conflict and identifies four stages according to increasingly overt actions of violence (see Chapter 7). Unfortunately, Wright says little about the subjective aspects in conflict escalation such as attitudes and patterns of interaction. This deficit is counterbalanced by the work of Glasl and of Prein, which directly consider perceptual distortions, communication problems, and relationship issues along with substantive differences.

Using these various contributions, it is possible to develop a basic stage model of conflict escalation and an initial contingency approach for third party intervention (Keashly & Fisher, 1989). The stage model (see Table 9-5) distinguishes four stages: Discussion, Polarization, Segregation, and Destruction. These are identified by significant changes in the nature of communication, the parties' perceptions and images of each other and their relationship, the overt issues in the dispute, the perceived possible outcomes, and the appropriate approach to managing the conflict. The stage model bears overall similarity to the eclectic model of conflict presented in Chapter 5, particularly with regard to the system states of low intensity and high intensity conflict. Specifically, Stages I and II roughly correspond to the low intensity system state, whereas Stages III and IV are more or less captured by the high intensity system state. This is especially true with regard to the nature of communication within the intergroup relationship, the cognitive functioning of the parties, and the basic issues that are seen to lie at the source of the conflict.

Briefly, as conflict escalates, communication moves from direct discussion and debate between the parties to reliance on the interpretation of actions rather than words, to the use of threats, and finally to direct attacks. Thus, communication is carried out through increasingly aggressive forms of interaction between the parties. Accompanying this breakdown in open and direct communication is the replacement of accurate perceptions with negative and simplified stereotypes to the point where the other party is regarded as evil and nonhuman. The relationship moves from one of trust, respect, and commitment to one of mistrust, disrespect, and, finally, hopelessness in terms of possible improvements. In terms of issues fueling the conflict, the emphasis shifts from substantive interests and positions to concerns regarding the relationship, to basic needs or values, and ultimately to the very survival of the parties. In line with these changes, the possible outcomes begin with joint gain, or win–win, options, move to compromises, then to win–lose results, and finally to lose–lose results, in which the objective is to minimize one's own losses while inflicting maximum costs on the other party. In attempting to achieve these outcomes, the parties' preferred methods of conflict management move from joint decision making, through negotiation to defensive competition, and ultimately to outright attempts at destruction. Although the stage model presents a simplified picture of conflict escalation, it does provide an accurate and detailed enough picture so that different third party interventions can be linked to the different stages, which is the essence of the contingency approach.

The overall strategy of a contingency approach to third party intervention is to de-escalate conflict back down through the identified stages. This is potentially accomplished not only by matching particular interventions to specific stages, but also by combining interventions in appropriate sequences to further de-escalate the conflict. The initial contingency model is given in Figure 9-2. In the first stage, the key dimension of concern is the nature of communication, because perceptions are still accurate, commitment to the relationship strong, and belief in possible joint gain predominant. Thus, conciliation is the third-party intervention of choice to facilitate clear and open communication on interests and positions so that the way is paved toward negotiations directly between the parties. In the second stage, relationship issues become central as trust and respect are threatened, and distorted perceptions and simplified stereotypes emerge. At this point, consultation becomes most appropriate because it uniquely deals directly with relationship issues, including perceptions and attitudes between the parties. Once a problem-solving orientation is developed or redeveloped, it becomes possible to deal effectively with the substantive issues. Thus, consultation would appropriately be followed by media-

A Contingency Approach to Third Party Intervention 237

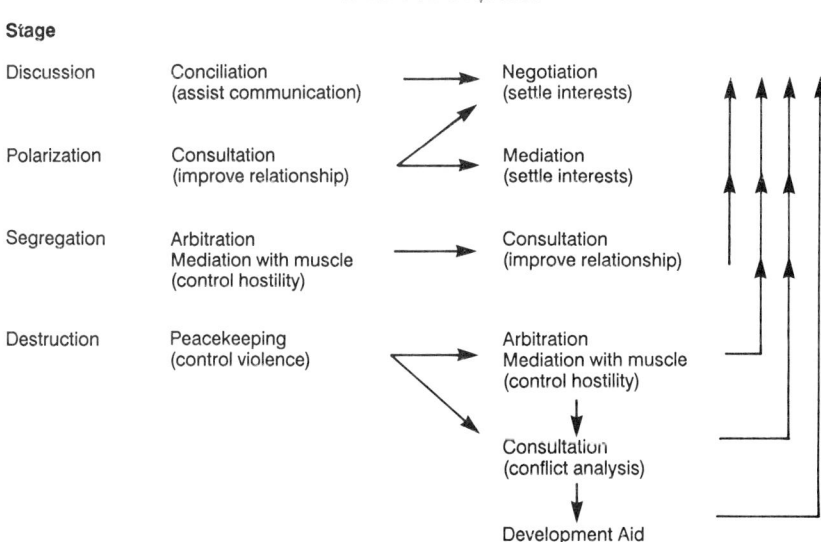

Figure 9-2. A contingency model of third party intervention.

tion or, if possible, by direct negotiation, thereby returning the conflict to the first stage. It is in this vein that consultation in the form of problem-solving discussions can potentially serve a very useful prenegotiation function (Fisher, 1989). In the third stage, competition and hostility are main themes and the conflict is now perceived as threatening basic needs. Thus, some immediate form of control is necessary to halt escalation and to demonstrate to the parties that agreement is still possible on substantive issues. The third party intervention of choice would be arbitration, assuming that it can be effectively introduced, in order to effect at least a partial settlement and halt spiraling hostility and aggression. A second alternative, midway between arbitration and mediation, is that of mediation with muscle, in which the mediator has the power to influence the parties toward agreement through inducing costs, present or future, or by providing positive inducements such as development aid. Once escalation is controlled, consultation would be provided to assist the parties in a full analysis of the conflict and the improvement of the relationship back to the first stage. In the fourth, and final, stage, the primary intent of the parties is to destroy or at least subjugate each other through the use of violence, typically expressed by war at the intercommunal and international levels. Given that destruction is the mutual intent of the parties, a power intervention by the third party is initially necessary to forcefully separate the parties and control escalating violence. The impartial and pacific form of such an intervention is that of peacekeeping, in which a ceasefire is monitored and maintained by forces organized by the third party. If the relationship can be stabilized and an initial commitment to joint effort obtained, the way is cleared for the implementation of other interventions depending on the parties' receptivity and sense of critical issues. Thus, subsequent to peacekeeping, arbitration or mediation with muscle might be instituted to control hostility and increase hope that peaceful settlements are possible. This could be followed by consultation for conflict analysis and for improving the relationship. Alternatively, consultation might be instituted subsequent to peacekeeping to identify key issues and to improve the relationship to the point where mediation or negotiation could be initiated. In addition, the provision of economic or social aid, but without the strings attached to settlement as in mediation with muscle, could be a complementary strategy to help deal with the structural inequity that is common in protracted intercommunal and international conflict (see Chapter 7).

Thus, the initial contingency model envisages the application and sequencing of third party interventions at the most propitious points in the escalatory spiral of conflict. It is also possible to envision the simultaneous and hopefully coordinated application of different strategies. There is little evidence that these types of deliberate efforts occur in the real world, at any level of conflict. Therefore, it is likely that one of the reasons for failures of third party interventions is their inappropriate application with regard to the stage of conflict. Another reason may be that there is a lack of follow-up using additional interventions designed to deal with the elements or issues that were not focused on by the initial or previous intervention. The contingency model thus raises the possibility that third party interventions could be applied singly and in combination with much greater effectiveness than at present. After gaining a reasonable degree of conceptual consensus, it is incumbent upon the field of conflict resolution to begin searching for the empirical and practical evidence that would support or refute the ideas inherent in the contingency model. Given the almost absolute paucity of work in this area, the agenda is as formidable as it is timely.

Chapter 10
Conclusion: Paths Toward a Peaceful World

The primary thesis of this book is that the discipline of social psychology has much to offer to the understanding and resolution of destructive intergroup and international conflict. A variety of themes running throughout the book demonstrate this richness in terms of theory, research, and practice. After discussing these themes briefly, this chapter will consider the implications of the social-psychological approach for conflict de-escalation and resolution. It will be made clear that a number of alternate paths toward a more peaceful world are available based on a social-psychological analysis. Finally, some thoughts about the agenda for the future will be brought forward. These will relate primarily to the need for the accelerated development and institutionalization of innovative methods of practice developed from a social-psychological base so that these can take a place alongside established methods of conflict management.

Major Themes

In line with the phenomenological perspective, the power of perceptual and cognitive processes to influence the course of intergroup conflict is all too apparent. Intergroup perceptions, images, and attitudes fall prey to both motivational and cognitive biases resulting in a selective and distorted view of the social world. The power of categorization and the push toward stereotyping lead to a skewed picture of positive in-group similarity in contrast to a distant and negative out-group homogeneity. Once formed, cognitive structures (beliefs, expectations, stereotypes, frameworks) have a very powerful influence on how incoming information is perceived, interpreted, and assimilated. The phenomenon of ethnocentrism is a concomitant of these processes in which in-groups are seen as legitimately superior and righteous whereas out-groups are targets of derogation and hostility. The ultimate influence of perceptual and cognitive processes is seen in the functioning of self-confirming expectations in which biased cognitions help produce skewed behavior that elicits the expected response. Thus, the self-perpetuating nature of social stereotypes produces an insidious dynamic that is extremely difficult to reveal or to counteract. A variety of distorted and self-justifying images of own and other group take the place of reality and ultimately create their own reality.

The importance of cognitive processes is enhanced through linkages with the concept of identity, a central construct in social identity and self-categorization theories. Social identity is a pivotal concept that helps us understand individual cognitive processes in the group context while at the same time it informs our understanding of intergroup behavior. Invidious comparisons between groups are inextricably linked with the need for a positive social identity more so than for personal identity. Social identity theory thus becomes an important complement to realistic group conflict theory for understanding the sources of intergroup conflict. In relation to the phenomenon of protracted social conflict, identity is one of the compelling universal needs, the frustration of which both causes and perpetuates destructive intergroup conflict. Identity is further linked to one of the basic types of intergroup conflict, that is, value conflict, by realizing that the values or ideology of a group or nation are an integral part of its identity and as such are not amenable to compromise or repudiation. The concept of social identity therefore plays an essential linking role between the individual, group, and intergroup levels of analysis.

The importance of group-level processes in the development and escalation of intergroup conflict must not be lost sight of, as many treatments concentrating on the individual level are wont to do. Along with the impact of social identity, the influence of group cohesion and conformity support an ethnocentric perspective of intergroup relations. These forces drive a faulty and insidious process of decision making that is the central contributor of group dynamics to destructive intergroup conflict. The model of groupthink provides a comprehensive and integrated explication of the ways in which a cohesive group fosters concurrence seeking in place of the realistic appraisal of alternatives. This model also integrates the effects of certain cognitive biases and organizational factors into its central focus on group-level variables. Along with the consideration of leadership and constituent pressure on representatives, all of these group-level concepts have significant implications for the escalation and de-escalation of intergroup conflict.

The eclectic model of intergroup conflict is a direct response to the clear need for multilevel, integrative theorizing based in the social-psychological perspective. Developed through a systematic approach to theory construction and sensitive to both static and dynamic variables, the eclectic model is an initial attempt to capture the essential reality of the causation and escalation of intergroup conflict. It is less sensitive to the mechanisms of de-escalation and in that way mirrors an imbalance in the field as a whole. The portrayal of the two system states of low and high intensity goes part way to correcting this deficiency. The eclectic model is also inadequate at the top end, or higher levels, of analysis; that is, it says very little about organizational, communal, societal, and global determinants and elements of intergroup and international conflict. Many of the variables at these levels can of course be addressed in the case study description and analysis of particular conflicts. Nonetheless, there are generic structures and processes at these levels that are necessary for understanding the process and outcomes of intergroup conflict in

Major Themes 241

organizational, community, and international settings. By concentrating on individual, group, and intergroup variables, the electic model encompasses a good deal of the social-psychological reality of intergroup conflict and of international conflict as shown by the present analysis. However, in taking this focus, it also ignores a great deal of the social world. There is therefore a strong need for the development of additional models at each higher level of analysis that would give appropriate attention to structures and processes at that level. Thus, a series of complementary models should be developed to do full justice to the complexity of intergroup and international conflict. The current model is seen as an essential step in that direction.

Approaching the understanding of intergroup conflict from a systems perspective carries some important and demanding implications for the manner in which research is conducted. Research paradigms and methods must be developed and used that can capture a reasonable amount of the complexity of the phenomenon. It is essential to study a variety of variables as they interrelate over time. Research endeavors that are limited in scope and time, such as laboratory games, are not likely to add substantially to our understanding, although they can be useful for studying specific causal relationships among variables in a way that may cumulate toward general principles over the long haul. As noted in Chapter 1, the complementarity of findings from different methods is one road toward greater external validity. Another is to build more complex and yet controlled methods for laboratory study.

The Intergroup Conflict Simulation (ICS) is seen as a step in this direction. The design of the ICS allows for the tracking of a variety of essential variables over time, and is open to the manipulation of other variables in order to study causal relationships directly. The initial results presented in Chapter 6 demonstrate the internal validity of the ICS in terms of group development and conflict intensity. The use of the ICS to compare different methods of third party intervention in Chapter 9 provides an example of how the paradigm may be used to yield unique and useful results. These data provide the first detailed, controlled, and complex comparison between third party consultation and mediation available in the conflict resolution literature. Now that the methodology has been developed and demonstrated to be useful, it can be made available for the testing of a variety of relationships among variables within a systems perspective. The strength of the ICS for studying reciprocal and multiple causation among variables, using appropriate multivariate statistical analyses, is particularly noteworthy. More specifically, the ICS can now be used for the assessment of many of the principles and propositions specified in the eclectic model. Such assessments should focus especially on interactive processes that occur during conflict escalation. Greater understanding in this area would be invaluable in charting the course that conflict de-escalation may need to take.

In the broader flow of conflict research, simulations like the ICS provide a valuable middle ground between laboratory games and content analyses of real-world interaction between conflicting groups and/or nations. Moving from the simpler to the more complex methods provides greater external validity with decreasing internal validity. Thus, the overall combination of methods may produce results that are adequately valid on both counts. The hope is that the same relationships and processes of interaction can be studied using all three methods, as well as others, thereby testing our propositions and models in a much more demanding fashion. The ultimate yield will be better theories about intergroup and international conflict as well as more powerful and useful implications for practice in the areas of de-escalation and resolution. Such developments would be a direct response to the challenge to integrate theory, research, and practice as discussed in Chapter 1.

Implications for Conflict De-Escalation and Resolution

In considering the implications of this work for addressing questions of amelioration, acknowledgment must first be given to the wider field of intergroup relations, which has much to offer the study of conflict resolution. In terms of understanding, generic conceptualizations, such as the cognitive theories covered in chapter 3, can be effectively applied to illuminate essential elements of intergroup conflict. A similar comment can be made with regard to much of the theorizing and research done in the areas of prejudice, discrimination, and racism (e.g., P.A. Katz & Taylor, 1988). On a broader scale, theories of intergroup relations can provide some of the wider analysis required at the societal level to explain intergroup conflict between various types of identity groups. In particular, most theories of intergroup relations deal more directly with relations between groups of unequal power than does the eclectic model. Unfortunately, as noted earlier, what some theories of intergroup relations lack is an explanatory focus that goes much beyond the individual level of analysis (D.M. Taylor & Moghaddam, 1987). Nonetheless, it is essential to keep the channels open so that the wider work on intergroup relations continues to inform the study of intergroup conflict and the practice of conflict resolution.

With regard to the question of practice, work in the field of intergroup relations on the facilitative conditions of intergroup contact has significant implications for conflict de-escalation and resolution. This is because the contact hypothesis delineates the broad parameters within which face-to-face interaction between members of conflicting groups is more likely to be useful. This significance is underscored by accepting Kelman's proposition that actual behavioral interaction among antagonists is a necessary requirement for conflict resolution (see Chapter 8). Thus, de-escalation may be possible through indirect and distanced interaction (i.e., communication) by decision makers, but movement toward resolution in the sense of searching toward creative, mutually acceptable, and self-sustaining solutions may only come about through direct dialogue between influential representatives of conflicting parties. Thus, the facilitative conditions of intergroup contact must be taken into account in the design and implementation of any form of contact between members of antagonistic groups or nations in order to increase the likelihood of productive outcomes. As noted in Chapter 8, more understanding of and attention to the intercultural dynamics of such contact, as provided for example by Brislin, Cushner, Cherrie, and Yong (1986), is also essential.

Another implication of the present work is to underscore the power of the norm of reciprocity in both the escalation and the resolution of intergroup and international conflict. As captured in Deutsch's crude law of social relations, reciprocity determines that competition breeds competition, whereas cooperation breeds cooperation. As mutually competitive orientations feed the perception of threat, escalation begins to move the relationship toward the malignant social process. A number of the critical variables in this reality are captured by the eclectic model, but underlying them all is the powerful pull of reciprocity. Nowhere is this more evident or significant than in international relations where mutual policies of deterrence tend to fuel arms races that make the likelihood of war greater rather than smaller.

Part of the key in conflict resolution, then, becomes reliance on reciprocity to facilitate the process of de-escalation. Unfortunately, for many reasons discussed in this work, it appears much easier to go up the conflict spiral than down it. Nonetheless, the positive influence of a strategy of reciprocity has been consistently demonstrated in a variety of contexts. In both games research and internation interaction, a tit-for-tat strategy appears effective in inducing de-escalation, maximizing joint gains, and avoiding mutually destructive outcomes. In studies of integrative complexity in internation communication, there is some indication of reciprocity effects: the complexity of the statements from one nation's policy makers appears to be partly dependent on preceding statements from those of the other. Thus, in a crisis, if one nation purposely increases the complexity of its communication, this may have a beneficial effect on the situation. The norm of reciprocity finds direct expression in the GRIT strategy, wherein a series of conciliatory moves by one party are expected to be eventually reciprocated by the other. This strategy is likely the strongest test of faith in reciprocity, because the initial moves are costly, may involve some increase in vulnerability, and cannot be easily withdrawn. Based on laboratory research, there are some indications that the GRIT strategy is even more effective than tit-for-tat in inducing cooperation. This raises the possibility that reciprocity sweetened with some conciliatory moves may be the best route toward de-escalation.

A number of theorists, mainly at the international level, have brought forward strategies for de-escalation that are firmly rooted in the principle of reciprocity (see Chapters 7 and 8). Kriesberg supports the tit-for-tat strategy as a combination of firmness and conciliation in which the sequencing of coercive and noncoercive moves is handled carefully in relation to the stage that the conflict is in, that is, prior to negotiation or at the initiation of or during negotiation. Patchen concludes that a successful policy for de-escalation combines firmness with cooperation and flexibility, that is, reciprocating coercive moves, but also reciprocating and sometimes initiating conciliatory moves. This is then a combination of tit-for-tat with GRIT. Deutsch also speaks of combining firmness with friendliness, and White proposes the maintenance of minimal deterrence with drastic tension reduction based on unilateral initiatives. Finally, Kaplowitz suggests that a firm-but-cooperative strategy will lead to de-escalation when paired with a deterrence or competitive strategy, because concerns about security are eased at the same time that exploitation is resisted. As with all these recommended approaches, attempts are made to elicit rather than force desired behavior and the assumption is made that the reciprocation of cooperation will eventually unfold. As noted in Chapter 8, the firm-but-cooperative strategy is the only one identified by Kaplowitz at the international level that lies on the integrative dimension of the two-dimensional model of conflict management. It is only a half step further to joint problem solving, or collaboration, which is generally the preferred strategy in interpersonal relations and organizational settings, increasingly within the context of a contingency approach. It is therefore quite clear that there is a great deal of commonality among those taking a social-psychological approach to intergroup and international conflict resolution: a combination of reciprocity and cooperation underlies the paths to a peaceful world.

Given the intractable nature of intense and protracted social conflict, the question has been raised as to whether the parties themselves will, in the foreseeable future, be able to successfully initiate moves toward de-escalation and resolution. In addition to the internal resistance that must be overcome for decision makers to take cooperative or conciliatory action, it is also predictable that exploitation rather than reciprocation will be the likely immediate response, given the intense competitive orientations in a highly escalated conflict. This sobering reality opens the door to the potential of various forms of third party intervention in situations where the parties are unable or unwilling to take steps toward de-escalation, settlement, or resolution.

In terms of third party methods, arbitration is seldom appropriate or effective in protracted intergroup and international conflicts, because the parties exist in an anarchic situation in which the rule of law is severely limited or nonexistent. Peacekeeping can be a useful stopgap measure for containing violence, but is not a route toward settlement, and may in fact be accepted by the parties for this very reason. That is, a controlled stalemate is preferable to a poor settlement. It is partly for this same reason that mediation is often resisted or rendered ineffective by the parties. In an escalated conflict, the mutual mistrust, ethnocentrism, and competitive orientations put a severe strain on mediation to produce results, primarily because any genuinely cooperative moves are extremely difficult, if not impossible, for the parties to initiate or to reciprocate. Mediation with muscle, in which the third party offers inducements or threatens punishments to elicit settlement, may meet with some success, but only in the short run. Third party interventions designed to facilitate the settlement of substantive issues, such as arbitration and mediation, typically fail to deal with fundamental needs of the parties and underlying issues in the relationship. Thus, they are ineffective in dealing with protracted social conflicts in the sense of reaching a long-term resolution that is mutually acceptable to the parties and that is sustainable until conditions change.

These considerations lay part of the basis for the proposition that third party consultation may be the most effective method for approaching the enigma of protracted social conflict in intergroup and international relationships. In particular, the problem-solving workshop provides a unique and attractive opportunity for the parties to undertake an analysis of their conflict and to search for creative solutions along the integrative dimension. Within a contingency approach, consultation may be the key to breaking out of the dilemma of stalemate frozen by peacekeeping— there is no widespread violence, yet there is no move toward true peace. In these situations, arbitration is usually impossible and mediation is extremely difficult, even though they make conceptual sense in terms of a contingency model. What is likely to be required is a mutual and full analysis of the conflict in both process and content terms, leading to further problem solving directed toward improving the intergroup relationship. For reasons of both motivation and competence, these types of initiatives are best designed and implemented with the assistance of an impartial and skilled team of facilitators in the third party role. Following the improvement of the intergroup relationship and the possible discovery of some creative solutions to substantive issues, either mediation or direct negotiation between the parties can be implemented to settle the remaining points of difference on interests. The implication is that a great deal of work needs to be done to further develop methods of third party intervention, especially consultation, within the context of a contingency approach to the management and resolution of intergroup and international conflict.

The Agenda for the Future

As the social-psychological study of intergroup and international conflict moves into the future, a prime consideration is to how better meet the challenges outlined in Chapter 1. Continuing developments are required to remedy a number of deficiencies that have been identified throughout this work. Briefly put, there is a strong need for multimethod research and multilevel theorizing. There needs to be corroboration and integration of results from different and complementary studies and there needs to be the construction of comprehensive and dynamic models. Within these activities, the intergroup level, rather than the individual or interpersonal levels, of analysis needs to be the primary focus. At the same time, group-level variables must be given their due. The overall approach must be integrative rather than reductionist.

In the broader interdisciplinary context of social science, the social-psychological approach must acknowledge and, where possible, take account of higher level structures and processes. In communal conflict, the role of historical and cultural factors, sometimes over centuries of interaction, is crucial to understanding the present situation. In international conflict, the influence of domestic politics is usually central in affecting the interaction between the parties. At the global level, not only must the complexity of reality be acknowledged, but attention must also be given to the normative possibilities of what could be. For example, the humanistic value base of applied social psychology is quite compatible with the creation of a world order based on a common set of values as outlined by a multinational and multidisciplinary team of scholars (Mendlowitz, 1975). The basic values identified include peace (the absence of violent conflict), ecological stability (harmonious interaction with the environment), economic well-being (reorganization of the economic system to drastically reduce inequity), participation (shared power in decision making), and social justice (the provision of basic rights and freedoms for all). It is in this broader context that the social-psychological approach to understanding and resolving conflict makes the most sense.

There is a need to develop more effective mechanisms for the dissemination of social scientific knowledge about conflict and its resolution to policy makers and practitioners. Although this is a complex and difficult process (Glaser, Abelson, & Garrison, 1983), institutional structures are one important mechanism for dissemination and utilization. Interdisciplinary research centers at universities for the study of conflict have an important role to play in fostering utilization, especially if they encourage interaction among scholars and policy makers. The first such center in the Western world was established at the University of Michigan in the mid-1950s, but was unfortunately dissolved in the early 1970s. One important legacy was the initiation of the *Journal of Conflict Resolution*, which continues to provide a forum for scholarly research from a variety of disciplines. Contemporary and noteworthy examples of this type of institutional structure are the Center for Conflict Analysis and Resolution at George Mason University and the Center for International Development and Conflict Resolution at the University of Maryland.

In the public domain, both the United States and Canadian governments moved in the mid-1980s to establish independent institutes concerned with peace. The United States Institute of Peace has the overall purpose of engendering research, training, and education in peaceful methods of conflict resolution. Its designated activities include the development and provision of continuing education and training programs in international conflict resolution for policy makers and practitioners. The Canadian Institute for International Peace and Security has the mandate of increasing knowledge and understanding of issues from a Canadian perspective with a particular emphasis on arms control, disarmament, defense, and conflict resolution. This institute supports policy-relevant research and analysis, disseminates information, and sponsors conferences that bring together researchers and practitioners. These institutional initiatives thus provide new opportunities for linkages between the social science community and government policy makers and diplomatic practitioners.

The appealing aspect of increased interaction among scientists and practitioners is that the connections among theory, research, and practice can be more directly and effectively examined. The policy and practice implications of social science theory and research on conflict can be brought forward and scrutinized for their potential utility in the real world. The principles underlying current practice can likewise be examined for their compatibility with social scientific understanding of conflict and its resolution. The potential utility of social-psychological approaches to handling intergroup and international conflict can be assessed and the implications for developing a wider array of practice options can be developed. More specifically, training programs based on social science understanding could be offered to policy makers and practitioners in a number of areas. Janis and Mann (1977), for example, describe a workshop on decision making that would assist participants in avoiding the pitfalls of poor decision making such as occur in groupthink. A variety of training experiences are now available in the area of negotiation, and similar workshops could be developed that focus on intergroup problem solving. The workshop format allows for the sharing of the experience and expertise of practitioners with the knowledge of conflict processes and alternative methods of management brought

The Agenda for the Future 247

forward by the social scientists. The emphasis in all these activities would be the more effective blending of theory, research, and practice toward the de-escalation and resolution of intergroup and international conflict.

There is a definite need for the further development of practice in conflict resolution through the active involvement of social scientists themselves in the role of scientist/practitioners. This is not an attempt to take over the traditional and existing roles of practitioners, be they diplomats, mediators, or whatever. It is a call for the creation of new roles within the social science community directed toward the study and resolution of intergroup and international conflict. The clearest example is the role of third party consultant, which has emerged out of the pioneering efforts of scholars such as Blake, Burton, Doob, and Kelman in intergroup and international problem solving (see Chapters 8 and 9). This role is uniquely suited to the identity of the scholar who acquires the necessary practice skills to design and facilitate direct confrontation between conflicting parties. Unfortunately, very little attention has been directed toward the selection and training of third party consultants, especially at the international level (Fisher, 1983). Some initial and general ideas on training are offered by Fisher (1976), suggesting that consultants need conceptual understanding of human social behavior at several levels of analysis and human relations skill training in a number of areas including interpersonal communication, small group processes, conflict management, consultation, and intergroup problem solving. Professional training opportunities, which exist in organization development and community development, can be useful starting points, but little exists for scholars interested in international conflict resolution. A recent and laudable initiative is the offering of graduate study at both the MA and PhD levels, specifically in conflict resolution, at George Mason University through the interdisciplinary Center for Conflict Analysis and Resolution. It is to be hoped that similar developments will occur elsewhere. Given the complexity of the third party consultant role, it is not expected that any one training program or any one individual can encompass all the requisite knowledge and skills. For this reason, team practice is highly recommended, and this creates an opportunity for apprenticeship experiences through which beginning scientist/practitioners can further develop their expertise. Hopefully, the development and dissemination of practice will be paralleled by improvements in theory and research as noted in Chapter 9 and discussed by Fisher (1983).

The final step in the development of practice is that of institutionalization, that is, the formation of organizational structures that offer the provision of services with the usual assurances of competence, consistency, and ethical conduct. Whereas forces of bureaucratization and stultification need to be resisted, the institutionalization of third party consultation services at the intergroup and international levels is an ultimate goal that should be pursued with vigor. There are various mechanisms by which this could be accomplished. At the organizational level, many consulting firms include intergroup problem solving in their repertoire of services. At the community level, a growing number of mediation centers offer conflict resolution services that appear to mix consultation with mediation, although much of their focus is interpersonal (e.g., disputes between neighbors or within families) rather than intergroup (e.g., conflict between ethnic groups). In the public and environmental domains, organizations such as the Conflict Clinic at George Mason University are being formed to offer a mixture of mediation and consultation services to conflicting parties on a variety of issues. These innovative developments in handling conflict within societies are part of a growing social movement known as "alternative dispute resolution," or ADR (Mitchell & Webb, 1988). This movement involves new institutional settings for conflict management and new, often hybrid, third party roles and functions. According to Sandholde (1988), ADR may represent the beginning of a paradigm shift away from political realism and competitive, adversarial processes for dealing with conflict and toward cooperative, noncoercive problem solving that blends traditional and innovative methods. A variety of perspectives and developments contained within this social movement or paradigm shift are described by Sandhole and Sandhole-Staroste (1987).

At the international level, third party consultation efforts have largely been initiated by academics working individually or through conflict research centers such as those mentioned above. This initial form of institutionalization is to be most encouraged at the present, because it is inherently supportive of developing theory and research alongside practice. Thus, research centers can sponsor pilot programs of consultation and use their scientific skills to rigorously and systematically evaluate such initiatives. This would make it possible, for example, to compare different workshop formats in terms of process and outcomes both among themselves and with control conditions, such as nondiscussion groups that would enter into problem solving at a later time. Furthermore, research projects could be designed to gauge the relative effectiveness of different components of the method. Simulations such as the ICS would be ideal for this purpose. Results would be very useful in informing both our theoretical understanding of intergroup conflict and our models of practice for conflict resolution.

Other forms of institutionalization are also to be encouraged as we move into the future. At the international level, the United Nations, particularly the Office of the Secretary General, is the most appropriate locus for development. In addition to mediation, the Secretariat of the UN could develop and offer services in third party consultation in ways that would be highly complementary to existing diplomatic practice. On a smaller scale, the various regional organizations could develop and offer consultation services within their spheres of interest and legitimacy. Finally, it would not be inappropriate for nationally based organizations, such as the publicly mandated peace institutes, to acquire and provide consultation to other countries or factions that perceive the institutes' national identity as impartial. Initially, and perhaps in the longer run as well, such initiatives should be in the form of action research rather than solely as practice for its own sake.

Third party consultation is a logical extension of the social-psychological approach to understanding destructive intergroup and international conflict. The method is based on a rationale derived primarily from the discipline of social psychology and is highly compatible with the humanistic value base of applied social psychology. Consultation provides a heretofore unavailable option in the management and resolution of intergroup and international conflict, and as such is the missing link in the contingency model of third party intervention. The full development of third party consultation will provide to the world of human affairs a unique opportunity to utilize the knowledge and expertise of social psychology and, more generally, social science. This eventuality will in turn provide these disciplines with greater understanding about protracted social conflict. Thus, all constituencies of humankind can benefit in a collaborative search toward solving the perplexing and costly enigma of intergroup conflict.

References

Abelson, R.P. (1981). Psychological status of the script concept. *American Psychologist, 36,* 715-729.
Adorno, T.W., Frenkel-Brunswik, E., Levinson, D.J., & Sanford, R.N. (1950). *The authoritarian personality.* New York: Harper & Row.
Alderfer, C.P. (1977). Improving organizational communication through long-term intergroup intervention. *Journal of Applied Behavioral Science, 13,* 193-210.
Alevy, D.I., Bunker, B., Doob, L.W., Foltz, W.J., French, N., Klein, E.B., & Miller, J.C. (1974). Rationale, research, and role relations in the Stirling Workshop. *Journal of Conflict Resolution, 18,* 276-284.
Allison, G.T. (1971). *Essence of decision: Explaining the Cuban missile crisis.* Boston: Little, Brown.
Allport, G.W. (1954). *The nature of prejudice.* Cambridge, MA: Addison-Wesley.
Allport, G.W., & Postman, L.J. (1945). The basic psychology of rumor. *Transactions of the New York Academy of Sciences, Series II, 8,* 61-81.
Altemeyer, R. (1981). *Right-wing authoritarianism.* Winnipeg, Canada: The University of Manitoba Press.
Amir, Y. (1969). Contact hypothesis in ethnic relations. *Psychological Bulletin, 71,* 319-342.
Amir, Y. (1976). The role of intergroup contact in change of prejudice and ethnic relations. In P.A. Katz (Ed.), *Towards the elimination of racism.* New York: Pergamon.
Anderson, J.C. (1981). The impact of arbitration: A methodological assessment. *Industrial Relations, 20,* 129-148.
Angell, R.C. (1965). The sociology of human conflict. In E.B. McNeil (Ed.), *The nature of human conflict.* Englewood Cliffs, NJ: Prentice-Hall.
Aronson, E., Blaney, N.N., Stephan, C., Sikes, J., & Snapp, M. (1978). *The jigsaw classroom.* Beverly Hills, CA: Sage.
Aronson, E., & Osherow, N. (1980). Cooperation, social behavior, and academic performance: Experiments in the desegregated classroom. In L. Bickman (Ed.), *Applied social psychology annual: Vol. 1.* Beverly Hills, CA: Sage.
Asch, S.E. (1956). Studies of independence and conformity: I. A minority of one against a unanimous majority. *Psychological Monographs, 70,* (No. 416).
Austin, W.G., & Worchel, S. (Eds.). (1979). *The social psychology of intergroup relations.* Monterey, CA: Brooks/Cole.
Axelrod, R. (Ed.). (1976). *Structure of decision: The cognitive maps of political elites.* Princeton, NJ: Princeton University Press.
Axelrod, R. (1980). Effective choice in the Prisoner's Dilemma. *Journal of Conflict Resolution, 24,* 3-26.

Axelrod, R. (1984). *The evolution of co-operation*. New York: Basic Books.
Azar, E.E. (1983). *The theory of protracted social conflict and the challenge of transforming conflict situations*. (Monograph Series in World Affairs, 20, #M2, 81-99). University of Denver.
Azar, E.E., & Burton, J.W. (Eds.). (1986). *International conflict resolution: Theory and practice*. Brighton, U.K.: Wheatsheaf.
Azar, E.E., & Farah, N. (1981). The structure of inequalities and protracted social conflict: A theoretical framework. *International Interactions, 7*, 317-335.
Bales, R.F. (1950). A set of categories for the analysis of small group interaction. *American Sociological Review, 15*, 257-263.
Banks, M. (1984). The evolution of international relations theory. In M. Banks (Ed.), *Conflict in world society*. New York: St. Martin's Press.
Banks, M. (1986). The international relations discipline: Asset or liability for conflict resolution: In E.E. Azar and J.W. Burton (Eds.), *International conflict resolution: Theory and practice*. Brighton, U.K.: Wheatsheaf.
Bartenuk, J.M., Benton, A.A., & Keys, C.B. (1975). Third party intervention and the bargaining behavior of group representatives. *Journal of Conflict Resolution, 19*, 532-557.
Bartlett, F.C. (1932). *Remembering: A study in experimental and social psychology*. Cambridge: University of Cambridge Press.
Bay, C. (1958). *The structure of freedom*. Stanford, CA: Stanford University Press.
Bell, E.C., & Blakeney, R.N. (1977). Personality correlates of conflict resolution modes. *Human Relations, 30*, 849-857.
Bell, R.L., Cleveland, S.E., Hanson, P.G., & O'Connell, W.E. (1969). Small group dialogue and discussion: An approach to police-community relationships. *Journal of Criminal Law, Criminology, and Police Science, 60*, 242-246.
Ben-Ari, R., & Amir, Y. (1986). Contact between Arab and Jewish youth in Israel: Reality and potential. In M. Hewstone & R. Brown (Eds.), *Contact and conflict in intergroup encounters*. Oxford: Blackwell.
Benne, K.D., & Sheats, P. (1948). Functional roles of group members. *Journal of Social Issues, 4*(2), 41-49.
Bennis, W.G., Benne, K.D., & Chin R. (Eds.). (1985). *The planning of change* (4th ed.). New York: Holt, Rinehart & Winston.
Bercovitch, J. (1985). Third parties in conflict management: The structure and conditions of effective mediation in international relations. *International Journal, 40*, 736-752.
Beres, M.E., & Schmidt, S.M. (1982). The conflict carousel: A contingency approach to conflict management. In G.B.J. Bomers & R.B. Peterson (Eds.), *Conflict management and industrial relations*. Boston: Kluwer-Nijhof Publishing.
Berry, J.W. (1984). Multicultural policy in Canada: A social psychological analysis. *Canadian Journal of Behavioural Science, 16*, 353-370.
Berry, J.W., Kalin, R., & Taylor, D.M. (1977). *Multiculturalism and ethnic attitudes in Canada*. Ottawa: Minister of State for Multiculturalism.
Bigoness, W.J. (1976). The impact of initial bargaining position and alternative modes of third party intervention in resolving bargaining impasses. *Organizational Behavior and Human Performance, 17*, 185-198.
Billig, M., & Tajfel, H. (1973). Social categorization and similarity in intergroup behavior. *European Journal of Social Psychology, 3*, 27-52.
Bixenstine, V.E., & O'Reilly, E.F. (1966). Money versus electric shock as payoff in a Prisoner's Dilemma game. *Psychological Record, 16*, 251-264.
Blake, R.R., & Mouton, J.S. (1961). *Group dynamics: Key to decision-making*. Houston, TX: Gulf.
Blake, R.R., & Mouton, J.S. (1964). *The managerial grid*. Houston, TX: Gulf.
Blake, R.R., & Mouton, J.S. (1984). *Solving costly organizational conflicts*. San Francisco, CA: Jossey-Bass.

Blake, R.R., Mouton, J.S., & Sloma, R.L. (1965). The union-management intergroup laboratory. *Journal of Applied Behavioral Science, 1*, 25–57.

Blake, R.R., Shepard, H.A., & Mouton, J.S. (1964). *Managing intergroup conflict in industry.* Houston, TX: Gulf.

Boehringer, G.H., Zeruolis, V., Bayley, J., & Boehringer, K. (1974). Stirling: The destructive application of group techniques to a conflict. *Journal of Conflict Resolution, 18*, 257–275.

Bonham, M.G. (1971). Simulating international disarmament negotiations. *Journal of Conflict Resolution, 15*, 299–315.

Bonoma, T.V. (1975). *Conflict: Escalation and deescalation.* Beverly Hills, CA: Sage.

Boulding, K.E. (1962). *Conflict and defense: A general theory.* New York: Harper.

Branthwaite, A., Doyle, S., & Lightbown, N. (1979). The balance between fairness and discrimination. *European Journal of Social Psychology, 9*, 149–163.

Branthwaite, A., & Jones, J.E. (1975). Fairness and discrimination: English versus Welsh. *European Journal of Social Psychology, 5*, 323–338.

Brett, J.M., & Goldberg, S.B. (1983). Mediator–advisers: A new third-party role. In M.H. Bazerman & R. Lewicki (Eds.), *Negotiating in organizations.* Beverly Hills, CA: Sage.

Brett, J.M., Goldberg, S.B., & Ury, W. (1980). Mediation and organizational development: Models for conflict management. *Proceedings of the 33rd Annual Meeting of the Industrial Relations Association.* Madison, WI: Industrial Relations Research Associates.

Brewer, M.B. (1979). Ingroup bias in the minimal intergroup situation: A cognitive-motivational analysis. *Psychological Bulletin, 86*, 307–324.

Brewer, M.B., & Kramer, R.M. (1985). The psychology of intergroup attitudes and behavior. *Annual Review of Psychology, 36*, 219–243.

Brewer, M.B., & Miller, N. (1984). Beyond the contact hypothesis: Theoretical perspectives on desegregation. In N. Miller & M.B. Brewer (Eds.), *Groups in contact: The psychology of desegregation.* New York: Academic Press.

Brewer, W.F., & Nakamura, G.V. (1984). The nature and functions of schemes. In R.S. Wyer & T.K. Srull (Eds.), *Handbook of social cognition: Vol. 1.* Hillsdale, NJ: Erlbaum.

Brigham, J.C. (1971). Ethnic stereotypes. *Psychological Bulletin, 76*, 15–38.

Brilhart, J.K. (1982). *Effective group discussion* (4th ed.). Dubuque, IW: W.C. Brown.

Brislin, R.W. (1978). Structured approaches to dealing with prejudice and intercultural misunderstanding. *International Journal of Group Tensions, 8*, 33–48.

Brislin, R.W. (1981). *Cross-cultural encounters: Face-to-face interaction.* Elmsford, NY: Pergamon.

Brislin, R.W., Cushner, K., Cherrie, C., & Yong, M. (1986). *Intercultural interactions: A practical guide.* Beverly Hills, CA: Sage.

Brockner, J., & Rubin, J.Z. (1985). *Entrapment in escalating conflicts: A social psychological analysis.* New York: Springer-Verlag.

Bronfenbrenner, U. (1961). The mirror image in Soviet–American relations: A social psychologist's report. *Journal of Social Issues, 17*(3), 45–56.

Brown, R.J., & Turner, J.C. (1981). Interpersonal and intergroup behavior. In J.C. Turner & J. Giles (Eds.), *Intergroup Behavior.* Oxford: Blackwell.

Brown, R.J., & Wade, G. (1987). Superordinate goals and intergroup behavior: The effect of role ambiguity and status on intergroup attitudes and task performance. *European Journal of Social Psychology, 17*, 131–142.

Brown, R.J., Wade, G., Mathews, A., Condor, S., & Williams, J. (1983). *Group identification and intergroup differentiation.* Paper presented at the Annual Conference of the British Psychological Society, Sheffield, U.K.

Bruner, J.S. (1957). On perceptual readiness. *Psychological Review, 64*, 123–152.

Bruner, J.S., & Perlmutter, J.V. (1957). Compatriot and foreigner: A study of impression formation in three countries. *Journal of Abnormal and Social Psychology, 55*, 253–260.

Burke, R.J. (1970). Methods of resolving superior–subordinate conflict: The constructive use of subordinate differences and disagreements. *Organizational Behavior and Human Performance, 5*, 393–411.

Burke, W.W. (1974). Managing conflict between groups. In J.D. Adams (Ed.), *Theory and method in organization development: An evolutionary process*, Arlington, VA: NTL Institute.
Burton, J.W. (1962). *Peace theory*. New York: Knopf.
Burton, J.W. (1965). *International relations: A general theory*. London: Cambridge University Press.
Burton, J.W. (1968). *Systems, states, diplomacy and rules*. London: Cambridge University Press.
Burton, J.W. (1969). *Conflict and communication: The use of controlled communication in international relations*. London: MacMillan.
Burton, J.W. (1972). *World society*. London: Cambridge University Press.
Burton, J.W. (1979). *Deviance, terrorism & war: The process of solving unsolved social and political problems*. New York: St. Martin's Press.
Burton, J.W. (1982). Decision-making processes and conflict. In G.B.J. Bomers & R.B. Peterson (Eds.), *Conflict management and industrial relations*. Boston, MA: Kluwer-Nijhof Publishing.
Burton, J.W. (1984). *Global conflict: The domestic sources of international conflict*. Brighton, U.K.: Wheatsheaf.
Burton, J.W. (1985a). The history of international conflict resolution. *International Interactions, 12*, 45–57.
Burton, J.W. (1985b, February). *Second track diplomacy: History and practice*. Paper presented to the Foreign Service Institute, Washington, D.C.
Burton, J.W. (1987a). *Resolving deep-rooted conflict: A handbook*. Lanham, MD: University Press of America.
Burton, J.W. (1987b). Track two: An alternative to power politics. In J.W. McDonald & D.B. Bendahmane (Eds.), *Conflict resolution: Track two diplomacy*. Washington, D.C.: Foreign Service Institute.
Burton, J.W. (1988a). *The need for needs theory*. Unpublished manuscript, George Mason University, Fairfax, VA.
Burton, J.W. (1988b, July). *Needs theory and conflict resolution*. Paper presented at Conference on Needs Theory, George Mason University, Fairfax, VA.
Campbell, D.T. (1958). Common fate, similarity, and other indices of the status of aggregates of persons as social entities. *Behavioral science, 3*, 14–25.
Campbell, D.T. (1965). Ethnocentrism and other altruistic motives. In D. Levine (Ed.), *Nebraska symposium on motivation, Vol. 13*. Lincoln: University of Nebraska Press.
Campbell, D.T., & McCandless, B.R. (1951). Ethnocentrism, xenophobia and personality. *Human Resolutions, 4*, 185–192.
Cantor, N,. & Mischel, W. (1977). Traits as prototypes: Effects on recognition memory. *Journal of Personality and Social Psychology, 35*, 38–48.
Carnevale, P.J.D. (1986). Strategic choice in mediation. *Negotiation Journal, 2*, 41–56.
Cartwright, D. (1971). Risk-taking by individuals and groups. An assessment of research involving choice dilemmas. *Journal of Personality and Social Psychology, 20*, 361–378.
Chanin, M.N., & Schneer, J.A. (1984). A study of the relationship between Jungian personality dimensions and conflict-handling behavior. *Human Relations, 37*, 863–879.
Chesler, M.A. (1965). Ethnocentrism and attitudes toward the physically disabled, *Journal of Personality and Social Psychology, 2*, 877–882.
Chin, R., & Benne, K.D. (1985). General strategies for effecting change in human systems. In W.G. Bennis, K.D. Benne, & R. Chin (Eds.), *The planning of change* (4th ed.). New York: Holt, Rinehart & Winston.
Cobbs, P.M. (1972). Ethnotherapy in groups. In L. Solomon & B. Berzon (Eds.), *New perspectives on encounter groups*. San Francisco: Jossey-Bass.
Cohen, E. (1984). The desegregated school: Problems of status, power, and interethnic climate. In N. Miller & M. Brewer (Eds.), *Groups in contact: The psychology of desegregration*. New York: Academic Press.

Cohen, S.P., Kelman, H.C., Miller, F.D., & Smith, B.L. (1977). Evolving intergroup techniques for conflict resolution: An Israeli–Palestinian pilot workshop. *Journal of Social Issues, 33* (1), 165–189.

Condor, S., & Brown, R. (1988). Psychological processes in intergroup conflict. In W. Stroebe, A.W. Kruglanski, D. Bar-Tal, & M. Hewstone (Eds.), *The social psychology of intergroup conflict*. New York: Springer-Verlag.

Cook, S.W. (1970). A preliminary study of attitude change. In M. Wertheimer (Ed.), *Confrontation: Psychology and the problems of today*. Glenview, IL: Scott, Foresman.

Cook, S.W. (1979). Social science and school desegregration: Did we mislead the Supreme Court? *Personality and Social Psychology Bulletin, 5*, 420–437.

Cook, S.W. (1984). Cooperative interaction in multiethnic contexts. In N. Miller & M.B. Brewer (Eds.), *Groups in contact*. New York: Academic Press.

Coser, L.A. (1956). *The functions of social conflict*. Glencoe, IL: Free Press.

Courtwright, J.A. (1976). *Groupthink and communication processes: An initial investigation*. Unpublished Doctoral Dissertation, University of Iowa.

Crow, W.J. (1963). A study of strategic doctrines using the Inter-Nation Simulation. *Journal of Conflict Resolution, 7*, 580–598.

Crutchfield, R.S. (1955). Conformity and character. *American Psychologist, 10*, 191–198.

Cyert, R.M., & March, J.G. (1963). *A behavioral theory of the firm*. Englewood Cliffs, NJ: Prentice-Hall.

Darley, J.M., & Fazio, R.H. (1980). Expectancy confirmation processes arising in the social interaction sequence. *American Psychologist, 35*, 867–881.

Dean J.P., & Rosen, A.A. (1955). *A manual of intergroup relations*. Chicago: University of Chicago Press.

Deaux, K. (1976). Sex: perspective on the attribution process. In J.H. Harvey, W.J. Ickes, & R.F. Kidd (Eds.), *New directions in attribution research: Vol. 1*. Hillsdale, NJ: Erlbaum.

Dedring, J. (1976). *Recent advances in peace and conflict research: A critical survey*. Beverly Hills, CA: Sage.

de Reuck, A.V.S. (1974). Controlled communication: Rationale and dynamics. *The Human Context, VI* (1), Spring, 64–80.

de Reuck, A.V.S. (1983). A theory of conflict resolution by problem solving. *Man, Environment, Space and Time, 3* (1), 53–69.

Deschamps, J.C., & Brown, R. (1983). Superordinate goals and intergroup conflict. *British Journal of Social Psychology, 22*, 189–195.

de Sola Pool, I. (1965). Effects of cross-national contact on national and international images. In H.C. Kelman (Ed.), *International behavior: a social-psychological analysis*. New York: Holt, Rinehart & Winston.

Deutsch, M. (1973). *The resolution of conflict: Constructive and destructive processes*. New Haven, CT: Yale University Press.

Deutsch, M. (1980). Fifty years of conflict. In L. Festinger (Ed.), *Four decades of social psychology*, Oxford U.K.: Oxford University Press.

Deutsch, M. (1983). The prevention of World War III: A psychological perspective. *Political Psychology, 4*, 3–32.

Diab, L.N. (1970). A study of intragroup and intergroup relations among experimentally produced small groups. *Genetic Psychology Monographs, 82*, 49–82.

Dion, K.L. (1973). Cohesiveness as a determinant of ingroup–outgroup bias. *Journal of Personality and Social Psychology, 28*, 163–171.

Dion, K.L. (1979). Intergroup conflict and intergroup cohesiveness. In W.G. Austin & S. Worchel (Eds.), *The social psychology of intergroup relations*. Monterey, CA: Brooks/Cole.

Dion, K.L, (1986). Response to perceived discrimination and relative deprivation. In J.M. Olson, C.P. Herman, & M.P. Zanna (Eds.), *Relative deprivation and social comparison: The Ontario symposium: Vol. 4*. Hillsdale, NJ: Erlbuam.

Doise, W., Deschamps, J.C., & Meyer, G. (1978). The accentuation of intra-category similarities. In H. Tajfel (Ed.), *Differentiation between social groups: Studies in the social psychology of intergroup relations*. London: Academic Press.
Doob, L.W. (Ed.). (1970). *Resolving conflict in Africa: The Fermeda workshop*. New Haven, CT: Yale University Press.
Doob, L.W. (1981). *The pursuit of peace*. Westport, CT: Greenwood Press.
Doob, L.W., & Foltz, W.J. (1973). The Belfast Workshop: An application of group techniques to a destructive conflict. *Journal of Conflict Resolution, 17*, 489–512.
Doob, L.W., & Foltz, W.J. (1974). The impact of a workshop upon grassroots leaders in Belfast. *Journal of Conflict Resolution, 18*, 237–256.
Doob, L.W., & Foltz, W.J. (1975). Voices from a Belfast workshop. *Social Change, 5* (3), 1–3, 6–8.
Douglas, A. (1962). *Industrial peacemaking*. New York: Columbia University Press.
Druckman, D. (1968). Ethnocentrism in the Inter-Nation Simulation. *Journal of Conflict Resolution, 12*, 45–68.
Druckman, D. (1973). Human factors in international negotiations: Social-psychological aspects of international conflict. *A Sage Professional Paper: International Studies Series, 2*, 02–020.
Druckman, D. (Ed.). (1977). *Negotiations: Social-psychological perspectives*. Beverly Hills, CA: Sage.
Druckman, D. (1983). Social psychology in international negotiations. In R.F. Kidd & M.J. Saks (Eds.), *Advances in applied social psychology: Vol. 2*. Hillsdale, NJ: Erlbaum.
Druckman, D., & Mahoney, R. (1977). Processes and consequences of international negotiation. *The Journal of Social Issues, 33* (1), 60–87.
Dubin, R.V. (1969). *Theory building*. New York: The Free Press.
Dubin, R. (1976). Theory building in applied areas. In M.D. Dunnette (Ed.), *Handbook of Industrial and Organizational Psychology*. Chicago: Rand-McNally.
Duncan, B.L. (1976). Differential social perception and attribution of intergroup violence: Testing the lower limits of stereotyping of blacks. *Journal of Personality and Social Psychology, 34*, 590–598.
Ehrlich, H.J. (1964). Instrument error and the study of prejudice. *Social Forces, 43*, 197–206.
Ehrlich, P.R. (1983). Long-term biological consequences of nuclear war. *Science, 222*, 1293–1300.
Epp-Tiessen, E. (1987). *Missiles and malnutrition: The links between militarization and underdevelopment*. Waterloo, Ontario: Project Ploughshares.
Erikson, B., Holmes, J.G., Frey, R., Walker, L., & Thibaut, J. (1974). Functions of a third party in the resolution of conflict: The role of a judge in pre-trial conferences. *Journal of Personality and Social Psychology, 30*, 293–306.
Etzioni, A. (1962) *The hard way to peace*. New York: Collier.
Etzioni, A. (1967). The Kennedy experiment. *The Western Political Quarterly, 20*, 361–380.
Festinger, L. (1957). *A theory of cognitive dissonance*. Evanston, IL: Row, Peterson.
Fiedler, F.E. (1967). *A theory of leadership effectiveness*. New York: McGraw-Hill.
Filley, A.C. (1975). *Interpersonal conflict resolution*. Glenview, IL: Scott, Foresman.
Filley, A.C. (1978). Some normative issues in conflict management. *California Management Review, 21* (2), 61–66.
Fink, C.F. (1968). Some conceptual difficulties in the theory of social conflict. *Journal of Conflict Resolution, 12*, 412–460.
Fisher, R. (1986). Dealing with conflict among individuals and nations: Are there common principles? *Psychoanalytic Inquiry, 6* (2), 143–153.
Fisher, R., & Ury, W. (1981). *Getting to "yes": Negotiating agreement without giving in*. Boston: Houghton Mifflin.
Fisher, R.J. (1968). *Ingroup loyalty, ingroup glorification and outgroup rejection: A partial re-evaluation of ethnocentrism*. Unpublished Masters Thesis, University of Saskatchewan, Saskatoon, Canada.

Fisher, R.J. (1972). Third party consultation: A method for the study and resolution of conflict. *Journal of Conflict Resolution, 16*, 67-94.
Fisher, R.J. (1976). Third party consultation: A skill for professional psychologists in community practice. *Professional Psychology, 7*, 344-351.
Fisher, R.J. (1980). A third-party consultation workshop on the India-Pakistan conflict. *Journal of Social Psychology, 112*, 191-206.
Fisher, R.J. (1981). Training in applied social psychology: Rationale and core experiences. *Canadian Psychology, 22*, 250-259.
Fisher, R.J. (1982). *Social psychology: An applied approach.* New York: St. Martin's Press.
Fisher, R.J. (1983). Third party consultation as a method of intergroup conflict resolution: A review of studies. *Journal of Conflict Resolution, 27*, 301-344.
Fisher, R.J. (1985, June). *The social psychology of intergroup conflict: Toward eclectic theory and effective practice.* Paper presented at the Annual Meeting of the Canadian Psychological Association, Halifax, Nova Scotia.
Fisher, R.J. (1988, July). *Needs theory, social identity, and an eclectic model of conflict.* Paper presented at the Conference on Needs Theory, George Mason University, Fairfax, VA.
Fisher, R.J. (1989). Prenegotiation problem-solving discussions: Enhancing the potential for successful negotiation. *International Journal, XLIV*, Spring, 442-474.
Fisher, R.J., & Grant, P.R. (1985). *A simulation study of intergroup conflict.* Social Sciences and Humanities Research Council Grant Proposal.
Fisher, R.J., & Keashly, L. (1988). Distinguishing third party intervention in intergroup conflict: Consultation is not mediation. *Negotiation Journal, 4*, 381-393.
Fisher, R.J., & White, J.H. (1976a). Intergroup conflicts resolved by outside consultants. *Journal of the Community Development Society, 7*, 88-98.
Fisher, R.J., & White, J.H. (1976b). Reducing tensions between neighbourhood housing groups: A pilot study in third party consultation. *International Journal of Group Tensions, 6*, 41-52.
Flowers, M.L. (1977). A laboratory test of some implications of Janis's groupthink hypothesis. *Journal of Personality and Social Psychology, 35*, 888-896.
Folberg, J., & Taylor, A. (1984). *Mediation: A comprehensive guide to solving conflicts without litigation.* San Francisco: Jossey-Bass.
Forster, C.L. (1989). *Group mediators of intergroup conflict resolution.* Unpublished Manuscript. University of Saskatchewan, Saskatoon, Canada.
Fouraker, L., & Siegel, S. (1963). *Bargaining behavior.* New York: McGraw-Hill.
Fox, W.T.R. (1984). World politics as conflict resolution. In R.O. Matthews, A.G. Rubinoff, & J.G. Stein (Eds.), *International conflict and conflict management.* Scarborough, Ontario: Prentice Hall of Canada.
French, W.L., & Bell, C.H. (1984). *Organization development* (3rd. ed.). Englewood Cliffs, NJ: Prentice-Hall.
Freud, S. (1930). *Civilization and its discontents.* London: Hogarth Press.
Freud, S. (1948). *Group psychology and the analysis of the ego.* London: Hogarth Press.
Galtung, J. (1965). Institutionalized conflict resolution. A theoretical paradigm. *Journal of Peace Research, 2*, 348-396.
Galtung, J. (1969). Violence, peace and peace research. *Journal of Peace Research, 6*, 167-191.
Galtung, J. (1980). The basic needs approach. In K. Lederer (Ed.), *Human needs.* Cambridge, MA: Oelsgeschlager, Gunn & Hain.
Glaser, E.M., Abelson, H.H., & Garrison, K.N. (1983). *Putting knowledge to use.* San Francisco: Jossey-Bass.
Glasl, F. (1982). The process of conflict escalation and roles of third parties. In G.B.J. Bomers & R.B. Peterson (Eds.), *Conflict management and industrial relations.* Boston: Kluwer-Nijhof Publishing.
Granberg, D. (1978). GRIT in the final quarter: Reversing the arms race through unilateral initiatives. *Bulletin of Peace Proposals, 9*, 210-221.

Grant, P.R. (1980). *Descriptive and affective distancing of an outgroup: The formation and use of group images under threat*. Unpublished Doctoral Dissertation, University of Waterloo, Waterloo, Canada.

Grant, P.R. (1987, July). *The relationship between social identity theory and realistic conflict theory*. Paper presented at the International Conference on Social Identity Theory, University of Exeter, Exeter, U.K.

Grigsby, D.W., & Bigoness, W.J. (1982). Effects of mediation and alternative forms of arbitration on bargaining behavior: A laboratory study. *Journal of Applied Psychology, 67*, 549-554.

Groom, A.J.R. (1986). Problem solving in international relations. In E.E. Azar & J.W. Burton (Eds.), *International conflict resolution: Theory and practice*. Brighton, U.K.: Wheatsheaf.

Guetzkow, H., Alger, C.F., Brody, R.A., Nell, R.C., & Snyder, R.C. (1963). *Simulation in international relations*. Englewood Cliffs, NJ: Prentice-Hall.

Geutzkow, H., & Gyr, J. (1954). An analysis of conflict in decision-making groups. *Human Relations, 7*, 367-382.

Hackman, J.R. (1976). Group influences on individuals. In M.D. Dunnette (Ed.), *Handbook of industrial and organizational psychology*. Chicago: Rand-McNally.

Hall, D.G. (1986). *The development of a comprehensive simulation of intergroup conflict*. Unpublished Doctoral Dissertation, University of Saskatchewan, Saskatoon, Canada.

Hall, D.G., Fisher, R.J., & Grant, P.R. (1986, August). *The development and testing of a comprehensive intergroup conflict simulation*. Paper presented at the Annual Convention of the American Psychological Association, Washington, D.C.

Hameed, S., & Sen, J. (1987). A power theory of third party intervention in labour management relations. *Relations Industrielles, 42*, 243-253.

Hamilton, D.L. (1979). A cognitive-attributional analysis of stereotyping. In L. Berkowitz (Ed.), *Advances in experimental social psychology: Vol. 12*. New York: Academic Press.

Hamilton, D.L. (Ed.) (1981). *Cognitive processes in stereotyping and intergroup behavior*. Hillsdale, NJ: Erlbaum.

Hamilton, D.L., & Rose, T.L. (1980). Illusory correlation and the maintenance of stereotypic beliefs. *Journal of Personality and Social Psychology, 39*, 832-845.

Han, G., & Lindskold, S. (1985). *Responsiveness and conciliation in conflict*. Paper presented at the Annual Meeting of the Midwestern Psychological Association, Chicago.

Haney, C., Banks, W.C., & Zimbardo, P.G. (1973). Interpersonal dynamics in a simulated prison. *International Journal of Criminology and Penology, 1*, 69-97.

Hartley, E.L. (1946). *Problems in prejudice*. New York: King's Crown Press.

Harvey, O.J., Hunt, D.E., & Schroder, H.M. (1961). *Conceptual systems and personality organization*. New York: Wiley.

Haythorn, W., & Altman, I. (1967). Together in isolation. *Trans-action, 4* (3), 18-22.

Heider, F. (1958). *The psychology of interpersonal relations*. New York: Wiley.

Hewstone, M. (1988a). Attributional bases of intergroup conflict. In W. Stroebe, A.W. Kruglanski, D. Bar-Tal, & M. Hewstone (Eds.), *The social psychology of intergroup conflict*. New York: Springer-Verlag.

Hewstone, M. (1988b). Causal attribution: From cognitive processes to collective beliefs. *The Psychologist: Bulletin of the British Psychological Society, 8*, 323-327.

Hewstone, M., & Brown, R. (Eds.) (1986a). *Contact and conflict in intergroup encounters*. Oxford: Blackwell.

Hewstone, M., & Brown, R. (1986b). Contact is not enough: An intergroup perspective on the "contact hypothesis." In M. Hewstone & R. Brown (Eds.), *Contact and conflict in intergroup encounters*. Oxford: Blackwell.

Hill, B.J. (1982). An analysis of conflict resolution techniques: From problem-solving workshops to theory. *Journal of Conflict Resolution, 26*, 109-138.

Hinkle, S., & Schopler, J. (1979). Ethnocentrism in the evaluation of group products. In W.G. Austin & S. Worchel (Eds.), *The social psychology of intergroup relations*. Monterey, CA: Brooks/Cole.

References

Holmes, J.G. (1975). *Group reactions to perceived threat.* Research Grant Application to the Canada Council.

Holmes, J.G., Ellard, J.H., & Lamm, H. (1986). Boundary roles and intergroup conflict. In S. Worchel & W.G. Austin (Eds.), *Psychology of intergroup relations* (2nd ed.). Chicago: Nelson-Hall.

Holmes, J.G., & Grant, P. (1979). Ethnocentric reactions to social threat. In L.H. Strickland (Ed.), *Social psychology: East-West perspectives*, Oxford: Pergamon.

Holsti, O.R. (1979). Theories of crisis decision making. In P.G. Lauren (Ed.), *Diplomacy: New approaches in history, theory and policy.* New York: The Free Press.

Holsti, O.R., Brody, R.A., & North, R.C. (1964). The management of international crisis: Affect and action in American-Soviet relations. *Journal of Peace Research, 3-4,* 170–190.

Hovland, C.I., Janis, I., & Kelley, H.H. (1953). *Communication and persuasion.* New Haven, CT: Yale University Press.

Ikle, F.C. (1964). *How nations negotiate.* New York: Harper.

Jackson, D. (1970). *The Jackson Personality Inventory.* Goshen, NY: Research Psychologists Press.

Janis, I.L. (1972). *Victims of groupthink.* Boston: Houghton Mifflin.

Janis, I.L. (1982). *Groupthink* (2nd ed.). Boston: Houghton Mifflin.

Janis, I.L. (1986). Problems of international crisis management in the nuclear age. *Journal of Social Issues, 42* (2), 201–220.

Janis, I.L., & Mann, L. (1977). *Decision making: A psychological analysis of conflict, choice, and commitment.* New York: The Free Press.

Jervis, R. (1976). *Perception and misperception in international politics.* Princeton, NJ: Princeton University Press.

Jervis, R., Lebow, R.N., & Stein, J.G. (1985). *Psychology and deterrence.* Baltimore, MD: John Hopkins University Press.

Johnson, D.F., & Tullar, W.L. (1972). Style of third party intervention, face-saving and bargaining behavior. *Journal of Experimental Social Psychology, 8,* 319–330.

Johnson, D.W., & Johnson, R.T. (1983). The socialization and achievement crisis: Are cooperative learning experiences the solution? In L. Bickman (Ed.), *Applied Social Psychology Annual: Vol. 4.* Beverly Hills, CA: Sage.

Jones, E.E., & McGillis, D. (1976). Correspondent inferences and the attribution cube: a comparative reappraisal. In J.H. Harvey, W.J. Ickes, & R.F. Kidd (Eds.), *New directions in attribution research: Vol. 1.* Hillsdale, NJ: Erlbaum.

Jones, R.E. & Melcher, B.H. (1982). Personality and the preference for modes of conflict resolution. *Human Relations, 35,* 649–658.

Jussim, L. (1986). Self-fulfilling prophecies: A theoretical and integrative review. *Psychological Review, 93,* 429–445.

Kahn, A., & Ryen, A.H. (1972). Factors influencing bias toward one's own group. *International Journal of Group Tensions, 2,* 35–50.

Kaplowitz, N. (1984). Psychopolitical dimensions of international relations: The reciprocal effects of conflict strategies. *International Studies Quarterly, 28* (4), 373–406.

Katz, D. (1960). The functional approach to the study of attitudes. *Public Opinion Quarterly, 24,* 163–204.

Katz, D. (1965). Nationalism and strategies of international conflict resolution. In H.C. Kelman (Ed.), *International behavior: A social-psychological analysis.* New York: Holt, Rinehart & Winston.

Katz, D., & Braly, K. (1933). Racial stereotypes in one hundred college students. *Journal of Abnormal and Social Psychology, 28,* 280–290.

Katz, D., & Braly, K. (1935). Racial prejudice and racial stereotypes. *Journal of Abnormal and Social Psychology, 30,* 175–193.

Katz, D., & Kahn, R.L. (1978). *The social psychology of organizations* (2nd ed.). New York: Wiley.
Katz, P.A. (Ed.) (1976). *Towards the elimination of racism*. New York: Pergamon.
Katz, P.A., & Taylor, D.A. (1988). *Eliminating racism*. New York: Plenum.
Keashly, L. (1988). *A comparative analysis of third party interventions in intergroup conflict*. Unpublished Doctoral Dissertation, University of Saskatchewan, Saskatoon, Canada.
Keashly, L., & Fisher, R.J. (1989, January). *Toward a contingency approach to third party intervention in regional conflict*. Paper presented at the conference on Managing Regional Conflict: Regimes and Third Party Mediators, Canadian Institute for International Peace and Security, Ottawa.
Keashly, L., Fisher, R.J., & Grant, P.R. (1989). *The comparative effectiveness of third party consultation versus mediation within a complex simulation of intergroup conflict*. Unpublished Manuscript. University of Saskatchewan, Saskatoon, Canada.
Kelman, H.C. (Ed.). (1965). *International behavior: A social-psychological analysis*. New York: Holt, Rinehart & Winston.
Kelman, H.C. (1972). The problem-solving workshop in conflict resolution. In R.L. Merritt (Ed.), *Communication in international politics*. Urbana: University of Illinois Press.
Kelman, H.C. (1978). Israelis and Palestinians: Psychological prerequisites for mutual acceptance. *International Security, 3*, 162–186.
Kelman, H.C. (1982). Creating the conditions for Israeli-Palestinian negotiations. *Journal of Conflict Resolution, 26*, 39–75.
Kelman, H.C. (1985, November). A behavioral-science perspective on the study of war and peace. Lecture at the University of Colorado. Denver, Co.
Kelman, H.C., & Cohen, S.P. (1976). The problem-solving workshop: A social-psychological contribution to the resolution of international conflict. *Journal of Peace Research, 13*, 79–90.
Kelman, H.C., & Cohen, S.P. (1986). Resolution of international conflict: An interactional approach. In S. Worchel and W.G. Austin (Eds.), *Psychology of intergroup relations* (2nd ed.). Chicago: Nelson-Hall.
Kende, (1978). Wars of ten years: 1967–1976. *Journal of Peace Research, 15*, 227–241.
Kilmann, R.H., & Thomas, K.W. (1975). Interpersonal conflict-handling behavior as reflections of Jungian personality dimensions. *Psychological Reports, 37*, 971–980.
Kilmann, R.H., & Thomas, K.W. (1977). Developing a forced choice measure of conflict-handling behavior: The "MODE" instrument. *Educational and Psychological Measurement, 37*, 309–325.
Kinder, D.R., & Weiss, J.A. (1978). In lieu of rationality: Psychological perspectives on foreign policy decision making. *Journal of Conflict Resolution, 22*, 707–735.
Klimoski, R.J. (1972). The effects of intragroup forces on intergroup conflict resolution. *Organizational Behavior and Human Performance, 8*, 363–383.
Klimoski, R.J. (1978). Simulation methodologies in experimental research on negotiations by representatives. *The Journal of Conflict Resolution, 22*, 61–78.
Kolb, D.M. (1983). *The mediators*. Cambridge, MA: MIT Press.
Kolb, D.M. (1985). To be a mediator: Expressive tactics in mediation. *Journal of Social Issues, 41* (2), 11–26.
Kressel, K. (1972). *Labor mediation: An exploratory survey*. Albany, NY: Association of Labor Mediation Agencies.
Kriesberg, L. (1982). *Social conflict* (2nd. ed.). Englewood Cliffs, NJ: Prentice-Hall.
Kriesberg, L. (1984). Social theory and the de-escalation of international conflict. *Sociological Review, 32*, 471–491.
Kriesberg, L. (1987). Carrots, sticks, de-escalation: U.S.–Soviet and Arab-Israeli relations *Armed Forces and Society, 13* (3), Spring, 403–423.
Kriesberg, L. (1988). Strategies of negotiating agreements: Arab–Israeli and American–Soviet cases. *Negotiation Journal; 4*, 19–29.
Lakin, M., Lomranz, J., & Lieberman, M.A. (1969). *Arab & Jew in Israel: A case study in*

a human relations approach to conflict. Washington, D.C.: NTL Institute for Applied Behavioral Science.
Lall, A. (1966). *Modern international negotiation*. New York: Columbia University Press.
Lebow, R.N. (1981). *Between peace and war*. Baltimore, MD: John Hopkins University Press.
Lebow, R.N., & Stein, J.G. (1987). Beyond deterrence. *Journal of Social Issues, 43* (4), 5–71.
Lederer K. (Ed.) (1980). *Human needs*. Cambridge, MA: Oelgeschlager, Gunn & Hain.
Lemaine, G. (1974). Social differentiation and social originality. *European Journal of Social Psychology, 4*, 17–52.
Lemaine, G., Kastersztein, J., & Personnaz, B. (1978). Social differentiation. In H. Tajfel (Ed.), *Differentiation between social groups: Studies in the social psychology of intergroup relations*. London: Academic Press.
Lemyre, L., & Smith, P.M. (1985). Intergroup discrimination and self-esteem in the minimal group paradigm. *Journal of Personality and Social Psychology, 49*, 660–670.
Leng, R.J., & Wheeler, H.G. (1979). Influence strategies, success, and war. *Journal of Conflict Resolution, 23*, 655–684.
Levine, R.A., & Campbell, D.T. (1972). *Ethnocentrism: Theories of conflict, ethnic attitudes and group behavior*. New York: Wiley.
Levinson, D.J. (1954). The intergroup relations workshop: Its psychological aims and effects. *Journal of Psychology, 38*, 103–126.
Levinson, D.J., & Schermerhorn, R.A. (1951). Emotional–attitudinal effects of an intergroup relations workshop on its members. *Journal of Psychology, 31*, 243–256.
Lewin, K. (1935). *Dynamic theory of personality*. New York: McGraw-Hill.
Lewin, K. (1947). Group decision and social change. In T.M. Newcomb & E.L. Hartley (Eds.), *Readings in Social Psychology*. New York: Holt, Rinehart & Winston.
Lewin, K. (1948). *Resolving social conflict*. New York: Harper.
Lewin, K. (1951). *Field theory in social science*. New York: Harper.
Likert, R. (1932). A technique for the measurement of attitudes. *Archives of Psychology*, No. 140.
Likert, R., & Likert, J.G. (1976). *New ways of managing conflict*. New York: McGraw-Hill.
Likert, R., & Likert, J.G. (1978). A method for coping with conflict in problem-solving groups. *Group & Organization Studies, 3*, 427–434.
Lindskold, S. (1978). Trust development, the GRIT proposal, and the effects of conciliatory acts on conflict and cooperation. *Psychological Bulletin, 85*, 772–793.
Lindskold, S. (1979). Conciliation with simultaneous or sequential interaction. *Journal of Conflict Resolution, 23*, 704–714.
Lindskold, S. (1986). GRIT: Reducing distrust through carefully introduced conciliation. In S. Worchel and W.G. Austin (Eds.), *Psychology of intergroup relations* (2nd ed.). Chicago: Nelson-Hall.
Lindskold, S., Betz, B., & Walters, R.S. (1986). Transforming competitive or cooperative claimants. *Journal of Conflict Resolution, 30*, 99–114.
Lindskold, S., & Collins, M.G. (1978). Inducing co-operation by groups and individuals: Applying Osgood's GRIT strategy. *Journal of Conflict Resolution, 22*, 679–690.
Lindskold, S., & Finch, M.L. (1981). Styles of announcing conciliation. *Journal of Conflict Resolution, 25*, 145–155.
Lindskold, S., Han, G., & Betz, B. (1986). The essential elements of communication in the GRIT strategy. *Personality and Social Psychology Bulletin, 12*, 179–186.
Lindskold, S., Walters, P.S., & Koutsourais, H. (1983). Cooperators, competitors, and response to GRIT. *Journal of Conflict Resolution, 27*, 521–532.
Lingle, J.H., Altom, M.W., & Medin, D.L. (1984). Of cabbages and kings: Assessing the extendibility of natural object concept models to social things. In R.S. Wyer & T.K. Srull (Eds.), *Handbook of Social Cognition: Vol. 1*. Hillsdale, NJ: Erlbaum.
Lippitt, G., & Lippitt, R. (1986). *The consulting process in action* (2nd ed.). San Diego: University Associates.

Lippitt, R. (1949). *Training in community relations.* New York: Harper & Brothers.
Lippitt, R., Watson, J., & Westley, B. (1958). *The dynamics of planned change.* New York: Harcourt Brace Jovanovich.
Lockhart, C. (1973). The efficacy of threats in international interaction strategies. *A Sage Professional Paper: International Studies Series, 2,* 02–023.
Longley, J., & Pruitt, D.G. (1980). A critique of Janis's theory of groupthink. In L. Wheeler (Ed.), *Review of Personality and Social Psychology, Vol. 1.* Beverly Hills, CA: Sage.
Love, R.L., Rozelle, R.M., & Druckman, D. (1983). Resolving conflicts of interests and ideologies: A simulation of political decision-making. *Social Behavior and Personality, 11* (2), 23–28.
Mack, R.W., & Snyder, R.C. (1957). The analysis of social conflict—Toward an overview and synthesis. *Journal of Conflict Resolution, 1,* 212–248.
Maier, N.R.F. (1963). *Problem-solving discussions and conferences.* New York: McGraw-Hill.
Maier, N.R.F. (1967). Assets and liabilities in group problem solving: The need for an integrative function. *Psychological Review, 74,* 239–249.
Maier, N.R.F. (1970). *Problem solving and creativity in individuals and groups.* Belmont, CA: Brooks/Cole.
March, J.D., & Simon, H.A. (1958). *Organizations.* New York: Wiley.
Markus, J., & Zajonc, R.B. (1985). The cognitive perspective in social psychology. In G. Lindzey & E. Aronson (Eds.), *Handbook of social psychology: Vol. 1.* New York: Random House.
Marx, M.H. (1963). *Theories in contemporary psychology.* New York: MacMillan.
Matthews, R.O., Rubinoff, A.G., & Stein, J.G. (Eds.) (1984). *International conflict and conflict management.* Scarborough, Ontario: Prentice-Hall of Canada.
McCann, L.M. (1985). *The effect of male group threat and female group distinctiveness on conflict between women's groups.* Unpublished Masters Thesis, University of Saskatchewan, Saskatoon, Canada.
McClelland, D.C. (1961). *The achieving society.* Princeton, NJ: Van Nostrand.
McClelland, D.C. (1975). *Power: The inner experience.* New York: Irvington.
McDonald, J.W., & Bendahmane, D.B. (Eds.). (1987). *Conflict resolution: Track two diplomacy.* Washington, D.C.: Foreign Service Institute.
McGillicuddy, N.B., Welton, G.L., & Pruitt, D.G. (1987). Third party intervention: A field experiment comparing three different models. *Journal of Personality and Social Psychology, 53,* 104–112.
McGrath, J.E., & Altman, I. (1966). *Small group research: A synthesis and critique of the field.* New York: Holt, Rinehart & Winston.
McGuire, W.J. (1973). The Yin and Yang of progress in social psychology: Seven Koan. *Journal of Personality and Social Psychology, 26,* 446–456.
McGuire, W.J. (1979, September). *Toward social psychology's second century.* Paper presented at the Annual Convention of the American Psychological Association, New York.
Mendlowitz, S.H. (Ed.). (1975). *On the creation of a just world order.* New York: Free Press.
Mervis, C.B., & Rosch, E. (1981). Categorization of natural objects. *Annual Review of Psychology, 32,* 89–115.
Milburn, T.W. (1977). The nature of threat. *The Journal of Social Issues, 33* (1), 126–139.
Miller, N., & Brewer, M.B. (1984). (Eds.). *Groups in contact: The psychology of desegregation.* New York: Academic Press.
Mitchell, C.R. (1981a). *The structure of international conflict.* London: Macmillan.
Mitchell, C.R. (1981b). *Peacemaking and the consultant's role.* Westmead, U.K.: Gower.
Mitchell, C.R., & Webb, K. (1988). *New approaches to international mediation.* New York: Greenwood Press.
Moore, C.W. (1986). *The mediation process: Practical strategies for resolving conflict.* San Francisco: Jossey-Bass.
Morgan, P.M. (1983). *Deterrence: A conceptual analysis.* Beverly Hills, CA: Sage.
Morris, W.C., & Sashkin, M. (1976). *Organization behavior in action: Skill building*

experiences. St. Paul, MN: West.
Moscovici, S., & Zavalloni, M. (1969). The group as a polarizer of attitudes. *Journal of Personality and Social Psychology, 12*, 125–135.
Murray, H.A. (1938). *Explorations in personality*. New York: Oxford University Press.
Myers, A. (1962). Team competition, success, and the adjustment of group members. *Journal of Abnormal and Social Psychology, 65* (5), 325–332.
Myers, D.G. & Lamm, H. (1975). The polarizing effect of group discussion. *American Scientist, 63*, 297–303.
Napier, R.W., & Gershenfeld, M.K. (1973). *Groups: Theory and experience*. Boston: Houghton Mifflin.
Napier, R.W., & Gershenfeld, M.K. (1985). *Groups: Theory and experience* (3rd ed.). Boston: Houghton Mifflin.
Naroll, R., Bullough, V.L., & Naroll, F. (1974). *Military deterrence in history: A pilot cross-historical survey*. Albany: State University of New York Press.
Newcomb, T.M. (1943). *Personality and social change*. New York: Holt, Rinehart & Winston.
Newcomb, T.M. (1953). An approach to the study of communicative acts. *Psychological Review, 60*, 393–404.
Newcomb, T.M. (1961). *The acquaintance process*. New York: Holt, Rinehart & Winston.
Newcomb, T.M. (1968). Interpersonal balance. In R.P. Abelson, E. Aronson, W.J. McGuire, T.M. Newcomb, M.J. Rosenberg, & P.H. Tannenbaum (Eds.), *Theories of cognitive consistency: A sourcebook*. Chicago: Rand McNally.
Newcombe, H. (1982). Unilateral initiatives, inviting reciprocation (GRIT). *Peace Research Reviews, IX* (3), 1–34.
North, R.C., Brody, R.A., & Holsti, O.R. (1964). Some empirical data on the conflict spiral. *Peace Research Society (International) Papers, 1*, 1–14.
Oakes, P., & Turner, J.C. (1980). Social categorization and intergroup behavior: Does minimal intergroup discrimination make social identity more positive? *European Journal of Social Psychology, 10*, 295–301.
Osgood, C.E. (1962). *An alternative to war or surrender*. Urbana: University of Illinois Press.
Osgood, C.E. (1979). GRIT for MBFR: A proposal for unfreezing force-level postures in Europe. *Peace Research Reviews, 8* (2), 77–92.
Oskamp, S. (1984). *Applied social psychology*. Englewood Cliffs, NJ: Prentice-Hall.
Oskamp, S. (Ed.) (1985). International conflict and national public policy issues. *Applied social psychology annual Vol. 6*. Beverly Hills, CA: Sage.
Patchen, M. (1987). Strategies for eliciting cooperation from an adversary: Laboratory and internation findings. *Journal of Conflict Resolution, 31*, 164–185.
Patchen, M. (1988). *Resolving disputes between nations*. Durham, NC: Duke University Press.
Peabody, D. (1967). Trait inferences: Evaluative and descriptive aspects. *Journal of Personality and Social Psychology Monograph, 7* (4).
Pettigrew, T.F. (1971). *Racially separate or together?* New York: McGraw-Hill.
Pettigrew, T.F. (1979). The ultimate attribution error: Extending Allport's cognitive analysis of prejudice. *Personality and Social Psychology Bulletin, 5*, 461–476.
Pettigrew, T.F. (1986). The intergroup contact hypothesis reconsidered. In M. Hewstone & R. Brown (Eds.), *Contact and conflict in intergroup encounters*. Oxford: Blackwell.
Pfeiffer, J.W., & Jones, J.E. (Eds.) (1974). *A handbook of structured experiences for human relations training*. La Jolla, CA: University Associates.
Popper, K.R. (1961). *The logic of scientific discovery*. New York: Science Editions.
Prein, H.C. (1984). A contingency approach for conflict intervention. *Group & Organization Studies, 9*, 81–102.
Prothro, E.T. (1952). Ethnocentrism and anti-Negro attitudes in the deep south. *Journal of Abnormal and Social Psychology, 47*, 105–108.
Pruitt, D.G. (1981). *Negotiation behavior*. New York: Academic Press.
Pruitt, D.G. (1986). Achieving integrative agreements in negotiation. In R.K. White (Ed.), *Psychology and the prevention of nuclear war*. New York: New York University Press.

Pruitt, D.G., & Kimmel, M.J. (1977). Twenty years of experimental gaming: Critique, synthesis and suggestions for the future. *Annual Review of Psychology, 28,* 363-392.

Pruitt, D.G., & Kressel, K. (1985). The mediation of social conflict: An introduction. *Journal of Social Issues, 41* (2), 1-10.

Pruitt, D.G., & Rubin, J.Z. (1986). *Social conflict: Escalation, stalemate, and resolution.* New York: Random House.

Quattrone, G.A. (1986). On the perception of a group's variability. In S. Worchel, & W.G. Austin (Eds.), *Psychology of intergroup relations* (2nd ed.). Chicago: Nelson-Hall.

Rabbie, J.M., & Huygen, K. (1974). Internal disagreements and their effects on attitudes toward in- and out-groups. *International Journal of Group Tensions, 4,* 222-246.

Rabbie, J.M., & Wilkens C. (1971). Intergroup competition and its effect on intragroup and intergroup relations. *European Journal of Social Psychology, 1,* 215-234.

Read, S.J. (1987). Constructing causal scenarios: A knowledge structure approach to causal reasoning. *Journal of Personality and Social Psychology, 52,* 288-302.

Rokeach, M. (1960). *The open and closed mind.* New York: Basic Books.

Rosch, E. (1975). Cognitive representations of semantic categories. *Journal of Experimental Psychology: General, 104,* 192-233.

Rosch, E. (1978). Principles of categorization. In E. Rosch & B.B. Lloyd (Eds.), *Cognition and categorization.* Hillsdale, NJ: Erlbaum.

Rosenberg, M. (1965). *Society and the adolescent self-image.* Princeton, NJ: Princeton University Press.

Rothbart, M., Dawes, R., & Park, B. (1984). Stereotyping and sampling biases in intergroup perception. In J.R. Eiser (Ed.), *Attitudinal Judgment.* New York: Springer-Verlag.

Rothbart, M., Evans, M., & Fulero, S. (1979). Recall for confirming events: Memory processes and the maintenance of social stereotypes. *Journal of Experimental Social Psychology, 15,* 343-355.

Rubin, J.Z. (1980). Experimental research on third party intervention in conflict: Toward some generalizations. *Psychological Bulletin, 87,* 379-391.

Rubin, J.Z. (Ed.) (1981). *Dynamics of third party intervention: Kissinger in the Middle East.* New York: Praeger.

Rubin, J.Z. (1983). Negotiation. *American Behavioral Scientist, 27* (2), 135-147.

Rubin, J.Z., & Brown, B. (1975). *The social psychology of bargaining and negotiation.* New York: Academic Press.

Ruble, T.L., & Thomas, K.W. (1976). Support for a two-dimensional model of conflict behavior. *Organizational Behavior and Human Performance, 16,* 143-155.

Rumelhart, D.E. (1984). Schemata and the cognitive system. In R.S. Wyer & T.K. Srull (Eds.), *Handbook of Social Cognition: Vol. 1.* Hillsdale, NJ: Erlbaum.

Russett, B.M. (Ed.). (1972). *Peace, war, and numbers.* Beverly Hill, CA: Sage.

Ryen, A.H., & Kahn, A. (1975). Effects of intergroup orientation on group attitudes and proxemic behavior. *Journal of Personality and Social Psychology, 31,* 302-310.

Sagan, C. (1983). Nuclear war and climatic catastrophe: Some policy implications. *Foreign Affairs, 62,* 257-292.

Sandhole, D.J.D. (1968). Paradigms, movements and shifts: Indicators of a social invention. In C.R. Mitchell & K. Webb (Eds.), *New approaches to international mediation.* New York: Greenwood Press.

Sandhole, D.J.D., & Sandhole-Staroste, I. (1987). *Conflict management and problem solving: Interpersonal to international applications.* London: Frances Pinter.

Sawyer, J., & Guetzkow, J. (1965). Bargaining and negotiation in international relations. In H.C. Kelman (Ed.), *International behavior: A social-psychological analysis.* New York: Holt, Rinehart & Winston.

Schacter, S. (1959). *The psychology of affiliation.* Stanford, CA: Stanford University Press.

Schlenker, B.R., & Bonoma, T.V. (1978). Fun and games: The validity of games for the study of conflict. *Journal of Conflict Resolution, 22,* 7-38.

Scott, W.A. (1965). Psychological and social correlates of international images. In H.C.

Kelman (Ed.), *International behavior: A social-psychological analysis*. New York: Holt, Rinehart & Winston.

Shapiro, D., Dreighe, R., & Brett, J. (1985). Mediator behavior and the outcome of mediation. *Journal of Social Issues, 41* (2), 101–114.

Sharan, S. (1980). Cooperative learning in small groups: Recent methods and effects on achievement, attitudes and ethnic relations. *Review of Educational Research, 50*, 241–271.

Sharan, S., Kussell, P., Hertz-Lazarowitz, R., Bejarano, Y., Raviv, S., & Sharan, Y. (1984). *Cooperative learning in the classroom: Research in desegregated schools*. Hillsdale, NJ: Erlbaum.

Shaw, M.E. (1981). *Group dynamics: The psychology of small group behavior* (3rd ed.). New York: McGraw-Hill.

Shaw, M.E., & Costanzo, P.R. (1970). *Theories of social psychology*. New York: McGraw-Hill.

Shaw, M.E., & Wright, J.M. (1967). *Scales for the measurement of attitudes*. New York: McGraw-Hill.

Sheppard, B.H. (1984). Third party conflict intervention: A procedural framework. *Research in Organizational Behavior, 6*, 141–190.

Sherif, M. (1936). *The psychology of group norms*. New York: Harper & Row.

Sherif, M. (1966). *In common predicament: Social psychology of intergroup conflict and cooperation*. Boston: Houghton Mifflin.

Sherif, M., Harvey, O.J., White, B.J., Hood, W.R., & Sherif, C.W. (1961). *Intergroup conflict and cooperation: The Robber's Cave experiment*. Norman: University of Oklahoma Book Exchange.

Sherif, M., & Sherif, C.W. (1979). Research on intergroup relations. In W.G. Austin & S. Worchel (Eds.), *The social psychology of intergroup relations*. Monterey, CA: Brooks/Cole.

Silbey, S., & Merry, S. (1986). Mediator settlement strategies. *Law and Policy, 8* (1), 7–32.

Simmel, G. (1955). *Conflict and the web of group affiliations*. New York: Free Press.

Simpson, G.E., & Yinger, M.J. (1972). *Racial and cultural minorities: An analysis of prejudice and discrimination* (4th ed.). New York: Harper & Row.

Singer, J.D. (1970). Escalation and control in international conflict: A simple feedback model. *General Systems, 15*, 163–173.

Singer, J.D. (Ed.). (1979). *Explaining war*. Beverly Hills, CA: Sage.

Singer, J.D., & Ray, P. (1966). Decision-making in conflict: From inter-personal to international relations. *Menninger Clinic Bulletin, 30*, 300–312.

Singer, J.E., Radloff, L.S., & Work, D.M. (1963). Renegades, heretics, and changes in sentiment. *Sociometry, 26*, 178–179.

Sites, P. (1973). *Control: The basis of social order*. New York: Dunellen.

Sivard, R.L. (1986). *World military and social expenditures (1986)*. Leesburg, VA: World Priorities.

Slavin, R.E. (1980). Cooperative learning. *Review of Educational Research, 50*, 315–342.

Slavin, R.E. (1985). Cooperative learning: Applying contact theory in desegregated schools. *Journal of Social Issues, 41* (3), 45–61.

Smith, C.G. (1979). Studies in international conflict: Recent contributions of the behavioral sciences. *International Journal of Group Tensions, 9* (1–4), 86–109.

Snyder, M. (1981). On the self-perpetuating nature of social stereotypes. In E.T. Higgins, C.P. Herman, & M.P. Zanna (Eds.), *Social cognition: The Ontario symposium: Vol. 1*. Hillsdale, NJ: Erlbaum.

Snyder, M. (1984). When belief creates reality. In L. Berkowitz (Ed.), *Advances in experimental social psychology: Vol. 18*. New York: Academic Press.

Snyder, M., & Uranowitz (1978). Reconstructing the past: Some cognitive consequences of person perception. *Journal of Personality and Social Psychology, 36*, 941–950.

St. John, N.H. (1975). *School desegregation: Outcomes for children*. New York: Wiley.

Stagner, R. (Ed.). (1967). *The dimensions of human conflict*. Detroit: Wayne State University Press.

Stein, A.A. (1976). Conflict and cohesion. A review of the literature. *Journal of Conflict Resolution, 20*, 143-172.
Steiner, I.D. (1974). Whatever happened to the group in social psychology? *Journal of Experimental Social Psychology, 10*, 94-108.
Steiner, I.D. (1986). Paradigms and groups. In L. Berkowitz (Ed.), *Advances in Experimental Social Psychology: Vol. 19.* New York: Academic Press.
Stephan, W.G. (1978). School desegregation: An evaluation of predictions made in Brown vs. Board of Education. *Psychological Bulletin, 85*, 217-238.
Stephan, W.G. (1985). Intergroup relations. In G. Lindzey & E. Aronson (Eds.), *Handbook of social psychology: Vol. III.* New York: Random House.
Stephan, W.G., & Brigham, J.C. (1985). Intergroup contact: Introduction. *Journal of Social Issues, 41* (3), 1-8.
Stephan, W.G., & Stephan, C.W. (1984). The role of ignorance in intergroup relations. In N. Miller & M.B. Brewer (Eds.), *Groups in contact: The psychology of desegregation.* Orlando, FL: Academic Press.
Stephan, W.G., & Stephan, C.W. (1985). Intergroup anxiety. *Journal of Social Issues, 41* (3), 157-175.
Stephenson, C.M. (Ed.) (1982). *Alternative methods for international security.* Washington, D.C.: University Press of America.
Stephenson, G.M. (1981). Intergroup bargaining and negotiation. In J.C. Turner & H. Giles (Eds.), *Intergroup behavior.* Oxford: Blackwell.
Stevens, S.S. (1963). Operationism and logical positivism. In M.H. Marx (Ed.), *Theories in contemporary psychology.* New York: MacMillan.
Stockholm International Peace Research Institute (1987). *World armaments and disarmament.* Stockholm, Sweden: SIPRI.
Stroebe, W., Kruglanski, A.W., Bar-Tal, D., & Hewstone, M. (Eds.) (1988). *The social psychology of intergroup conflict.* New York: Springer-Verlag.
Suedfeld, P., & Tetlock. P. (1977). Integrative complexity of communications in international crises. *Journal of Conflict Resolution, 21*, 169-184.
Suedfled, P., Tetlock, P.E., & Raminez, C. (1977). War, peace, and integrative complexity: UN speeches on the Middle East problem, (1947-1976). *Journal of Conflict Resolution, 21*, 427-441.
Sumner, W.G. (1906). *Folkways.* Boston: Ginn & Co.
Taft, S.H. (1987). Use of the collaborative ethic and contingency theories in conflict management. In J.W. Pfeiffer (Ed.), *The 1987 annual: Developing human resources.* San Diego, CA: University Associates.
Tajfel, H. (1969). Cognitive aspects of prejudice. *Journal of Social Issues, 25*, 79-97.
Tajfel, H. (1970). Experiments in intergroup discrimination. *Scientific American, 223* (5) 96-102.
Tafjel, H. (1978). *Differentiation between social groups: Studies in the social psychology of intergroup relations.* London: Academic Press.
Tajfel, H. (1981). *Human groups and social categories: Studies in social psychology.* Cambridge: Cambridge University Press.
Tajfel, H. (1982). Social psychology of intergroup relations. *Annual Review of Psychology, 33*, 1-39.
Tajfel, H., Flament, C., Billig, M., & Bundy, R. (1971). Social categorization and intergroup behavior. *European Journal of Social Psychology, 1*, 149-177.
Tajfel, H., & Turner, J. (1979). An integrative theory of intergroup conflict. In W.G. Austin & S. Worchel (Eds.), *The social psychology of intergroup relations.* Monterey, CA: Brooks/Cole.
Tajfel, H., & Wilkes, A.L. (1963). Classification and quantitative judgement. *British Journal of Psychology, 54*, 101-114.
Taylor, D.M., & Jaggi, V. (1974). Ethnocentrism and causal attribution in a South Indian context. *Journal of Cross-Cultural Psychology, 5*, 162-172.

Taylor, D.M, & McKirnan, D.J. (1984). A five-stage model of intergroup relations. *British Journal of Social Psychology, 23*, 291-300.
Taylor, D.M., & Moghaddam, F.M. (1987). *Theories of intergroup relations. International social psychological perspectives*. New York: Praeger.
Taylor, D.M., & Simard, L.M. (1979). Ethnic identity and intergroup relations. In D.J. Lee (Ed.), *Emerging ethnic boundaries*. Ottawa, Canada: University of Ottawa Press.
Taylor, S.E., & Crocker, J. (1981). Schematic bases of social information processing. In E.T. Higgins, C.P. Herman, & M.P. Zanna (Eds.), *Social cognition: The Ontario symposium: Vol. 1*. Hillsdale, NJ: Erlbaum.
Taylor, S.E., & Fiske, S.T. (1978). Salience, attention, and attribution: Top of the head phenomena. In L. Berkowtiz (Ed.), *Advances in experimental social psychology: Vol. II*. New York: Academic Press.
Taylor, S.E., Fiske, S.T., Etcoff, N.L., & Ruderman, A.J. (1978). Categorical and contextual basis of person memory and stereotyping. *Journal of Personality and Social Psychology, 36*, 778-793.
Tetlock, P.E. (1983). Policymakers' images of international conflict. *Journal of Social Issues, 39* (1), 67-86.
Tetlock, P.E. (1985). Integrative complexity of American and Soviet Foreign policy rhetoric: A time-series analysis. *Journal of Personality and Social Psychology, 49*, 1565-1585.
Tetlock, P.E. (1988). Monitoring the integrative complexity of American and Soviet policy rhetoric: What can be learned? *Journal of Social Issues, 44* (2), 101-131.
Tetlock, P.E., & McGuire, C.B. (1985). Cognitive perspectives on foreign policy. In S. Long (Ed.), *Political Behavior Annual*. Boulder, CO: Westview.
Thomas, K.W. (1976). Conflict and conflict management. In M. Dunnette (Ed.), *Handbook of industrial and organization psychology*. Chicago: Rand-McNally.
Thomas, K.W., & Kilmann, R.H. (1974). *The Thomas-Kilmann Conflict MODE Instrument*. Tuxedo Park, NY: Xicom.
Thurstone, L.L., & Chave, E.J. (1929). *The measurement of attitudes*. Chicago: University of Chicago Press.
Touval, S., & Zartman, I.W. (Eds.). (1985). *International mediation in theory and practice*. Boulder, CO: Westview.
Turco, R.P., Toon, O.B., Ackerman, T.P., Pollack, J.B., & Sagan, C. (1983). Nuclear winter: Global consequences of multiple nuclear explosions. *Science, 222*, 1283-1292.
Turner, J.C. (1981). The experimental social psychology of intergroup behavior. In J.C. Turner & H. Giles (Eds.), *Intergroup behavior*. Oxford: Blackwell.
Turner, J.C. (1982). Towards a cognitive redefinition of the social group. In H. Tajfel (Ed.), *Social identity and intergroup relations*. Cambridge: Cambridge University Press.
Turner, J.C. (1985). Social categorization and the self-concept: A social cognitive theory of group behavior. In E.J. Lawler (Ed.), *Advances in group processes: Vol. 2*. Greenwich, CT: JAI Press.
Turner, J.C., Hogg, M.A., Oakes, P.J., Reicher, S.D., & Wetherell, M.S. (1987). *Rediscovering the social group: A self-categorization theory*. Oxford: Blackwell.
Tversky, A. (1977). Features of similarity. *Psychological Review, 84*, 327-352.
Tzinier, A. (1982). Group cohesiveness: A dynamic perspective. *Social Behavior and Personality, 10*, 205-211.
Ury, W.L. (1987). Strengthening international mediation. *Negotiation Journal, 3*, 225-229.
Wall, J.A. (1981). Mediation: An analysis, review and proposed research. *Journal of Conflict Resolution, 25*, 157-180.
Wallace, M.D. (1979). Arms race and escalation: Some new evidence. *Journal of Conflict Resolution, 23*, 3-16.
Walton, R.E. (1969). *Interpersonal peacemaking: Confrontations and third party consultation*. Reading, MA: Addison-Wesley.
Wang, R.S. (1977). External hostility and internal conflict: Group cohesion theory in international politics. *Dissertation Abstracts International, 37*, 7954A.

Webb, J.C. (1979). Behavioral studies of third party intervention. In G.M. Stephenson & C.J. Brotherton (Eds.), *Industrial relations: A social psychological approach*. New York: Wiley.
Webb, N.M. (1982). Student interaction and learning in small groups. *Review of Educational Research, 52*, 421-445.
Weiner, B. (1985). An attributional theory of achievement motivation and emotion. *Psychological Review, 92*, 548-573.
Weyant, J.M. (1986). *Applied social psychology*. New York: Oxford University Press.
White, R.K. (1965). Images in the context of international conflict: Soviet perceptions of the U.S. and U.S.S.R. In H.C. Kelman (Ed.), *International behavior: A social-psychological analysis*. New York: Holt, Rinehart & Winston.
White, R.K. (1966). Misperception and the Vietman War. *Journal of Social Issues, 22* (3), 1-164.
White, R.K. (1970). *Nobody wanted war: Misperception in Vietnam and other wars*. Garden City, NY: Doubleday.
White, R.K. (1977). Misperception in the Arab-Israeli conflict. *Journal of Social Issues, 33* (1), 190-221.
White, R.K. (1984). *Fearful warriors: A psychological profile of U.S.-Soviet relations*. New York: The Free Press.
White, R.K. (1985). Ten psychological contributions to the prevention of nuclear war. In S. Oskamp (Ed.), *International conflict and national public policy issues: Applied social psychology annual: Vol. 6*. Beverly Hills, CA: Sage.
White, R.K. (1988). Specifics in a positive approach to peace. *Journal of Social Issues, 44* (2), 191-202.
Wilder, D.A. (1984). Predictions of belief homogeneity and similarity following social categorization. *British Journal of Social Psychology, 23*, 323-333.
Wilder, D.A. (1986). Social categorization: Implications for creation and reduction of intergroup bias. In L. Berkowitz (Ed.), *Advances in experimental social psychology: Vol. 19*. New York: Academic Press.
Wilder, D.A., & Allen, V.L. (1978). Group membership and preference for information about others. *Personality and Social Psychology Bulletin, 4*, 106-110.
Winham, G.R. (1977). Negotiation as a management process. *World Politics, 30* (1), October, 87-114.
Withey, S., & Katz, D. (1965). The social psychology of human conflict. In E.B. McNeil (Ed.), *The nature of human conflict*. Englewood Cliffs, NJ: Prentice-Hall.
Worchel, S., & Austin, W.G. (Eds.). (1986). *Psychology of intergroup relations* (2nd ed.). Chicago: Nelson-Hall.
Workie, A. (1967). *The effect of cooperation and competition on productivity*. Unpublished doctoral dissertation, Teachers College, Columbia University, New York.
Wright, Q. (1965a). *A study of war* (2nd ed.). Chicago: University of Chicago Press.
Wright, Q. (1965b). Escalation of international conflicts. *Journal of Conflict Resolution, 9*, 434-449.
Wyer, R.S., & Gordon, S.E. (1982). The recall of information about persons and groups. *Journal of Experimental Social Psychology, 18*, 128-164.
Wyer, R.S., & Gordon, S.E. (1984). The cognitive representation of social information. In R.S. Wyer & T.K. Srull (Eds.), *Handbook of Social Cognition: Vol. 2*. Hillsdale, NJ: Erlbaum.
Young, O.R. (1967). *The intermediaries: Third Parties in International Crisis*. Princeton, NJ: Princeton University Press.
Zander, A. (1979). The psychology of group processes. *Annual Review of Psychology, 30*, 417-451.
Zartman, I.W. (1977). Introduction: Special issue on negotiation. *Journal of Conflict Resolution, 21*, 563-564.

Author Index

Abelson, H.H., 246
Abelson, R.P., 50
Ackerman, T.P., 3
Adorno, T.W., 22, 23, 92, 104, 132
Alderfer, C.P., 204
Alevy, D.I., 206
Allen, V.L., 41
Allison, G.T., 81, 101
Allport, G.W., 21, 180, 182
Altemeyer, B., 104, 132
Altman, I., 60, 104
Altom, M.W., 45
Amir, Y., 55, 57, 114, 180
Anderson, J.C., 223, 228
Angell, R.C., 4, 107
Aronson, E., 55, 56
Asch, S.E., 69
Austin, W.G., 21, 27, 87
Axelrod, R., 80, 200
Azar, E.E., 4, 5, 99, 111, 147

Bales, R.F., 59
Banks, M., 143
Banks, W.C., 25, 28
Bar-Tal, D., 178
Bartenuk, J.M., 230
Bartlett, F.C., 50
Bay, C., 149
Bayley, J., 206
Bell, C.H., 204
Bell, E.C., 104
Bell, R.L., 204

Ben-Ari, R., 57
Bendahmane, D.B., 145
Benne, K.D., 15, 60
Bennis, W.G., 15
Benton, A.A., 230
Bercovitch, J., 224
Beres, M.E., 4, 234
Berry, J.W., 21, 179
Betz, B., 199, 200
Bigoness, W.J., 223, 228, 230
Billig, M., 29, 44, 67
Bixenstine, V.E., 92
Blake, R.R., 11, 13, 15, 25–27, 35, 36,
   68, 69, 82, 83, 94, 99, 101, 111, 117,
   135, 184, 188–191, 203, 204, 214,
   216, 226, 230, 246
Blakeney, R.N., 104
Blaney, N.N., 56
Boehringer, G.H., 206
Boehringer, K., 206
Bonham, M.G., 169
Bonomo, T.V., 13, 170
Boulding, K.E., 24, 99
Braly, K., 21, 41
Branthwaite, A., 45
Brett, J.M., 212, 223
Brewer, M.B., 30, 45, 46, 48, 57, 102,
   181
Brewer, W.F., 42, 49, 50, 55
Brezhnev, L., 197
Brigham, J.C., 41, 180, 181
Brilhart, J.K., 132, 133

Brislin, R.W., 149, 185, 242
Brockner, J., 111
Brody, R.A., 160
Bronfenbrenner, U., 151
Brown, B., 163
Brown, R.J., 6, 8, 12, 30, 37, 55–57, 181–186
Bruner, J.S., 39, 45, 53
Bullough, V.L., 160
Bundy, R., 29, 44
Bunker, B., 206
Burke, R.J., 190
Burke, W.W., 204
Burton, J.W., 5, 99, 111, 112, 144, 147, 148, 159, 162, 187, 204–206, 212, 214, 226, 227, 230, 234, 246

Campbell, D.T., 23, 24, 45, 48–50, 53, 54, 62, 65, 99
Cantor, N., 52
Carnevale, P.J.D., 228
Cartwright, D., 69
Chanin, M.N., 94
Chave, E.J., 21
Cherrie, C., 242
Chesler, M.A., 23
Chin, R., 15
Cleveland, S.E., 204
Cobbs, P.M., 203
Cohen, E., 181
Cohen, S.P., 145, 206, 207, 219, 227, 230
Collins, M.G., 198, 201
Condor, S., 6, 8, 30, 184
Cook, S.W., 114, 180–183
Coser, L.A., 24, 33, 64, 65, 66, 99, 101, 102
Costanzo, P.R., 89
Courtwright, J.A., 73
Crocker, J., 42, 50, 51, 53
Crow, W.J., 13, 197, 198, 201
Crutchfield, R.S., 69
Cushner, K., 242
Cyert, R.M., 81

Dahrendorf, R., 4, 32, 107
Darley, J.M., 43
Dawes, R., 41
Dean, J.P., 202
Deaux, K., 44

Dedring, J., 159
de Reuck, A.V.S., 207, 221, 222
Deschamps, J.C., 40, 56
de Sola Pool, I., 149
Deutsch, M., 6, 7, 10, 27, 31, 32, 35–37, 96, 99, 100, 108, 111, 114, 159, 175, 177, 178, 188, 191, 194, 200, 212, 243
Diab, L.N., 66, 184
Dion, K.L., 27, 48, 54, 65–68, 93, 101, 102
Doise, W., 40, 46
Doob, L.W., 112, 205, 206, 214, 230, 246
Douglas, A., 227, 228
Doyle, S., 45
Drieghe, R., 223
Druckman, D., 13, 14, 67, 94, 163–167, 169
Dubin, R.V., 88–91, 97, 105, 108, 112
Duncan, B.L., 41

Ehrlich, H.J., 23
Ehrlich, P.R., 3
Ellard, J.H., 61
Epp-Tiessen, E., 3
Erikson, B., 127, 130
Etkoff, N.L., 40
Etzioni, A., 111, 196, 197
Evans, M., 42

Farah, N., 147
Fazio, R.H., 43
Fiedler, F.E., 68, 94, 130
Filley, A.C., 188, 212
Finch, M.L., 198
Fink, C.F., 31–33
Fisher, R., 169, 234
Fisher, R.J., 5, 8, 10, 11, 15, 23, 60, 74, 112, 114, 117, 118, 132, 134, 145, 149, 150, 156, 159, 178, 180, 196, 207, 212, 214–216, 218, 219, 221, 224–228, 230, 231, 235, 237, 246
Fiske, S.T., 40, 42, 52
Flament, C., 29, 44
Flowers, M.L., 73
Folberg, J., 212, 225
Foltz, W.J., 205, 206
Forster, C.L., 68

Author Index

Fouraker, L., 163
Fox, W.T.R., 143
French, N., 206
French, W.L., 204
Frenkel-Brunswik, E., 22
Freud, S., 63
Frey, R., 127
Fromm, E., 63
Fulero, S., 42

Galtung, J., 3, 148, 149
Garrison, K.N., 246
Gershenfeld, M.K., 60, 62, 81, 123
Glaser, E.M., 246
Glasl, F., 235
Goldberg, S.B., 212, 223
Gorbachev, M., 197
Gordon, S.E., 42, 49–52
Granberg, D., 197
Grant, P.R., 49, 53, 54, 68, 95, 100, 118, 132, 133, 139, 231
Grigsby, D.W., 223, 228
Groom, A.J.R., 207, 220, 221
Guetzkow, H., 13, 60, 67, 163–165, 169, 197
Gyr, J., 60

Hackman, J.R., 60
Hall, D.G., 118, 119, 132, 133
Hameed, S., 223
Hamilton, D.L., 41, 50, 52
Han, G., 199, 201
Haney, C., 25, 28
Hanson, P.G., 204
Hartley, E.L., 23
Harvey, O.J., 25, 156
Haythorn, W., 104
Heider, F., 48, 53
Herek, G., 79
Hewstone, M., 12, 43, 44, 55–57, 178, 181–186
Hill, B.J., 230
Hinkle, S., 102
Hogg, M.A., 46
Holmes, J.G., 49, 54, 61, 68, 95, 100, 127
Holsti, O.R., 81, 145, 160
Hood, W.R., 25
Horney, K., 63
Hovland, C.I., 21

Hunt, D.E., 156
Huth, P., 79
Huygen, K., 67

Ikle, F.C., 163

Jackson, D., 132
Jaggi, V., 43
Janis, I.L., 21, 69–81, 83–85, 103, 145, 246
Jervis, R., 76, 80, 145, 150, 153, 159, 160
Johnson, D.F., 230
Johnson, D.W., 55
Johnson, R.T., 55
Jones, E.E., 50
Jones, J.E., 45, 132, 133
Jones, R.E., 94
Jussim, L., 43

Kahn, A., 66–68
Kahn, R.L., 61, 75, 81, 99, 130
Kalin, R., 21
Kaplowitz, N., 191–195, 201, 243, 244
Kastersztein, J., 56
Katz, D., 12, 21, 33, 41, 61, 63, 75, 81, 99, 130, 146, 147, 149, 171
Katz, P.A., 21, 242
Keashly, L., 133, 224, 225, 230, 231, 235
Kelley, H.H., 21
Kelman, H.C., 10, 112, 144, 145, 151, 191, 206, 207, 219, 221, 222, 227, 230, 242, 246
Kende, I., 2
Kennedy, J.F., 196
Keys, C.B., 230
Kilmann, R.H., 94, 130, 189, 190, 195
Kimmel, M.J., 11, 13, 118
Kinder, D.R., 80
Klein, E.B., 206
Klimoski, R.J., 118
Kolb, D.M., 223, 227, 229
Koutsourais, H., 198
Kramer, R.M., 181
Kressel, K., 228
Kriesberg, L., 111, 163, 170–172, 243
Kruglanski, A.W., 178
Krushchev, N., 196

Lakin, M., 203
Lall, A., 163
Lamm, H., 61
Lebow, R.N., 74, 76, 77, 80, 85, 145, 160
Lederer, K., 148, 178
Lemaine, G., 56
Lemyre, L., 93
Leng, R.J., 200, 201
Levine, R.A., 24, 45, 48, 49, 54, 62, 65, 99
Levinson, D.J., 22, 203
Lewin, K., 21, 60, 75, 77, 89
Lieberman, M.A., 203
Lightbown, N., 45
Likert, J.G., 83
Likert, R., 21, 83, 226
Lindskold, S., 14, 198–202
Lingle, J.H., 45, 51
Lippitt, G., 224, 225
Lippitt, R., 15, 202, 203, 224, 225
Lockhart, C., 161
Lomranz, J., 203
Longley, J., 73, 74
Love, R.L., 13

Mack, R.W., 30–34
Mahoney, R., 94, 163, 165, 166
Maier, N.R.F., 62, 80–82
Mann, L., 72, 75–81, 84, 246
March, J.G., 75, 80, 81
Markus, J., 50–53
Marx, K., 32
Marx, M.H., 89
Maslow, A.H., 149
Mathews, A., 30
Matthews, R.O., 143
McCandless, B.R., 23
McCann, L.M., 132
McClelland, D.C., 93
McDonald, J.W, 145
McGillicuddy, N.B., 223
McGillis, D., 50
McGrath, J.E., 60
McGuire, C.B., 145, 151
McGuire, W.J., 117
McKirnan, D.J., 54, 108, 177
Medin, D.L., 45
Melcher, B.W., 94

Mendlowitz, S.H., 245
Merry, S., 212
Mervis, C.B., 46
Meyer, G., 45
Milburn, T.W., 161
Miller, D., 63
Miller, F.D., 207
Miller, J.C., 206
Miller, N., 55, 57
Mischel, W., 52
Mitchell, C.R., 144, 187, 212, 234, 248
Moghaddam, F.M., 6, 30, 87, 147, 177, 242
Moore, C.W., 230
Morgan, P.M., 159
Morris, W.C., 62, 81, 226
Mouton, J.S., 11, 13, 15, 25–27, 35, 36, 68, 69, 82, 83, 94, 99, 101, 112, 117, 135, 184, 188–191, 203, 204, 214, 216, 226, 230
Moscovici, S., 69
Murray, H.A., 93
Myers, A., 66
Myers, D.G., 69

Nakamura, G.V., 42, 49, 50
Napier, R.W., 60, 62, 81, 123
Naroll, F., 160
Naroll, R., 160
Newcomb, T.M., 48, 49, 53, 69, 182
Newcombe, H., 202
North, R.C., 160

Oakes, P.J., 46, 64
O'Connell, W.E., 204
O'Reilly, E.F., 92
Osgood, C.E., 12, 111, 114, 160, 175, 196–198, 201
Osherow, N., 55
Oskamp, S., 10, 145

Park, B., 41
Parsons, T., 32
Patchen, M., 14, 173–176, 194, 234
Peabody, D., 132
Perlmutter, J.V., 39
Personnaz, B., 56
Pettigrew, T.F., 43, 178, 182, 183

Author Index

Pfeiffer, J.W., 132, 133
Physicians for Social Responsibility, 3
Pollack, J.B., 3
Popper, K.R., 91
Postman, L.J., 21
Prein, H.C., 212, 235
Prothro, E.T., 23
Pruitt, D.G., 11, 13, 73, 74, 83, 100, 105, 111, 118, 145, 159, 160, 162, 163, 167, 168, 223, 225

Quattrone, G.A., 40, 41

Rabbie, J.M., 27, 67
Radloff, L.S., 67
Raminez, C., 156, 157
Ray, P., 169
Read, S.J., 50
Reicher, S.D., 46
Rogers, C., 63
Rokeach, M., 24
Rosch, E., 39, 45, 46, 51, 53
Rose, T.L., 52
Rosen, A.A., 202
Rosenberg, M., 132
Rothbart, M., 41, 42
Rozelle, R.M., 13
Rubin, J.Z., 83, 100, 105, 111, 145, 159, 160, 162, 163, 167, 211, 212, 225, 229
Rubinoff, A.G., 143
Ruble, T.L., 190
Ruderman, A.J., 40
Rumelhart, D.E., 49
Russett, B.M., 145
Ryen, A.H., 66–68

Sagan, C., 3
Sandhole, D.J.D., 248
Sandhole-Staroste, I., 248
Sanford, R.N., 22
Sashkin, M., 62, 81, 226
Sawyer, J., 163–165, 169
Schachter, S., 66
Schlenker, B.R., 13
Schmidt, S.M., 4, 234
Schneer, J.A., 94
Schopler, J., 102
Schroder, H.M., 156

Scott, W.A., 151
Sen, J., 223
Shapiro, D., 223, 228
Sharan, S., 55
Shaw, M.E., 21, 60, 89, 107
Sheats, P., 60
Shepard, H.A., 11, 15, 83, 112, 184, 188, 190, 191, 203, 214, 216, 226, 230
Sheppard, B.H., 224, 225, 228, 229
Sherif, C.W., 25, 117
Sherif, M., 11, 13, 24, 25–27, 35, 36, 49, 53, 62, 65, 68, 69, 82, 91, 99–102, 105–107, 111, 114, 117, 184, 185, 203
Shermerhorn, R.A., 203
Siegel, S., 163
Sikes, J., 56
Silbey, S., 212
Simard, L.M., 185
Simmel, G., 64, 65
Simon, H.A., 75, 81
Simpson, G.E., 180
Singer, J.D., 145, 159, 169
Singer, J.E., 67
Sites, P., 148
Sivard, R.L., 3
Slavin, R.E., 55, 181
Sloma, R.L., 203
Smith, B.L., 207
Smith, C.G., 147
Smith, P.M., 93
Snapp, M., 56
Snyder, M., 42, 43
Snyder, R.C., 30–34
Stagner, R., 108, 203
Stein, A.A., 65–67
Stein, J.G., 143, 145, 160
Steiner, I.D., 60
Stephan, C.W., 56, 181, 185, 220
Stephan, W.G., 40–43, 45, 50–52, 55, 180, 185, 220
Stephenson, C.M., 145
Stephenson, G.M., 117
Stevens, S.S., 90
St. John, N.H., 181
Stroebe, W., 178
Suedfeld, P., 156, 157
Sullivan, H.S., 63
Sumner, W.G., 22, 65

Taft, S.H., 195
Tajfel, H., 21, 28–29, 37, 39, 44–47, 53, 54, 62, 64, 66–69
Taylor, A., 212, 225
Taylor, D.A., 242
Taylor, D.M., 6, 21, 30, 43, 54, 87, 108, 147, 177, 185, 242
Taylor, S.E., 40, 42, 50–53
Tetlock, P.E., 145, 151, 156–159, 161, 162
Thibaut, J., 127
Thomas, K.W., 11, 83, 94, 99, 115, 117, 130, 135, 188–190, 195
Thurstone, L.L., 21
Toon, O.B., 3
Touval, S., 145
Tullar, W.L., 230
Turco, R.P., 3
Turner, J.C., 12, 27, 28, 37, 45–48, 50–54, 57, 64, 182
Tversky, A., 39, 45, 46, 50, 53
Tzinier, A., 68

Uranowitz, S.W., 42
Ury, W.L., 169, 212

Wade, G., 30, 56
Walker, L., 127
Wall, J.A., 211, 212, 225, 227, 228
Wallace, M.D., 160
Walters, R.S., 198, 200
Walton, R.E., 211, 213, 214
Wang, R.S., 66
Watson, J., 15
Webb, J.C., 225, 227

Webb, K., 248
Webb, N.M., 55
Weiner, B., 43
Weiss, J.A., 80
Welton, G.L., 223
Westley, B., 15
Wetherell, M.S., 46
Weyant, J.M., 10
Wheeler, H.G., 200, 201
White, B.J., 25
White, J.H., 216
White, R.K., 145, 152–156, 175, 194
Wilder, D.A., 40, 41, 43, 48, 51, 55, 56
Wilkens, C., 27, 67
Wilkes, A.L., 39
Williams, J., 30
Winham, G.R., 163
Withey, S., 12
Worchel, S., 21, 27, 87
Work, D.M., 67
Workie, A., 36
Wright, J.M., 21
Wright, Q., 21, 143, 159, 235
Wyer, R.S., 42, 49–52

Yinger, M.J., 180
Yong, M., 242
Young, O.R., 211

Zajonc, R.B., 50–53
Zander, A., 60
Zartman, I.W., 145, 163
Zavalloni, M., 69
Zeruolis, V., 206
Zimbardo, P.G., 25, 28

Subject Index

Aggressor-defender model, 159–162
Alternate dispute resolution, 248
Antecedent variables, 92
Anti-semitism, 22–23
Applied social psychology, 5, 9, 10, 248
Arbitration, 212, 223
Arms race, 2, 160, 194
Assimilation, 150
Attributions, 43
Authoritarian personality, 22, 23, 24, 92, 104

Balance theory, 48, 53
Boundaries (of a model), 89, 105–108
Boundary role, 61

Canadian Institute for International Peace and Security, 246
Categorization, 150
Categorization theory, 45
Center for Conflict Analysis and Resolution, 246, 247
Center for International Development and Conflict Resolution, 246
Cognitive consistency, 48, 76, 80, 150, 220
Cognitive differentiation hypothesis, 48
Cohesion, 60, 64–68, 93, 94, 101–103
Communication networks, 61
Competition, 32, 66–68, 93
Competitive orientation, 35, 36, 93, 96, 99, 100, 176

Conciliation, 212
Conflict Clinic, 248
Conflict, definitions, 6, 30–31
Conflict intensity, 109, 170, 200
Conflict, sources, 33, 34, 93, 99, 146–149, 192
Conflict spiral model, 159–162
Conflict-theory model of decision making, 77–79
Conformity, 68–69
Constituent pressure, 11, 27, 82, 83, 93, 95, 101, 102
Content Control, 224
Contingency approach, 194, 234–238
Contingency Model, 237, 238
Contrient interdependence, 35, 99
Controlled communication, 204
Crude law of social relations, 36, 99, 200
Cuban missile crisis, 74
Cultural Differences, 149, 166, 185
Cultural Identity, 149

Decision making, 74–82, 84–85
Decision making criteria, 79
De-escalation, 84, 111, 114, 185, 242
Defensively motivated aggression, 153
Desegregation, 178, 180
Deterrence model, 159–162, 193, 194
Diabolical enemy image, 152, 153
Diffusion of Responsibility, 61
Dogmatism, 24
Domain of a model, 105, 108

Eclectic model of intergroup conflict, 87, 98, 115, 117, 155, 162, 170, 178, 236, 240
Economic conflict, 33, 99, 146
Empirical indicators, 90
Empirical theories, 89
Escalation, 34–36, 84, 100, 111, 159–162, 170, 193, 235
Ethnocentrism, 22, 62–64, 93, 95, 100–104, 223
  definition, 22
  Scale, 23
Exaggerated fear, 153
Expectancies, 42, 43

F (Facism) Scale, 23, 132
Facilitative conditions of intergroup contact, 114, 180–187, 202, 207, 208, 222, 242
Feature Matching Model, 45
Focusing hypothesis, 45
Functional Theory of Attitudes, 63, 220
Fundamental attribution error, 151

Gradualism, 196
Graduated Reciprocation in Tension-reduction (GRIT), 12, 13, 14, 19, 111, 171, 176, 196–202, 242
Group dynamics, 59–62, 70, 84, 85, 222
Group-level variables, 94, 95, 177
Groupthink, 68–74, 83–85, 103

Hypotheses, 91

Identity, 59, 62–64, 93, 94, 102, 103, 107, 148, 149, 154, 155, 178, 182, 185, 205, 240
Image, 151, 152, 161, 162, 191, 192, 204, 223
Individual-level variables, 92, 177, 178
In-group bias, 29, 44, 47
Integrative complexity, 156–158
Interaction process analysis, 217
Interface Conflict-Solving Model, 204
Intergroup anxiety, 180, 185, 207, 222
Intergroup Contact Hypothesis, 54–57, 180–187, 222, 242

Intergroup Conflict Simulation (ICS), 18, 19, 119, 141, 142, 198, 229–233, 241, 248
Intergroup-level variables, 95
Intergroup relations, 21, 54, 57, 59, 87, 90, 105, 106, 177, 180, 181, 202, 203, 242
Inter-Nation Simulation, 13, 67, 197, 198
Interpersonal attraction, 182, 201
Irrational consistency, 150

Jackson Personality Inventory, 132
Journal of Conflict Resolution, 246

Launch-on-warning policy, 176
Laws, 89, 97
Leadership, 61, 82, 83, 94
League of Nations, 143
Levels of analysis, 92
Liberalism, 143

Macho pride, 153
Malignant social process, 36, 111, 159, 176, 178
Mediation, 212, 223
Minimal group paradigm, 29, 44, 64, 149
Mirror image, 151
Moral self image, 152, 153
Multiculturalism, 178, 179, 208
Mutual example, 197

Nationalism, 146, 147, 222
Need for achievement, 93, 94, 104
Need for affiliation, 93, 94
Need for power, 93, 104
Needs theory, 111, 147–149, 178, 179, 205
Negotiation, 96, 127, 163–170, 172, 207
No-first-use policy, 176
Norms, 60–61, 68, 122, 221

Orientations, 92, 192
Outcome control, 224
Outcome variables, 92, 192

Peacekeeping, 237
Phenomenology, 6, 177
Planned change, 15

Subject Index

Pluralism, 144, 178
Polarization, 68, 69
Power conflict, 34, 99, 146, 147
Prenegotiation, 207, 237
Principles, 89, 97–105
Prisoner's Dilemma, 13, 35, 117, 198, 199–201
Problem solving, 61, 74–82, 93, 95, 101, 103, 105, 203, 221, 226
Problem-solving workshop, 171, 202–208, 213, 219
Process control, 224
Process variables, 92
Promotive interdependence, 35
Propositions, 90, 112–115
Protracted social conflict, 3, 147, 148, 179, 184, 240, 244

Realism, 144, 248
Realistic Group Conflict Theory (RCT), 22, 24, 26, 28, 49, 63, 65, 95–97, 99, 100, 114, 155, 240
Reciprocity, norm of, 178, 187, 198–201, 221, 242
Reference group, 107
Resolution effects, 97
Risky shift, 69
Role, 61

Satisficing, 75, 80
Schema Theory, 49–54
Security dilemma, 160, 162
Self-Categorization Theory, 46, 51–53
Self-esteem, 62–64, 72, 73, 92, 93, 94, 101, 103, 104
Self-fulfilling Prophecy, 43, 56, 152, 161, 187, 220
Sensitivity training (see T-group)
Simulation, 37, 118
Social Identity Theory (SIT), 28–30, 44, 47, 62, 102, 177, 178
Stages of conflict escalation, 235

Statism, 147
Stereotypes, 21, 36, 41, 46, 50, 52, 56, 70, 185, 220, 236
Stockholm International Peace Research Institute, 2
Strategic Simulation, 118
Structuralism, 144
Superordinate goal, 25, 27, 111, 184
System states, 90, 105, 108–112

Tavistock group, 205
Taxonomy of third party intervention, 223–229
T-group, 202, 205, 221
Theory building, 88–91
Threat, 66, 68, 71, 93, 95, 100, 103, 104, 159–161, 193, 236
Third party consultation, 112, 207, 211–223, 247–249
Third party intervention, 211–213, 223–229
Thomas-Kilmann Conflict Mode Instrument, 130, 135
Tit-for-tat strategy, 172, 174, 200, 201, 242
Track two diplomacy, 205
Trust, 93, 96, 100, 199, 201, 202, 220, 232, 236
Turning points in negotiation, 167
Two-dimensional model of conflict management, 188–190, 208

Ultimate Attribution Error, 43
United Nations, 3, 248
United States Institute of Peace, 246
Units, 89

Value conflict, 34, 99, 146
Virile self image, 152

War, 2, 143, 144, 200
World society paradigm, 144